POLITICS AND VISION

Politics and Vision:

THE ADA AND AMERICAN LIBERALISM, 1947–1985

Steven M. Gillon

New York   Oxford
Oxford University Press
1987

Oxford University Press

Oxford   New York   Toronto
Delhi   Bombay   Calcutta   Madras   Karachi
Petaling Jaya   Singapore   Hong Kong   Tokyo
Nairobi   Dar es Salaam   Cape Town
Melbourne   Auckland

and associated companies in
Beirut   Berlin   Ibadan   Nicosia

Published by Oxford University Press, Inc.,
200 Madison Avenue, New York, New York 10016

Oxford is a registered trademark of Oxford University Press

Library of Congress Cataloging-in-Publication Data

Gillon, Steven M.
Politics and vision.

Bibliography: p.
Includes index.
1. Americans for Democratic Action.   2. Liberalism—
United States—History—20th century.   3. United
States—Politics and government—1945—   . I. Title.
E743.G45   1987   324.273′3   86–31259
ISBN 0–19–504973–X

2 4 6 8 10 9 7 5 3 1

Printed in the United States of America
on acid-free paper

To my parents
June C. Gillon
Francis M. Gillon

Preface

"For all its belief in innovation, American society at the beginning of the 1960s was still conservative," noted the British journalist Godfrey Hodgson. "People wanted change," he continued; "they did not want to be changed." Although obviously impressionistic, Hodgson's observation is not without merit. Many scholars have pointed out that for a variety of reasons—the absence of feudalism, the abundance of free land, the shortage of manpower, the possibility of upward social mobility, and the prevalence of Lockian values of individualism, equality, and liberty—the United States never developed the antagonistic class-conscious politics common in Europe. Instead, American politics has been characterized by a fairly broad consensus on basic issues.[1]

The historians Louis Hartz and Daniel Boorstin, as well as the sociologist Daniel Bell, gave this consensus approach to American history forceful expression in the 1950s. These scholars rejected the progressive view that depicted history as progress toward the realization of a democratic ideal through a cycle of economic conflict. Instead, consensus historians emphasized the durability of America's political culture and saw unity and coherence rather than division and transformation as the central features of that culture. Despite this important contribution, these scholars underrated both the degree of ethnic, racial, and class conflict in America and the importance of ideology. As early as 1955, however, Richard Hofstadter showed, with the publication of his seminal book *The Age of Reform,* that consensus history need not be simple and one-dimensional—that consensus need not require a celebration of the American condition, only the recognition of shared values.[2]

In recent years a number of scholars have developed a more sophisticated variation of the consensus model, which, while emphasizing the dominant forces of centralization and homogenization, also recognizes, in Alan Brinkley's words, "the striking persistence, in the face of these powerful homogenizing forces, of diversity, differences, divisions." To understand American society properly, Brinkley claims, the historian must understand not only the "things that have drawn American society more tightly together" but also "those that continue to drive it apart." In other words, while recognizing the existence of a coherent national political culture, historians should not blind themselves to the perpetual struggle among numerous subcultures—ethnic, religious, class, and so on—to challenge the hegemony of the dominant view.[3]

Many scholars, influenced by new organizational and pluralist schools of thought, have refined this version of the consensus approach. Not surprisingly, Brinkley in *Voices of Protest* has shown how two radicals, Father Coughlin and Huey Long, attempted, unsuccessfully, to "defend the autonomy of the individual and the independence of the community against encroachments from the modern industrial state." David Kennedy, in his analysis of the impact of World War I on American society, has shown how the national obsession with voluntarism and consensus frustrated liberal attempts to create a national community spirit. James Patterson's study of the federal government's response to poverty in the twentieth century traces "the persistence of attitudes popular among the middle class" and concludes that, despite the rise of powerful interest groups on behalf of the poor, "the 'social philosophy' of Americans had not changed much in eighty years."[4]

These scholars have noted the persistence of conservative American social and political values even in the face of powerful forces of nationalization and centralization. This tension presents special problems to those committed to challenging established institutions. America's conservative political culture has impaled reformers on the horns of a dilemma. David Kennedy's description of the plight of liberals prior to America's entry into World War I captures the dilemma that confronts all of those committed to political reform in America. Liberals, Kennedy has claimed, had to decide "whether to oppose a distasteful policy on principle and work against it whatever the pain, or to swallow the bitter pill, seek somehow to make it palatable, retain one's 'effectiveness,' and push for good policies to counter-balance the bad."[5]

Scholars from diverse fields have observed this tension. Max Weber wrote about a tension between "substantive rationality," involving the ultimate values sought, and "functional rationality," dealing with the means to attain a given goal. Social action groups, he argued, were divided between *Zweckrationalität,* which emphasized the "ethics of responsibility," and *Wertrationalität,* which was committed to the "ethics of absolute ends." Sheldon Wolin has referred to the inevitable tension between vision, which poses "a futurist quality, a projection of the political order into a time that is yet to be," and politics, which is committed "to lessening the gap between the possibilities grasped through political imagination and the actualities of political experience." Most scholars agree that both forms of rationality—politics and vision—are necessary for a healthy society. As the political scientist Seymour Martin Lipset has commented, "a society cannot maintain its pursuit of rational means-ends relationships except in the context of a set of absolute values which anchor and direct the search for means."[6]

This study analyzes how one representative group, the Americans for Democratic Action, responded to this dilemma. Founded in January 1947, the ADA was at the forefront of the movement toward "Vital Center" liberalism and for the next two decades emerged as the most forceful advocate of many ideas cherished by political liberals. The ADA's national leadership included many of the nation's chief labor leaders like Walter Reuther and David Dubinsky; New Dealers eager to continue the Roosevelt tradition like Eleanor Roosevelt, John Kenneth Galbraith, and Robert Nathan; and prominent members of the liberal anti-Communist Left like James Loeb, Arthur Schlesinger, Jr., Joseph Rauh, and Reinhold Niebuhr. The ADA functioned as a national lobbying group for liberal legislation, a source of liberal policy alternatives, and a grass roots organization devoted to social change.[7]

Apart from the impressive list of luminaries who joined the ADA, most of the organization's members shared remarkably similar social backgrounds. The overwhelming majority of ADA members were white, college-educated, Jewish men from the middle or upper-middle class. Despite the organization's strong advocacy of civil rights and labor issues, it attracted little support from either blacks or rank-and-file unionists. Along with their similar social background, what characteristics can help identify "ADA-type liberals"? It would appear the New Deal served as the unifying force. For onetime Socialists the New Deal had offered the prospect of achieving meaningful change without sacrificing political influence. For the many liberals and intellectuals originally aroused to political activity by Roosevelt, the New Deal afforded both influence and prestige. Many of those who identified with the New Deal became increasingly frustrated after 1945 by the changing tide of national and international events and, perhaps, by their own declining influence in the Truman administration. Their commitment to extending the New Deal and their desire to be involved in the nation's political life was to unite them for the next twenty years.[8]

A common social background and a shared commitment to the New Deal did not prevent serious disagreement among ADA members over goals and strategy. Most of the labor representatives and a few intellectuals wanted the organization to serve as an appendage of the Democratic party, providing ideas but avoiding heavy involvement in politics. They also hoped to keep the organization firmly rooted in the bread-and-butter issues of the New Deal and were militantly anti-Communist. A much larger group of intellectuals and professionals wanted the organization to work as a source of new ideas for the party and as an effective political pressure group. While committed to the New Deal, these members hoped to expand the liberal coalition by addressing such controversial social issues as civil rights and civil liberties. In the 1960s the differences between labor and intellectuals in the organization were dwarfed by the rise of the "New Politics" group. These new, younger reformers, who grew up in the relative affluence of the postwar period, abandoned the organization's ties to the New Deal agenda and advocated sweeping changes in American institutions and values. Although of the same social standing as older ADA members, they were not concerned with the same issues that had motivated middle-class reformers in the 1940s and 1950s.[9] Rather than identifying with the aspirations of the emerging middle class, they empathized with the plight of the poor and outcasts in American society.[10]

The ADA provides an excellent case study of the vicissitudes of postwar

American liberalism. Most studies of the plight of liberalism tend to be period pieces, focusing either on the emergence of the Vital Center during the Truman years or on the fall of that consensus during the 1960s. Such monographs provide only static glimpses of a dynamic process, and no sense of movement and change. Other studies look to the presidential administrations of Harry S Truman, John F. Kennedy, and Lyndon B. Johnson to define the liberal reform impulse. Yet, even the policies of progressive presidents are not always representative of liberal ideas. Their programs tend to be diluted by the give-and-take of negotiation and compromise with Congress and rarely live up to liberal expectations. Also, most liberals argue, with considerable justification, that they were never as influential as they or their detractors would have one believe. "The reality of American politics in the liberal era," commented Gus Tyler of the International Ladies Garment Workers Union, "is that the Legislative Branch of the Federal government was in the hands of a conservative coalition which could be petitioned, persuaded or pushed, but not commanded by a liberal majority."[11]

ADA liberals, chastened by the harsh reality of the Great Depression and fascism, disenchanted with Marxist polemics, and skeptical of ideal solutions, placed a premium on bargaining and compromise. Yet, they also fancied themselves as reformers with a responsibility to promote social and economic justice. Liberals who had come to prominence after World War II tried to strike a balance between their commitment to abstract ideals of social justice and their sense of the politically possible. Although they were able to maintain that balance for nearly twenty years, it began to be upset in the 1960s. The emergence of divisive issues like civil rights, which tugged at the moral sensibilities of most liberals, left little room for compromise. Adding to the problem was the appearance of a more militant younger generation who remembered neither the New Deal nor the Great Depression and were eager to assume moral leadership of the liberal movement. It was Vietnam, however, that, in Hodgson's words, "became the organizing principle around which all the doubts and disillusionments of the years of crisis since 1963, and all the deeper discontents hidden under the glossy surface of the confident years, coalesced into one great rebellion."

The Vietnam War forced liberals to put conviction over politics. The ADA did so in 1968 when it supported Eugene McCarthy over Hubert Humphrey for the Democratic nomination. However, it paid a high price. Choosing vision over politics left the organization, and liberalism in general, isolated from the mainstream of American politics. After a few years in the political wilderness, the organization was by 1978 beginning to reforge a new liberal-labor coalition. Whether its political strategy will succeed is uncertain. What is certain is that along the way the ADA has abandoned many of its old assumptions and refashioned the Vital Center consensus.

Like all writers, I have incurred numerous debts while completing this study. I gratefully acknowledge financial support from the Harry S Truman Foundation, a Moody Grant from the Lyndon B. Johnson Foundation, the Albert J. Beveridge Award from the American Historical Association, as well as grants from the scarce resources of the Brown University Graduate School.

While the financial support helped provide the resources for this study, my family, friends, and advisers provided the inspiration and the guidance. My parents, to whom this book is dedicated, have devoted most of their lives to providing for their children a better life full of richer opportunities. They have, along with my grandparents, Mrs. and Mr. Benjamin Waldov and the late Mrs. Alice Gillon, and siblings Franny, Mike, and Karen, provided me with emotional support and physical comfort. This book is a small token of my appreciation. Also, as both an undergraduate and graduate student, I have had the fortune of meeting dedicated and caring faculty members who took interest in both my personal and my intellectual development. At Widener College, Julian Skaggs, the late Mervin Lowe, and, especially, Lawrence Buck inspired me to continue the study of history. While at Brown, I spent two enjoyable years as a teaching assistant in Charles Neu's course in diplomatic history. Elmer Cornwell's cheerful disposition and friendly encouragement brightened many of my days. Both read the entire manuscript and made many helpful suggestions. Mark and Betty Garrison and Dan Caldwell, of the Center for Foreign Policy Development, extended me many kindnesses during my two years there.

No list could convey my gratitude to friends who have contributed to the manuscript. Charlie King, a former Brown University student, conceived the idea of writing a study of the ADA. Dave Heller of Oxford University and Gary Ginsberg of Columbia University School of Law read early drafts of the manuscript and saved me from many embarrassing errors. Other students and friends encouraged me throughout the nearly four years that I worked on this project. They include Gary Briggs, Salil Mehta, Grace Curley, Al Shehadi, Paul Croce, Dan and Sue Collins, John Kennedy, Andrew Hurwitz, Bill Ferraro, Steve Smith, Andy Wagner, Mike Hanrahan, Bill O'Farrell, and Dan Philips. A special thanks goes to Ken Orkin, who extended a helping hand when it was needed most. Like all Brown University American Civilization students, I owe a deep appreciation to Rheta Martin, the secretary–social director of the American Civilization Department, who retired in 1985.

John Thomas of Brown University, John Morton Blum of Yale, and Laura Kalman of the University of California, Santa Barbara, have given me the benefit of their advice. Arthur Schlesinger, Jr., in his dual role as historian and ADA member, and Leon Shull gave freely of their time to read the manuscript and answer questions. The ADA's national staff tolerated numerous inconveniences as I poked around in files and rummaged through their basement. Many other ADA members—especially John Kenneth Galbraith, John Roche, Robert Nathan, Leon Keyserling, Congressman Don Edwards, William Leuchtenburg, Michael Harrington, Ann Lewis, and Amy Isaacs—took time from their busy schedules to talk with me about the organization. I am especially indebted to Joseph Rauh, who gave generously of his time and insights for this study. His remarkable life story is still waiting to be told.

Most of all, I would like to thank James T. Patterson, who directed this book from beginning to end. He deftly gave perceptive criticism and gentle support when they were needed. But most of all, he forced me to do better, to push harder. He did so not through stentorian exhortation but by the gentle yet persuasive force of his example. He sets a standard of professionalism and dedication to teaching and scholarship that his students cannot help emulating. His support has gone beyond reading drafts and making comments. He has been a good friend, who has more than tolerated my unpolished manner and insipid humor.

New Haven   S.M.G.
September 1986

Contents

POLITICS AND VISION

1

Communists, Anti-Communists
and the Cold War

The Georgia sun climbed over Pine Mountain on April 12, 1945. In the valley below, Franklin D. Roosevelt, looking drawn and weak, sat contentedly in his leather chair in the living room of his cozy Warm Springs cottage. There were papers for him to sign before lunch—State Department nominations, postmaster appointments, citations for the Legion of Merit awards, and the bill to extend the life of the Commodity Credit Corporation. Around noon Roosevelt sat for an artist's sketching while his cousins Margaret Suckley and Laura Delano busied themselves on the other side of the cluttered room. Suckley glanced over and saw Roosevelt slump in his chair. "I have a terrific headache," he muttered. A few hours later, at 3:55 P.M., Franklin D. Roosevelt died.

Perhaps no president had so dominated the politics of his time as Franklin Roosevelt. He set the agenda for American political discourse for at least a generation. "All contemporary national politics descend from Franklin Roosevelt," observed Theodore White. Roosevelt's masterful fusion of liberal vision with practical politics left liberals unprepared for the postwar debates over the direction of the liberal movement. Roosevelt's immediate successor, Harry S Truman, one journalist noted, "walked, as completely as did the smallest laborer who had been a 'Roosevelt man,' in the long shadow of the dead President." Old New Dealers had difficulty accepting a slight, bespectacled figure as a substitute for the urbane and aristocratic father of the New Deal. Though Truman committed himself to carrying out his predecessor's policies, "the dry Missouri voice," Rex Tugwell wrote, "was a disastrous declination from the Roosevelt oratory which had familiarized Americans with a richness they had come to take for granted and now realized had been a golden gift they had not sufficiently valued."[1]

Truman appeared incapable of fulfilling the unconstrained and unrealistic liberal hopes for the postwar world. At home liberals, who had abandoned their traditional hostility toward big business, believed, as the former Office of Price Administration head Chester Bowles argued, that government spending beyond its income combined with "the increase of consumer spending" would provide "the basic and lasting solution of our economic future." At the same time even the most dour liberals hoped for world order and stability

3

based on U.S.-Soviet cooperation. "The war cannot be won unless America and Russia win it together," the columnist Max Lerner wrote in 1943. "The peace cannot be organized unless America and Russia organize it together."[2] As always, liberals looked to the presidency to fulfill their hopes and lead America into a prosperous and peaceful postwar era. Yet, whereas Roosevelt inspired and excited liberals, Truman never appeared able to transcend his cultural heritage as a provincial midwesterner groomed for political life by party bosses and professional politicians. Rather than providing the dynamic leadership of FDR, Truman, liberals complained, stumbled from one problem to the next without vision or insight.

The initial liberal dissatisfaction with Truman grew until 1948. Liberals watched as one venerable New Dealer after another left government only to be replaced by a more conservative appointee. Although Truman did make liberal appointments, the role of cronies like his advisers Harry Vaughn, Ed McKim, and Jake Vardaman and the appointments of the Missouri banker John Snyder as head of the Office of War Mobilization and Reconversion and the oilman Edwin Pauley as ambassador to the Allied Reparations Commission disappointed liberals. The columnist I. F. Stone complained that the Truman era was "the era of the moocher. The place was full of Wimpys who could be had for a hamburger."[3] The president also came up short on a number of issues that served as a litmus test for postwar liberals. His difficulties in providing strong leadership can be explained in part by the political climate, which was decidedly hostile—at least in Congress—to liberal legislation. A conservative coalition of Republicans and right-wing Democrats controlled both houses and was determined to thwart most presidential initiatives. Still, Harry Truman seemed weak to many liberals. He gave only halfhearted support, for example, to liberal demands for full-employment legislation, and he shocked liberals in May 1946 when he requested authority to draft striking railroad workers into the army. Max Lerner's response to Truman's action was typical of the horror felt by most liberals. The proposal, he sneered, was similar to "what happened when Hitler came into power and drafted workers into the labor battalions of the party." Many liberals probably agreed with the *Nation*'s characterization of Truman as a "weak, baffled, angry man."[4]

Truman also had to weather an embarrassing incident that seemed to call into question his commitment to civil rights. In December 1945 a black member of the Fair Employment Practices Commission (FEPC) resigned in public protest over the president's indifference to the committee's work. The incident concerned a controversial administration decision that prevented the committee from issuing an order banning discrimination in a District of Columbia transit company seized by the federal government. Truman tried to limit the damage by issuing a number of public statements expressing his personal support for the committee, but to liberals his actions were speaking louder than his words.

The president seemed to fare little better in the realm of foreign policy, where some observers found him indecisive and uncertain. Roosevelt's personalized diplomacy, his mixing of realpolitik with idealism, and his precarious, careful balancing of domestic and foreign pressures left his inexperienced and less charismatic successor with a serious problem. Truman spent the first year of his presidency trying a blend of negotiation, threat, and posturing to solve the Russian problem. The result was a policy that was often confused and contradictory and that served to heighten tension. While observers tried to determine whether Truman had repudiated Roosevelt's "Grand Design" or was simply overwhelmed by the office, Truman searched for a more stable policy.[5]

Truman wasted little time initiating his new policy. Although legally mandated to terminate lend-lease shipments at the end of the war, Truman's abrupt cancellation of assistance to the Soviet Union infuriated Stalin. Furthermore, the president refused to allow the Soviets a major role in the occupation of Japan, and he expressed concern over Soviet actions in the Middle East and in Turkey. Stalin's refusal to honor a promise made at Yalta to allow "free and unfettered elections" in Poland also angered the president. In October 1945 he publicly criticized Russian policy. "We believe," Truman declared, "that all peoples who are prepared for self-government should be permitted to choose their own form of government by their own freely expressed choice, without interference from any foreign source."

The new year brought no reprieve from hostility. On February 9, 1946, in Moscow, Joseph Stalin spoke of the incompatibility of communism and capitalism and implied that future wars were inevitable. *Time* described the speech as "the most warlike pronouncement uttered by any top-rank statesman since V-J Day." Two weeks after Stalin's speech George F. Kennan, the chargé d'affaires in Moscow, sent a long telegram to the State Department analyzing the motives behind Soviet behavior. America, Kennan argued, is confronted with "a political force committed fanatically to the belief that with [the] U.S. there can be no permanent *modus vivendi,* that it is desirable and necessary that the internal harmony of our society be broken, if Soviet power is to be secure." Arriving at a critical time, when Truman was reevaluating American policy toward the Soviets, Kennan's telegram provided intellectual justification for a new "get tough with Russia" approach.[6]

Soviet behavior, together with Kennan's perceptive analysis of it, convinced Truman and his advisers that Stalin was an ideological zealot determined to conquer the West. American officials seemed still willing to compromise, but from now on all the concessions would have to come from the other side. To a degree the American-Russian conflict was inevitable. Stalin saw the postwar situation as an opportunity to pursue traditional Russian goals—expanded influence in Iran, Manchuria, and Turkey and a secure buffer in Eastern Europe as protection against a rearmed Germany. Truman, expressing America's ingrained hostility toward communism, a belief in America's global mission, and a faith in military might, determined to stand firm. While Truman's compulsive desire to appear decisive and "tough" aggravated the problem, it tended to reflect the views of most of his countrymen.[7]

Increasing Cold War tensions sharpened differences among liberals. Many liberals had felt betrayed when, in August 1939, American Communists endorsed Stalin's decision to sign a nonaggression pact with Hitler. Until then Communists had worked as part of the Popular Front with liberals and radicals in fighting the spread of world fascism. Yet, when Hitler invaded the Soviet Union in June 1940, American Communists, again following the party line, quickly reversed their position and supported American entry into the war. During the war Communists opposed strikes, abandoned their status as a political party, and made important gains in local Democratic party organizations and in the trade union movement. "By the midpoint of the Second World War," Joseph Starobin has written, "American communism had reached its zenith in members, and its influence far exceeded its own strength." As many as eleven of the CIO's thirty-three affiliates had substantial Communist leadership, and a number of unions were led by party members. They also held key staff positions in the United Auto Workers and the CIO.[8]

Amid the growing hostility between the two countries, liberals needed to consider whether they should continue the wartime practice of working with Communists or whether the new Soviet hostility revealed a fundamental difference of purpose. Liberals divided on this basic issue. Anti-Communist liberals who clustered around the Union for Democratic Action (UDA), and later around the ADA, opposed the Popular Front and, while sympathetic with Truman's growing hard line toward the Soviets, found him indecisive and—compared with FDR, anyhow—incapable of the inspirational leadership they had come to expect from the presidency. Progressives, on the other hand, who later rallied around Henry Wallace and the Progressive Citizens of America, were committed to maintaining the Popular Front and blamed Truman for inciting the Cold War with Russia and ignoring the continued threat from fascism. For the next few years anti-Communist liberals and progressives would debate the direction of liberalism in the postwar era.

During the war progressive opinion enjoyed considerable support in the liberal community. There had been five major liberal groups in the United States during the war years; only one, the anti-Communist UDA, prevented Communists from becoming members or refused to participate in events sponsored by Communists. Progressive groups included the National Farmers Union, led by its spirited young president, James G. Patton. Imbued with a Jeffersonian spirit of the small farmer and a socialist faith in a class movement, its leadership attempted to forge a working-class coalition of farmers and laborers. Second was the CIO-PAC, headed by Sidney Hillman, formed in 1943 in response to the anti-union Smith-Connally Act, which prevented labor unions from contributing to political campaigns. It was the most effective group in mobilizing voters on election day. Affiliated with the CIO-PAC was a third group, the National Citizens Political Action Committee (NCPAC). Originally formed to promote a fourth term for Roosevelt, NCPAC evolved into a large and powerful force in postwar liberal politics. Its broad and impressive membership included liberal businessmen, journalists, and politicians, as well as notable progressives and civil rights leaders. Finally, the Independent Citizens Committee of the Arts, Sciences, and Professions (ICCASP), comprising stars from science, the arts, and show business, was the group most infiltrated by Communists.[9]

Progressives believed that continued American-Russian cooperation was essential to the preservation of the antifascist alliance in the postwar period. The goal of American foreign policy, the *New Republic* had editorialized in 1944, was to establish "genuine political cooperation of a sort that would convince Russia she can safely entrust her future to collective security underwritten by the two great Western powers." These liberals were certain that Soviet actions in Eastern Europe at the end of the war were inspired by legitimate security needs and did not present a serious threat to American interests. "Those who like to complicate the Russian issue and delight businessmen's clubs by lecturing on the enigma of the East and the mystery of the Russian soul should learn one simple fact," wrote J. Alvarez Del Vayo in the *Nation:* "Russia wants peace." Progressives feared that a strident American anti-Communist policy would have just the opposite effect from what it was intended to have. "An American foreign policy that is guided by the fear of Russian power," Max Lerner wrote, "must in the end—whatever its other pretensions—be guided by nothing else." Concern for justice in Spain, peace in China, and decency for the Jews in Palestine will be thrown out the window "because once you make the obsession with Russia your crucial test, nothing else counts except to give the Russians no possible advantage." Progressives blamed both the United States and the Soviet Union for attempting to crush democracy in the world. "In a universal vacuum of political morality," wrote the *New Republic* editor Michael Straight, "neither Russia nor America makes any claim to leadership."[10]

Henry A. Wallace emerged as the progressives' leader. Born on a small farm in Iowa in 1888, Wallace served first as secretary of agriculture from 1933 to 1940, then as vice-president until 1945, and finally as secretary of commerce. In his early New Deal days, reporters voted Wallace "the worst-dressed man" in government. In later years he acquired a more statesmanlike appearance, but to most Washington observers he remained an enigma. "He is a man who has read much but is not well read, thought much but is not a thinker, known too many people to have made many real friends," *Time* observed in 1946. "He is a scientist who is governed by his emotions, a believer who has rejected faith."[11]

But Wallace inspired many on the left. He had emerged as a liberal leader in May 1942 when he delivered his famous speech entitled "The Price of Free World Victory," arguing that the prime object of the war was to solve the problems of want. He called for a "people's revolution," based upon the revolutionary movements of the American and Latin American colonies, of France in 1789, of Germany in 1848, and of Russia in 1917.[12] Although as vice-president Wallace was unable to penetrate the internal power structure of the Senate, his public expressions of discontent with the conservative members of the administration increased his stature with liberals. Removed from the ticket in 1944, he became a martyr for progressive principles. After Roo-

sevelt's sudden death, most liberal attention and hope focused on Wallace's
plans for the future. While Truman in his early months as president appeared
to be moving away from Roosevelt's domestic and international policies, Wallace lifted liberal hopes with calls for economic development, full employment, and cooperation with the Soviet Union.

Truman grew increasingly annoyed at Wallace's public criticism of American foreign policy. The last straw was a confidential memorandum on foreign
affairs that Wallace had written to the president in July 1946 and released in
September. It was a scathing criticism of U.S. policy toward Russia. Wallace
charged "a school of military thinking" with advocating a "preventive war"
before Russia would perfect its own atomic bomb and denounced the U.S.
plan for atomic control as humiliating to the Russians. "The fundamental objective" of American foreign policy, he charged, "should be to allay any reasonable Russian grounds for fear, suspicion and distrust." At first Truman
seemed to believe that Wallace's views could be accommodated, and he gave
Wallace permission to speak his mind before a Popular Front rally at Madison Square Garden. The speech, however, revealed the split that had developed. The powerful Republican Senator Arthur Vandenberg of Michigan, who
with James Byrnes was negotiating with the Russians in Paris, cabled, "We
Republicans can cooperate with only one secretary of state at a time." A few
days later Truman abruptly fired Wallace.[13]

For many progressives Wallace's departure proved what they had suspected all along—that Truman had abandoned FDR's policies. His dismissal,
the CIO's National Maritime Union claimed, is "conclusive evidence that the
President has entirely abandoned the progressive foreign policies of Franklin
D. Roosevelt." "Henry Wallace has issued a summons to action and a platform to which all progressives can rally," commented Freda Kirchwey of
the Nation. "Only if we take up that challenge, and take it up with courage
and determination, can we check the steady drift in American reaction and
prevent a new war."[14]

For Wallace, removal from the cabinet merely accentuated his differences
with Truman. Now more than ever Wallace believed that peace with the Soviet Union was a prerequisite for fulfilling his hopes for the postwar world.
He accepted the essential benevolence of the Soviet people and the limited
goals of the Soviet state. While the administration and the American public
were becoming increasingly suspicious of Soviet intentions, Wallace refused
to view the Soviet Union as an ideological state committed to the cause of
world revolution. Yet, Wallace's dissent stemmed less from his admiration
of the Soviet Union than from his mystic faith in international brotherhood.
With his dream of postwar cooperation fading, Wallace lashed out at Truman as a convenient scapegoat for the dangerous state of international tensions. Truman's policy of containment, he claimed, with its emphasis on a
military rather than an economic challenge, was misplaced and would lead
only to further escalation of tensions. The best way to undercut Communist
appeal, he insisted, was through economic reform and by showing the essential vitality of capitalism. He believed that Americans had learned the

wrong lessons from Munich: communism and fascism were clearly distinguishable; Stalin was not the reincarnation of Hitler. Wallace wanted the United States to engage "in friendly economic competition rather than a deadly arms race with the Soviet Union." Because Wallace thought that fascism still posed the greatest threat to American security, he wanted to continue the Popular Front. Accepting Communist support, Wallace frequently attended Communist-sponsored functions and was openly critical of those who wanted to split the antifascist coalition.[15]

Among anti-Communist liberals who criticized the progressive faith in the Popular Front many were former Socialists who had dissented in 1939–40 from the strong pacifist convictions of their leader, Norman Thomas. Although the dissidents remained committed to the Socialist ideals of economic justice, they hoped to create a new party that would not only pursue domestic reform but also stand up to Hitler. While recognizing that fascism presented the gravest immediate threat to the West, many of these Socialists, particularly those of East European descent, were also skeptical of Soviet intentions. Unlike other liberal groups, they also planned to bar Communists from joining.

Murray Gross of the International Ladies Garment Workers, took charge and asked the theologian Reinhold Niebuhr if he would join a small group of disaffected Socialists and progressives. Niebuhr was an important ally for Gross. Already considered the leading theologian of American Protestantism, Niebuhr had amassed, through his extensive lectures, articles, and books, a considerable following in both liberal and Socialist circles. Niebuhr's experience with a lost peace, economic strife, and Nazi brutality shook his confidence in idealistic views of human nature. He concluded in 1939, "The whole of contemporary history proves that liberal culture has not seen the problem of mankind in sufficient depth to understand its own history." Consequently, he moved in the 1940s toward a new, more skeptical version of the liberal faith that was to find its fullest expression in *The Children of Light and the Children of Darkness,* published in 1944. He captured his new philosophy in a revealing aphorism: "Man's capacity for justice makes democracy possible; but man's inclination to injustice makes democracy necessary." In a political universe devoid of moral absolutes, Niebuhr reasoned, only a pluralistic democracy composed of delicately balanced conflicting interests could control the "moral cynicism" of the children of darkness and the utopian idealism of the children of light. Niebuhr's emphasis on gradualism and on pragmatism, along with his recognition of the role power played in society, marked a fundamental shift away from the idealism and moral absolutism of an earlier generation of liberals and toward a new, more tempered philosophical framework that would guide liberal intellectuals for years to come.[16]

Gross also invited Lewis Corey, a founding member of the American Communist party who became a staunch anti-Communist during the 1930s; John L. Childs, a professor at the Columbia Teachers College, in New York City; the former Socialist Gus Tyler, Alfred Baker Lewis, and Jack Altman;

as well as a number of liberal interventionists from liberal journals like Freda Kirchwey of the *Nation,* George Soule of the *New Republic,* and Alfred Bingham of *Common Sense.*[17]

On May 10, 1941, the group organized an overflow luncheon at the Town Hall Club of New York City and founded the Union for Democratic Action. Freda Kirchwey served as chairman. James B. Carey, secretary-treasurer of the CIO, Philip Randolph, president of the Brotherhood of Sleeping Car Porters, Louis Corey, and Reinhold Niebuhr addressed the session. In addition to the sponsors at the first meeting, UDA founders included Andrew Biemiller, a congressman from Wisconsin, Frank Graham, president of the University of North Carolina, and Mark Starr, educational director of the International Ladies Garment Workers Union (ILGWU).[18]

After helping to organize the new group, Gross decided to return to his position with the ILGWU. To take over the administrative responsibilities, the UDA hired James Loeb, a teacher of Romance languages at a local New York high school and a former Socialist. An intense, frequently dour man, Loeb had graduated from Dartmouth in 1929, taken his M.A. and Ph.D. in Romance languages at Northwestern, and then become active in the socialist trade movement in Spain during the 1930s. He, like others in the newly formed UDA, was a staunch antifascist. But he also loathed communism. It was during a summer in Spain that Loeb experienced firsthand the brutal tactics of Communists determined to overtake the government by any means possible—even by posing as patrons of democracy. It was a lesson he never forgot.[19]

Members of the newly constituted group had little difficulty adopting a platform. Niebuhr summed up the philosophy of the group at the inaugural meeting: "The overwhelming majority of the American people desire a triumphant democracy at home and abroad." To promote democracy abroad, the UDA accepted as its first priority U.S. participation in the war against fascism. It called for all-out aid to England and for American convoys to defend the shipping lanes. Many UDA members believed that the Soviet Union, which two years earlier had negotiated a nonaggression pact with Hitler, was just as corrupt and immoral as Nazi Germany, but not as immediately menacing as Hitler's rampaging army. Viewing communism and fascism as equal threats to democracy, they decided to "specifically exclude" the Communist party from all organizational activities. At home the UDA called for "basic economic changes and new social arrangements," including the "socialization of the great banks and industries," the formation of a national planning board, heavy taxes on income above $2,000, and government control of credit and investment.[20]

The UDA's attempt to forge a consensus on American entry into the war and its opposition to both Soviet and German foreign policy and domestic communism and fascism proved short-lived. Hitler's attack on Russian territory in June 1941 forced the United States into an "unholy alliance" with the Soviet Union. Two days after the invasion the executive committee released a statement declaring that Hitler was a greater menace than Stalin and that the United States should give the Soviet Union all necessary aid. The statement, however, claimed that the change should not result in lessened vigilance against "communist penetration into the liberal and labor movement." The UDA, Loeb warned, will now have to be on guard against "the infiltration that is bound to descend upon us." Niebuhr, meanwhile, urged members to continue "the process of eliminating Communism from union leadership and from all organizations which stand on the left wing of democracy," even though American foreign policy was, "for the moment, identical with that of the Communists."[21]

Loeb confessed to his friend James Wechsler, the *New York Post* columnist, that during the war the UDA was considered "the pariah of the liberal movement." Some progressives called them the "hang-back boys" because they refused to participate in many events solely because Communists were involved. "They were the things to do and we refused to do them," Loeb said. "We fought at meetings, we pleaded, we warned, and we were damned unpopular. We fought in the Teachers' Union, the labor unions, and all over the place. Tragically for the world, we were right about the way it turned out, but nobody ever loved Cassandra."[22]

The four progressive organizations—the National Farmers Union, CIO-PAC, the Independent Voters Committee of the Arts and Sciences, and the National Citizens Political Action Committee—dwarfed the ADA in both financial resources and membership. The UDA membership, optimistically estimated at ten thousand in 1946, was no match for NCPAC's fifty thousand. Financially, the UDA staggered from one crisis to another, sometimes forcing Loeb and his small staff to forgo their weekly paychecks. Having only a few chapters on the East Coast, in such cities as Philadelphia, Washington, and New York, and in a few other states nationwide, the UDA lacked the political muscle and financial support of the progressive groups.

Although UDA liberals had consistently rejected accommodation with Communists, the debate between anti-Communist liberals and progressives became esepecially sharp when progressives organized the "Win the Peace Conference" in Washington for early April 1946. Among the conference's organizers were many known Communists and fellow travelers, as well as important independent anti-Communist liberals. Niebuhr and Loeb issued a joint statement emphasizing that the conference should not be considered representative of American liberals. The UDA's stand against the conference attracted the attention of the *New Republic,* which asked Loeb to write a short piece addressing the question of whether non-Communists should work together with Communists. Loeb took the opportunity to attack the Communist party, which he called "a disciplined, semi-conspiratorial caucus whose aim is to retain or obtain control" of liberal organizations. The Popular Front, he argued, of which progressives were so fond, was destined to become a fragmented front. The inevitable consequence was that organizations that continued to associate with Communists could not "in the long run win political power through democratic means."[23]

Loeb decided to use the UDA's opposition to the Popular Front to help

launch a bold organizational drive to expand the UDA. Loeb recalled that
he and other national board members "had decided that UDA had just about
reached the end of its rope" and that they had to do something dramatic
to save it from extinction. In early May 1946 Loeb proposed that the UDA
executive committee support a conference in Washington during the last
weekend in November. The conference, he told the committee, would assess
the result of the congressional elctions and with other "democratic progressives" could then "work out a common program." He succeeded in gaining
the approval of the executive board, and the proposal was sent to the
UDA board of directors for final approval. At its next meeting the national
board of directors approved Loeb's proposal and instructed him to establish
a committee to write a program for the conference and to solicit support from
prominent liberals. Loeb established a planning committee that included the
journalist James Wechsler, the attorney Joseph Rauh, and the historian Arthur
Schlesinger, Jr. Meeting regularly at either Wechsler's apartment or Rauh's
home, these three men, previously strangers, were to become lifelong friends.
Meanwhile, Loeb went around Washington courting important political figures.
Shortly after publication of the letter, Loeb met with Eleanor Roosevelt, who
agreed to help by broaching the idea with Phillip Murray, the powerful leader
of the CIO.[24]

Loeb's timing was perfect, for in the summer and fall of 1946 a considerable ground swell of opposition to the Popular Front appeared within
liberal circles. Perhaps no one did more to articulate liberal passion over
the Communist threat than the gifted young historian and publicist Arthur
M. Schlesinger, Jr., did in a widely circulated article that appeared in *Life*
magazine. Considering a confrontation between Communists and anti-Communists inevitable, Schlesinger added an urgency to his appeal. Communists
are "working overtime," he warned, "to expand party influence, open and
covert, in the labor movement, among Negroes, among veterans, among organized liberals." Party members, Schlesinger claimed, are "lonely and frustrated people" who need discipline to provide them "with social, intellectual,
even sexual fulfillment they cannot obtain in existing society." In order to
understand the Communists, he continued, "you must think of them in terms,
not of a normal political party, but in terms of the Jesuits, the Mormons or
Jehovah's Witnesses." Conspiratorial and clandestine, they infiltrate unsus-
pecting hosts and then drain them of their political lifeblood. Because of
their secret ways, Schlesinger argued, they can hide "their true face from
American liberals," and prevent "honest discussion of the Communist issue
by raising the cry of 'red-baiting' and 'Rankinism.' "[25]

Other prominent liberals were reaching similar conclusions. Niebuhr
believed that Communist suppression of free elections in Romania and Poland in the winter of 1946 and the revival of the Comintern required a
strong American response. "Russian truculence," he declared, "cannot be
mitigated by further concessions. Russia hopes to conquer the whole of Europe strategically and ideologically." Eleanor Roosevelt's experiences in the
United Nations brought her to a similar recognition of the difficulties of

working with the Russians. The Russian abstention on the Declaration of Human Rights and their delaying tactics in the United Nations Atomic Energy Commission's deliberations over the Baruch plan left the former first lady disillusioned and bitter. Joseph and Stewart Alsop, political columnists for the *New York Herald Tribune,* and cousins of Eleanor Roosevelt, published a series of articles, bearing such ominous titles as "Tragedy of Liberalism" and such warnings as "The liberal movement is now engaged in sowing the seeds of its own destruction." Liberals, they charged, had "consistently avoided the great political reality of the present: the Soviet challenge to the West." Like most anti-Communist liberals, the Alsops believed that if liberals did not forsake their "self-delusions" concerning Soviet imperialism, they would be overrun by conservatives. "In the spasm of terror which will seize this country," they argued, "if we awake one morning with the sudden sensation of encirclement, it is the right—the very extreme right—which is most likely to gain victory." The Alsops warned that Wallace would "do to American liberals what Chamberlain and Simon did to the British Conservative party."[26]

Labor was crucial to any attempts to build a sustained liberal movement in America, and the years after the war witnessed anti-Communist stirrings in the CIO. The CIO had been the more radical wing of the labor movement ever since 1934, when it challenged the craft-oriented American Federation of Labor by organizing workers within industries. On the whole the CIO had been willing to work with Communists to further labor goals. During the war it worked closely with Popular Front organizations and had little in common with the UDA.

Nonetheless, the growing tension between the United States and the Soviet Union brought the Communist issue to the surface in the postwar period. In part it became an explosive issue because many CIO members were devout Catholics and were receptive to the Catholic Church's animosity toward the Communist party. The Communist issue also became caught in a personal struggle for power in the CIO. Walter Reuther was the key figure in the emergence of militant anti-communism in the CIO. A man of soaring and, usually, long-winded rhetoric, Reuther began his political career campaigning for the Socialist Norman Thomas in the 1932 presidential campaign. In 1936 he was elected to the UAW executive board in Detroit, where he organized a successful sit-down strike and developed a power base on the city's West Side. While leading successful strikes against General Motors at Flint, Michigan, and Henry Ford's River Rouge plant, Reuther began fighting for control of the UAW. Although his original support within the UAW drew from an alliance of Socialists, Communists, and other militant trade unionists, Reuther disavowed his Communist supporters because of the noninterventionist policy they adopted after the Nazi-Soviet pact.

Reuther's first attacks on the Communists in the UAW came at the St. Louis convention in August 1940. He continued his assault through 1946, when he challenged R. J. Thomas for the presidency of the UAW. Throughout the campaign Reuther not only charged Thomas with receiving Commu-

nist support but also made dire predictions of increased Communist influence if the rank and file elected his opponent. Winning by a narrow margin,
Reuther proceeded to consolidate his power by purging Communists from
the organization and dismissing more than 100 UAW staff members loyal
to the Communist party. The importance of Reuther's victory in turning the
UAW into an aggressively anti-Communist union can hardly be overestimated. Of the three largest CIO unions, only the 650,000-member United
Electrical Workers maintained close ties with Communists, and they were
now seriously outnumbered by the anti-Communist UAW and United Steel
Workers, each with over one million members.[27]

The CIO's president, Philip Murray, a Catholic and generally unsympa-
thetic to Communists, tried to play a unifying role during the postwar
struggles between Communists and anti-Communists. He had the support of
anti-Communists in the organization, particularly the Catholics, because of
his reputation for anticommunism; yet he established good relations with
the left wing through personnel as well as policy decisions.[28] In an attempt
to reach a compromise between the vying factions at the 1946 convention,
Murray appointed a special committee, composed of three right-wing and
three left-wing executive board members, to respond to "allegations contained in the newsprint . . . that this organization of ours . . . is Com-
munistically inclined." Not unexpectedly, the committee decided on a resolution stating, "[The CIO] resents and rejects efforts by the Communist
party or any other political party and their adherents in the affairs of the
CIO." However, it did not mention that Communists were working within
the CIO, and Murray was careful to note that the resolution "should not
be misconstrued to be a repressive measure, calculated to do things of a
repressive nature."[29] Yet, as pressure from Reuther and other anti-Communist unions increased, Murray found it harder to maintain his delicate balancing act.

Labor was not alone in its attempts to banish Communists from its ranks.
The postwar period also saw the unraveling of many Popular Front political
organizations. Perhaps the most significant development was the decline of
Communist influence in the Minnesota Farmer-Labor party and the emergence on the national scene of the young and dynamic mayor of Minneapolis,
Hubert H. Humphrey. Founded in 1918, the party had functioned as an
economic protest movement, an alternative source of ideas for public policy
issues, and an influential political party that nominated and endorsed candidates for office. The Republican triumph in the 1942 elections divided the
party into two factions: a moderate wing that believed that only a revitalized Farmer-Labor coalition working through the Democratic party could
prevent further Republican victories; and a more radical, Communist faction
that vigorously opposed any merger. Prior to 1935 the Communists had
been a small, disorganized faction in Minnesota politics barred from participation in the Farmer-Labor party. But in that year, following the dictates
of the Communist International Seventh World Congress, the party switched
tactics, moderated its views, and won acceptance into the Farmer-Labor
organization. Within two years disciplined and well-organized Communist

groups overwhelmed Farmer-Labor clubs and took control of influential CIO unions.[30]

Humphrey had appeared on the political scene in 1942, when, in his first, unsuccessful race for mayor against the incumbent, Marvin Kline, he built a broad coalition of support among intellectuals, unions, and moderate Farmer-Labor members. But Humphrey's struggles had only begun. In 1946 the Communist faction of the party headed by former Governor Elmer Benson encouraged Henry Wallace to seek the presidency on a third-party ticket. Humphrey, leading a more moderate reform faction, opposed any third-party challenge and supported Truman, or any other Democratic nominee. Ironically, just a few years earlier Humphrey had been one of Wallace's biggest admirers. Yet, by 1948 Humphrey could tolerate neither Wallace's criticisms of Truman's foreign policy nor his expressed willingness to accept Communist support.[31]

The clash between the two Farmer-Labor groups surfaced during the 1946 Democratic-Farmer Labor party state convention. The large Communist element jeered Humphrey as he rose to present the keynote address, and prevented the mayor from completing his speech by repeatedly interrupting him with cries of "fascist" and "warmonger." The experience came as a rude awakening to Humphrey, who quickly rallied his troops to win control over the party. He realized that the Communists sought to make Wallace the DFL presidential nominee and to force Truman to run in Minnesota as an independent. With military precision Humphrey prepared to take over the 1948 precinct caucuses, which were the first step in the complicated process of selecting state and national convention delegates. In his long and difficult struggle to purge the DFL of Communist elements, Humphrey looked nationally for support from others who shared his apprehension about Communist influence.

While all of these individuals and groups held similar convictions about the dangers of association with Communists, it took the Republican victories in the 1946 election to convince them of the political risks of maintaining the Popular Front. After the 1946 election, for the first time since 1930, the Republicans dominated both houses of Congress. Of the seventy-seven congressmen who had a *New Republic* liberal rating of at least 80 percent, only thirty-six were reelected. Republicans promised to cut excessive government interference in the lives of individuals through tax reductions and drastic cuts in federal spending. Among the new members of what liberals were to call the "infamous class of '46" were Representative Richard Nixon of California and Senators Joseph McCarthy of Wisconsin, John Bricker of Ohio, and William Knowland of California.[32] James Wechsler recalled the frustration that liberal anti-Communists felt after the congressional elections. "In Europe," he wrote, "there was a growing 'third Force,'" yet in America, "there was a rising Republican reaction, a pro-communist Left and nothing in between except the still inept, bumbling presidency of a man who wished he wasn't there."[33] Anti-Communists charged that Wallace misunderstood Soviet global ambitions and underestimated the seriousness of the Soviet threat. Reflexively, they disagreed with his attempt to maintain the Popular Front tactic of working with Communists. Not only would such an arrangement result in political suicide, they argued, but it was morally wrong because Communist objectives were quite different from liberal goals.

By the fall of 1946 two clear groups had emerged within the American Left. Both embraced the New Deal and hoped to save it from what they perceived as Truman's ineptitude and the callous Republican philosophy. It was mainly recent foreign policy issues that divided the Left. Divergent liberal views of Soviet international intentions led to sharp divisions in feelings about whether to work in a political coalition with Communists. The UDA and other anti-Communists were convinced that it was impossible to achieve liberal goals in an unholy alliance with totalitarians, while progressives were willing to work with all those interested in saving their program from the inevitable postwar reaction.

In December the two largest Popular Front organizations, NCPAC and ICCASP, plus representatives of eight other smaller groups merged to form the Progressive Citizens of America. Henry Wallace appeared at the first meeting and established himself as the leader of the new group, which presented itself as a clear challenge to the UDA. It could boast respected organizational leaders in the renowned sculptor Jo Davidson and the New York liberal leader Frank Kingdon; solid labor support in Vice-Chairman Philip Murray, Director Jack Kroll of the CIO-PAC, and the Brotherhood of Railway Trainmen head, A. F. Whitney; as well as New Deal support in Henry Wallace.

The two-day conference of progressives, held at the Hotel Commodore in Washington, included three hundred delegates from twenty-one states. Aware of the growing rift on the left, Wallace closed the conference by emphasizing the need for unity in fighting the forces of reaction, deflecting anti-Communist charges that he was a puppet of the Communist party and Soviet foreign policy. "We should have no allegiance outside the country of any sort," he warned, adding, "Except to One World, peaceful and prosperous." The progressive faith is so broad, he claimed, that it was wrong to be divided on minor issues. Using language similar to the UDA's, Wallace declared his intention of finding common ground between "Russian haters and the Russophiles." "We shall not allow the attacks of the enemy to stampede us into foolish Red-baiting," he said. "Nor shall we allow those who owe their primary allegiance to some foreign power to determine our course." Although he never mentioned Truman by name, the object of his criticism was clear. "The lukewarm liberals," he said, "are people who try to sit on not only two but three chairs at a time, and they are the people who get us into trouble. I would prefer to see an all-out, clear-cut reactionary like Senator Taft in high office than a lukewarm liberal."[34]

One week later, on January 4, 1947, a group of 130 anti-Communist liberals attended the UDA's long-awaited expansion meeting at the Willard Hotel in Washington, D.C. Among those in attendance were a number of New Dealers, anti-Communist labor leaders, intellectuals, journalists, and rising young politicians. Familiar faces from the UDA were there—James Loeb, Reinhold Niebuhr, Gus Tyler, Alfred Baker Lewis. Walter Reuther, the new president of the UAW and vice-president of the CIO, attended. Reuther was joined by another CIO vice-president, Emil Rieve, president of the Textile Workers Union of America, the fourth-largest union in the CIO, and by James Carey, a former president of the United Electrical, Radio, and Machine Workers of America (UE), defeated for reelection by a Communist-dominated wing of delegates, and currently the secretary-treasurer of the CIO.[35]

David Dubinsky, the dynamic and controversial head of the International Ladies Garment Workers Union, and Hugo Ernst, president of the Hotel and Restaurant Employees International Alliance and Bartenders International League of America, represented the AFL at the convention. A socialist from his days as a youth in Poland, Dubinsky was the first garment worker of European background to serve on the executive council of the conservative, craft-oriented AFL. Like the other leaders of the AFL, Dubinsky was a staunch anti-Communist. Having spent two years in a Soviet jail for organizing a successful strike at a bakery in Poland, Dubinsky developed an intense hatred of anything Russian. Once in the United States, he bitterly fought the Communist party for control of the ILGWU.

Among the other moving forces in the UDA expansion meeting were Joseph Rauh, an attorney and former deputy to Wilson Wyatt in the Veterans Emergency Housing Program. Rauh was raised in Cincinnati and educated at Harvard College and Harvard Law School. His first assignment out of school was as a legal assistant to the liberal Supreme Court justice Benjamin N. Cardozo. Rauh advocated American entry into the war against Hitler as early as 1939. "We were diddling while Hitler was conquering the world," he recalled. Although spared the internecine fights between Communists and socialists that scarred so many of his anti-Communist colleagues, Rauh believed that the difference between liberals and Communists were irreconcilable. After the Nazi-Soviet pact Rauh recalled how Communists who had been supporting Roosevelt started wearing Willkie buttons and condemned England as an "imperialist nation."[36] A relentless defender of the underdog—a skill James Wechsler claimed Rauh had learned well during his days on the lifeless Harvard basketball team—Rauh was new to the political battles on the left, yet he waged them with tenacity, intelligence, and commitment.

Joining Loeb and Rauh was the scholar-activist Arthur Schlesinger, Jr. Born in 1917, in Columbus, Ohio, and educated at Harvard, Schlesinger became a New Deal liberal and an early advocate of American entry into World War II. Later, he served with the Office of War Information and the Office of Strategic Studies. Schlesinger had a remarkable skill for turning a pithy phrase and writing eloquent and lofty speeches in one sitting at his typewriter. The precocious son of a family of distinguished historians, Schlesinger had in 1945, at the age of twenty-eight, won a Pulitzer Prize for his ground-breaking study of the age of Andrew Jackson. Like many liberal intellectuals, Schlesinger owed a great debt to the theologian and philosopher

Reinhold Niebuhr. Schlesinger recalled that Niebuhr provided him with "an interpretation of human nature and human history that gave a coherent frame to my own groping sense of the frailty of man and the inscrutability of events."[37]

Most impressive of all those gathered at the Willard was the constellation of New Deal stars who returned to carry on the Roosevelt tradition. If the new organization was successfully to compete with the Progressive Citizens of America (PCA) for the Roosevelt legacy, it had to attract well-known New Deal personalities. Loeb solicited the support of the only person who could effectively counterbalance Wallace's enormous appeal in the liberal community—Eleanor Roosevelt. The former first lady and her son, Franklin D. Roosevelt, Jr., both added their name and their prestige to the new organization.

Although sympathetic to Wallace's criticisms of America's "get tough" policy with the Russians, the former first lady's personal experience with Soviet truculence at the United Nations convinced her that more than simply misunderstanding had fostered postwar tensions. "She no longer believed," her biographer Joseph Lash has written, "that at the heart of Soviet aggressiveness were insecurity, fear, and a misunderstanding of U.S. intentions that genuine dialogue with her Soviet colleagues might help to overcome." Nurturing a healthy skepticism of the Popular Front, Mrs. Roosevelt became disenchanted with Wallace when he accepted Communist support without acknowledging Soviet responsibility for international tensions. While personally fond of Wallace, Mrs. Roosevelt found herself moving, albeit reluctantly, toward the anti-Communist position of the UDA. Unlike most other anti-Communist liberals who gathered at the founding convention, Mrs. Roosevelt still hoped that Wallace would abandon his Communist support and join the ADA in presenting a united liberal movement free of Communist influence.[38]

Many of the New Dealers who left the government in frustration during the Truman years saw the new organization as a way of creating a shadow New Deal. Elmer Davis, former head of the Office of War Information, in his opening remarks addressed the founding convention as "the New Deal in exile." Isador Lubin, previously director of the Bureau of Labor Statistics, was perhaps the best representative of those exiled New Dealers. According to David Lilienthal's diary account, Truman once bragged that all the New Deal people who left government in the year after FDR's death came back begging for jobs. He made specific mention of Lubin, who, according to Truman, pleaded for another government post. Although a little harsh, Truman was correct in noting how much many New Dealers yearned to influence policy. "I just can't stand it," Lubin said in reference to private business. "I want to be where something is going on."[39]

The new organization also attracted others destined to become important actors in the liberal anti-Communist cause. One was Leon Henderson, a boisterous and sometimes bellicose veteran of the Office of Price Administration, who was eager to put liberalism back on course. Henderson, whom

Raymond Moley called "the Falstaff of New Deal economists," was an early evangelical Keynesian who railed against business monopoly, demanded higher relief expenditures, and clamored for increased consumer purchasing power. A short and stocky man with broad shoulders and usually unkempt clothes, Henderson had been one of the more colorful personalities in the Roosevelt White House. Accompanying Henderson was Wilson W. Wyatt, a lanky Kentuckian, a successful corporate lawyer, and a former mayor of Louisville who had served under Truman for a brief term as Veterans Emergency Housing Program administrator until the president asked for his resignation in December 1946.

John Kenneth Galbraith, another attendee, had served as deputy administrator in charge of the price division of the OPA until forced to resign because of comments he made in testimony before a congressional committee. Galbraith became director of the U.S. Strategic Bombing Survey in 1945 and director of the State Department's Office of Economic Security Policy in 1946. Raised in an agricultural community of Scots in southwestern Ontario and educated at Berkeley, he was known for his wit, arrogance, and height—six feet eight inches.

Elmer Davis presided over the opening session on Saturday morning. The first order of business was to agree upon a set of principles for the new organization. The group's mandate, one member declared in obvious reference to the PCA, was to "draw distinctions between this meeting and other meetings recently held." Liberals attending the UDA expansion conference, he said, "should say that we are 'liberals' from the point of view of politics and 'progressives' from the point of view of economics." Schlesinger agreed, suggesting that the only way to be both liberal and progressive was to abstain from any third-party movement. "The consensus of opinion," Schlesinger told the group, "seems to be that the Democratic Party presents the most likely medium for the progressives in this country." Franklin Roosevelt, Jr., asserted "The surest way to make the Democratic Party a liberal party is to go into the Democratic Party. . . ." Leo Lerner of Illinois disagreed. "Politics is like poker," he said. "If we announce we are going to work within the Democratic Party, they will hold us at arm's length or actually push us out, as has been the experience with some before. The best thing is to hold back." Loeb seemed to side more with Lerner: "A political party is liberal because it finds it wise to be liberal." Their new organization, he declared, should "make it wise for parties to be liberal."[40]

The differences of opinion expressed at the founding conference over the new group's proper relationship with the Democratic party would continue throughout the organization's history. The conference participants found themselves trapped in a peculiar dilemma. Many who attended the expansion meeting were opposed to the idea of a third-party movement. Wallace's statements that he was considering forming a third party made it even more imperative for UDA liberals to work within the two-party system. Most agreed with Loeb that their new group could move the party in a more liberal direction through the force of its ideas. They were to find, however, that

the balancing of their commitment to liberal ideas with their interest in political action would be more difficult than anyone had imagined in January
1947.

The conference ran into some problems when the time came to write
a platform and agree on specific provisions. The journalist Marquis Childs
and the UDA board member Mortimer Hays wanted the conference to avoid
sounding too anti-Soviet. They feared that news coverage of the conference
would be headlined "Anti-Communist Group Meets." Hays pointed out that
the group was opposed to fascism and communism, yet some members
wanted to concentrate on criticism of Russia. "I don't think it is wise to
say that we are opposed to communism and fascism and then direct all our
criticism toward Russia," he said. "We must make it clear that we have
equal opposition to fascism in Spain and Latin America." Louis Fischer, a
fellow UDA board member, took issue with Hays. He defended an anti-
Russian emphasis as realistic, because it seized "the central problem of the
world—U.S. relations and Russia." "There is no separation," he continued,
"between the problem of Communism and fascism. They recruit for each
other, wash one another's hands." The United States, he concluded, was
engaged "in a clear, ideological war with Russia," and unless it won this
war, it would have "a military war." Eleanor Roosevelt gently yet firmly
undercut Fischer's harsh anti-Soviet speech. Despite our differences, the
former first lady informed the convention, "we must make peace with the
Russians."[41]

When it became obvious that the committee would not be able to agree
on a specific program, a number of members suggested that the group re-
strict itself to a general statement of principles. "We are in the habit of
dealing with specific things," Reuther said. "We can't hope for that out of
this conference." The basic question the conference needs to address, Reuther argued, is "whether it is possible to feed, clothe, and house people without putting their souls in chains." Most of the other committee members
agreed and broke for lunch.[42]

The first business after lunch was to decide upon a name for the new
organization. One member of the Committee on Continuations suggested a
title that contained the word "liberal," but some worried that the public
would confuse it with nineteenth-century laissez-faire liberalism. He suggested keeping the name Union for Democratic Action. But the UDA board
member Ethel Epstein, candidly admitting the UDA's lack of success, wanted
a fresh start and did not want the new organization confused with the UDA.
Some proposed substituting the word "progressive" for "liberal," but Franklin Roosevelt, Jr., noted that "progressive carries the connotation of third
partyism." Mrs. Lawrence Stapleton of Bryn Mawr agreed that "progressive"
was as "beclouded in the public mind" as the term "liberal." Finally, James
Carey, representing the labor caucus, suggested the name American Union
for Democratic Action, which, after a short debate, was abbreviated to
Americans for Democratic Action.[43]

Once the new name was selected, the ADA spent the remainder of the afternoon drawing up an organizational structure. The convention chose Leon Henderson and Wilson Wyatt as cochairmen. Loeb became the executive secretary. The organization voted to absorb the staff and facilities of the UDA's national office, beginning January 6, and decided that local UDA chapters would remain and affiliate with the ADA. A twenty-six member organizing committee, to meet periodically over the next few months, was established. Among its members were Humphrey, Niebuhr, Walter White, president of the NAACP, Dubinsky, Reuther, and Loeb. The conference also established the Committee of the Whole, charged with developing the ADA's legislative program. Its members included Robert Bendiner, Joseph Lash, Andrew Biemiller of the CIO-PAC, Bowles, Carey of the CIO, Galbraith, Rauh, Marvin Rosenberg, James Rowe, Jr., Arthur Schlesinger, Jr., and Wechsler.

For many of those present, one of the most memorable moments of the convention occurred just before the group adjourned for the evening. After sitting through a full day of deliberations, Mrs. Roosevelt stood to remind the assembled "best brains of liberalism" that they had said nothing about how to finance the new organization. "Now there's plenty of people with money in here who can make a substantial contribution to getting this thing going," she told the group. She volunteered the first $100 and pledged to raise another $1,000. Not to be outdone, David Dubinsky pledged $5,000, and soon all participants were reaching deep into their pockets for money. Although no one knew it at the time, the incident dramatized the financial problems that would plague the ADA throughout its history.[44]

Following Reuther's advice to stick with general statements, the new organization, at the end of the conference, issued a press release listing six "basic principles." In domestic policy the participants called for the extension of the New Deal "to insure decent levels of health, nutrition, shelter and education," as well as protection of civil liberties "from concentrated wealth and overcentralized government." Four of the principles concerned foreign policy. Still exuberant over the Allied victory, these liberals saw a new and expanded role for America. "Because the interests of the United States are the interests of free men everywhere," America should support "democratic and freedom-loving peoples the world over." This meant opposition to communism and fascism, both of which were "hostile to the principles of freedom and democracy on which the Republic has grown great." Claiming that any "sound foreign policy requires a healthy and prosperous domestic economy," the conference called for full support to the United Nations and endorsed the American plan for the control of atomic energy.[45]

Loeb was euphoric about the outcome of the conference. He confided to a friend that the five and a half years of previous work now seemed justified because they had "completely taken the ball away from the Communists in terms of the American liberal movement." The ADA's challenge to liberal fellow travelers was the culmination of the UDA's "historic function." "If we can follow through on it," he noted, "we have something of enormous proportions."[46] Loeb's optimism appeared justified when, in late January, the national board of the U.S. Student Assembly voted to accept the invitation of the National Board of ADA to become the ADA's student division, and changed its name to Students for Democratic Action. Most of the USSA's sixteen chapters subsequently voted to become SDA chapters.

Other prominent ADA members seemed to share Loeb's enthusiasm, and shortly after the founding convention many of the organization's best-known members traveled around the country establishing local chaters in as many major cities as possible. Arthur Schlesinger, Jr., Franklin Roosevelt, Jr., Eleanor Roosevelt, Loeb, and a young actor steeped in the New Deal tradition named Ronald Reagan toured extensively for the new organization. In the two months between the January meeting and the March convention, ADA leaders held organizational meetings in Chicago, Baltimore, Pittsburgh, and Philadelphia. On the West Coast there was a meeting in Seattle covering the states of Washington, Oregon, Idaho, and Montana, as well as one in Los Angeles for the state of California. In the Northeast, meetings were held in Massachusetts, Connecticut, New York, and New Jersey.[47]

Lukewarm public response in many of these cities forced Loeb to tone down his original optimism. He found public reception to the ADA generally "good" but also "spotty, particularly in terms of the situation in the left-of-center community." The problem was that in many of the larger cities where the ADA was trying to establish roots independent political groups were already in existence. In many of these cities the ADA was battling with the PCA for political loyalty. Loeb reported that in Detroit the Michigan Citizens Committee was a "united front organization" even though its leadership leaned more toward association with the ADA. The ADA decided that it "did not want affiliation of the group if there was a sizeable minority of communists in it." In Toledo, Ohio, the independent political group was noncommittal. Loeb admitted, "Our people have succeeded in keeping it out of PCA, but we can't move it into ADA yet." The ADA was especially interested in making gains in California but feared that an effective Wallace public relations campaign might have put the state out of reach. There was, one member reported, "great emotional attachment to Wallace in that area." The organization hoped to attract celebrities in order to counter Wallace's personal following in the state. Melvyn Douglas assumed responsibility for organizing fellow actors, making a special appeal to Danny Kaye, Frank Sinatra, Olivia de Havilland, Dinah Shore, and Bette Davis.[48]

The ADA could not expect much from the CIO in the immediate future. President Philip Murray was keeping his cards close to his chest, still unwilling to reveal his hand to either the ADA or the PCA. Murray sent a representative to the Willard Hotel in January, but his relationship with the ADA was not clear. Although he had earlier endorsed the PCA, Murray now saw the rival groups as a threat to the internal stability of his leadership in the CIO. To enforce his neutral position, Murray requested, and the CIO executive board on March 14, 1947, approved, a statement recommending that "the officers of the CIO . . . abstain from identifying themselves with either PCA or ADA and devote their time and attention to building CIO-PAC and strengthening its work." Underestimating the depth of the differences between the two groups, Murray hoped that in withholding CIO support, he would force the factions to merge.[49]

No membership data exist on the ADA in its early years, but later studies provide a clue as to the type of person the ADA attracted. They reveal that the "typical" member was a Jewish man, "somewhat under forty years of age, a professional holding a Bachelor's degree, married with just under two children per family" who lived in a single home which he owned or was purchasing. He was raised in middle- or upper- middle-class families where the father either owned his business, was engaged in a professional occupation or held a white-collar job. A study completed in 1964 of the national ADA confirmed these earlier findings, concluding that the organization was predominantly upper-middle class with an average income nearly twice the national average. Most members were professionals or owners or managers of a business.[50]

It is perhaps more revealing to identify those who did not join the ADA than to list those who did. Many liberals who expressed general sympathy with the ADA's attempt to create a non-communist alternative were offended by what they believed was the organization's excessive anticommunism. Both Thomas Amlie, Washington director of the UDA, and Chester Bowles attended the convention hoping the ADA would tone down its anticommunism as a first step toward a reconciliation with the non-communist elements of the PCA. Disappointed by the convention results, Amlie resigned from the UDA, while Bowles refused membership in the ADA for over a year. Amlie said he realized that the organization was going off in the wrong direction when he heard that "the boy wonder of Harvard, Mr. Arthur Schlesinger Jr.," planned to be "the key-note speaker at the preliminary meetings on the subject of foreign policy." Bowles, reflecting almost a year after the convention, reached a similar conclusion: "I thought that the ADA was concentrating too much of its time on opposing communism and not enough in opposing the Republican Party, which is the major threat in this country."[51]

Also absent were political party leaders and, with a few notable exceptions, Democratic elected officials. Also, while the national conference was able to attract a number of national labor leaders, the local chapters had difficulty enticing rank-and-file labor leaders into the organization. Like the PCA's, the ADA's membership was limited to a very small though influential segment of the Democratic party. Most party leaders wanted to keep the two organizations at a distance. Not only were they leery of both groups' declarations of independence, but they also felt culturally and emotionally distant from the programmatic and uncompromising liberalism of the PCA as well as the ADA. Unlike the PCA, however, whose conviction of independence from the party was clear, the ADA had an uncertain relationship with the party. The independent liberal community to which the ADA was trying to appeal was skeptical of the organization's avowed independence of party leaders; yet party leaders were put off by its proclamations of independence. Neither fish nor fowl, the ADA searched for a solution to its predicament.

Two liberal groups with strong roots in the New Deal were now vying for Roosevelt's legacy. Michael Straight of the *New Republic* commented later that the PCA and the ADA "moved into opposing trenches, and the ground between them became no-man's land." Observers speculated that a divided liberal movement could jeopardize New Deal programs. The *New York Times* editorialized that united the two groups "would perhaps be an important factor in national elections"; divided, however, they risked "the penalties of the proverbial house divided." Mayor Fiorello La Guardia of New York saw humor in the liberals' predicament. "The trouble with us liberals and progressives," he quipped, "is that we're not united. Let's not fool ourselves—we have more than fifty seven varieties."[52]

Members of the PCA resorted to print to emphasize the interests liberals shared and to plead with their anti-Communist rivals to work to overcome their minor differences. Freda Kirchwey wrote in the *Nation* that the ADA and the PCA were divided not over programmatic issues but over the question of communism. The "two organizations are so similar in purpose and in most personnel," she noted, "that their permanent separation" seems unnecessary as it is unfortunate." Kirchwey pleaded with the leaders of the two rival factions to meet in private, informal talks before "the lines of demarcation become too tightly drawn." Henry Wallace, by then editor of the *New Republic,* made a similar plea shortly after the ADA founding convention. In an article entitled "The Enemy Is Not Each Other," Wallace minimized liberal disunity while underscoring common values. "Liberals today," he wrote, "in the so-called warring groups are about 90% in agreement." If shared values were not enough, they should recognize they also had a mutual enemy—conservative reaction.[53]

In conjunction with its public efforts at reconciliation, the *New Republic* staff invited Arthur Schlesinger, Jr., to a luncheon meeting on February 20 to discuss the differences between the Progressive journal and the ADA. At the meeting Schlesinger debated Penn Kimball, Bruce Bliven, Henry Wallace, and Theodore White on the potential danger of the Communist party and the threat from Soviet expansionism. According to Schlesinger, White confronted him by asking, "What we want to find out is what the ADA has against the *New Republic.*" Schlesinger recounted a couple of grievances. First, the journal sent Helen Fuller, a vice-chairman of the PCA, to cover the ADA meeting. Second, Wallace reported erroneously in the journal that Mrs. Roosevelt was not a member of the ADA. From that point, Schlesinger recalled, the meeting got "rather heated." "From everything we can gather," Kimball shouted at Schlesinger, "ADA is obsessed with the Communist problem to the neglect of all the great fascist and war-making forces which are the real enemy of liberals." The *New Republic* position, Schlesinger claimed, is that "the most important thing in the world is to avoid war with Russia; the 'war party' . . . is trying to whip up public opinion in favor of this war; any attacks on American Communists or undue emphasis on the 'Communist problem' . . . simply strengthens the hand of the 'war party.' ADA is thus inevitably accelerating the drift toward war."[54]

The exchange between Schlesinger and the *New Republic* staff uncovered a deep crevice in the liberal landscape. The differences were ones not of style and tactics but of perceptions and goals. Wallace and his *New Republic* disciples believed that Soviet intransigence stemmed from a deep-seated fear of another invasion. Stalin's actions in Eastern Europe and the Middle East, they insisted, resulted from his desire to establish secure borders, and American actions had served only to aggravate his insecurity. Once Stalin was sure that American intentions were peaceful, he would be more compromising. Schlesinger and other anti-Communist liberals were critical of attempts to blame the United States for Soviet international behavior, believing that the Soviet Union was an ideological state that entertained notions of expanding its influence beyond its borders. The United States was simply responding in the only way possible to defend its interests without provoking a war.

While anti-Communist liberals and progressives bickered among themselves, Cold War tensions mounted, making any compromise between the two groups impossible. In February 1947 the British announced they would no longer provide economic and military aid to Greece and Turkey. Fearful that the Soviets would take advantage of the situation, Truman decided to assume the responsibility for the aid. He assembled a bipartisan group of congressional leaders and informed them of the administration's decision. After a lecture by Under Secretary of State Dean Acheson, who painted a vivid picture of a world divided into irreconcilable ideologies, Senator Arthur H. Vandenberg announced that he would support Truman's request only if the president made his position public. Vandenberg advised the president to go before Congress to dramatize the critical state of affairs—as he put it, to "scare hell out of the country."

Truman addressed Congress on March 12, 1947. He placed his proposal for assistance to Greece and Turkey in the broad and sweeping context of an ideological struggle between communism and democracy. "The very existence of the Greek state," he said, "is today threatened by the terrorist activities of several thousand armed men, led by Communists, who defy the government's authority." The United States, Truman declared, must "support peoples who are resisting attempted subjugation by armed minorities or by outside pressures. . . . The free peoples of the world look to us for support in maintaining their freedoms. If we falter in our leadership, we may endanger the peace of the world." Truman's shock therapy was meant to wake up Americans to the dangers of the postwar world. It succeeded.[55]

It appeared the Truman Doctrine would produce a revival of the fledgling Popular Front. Both the *New Republic* and the *Nation* opposed the president's new initiative. The PCA wasted no time denouncing the message as an invitation to war. In a statement released the day after Truman's address to Congress, it attacked the doctrine as marking "the end of an American policy based on one world" and presenting a policy that divided "the world into two camps." Henry Wallace was also quick to condemn Truman's policy. In a PCA-sponsored radio address, Wallace claimed that Truman's support for reactionary regimes in Greece and Turkey made him "the best spokesman Communism had." The policy means, he said, that there "is no regime too reactionary for us, provided it stands in Russia's path."[56]

While the PCA and other progressives were quick to denounce the Truman Doctrine, the ADA responded with mixed feelings. In one sense, it gave the ADA the issue it needed to separate itself from the PCA; yet, it was also difficult for liberals to digest any plan that emphasized military containment, called for unilateral action outside the purview of the United Nations, and supported countries that were far from democratic. Despite these reservations, anti-Communist liberals had been sounding the alarm about Soviet expansion for months, and Truman's plan appeared the only viable policy. Because of the potential divisiveness of the issue and because Truman's announcement came just two weeks before the ADA's national convention, Wyatt decided to reserve comment until the whole organization had a chance to deliberate on the issue.

The 250 delegates who assembled on top of the Hotel Washington on Saturday morning, March 27, had much work to do during their brief, two-day session. In addition to discussing the Truman Doctrine the delegates needed to develop a platform on domestic and foreign policy issues, one that would clearly demonstrate the ADA's differences with the PCA, to decide exactly what role the organization should play in partisan politics, and to elect officers and work out details of organizational structure and finances.

The Truman Doctrine, however, overshadowed all other issues. On the first day of the convention, more than half of the 250 delegates presented proposals before the foreign policy committee and its chairman, Marquis Childs. Meeting in closed session, Childs and the other committee members—Leon Henderson, Franklin Roosevelt, Jr., Arthur Schlesinger, Jr., the Reverend William Scarlett of St. Louis, Charles Bolte of the American Veterans Committee, and Thomas Finletter, a prominent New York lawyer—considered the proposals and wrote a statement, which Paul Porter, a former chairman of the Office of Price Administration and currently head of the American economic mission to Greece and Truman's personal envoy, read to the convention. The committee's platform claimed that there were democratic forces in Greece but that they needed economic assistance to flourish. Although the Greek government had "shortcomings," the committee's draft statement claimed, there was "still the friendly and untrammeled right of political discussion within Athens and within all Greece." Before discussing the foreign policy committee's report, delegates heard a speech by Porter, one of the most knowledgeable and persuasive advocates of the Truman Doctrine. Porter warned that if the United States refused to provide economic aid, he "would look for a complete economic collapse."[57]

As soon as Porter finished his speech, William Batt, Jr., rose to protest the committee resolution. Like other opponents of the doctrine, Batt saw a clear contradiction between the ADA's attempt to prevent Soviet expansion and its commitment to support democratic governments. Batt opposed the sending of military aid in a civil war that would "perpetuate an intolerable situation of Greeks killing Greeks with American arms." He presented a minority plank that opposed U.S. unilateral involvement in the Near East without UN sanction. Other members feared that paranoia over Soviet expansionism would force the United States "in the direction of support for every reactionary government in every country bordering on Russia or its satellites." One member charged that the ADA had a fanatical anti-Communist obsession: "I've met some of these anti-communists in various parts of the country, and my impression is that this hatred dominates their every political move." Mrs. James Downs, a member of the Baltimore board, accused the ADA of promoting "an emotional, negative policy dangerously close to being a crusade against Russia." It was obvious to her that the ADA hierarchy was "determined to make Russia appear as a devil with horns and tail."[58]

The comments of a New York delegate represented the majority point of view and showed how the hostility between the superpowers made liberals abandon their faith in one world and accept the existence of spheres of influence. The reality of the postwar situation, he said, is that the United States and the Soviet Union are engaged in a "power conflict." While liberals "would like to see one world . . . Russia has said that it cannot live in peace with capitalism or imperialism." Until the Russians provide some evidence of goodwill—some evidence that they have abandoned their quest for world conquest—liberals have to discard their ideal schemes for one world. It "would be foolish," he claimed, for the United States to ignore the existence of this power relationship and "give aid and relief on the basis of just humanitarian motives. We would be a laughing stock." The United States should provide "aid to Greece and Turkey because of that power fight not because of the nature of the government." Why, he asked, "should [we] try to democratize those nations"? While liberals did not like providing aid to regimes that were not democratic, they had, as Franklin Roosevelt, Jr., claimed, "to hold [their] noses" and give it.[59]

The delegates, convinced by those favoring the doctrine, passed a resolution stating, "Pending assumption of full responsibility by the United Nations, we believe that the United States must take action to achieve conditions in Greece under which free institutions may grow."[60]

The delegates expressed general agreement on most of the other political and domestic issues. The convention accepted resolutions declaring that the ADA was not the foundation for a third party, specified that Communists and fascists could not be members, and endorsed general and vague statements favoring "democratic planning and international cooperation." It also passed resolutions calling for government support of full employment; opposing elimination of industry-wide bargaining, compulsory arbitration, and prohibition of the closed shop; and advocating a comprehensive public housing law.[61]

With the question of the Truman Doctrine and domestic policy settled, the delegates turned their attention to the electing of officers and the writing of a constitution. The constitution created the officers of the organization. They included a national chairman, a chairman of the Executive Committee, and a treasurer, all to be elected by the delegates at the annual national convention. The delegates elected Wilson Wyatt chairman, Leon Henderson chairman of the Executive Committee, and Louis Harris treasurer. They also created the National Board, which was to meet four times a year and to be, according to the constitution, "the governing body of this organization between National Conventions." The board consisted of three executive officers, thirty-five members-at-large, five members from the student affiliate, one member from each local chapter having a minimum membership of one hundred, and one member from each state chapter. The annual convention could elect members to the National Board, or the Executive Committee could appoint members. Among those elected to the board in 1947 were the actor Melvyn Douglas, the labor leader David Dubinsky, the Wisconsin publisher William T. Evjue, Arthur M. Schlesinger, Jr., and Reinhold Niebuhr. The board also elected from its membership the Executive Committee, which was to "act on behalf of the Board between meetings." The Executive Committee, which met once a month, consisted of eight members, including Franklin D. Roosevelt, Jr., Hubert Humphrey, and the national officers.

The national convention held once a year was the "over-all" governing body of the ADA. Each of the local and state chapters was accorded delegates to the convention on the basis of the size of its membership. All national officers and members of the National Board were to be delegates; the student affiliate was also granted representation on the basis of membership; and the National Board could elect delegates-at-large, as long as they were members of the organization. The constitution required members to pay an annual membership fee of between three and five dollars, depending on the chapter. Each chapter also had to pay an annual charge of one dollar per member and to contribute an agreed-upon percentage of the chapter's income. The organization would grant local charters to any group of twenty-five or more that agreed to the general principles of the ADA constitution. Each chapter could "elect its own officers, determine policies on local issues, endorse local candidates and conduct their own activities in accordance with democratic procedures and the aims, policies and objectives of the National Organization."[62]

The convention also tried to define precisely the organization's role in American political life. Many labor leaders wanted the organization to serve as an American version of the British Fabian Society—a small, elite group of intellectuals, labor leaders, and politicians who would provide guiding principles for both political parties. They hoped to effect political change through long-term educational programs. They were not very enthusiastic about the ADA's becoming a "mass organization" with local chapters and a large membership. Another group, consisting primarily for former New Dealers and intellectuals, wanted the organization to be both a source of intellectual leadership and an effective political influence group.

The convention never satisfactorily resolved this debate over the ADA's role. Ernesto Galarza, a Washington chapter delegate, commented that it was "unquestionably the weak point of the conference" that "no written document on organizational aims and methods came out of the conference." One of the basic issues that went unresolved, Galarza complained, was whether the ADA was going to be a "leadership or a mass organization."[63] Galarza asked the crucial question that at one time or another confronts all organizations committed to social and political change: How does an organization maintain a balance between its "politics" and its "vision"? Organizations that conform to the societal consensus in order to participate successfully in the political debate can often find themselves compromising their ideals for the sake of short-run social change. But organizations that remain committed to their visionary goals can find themselves politically isolated and ineffective.[64] Although no one among the founders of the ADA could answer Galarza's query, the question would not go away.

The opposition to the Truman Doctrine within the ADA, along with the harsh treatment from the liberal press, dissuaded ADA leaders from taking a large role in backing it. There were no public rallies, no massive letter-writing campaigns, no membership drives organized around the decision. Support for the doctrine was hardly an act of callous political expediency; the decision actually left the ADA almost alone among liberal groups in America. What it did demonstrate was the growing similarity in worldview between America's largest anti-Communist liberal organization and the Truman administration.

The organization tried to distract attention from its support of the Truman Doctrine by commissioning an economic report that would put on display the ADA's strong New Deal heritage. Just a few days after the convention, Wyatt asked Chester Bowles to head a committee on economic stabilization to draft a "concrete plan to avert a possible economic depression." He gave the committee two weeks to deliberate and present its position. Supporting Bowles on the committee were Seymour Harris, John Kenneth Galbraith, and Alvin Hansen of Harvard and the veteran New Dealers Richard Gilbert and Robert Nathan. The ADA's recommendations were very similar to the Truman administration proposals. The committee called on Congress, in cooperation with the president, to establish a price adjustment board, which would work with industry on a "voluntary basis" to facilitate a 10 percent reduction of prices. Along with voluntary price reductions, it asked Congress to increase purchasing power by raising the federal minimum wage from forty to sixty-five cents per hour. The committee also advocated tax relief for lower-income taxpayers by raising individual exemptions from $500 to $700 and by lowering excise taxes; a new housing program that would cut construction costs by 20 percent; and a revised farm program that would extend wartime price supports, broaden crop insurance, and curb excessive speculation in farm products.[65] Not surprisingly, the administration reacted favorably to the report. Both Edwin Nourse, the chairman of the Council of Economic Advisers, and Leon Keyserling, also a council member, wrote Loeb to express their general acceptance of the ADA's program. It is "obvious to any careful reader,"

Nourse wrote, "that the essential part of the report parallels material made in the President's economic report and subsequent speeches, and in the written and spoken words of the Council."[66]

The ADA strategy may have paid off. The report diverted attention away from its support of the Truman Doctrine and briefly provided a much needed infusion of harmony. The *Nation* called the ADA's economic program "moderate and realistic." Even the *New Republic* gave the report favorable coverage, providing a detailed diagram of the committee's recommendations. The editors called the program "a comprehensive, detailed program designed to head off depression."[67]

The ADA's timely release of its economic report prevented the PCA from taking advantage of opposition to the ADA's support of the Truman Doctrine. The ADA, on the defensive and increasingly tied to the policies of the Truman administration, hoped for a dramatic initiative that would help rally public support for its program. It got its wish in June, when Secretary of State George Marshall used the occasion of a Harvard commencement address to announce a cooperative effort to rebuild the economy of all of Europe, including the Soviet Union. Marshall explained that his program was "directed not against any country or doctrine, but against hunger, poverty, desperation, and chaos." The Allies were enthusiastic about the plan, but the Russians were not. In July the Soviet foreign minister informed the United States that his country would not participate. The Soviets went further and also prevented other Communist eastern bloc countries from attending.

Although progressives were at first hopeful that the Marshall Plan marked a departure from the Truman Doctrine, they soon came to view it as a clever disguise of traditional Truman anticommunism. In October, Wallace wrote the PCA epitaph for the plan. Wallace saw the Marshall Plan as just another attempt to divide East from West and to impose "reactionary governments and influence the economic system of Western Europe to the benefit of Wall Street." It made matters worse that not only the idea but also the execution of the plan were flawed. Wallace claimed that the administration and Congress were simply unwilling to ask the hard questions necessary to stabilize Europe. "The heart of the problem is a shortage of 10 million tons of bread grains in Western Europe and 20 million tons of feed grains in the U.S.," he held. American farmers can make money by feeding their livestock wheat rather than corn while "Europe desperately needs wheat." Wallace wanted Congress to pass a law that would give the Commodity Credit Corporation authority to purchase wheat from farmers, to prohibit feeding wheat to livestock, and to ration meat and butter. "This is strong action," Wallace wrote, but "if we are to ward off chaos in Europe, such action will be necessary."[68]

While for the PCA the Marshall Plan was another Truman attempt to isolate the Russians and increase international tension, for the ADA, as the historian Alonzo Hamby has noted it "became an all-important rallying point, worthy of unreserved support on its merits and also a means of isolating the PCA." From the start the Marshall Plan provided the ADA with the perfect opportunity to play up its differences with the PCA and show, once and for all, that the PCA was subservient to the Communist line. The difference between the ADA and the PCA on the Marshall Plan, the ADA *World* observed, "should serve to clarify a difference which may have seemed obscure to some progressives."[69]

The Marshall Plan, the ADA claimed, "brings a moment of high hope to a world rapidly losing faith in its capacity to avoid the fatal drift toward suicidal war." Calling it the "last chance for world peace," the ADA urged "bold leadership" and "swift action" in order to enact the program. The plan, the ADA stated, is the "conclusive answer to those who have decried the 'negativism' of U.S. policy" and deserves "the vigorous support of all progressives in the legislative battles ahead." If the United States does not act, the penalty "will be the loss of Europe to freedom and the irrevocable division of the world." The president should make clear that

> We do not intend to keep Europe on the dole forever; but that we will make a major investment in the restoration of European productivity. We do not propose to help prop up the European economy, but to help rebuild it; not to prolong the prison rations and the hopeless days of the unhappy peoples of Europe, but to place a hopeful future in their grasp. Half-hearted authorizations, pinch-penny appropriations will not be enough. The task is in the magnitude of 30 billion dollars over a five year period.[70]

Whereas it quietly backed the Truman Doctrine, it publicly rallied its membership in support of European recovery. The Students for Democratic Action (SDA) tried to counter Wallace's appeal to the idealism of college students with "a vigorous and ambitious appeal to the responsible and most alert student leadership."[71]

Many ADA leaders had hoped that the organization's support of the Marshall Plan would increase its membership and strengthen it financially. Their hopes, however, were not realized. While statistics on ADA membership during these early years are sketchy at best, it appears the organization had only a handful of active and successful chapters, in New York, Philadelphia, Boston, and Chicago. The organization had little success in spreading outside of these urban centers, and no success at all in establishing new roots outside of the Northeast and Chicago.

Less than nine months after the euphoria of the Willard conference, the ADA faced a $20,000 debt, and many members worried that the organization could not survive without a generous infusion of money. The biggest problem, however, was the lack of labor support. The ADA was unable to make much headway with CIO members, because of Murray's ban against working with the PCA or the ADA. There was considerable disagreement over how the ADA should address this problem. Some union leaders in the ADA suggested the organization imitate Communist tactics of direct appeals to membership, while others argued that the only way to get results was to win over union leadership, a difficult task given Murray's restrictions. Only three unions contributed money to the ADA in 1947: the International Ladies Garment

Workers, which donated $13,500; the Hotel and Restaurant Employees, $5,000; and the International Association of Machinists, $2,000.[72]

As the eventful year came to an end, the ADA was searching for a way to solidify its relationship with the Truman administration, vanquish its PCA rival, and also solve its vexing financial problems. At a September 1947 National Board meeting, James Roosevelt seemed to point a way out of the predicament. Perhaps, he suggested, the organization should do something "glamorous," such as running a candidate for vice-president, to attract attention and distinguish itself from the PCA.[73] Unwittingly, Henry Wallace would give the ADA the opportunity it needed.

2

The ADA, Wallace, and the 1948 Election

The year 1948 provided the ADA with its first test in a national election. Although the organization hoped to win recognition and influence and, perhaps most important, to deal a decisive blow to its rival the PCA, its leaders were not blind to the risks involved. There was always the fear that Wallace would attract liberals frustrated with Truman's candidacy or that the divisions in the Democratic party would lead to a period of prolonged reaction. Still small, financially weak, and uncertain about its role in national politics, the ADA entered the election season with neither a candidate to support nor a clear strategy to follow.

In May and June of 1947, before announcing his candidacy, Wallace went on a coast-to-coast speaking tour. Surprisingly large crowds paid admission to hear him at PCA-sponsored rallies. In Chicago he drew 20,000 spirited fans; in Los Angeles, 27,000. Uplifted by the enthusiastic public reception, many Progressives speculated about a Wallace-led third party. Through the hot summer months, Wallace continued to travel and speak extensively, hinting at the possibility of a new party. "If the Democratic party is a war party, if my party continues to attack civil liberties, if both parties stand for high prices and depression," he told a PCA rally in September, "then the people must have a new party of liberty and peace."[1] On December 29, 1947, Wallace ended months of speculation by officially announcing his candidacy in a nationwide radio address. The Truman administration, he declared, was leading America toward fascism. "We are not for Russia and we are not for communism, but we recognize Hitlerite methods when we see them in our own land." He knew that he did not have a massive organization, but he had, he believed, "assembled a Gideon's Army, small in number, powerful in conviction."[2]

The American Communist party had special interest in Wallace's decision. Through the summer and early fall, while Wallace debated whether or not to run, the party spurned the idea of supporting a third-party challenge. A progressive, declared Eugene Dennis, the party chief, can win in 1948 only if the campaign "is so organized and so broadened as to bring about a situation in which there can be a coalition candidate, backed by the independent and third party forces, running as a Democrat." American Communists abandoned their cautious policy in October 1947, when the international party created the Cominform and advocated an organized counteroffensive against "American imperialism." Emboldened, party leaders now saw the Wallace candidacy as an opportunity to join the worldwide working-class movement against imperialism. Their official position changed from support of Wallace as an independent candidate on the Democratic ticket to encouragment of a third-party movement headed by Wallace. Chairman Dennis announced the new policy in a public address in February 1948. If the "Progressive party develops," he said, "we communists will seek to affiliate with it." Unfortunately for Wallace, Dennis kept his promise. "Communists everywhere supported the movement," recalled the labor radical Len De Caux. "They did much of the hard and thankless unpaid work, without seeking the public recognition that is one of its rewards."[3]

The Communists were the only organized group to express much interest in the Wallace movement. Wallace attracted little labor support, and only one prominent ex–New Dealer, Rexford Tugwell, associated himself with the campaign. Few liberals were eager to jump on the Wallace bandwagon. The Liberal party's chairman, Adolf Berle, Jr., and many liberal publications like *PM* and the *Nation* opposed his candidacy. Despite his attempt to appeal to minority groups—organized workers angry with inflation, Negroes and Jews fighting discrimination at home, and women fighting for equal rights—most of them did not support him.

But Wallace's fortunes seemed to rise in February, when in a New York special congressional election a Wallace-supported candidate, Leo Isacson, scored an impressive, two-to-one victory over a candidate backed by Ed Flynn, the Bronx Democratic machine boss, by Mrs. Roosevelt, and by Mayor William O'Dwyer. "If the special election in the Bronx can be taken as a test-tube event," *Newsweek* reported, "then it is evident that President Truman will perform a miracle if he carries New York State next November." Isacson's victory inflated Wallace's expectations and the ADA's fears. National expectations for the Wallace ticket zoomed, amid forecasts of up to four million votes. A *New York Times* survey completed after the New York election indicated that Wallace's support had risen in many other key industrial states, including Michigan, Pennsylvania, Illinois, and California. The survey concluded that Truman would have a difficult time carrying any of these states in November.[4]

Compounding Truman's already large problems in these states was his inconsistent policy toward the partition of Palestine. At the end of 1947 Truman had supported a plan that would, under United Nations auspices, divide Palestine into Jewish and Arab states. When the Arabs balked, the United States hedged. In March 1948 Truman abandoned the partition plan and instead called for a UN trusteeship until a new agreement could be reached. Truman's zigzag policy only confirmed suspicions that he was not really in control of foreign policy, and aroused fear among Jews in the United States that the president had fallen prey to a powerful cabal of Arab partisans in the State Department. The problem had a political dimension as well, because almost half of the five million Jews in the United States lived in New York, where they composed 17 percent of the state's population. They also made up approximately 5 percent of the population in Pennsylvania and Illinois—which, with New York, had a total of 110 electoral votes.

The ADA and its anti-Communist colleagues in labor and the Truman administration were uneasy about Wallace's candidacy. For the ADA the challenge was obvious: not only was Wallace the spokesman for the rival PCA, but his expressed willingness to work with Communists and his "appeasement" of the Soviet Union were anathema to anti-Communist liberals. As early as June 1947 Loeb wrote that the Wallace candidacy took the "Communist Party from the Texas League to the Majors in one jump." The ADA did not believe that Wallace could actually win the election, but it was afraid he could drain off enough Democratic votes to ensure a Republican victory. Loeb had told an ADA National Board meeting in June 1947 that it would be "short-sighted to overestimate Mr. Wallace's strength in the country as a whole, but it would be equally short-sighted to underestimate his following among liberals, even among liberals who disagree with much of his thinking."[5]

The ADA wasted no time attacking Wallace for his decision to seek the presidency. The day after Wallace announced, the ADA issued a press release affirming its opposition to a third-party movement. The statement revealed the ADA strategy for undercutting Wallace's appeal—paint a portrait of a well-intentioned Communist dupe whose political advice came directly from Moscow. Explaining that there was nothing wrong with "different American political parties," it called the Progressive party "an unholy alliance of Communists and reactionaries." Regardless of Wallace's intentions, it went on, "the goals of his sponsors are clear. They hope to divide progressives, create national confusion and insure the triumph of reactionary isolationism in 1948. They believe the achievement of these aims will serve the world interests of the international Communist movement."[6]

Much of organized labor also feared that a third party would "weaken the possibility of electing a progressive Congress." It had good reason to oppose Wallace's candidacy. Following the wave of strikes after the war in the basic industries of coal, steel, automobiles, and transportation, there was strong public outcry to "put labor in its place." In response to public pressure, Congress tried on a number of occasions to curb union abuses. Although unsuccessful in the Case bill of 1946, Congress did pass, and Truman signed, the Lea Act, aimed at curbing featherbedding practices in the musicians union. In July of 1946 Congress passed the Hobbs Anti-Racketeering Act, which made it a criminal offense to deny or interfere with the flow of interstate commerce by extortion.

Republicans in the elections of 1946 had taken advantage of the public frustration over inflation and the dearth of consumer goods, by campaigning on the issue of curbing union power. Having secured majorities in both houses of Congress, the Republican party in June of 1947 passed the Taft-Hartley

Act, which attempted to redress the balance of power that had shifted steadily in labor's favor since the passage of the Wagner Act. The bill identified unfair labor practices, required union officers seeking certification with the National Labor Relations Board to sign oaths that they were not Communists, and provided for "cooling off" periods if strikes threatened national health and safety. The provision outlawing the closed shop worried labor leaders most of all. On June 20 Truman went before a joint session of Congress to announce his veto of the bill. Within three days of Truman's message, both the House and the Senate garnered more than enough votes to override the veto.[7]

The ordeal over Taft-Hartley came as a shock to labor leaders grown complacent as a result of the federal beneficence under the New Deal. Labor realized that it could not disregard public opinion or rely too heavily upon the national government for support against an irate public. "It has led labor leaders," wrote Herbert Harris in the *New Republic,* "to reconsider basic policies and practices which have remained virtually unchanged since the days of Samuel Gompers." Labor leaders now know that they have "to go in harder for politics on a doorbell-ringing, ward-by-ward, year-round basis, and that the haphazard 'reward-your-friends, punish-your-enemies' strategy has to be supplanted by a more coherent set of political beliefs and purposes." Although unions had been active in politics prior to 1947, Taft-Hartley stimulated union political activity of unprecedented intensity and, perhaps more than any other single act, edged labor closer to the administration.[8]

For Philip Murray, Taft-Hartley meant not only that labor had to start flexing its political muscle but also that the public would not tolerate Communists in important labor positions. Most Americans, according to *Public Opinion Quarterly,* wanted Communists out of the labor unions. In October 1947 some 64 percent of the American public believed that avowed Communists should be banned from holding public office or executive positions in a labor union. The same percentage agreed with the provisions of Taft-Hartley that required officers of labor unions to swear they were not Communists.[9] For Murray the message was clear: the CIO had to abandon its Communist ties. With the public still harboring suspicions about the CIO's Communist heritage, Murray assumed the best defense was a good offense. In January 1948 the fifty-one-member CIO executive board passed a resolution denouncing the formation of a third party as "politically unwise," and shortly afterward the CIO-PAC published a pamphlet called "Third Party: Red Ally of Reaction," which hammered home the connection between Wallace and the Communists.[10]

Truman's chief political strategist, Special Counsel Clark Clifford, was not blind to either the political dangers or the oportunities that a Wallace candidacy presented. Clifford, a St. Louis attorney, had joined Truman's staff as a naval aide in 1945 only to become, within the year, one of his closest advisers. Polished and refined, Clifford was an excellent manager of people and had a talent for reconciling conflicting information. His famous forty-three-page memorandum, submitted to Truman on November 19, 1947, became the blueprint for Truman's reelection campaign. Although Wallace had not yet announced his candidacy, Clifford was so certain he would run that he based all his projections on a Wallace third-party challenge. Clifford advised Truman to undercut Wallace's support among liberals and progressives by moving to the left. Such a move, Clifford felt, could be accomplished with little backlash from the conservative South. Not only was the South a traditionally "safe" Democratic stronghold, but since Truman would never get any of his liberal programs through Congress anyway, the South would have nothing to hold against him.

Clifford warned Truman against assuming that only Communists supported Wallace. The former vice-president, Clifford insisted, also had a large following among young voters, pacifists, and the "lunatic fringe." Truman's task was to identify Wallace with the Communists while isolating his other potential supporters. Clifford recommended that Truman work around the "moribund" Democratic party organization and establish a direct relationship with labor and liberal leaders. The memorandum devoted considerable attention to labor and significantly less to the "amorphous group" called liberals. Clifford confirmed that Truman could not win without active labor support. The liberals, he wrote, although small in number, were also very influential. Clifford recognized that foreign policy issues were forcing liberals away from Wallace and into the Truman camp. Shrewdly, he advised the president to capitalize on this situation by emphasizing his differences with Wallace on these issues.

Clifford also warned that many liberals, especially ADA members, felt "cut off" from the government because of the influence of the southern wing of the party. He suggested that Truman appoint liberals to top-level positions, even if they could not be approved, and that he hit home on six issues, all dear to liberals: high prices, housing, the Marshall Plan, tax revision, conservation of natural resources in the West, and civil rights.[11]

Truman took most of Clifford's recommendations to heart. He opened his campaign with a State of the Union Message in January 1948 that made a direct appeal to the liberal-progressive voter. In his forty-three minutes on the speaker's rostrum, Truman presented a mail-order catalog of New Deal programs. He stressed his ten-point inflation control program, human rights, human resources, education, conservation, higher living standards, farm economy, and an income tax reduction. Truman followed up this address with specific messages to Congress advocating a far-reaching housing program, stronger rent control, a sweeping enlargement of Social Security coverage with higher benefits, and federal aid to education. The president then went on the offensive against the conservative Congress for not supporting his program. *Time* commented that, "except for universal military training and the European Recovery Program, there was little or nothing that Candidate Henry Wallace could not approve."[12]

As part of his plan to woo liberals, Clifford recruited William Batt, a founder of the Philadelphia chapter of the ADA, to organize a small research group within the Democratic National Committee. Batt spent a few weeks assembling a staff that included many of his friends from the Philadelphia chapter of the American Veterans Committee as well as the ADA. Ken Birkhead was a member of both groups; Dr. Johannes Hoeber helped organize the ADA in Philadelphia and later joined Mayor Joseph Clark's reform government; David Lloyd was the former head of the ADA's legislative and research department; and John Barriere was a Paul Douglas protégé from the University of Chicago. Living a cloistered life in a set of offices above Dupont Circle, Batt and his small staff prepared briefing books on labor, civil liberties, housing, and foreign policy. These books became useful references for Truman's speechwriters and a main source for the president's statements during the campaign.

The ADA had earned enough respect in the administration to draw more direct overtures. After his testimony before the Senate Foreign Relations Committee on behalf of the Marshall Plan, Paul Porter met with the DNC's chairman, Howard McGrath, and his assistant, Gael Sullivan, who was given the job of bringing liberals back into the Democratic mainstream. While there is no formal record of the discussion, Sullivan prepared a brief agenda he hoped would keep the discussion focused. Three items were on the agenda: financial aid for the ADA, the enlistment of ADA aid for the Democratic party, and a reciprocal show of interest in the ADA by Truman.[13]

Truman hoped that by moving to the left he could undercut the liberals' dissatisfaction and offer them an alternative to Wallace. While much of organized labor took the bait, the ADA did not. Most ADA leaders remained unconvinced that Truman was the best man for the job, even though at the time he was the only one available. Truman lacked the grace and magnetism that this generation of liberals, who looked to the White House for guidance and inspiration, had come to expect. For them, the presidency was a symbol of moral leadership as well as a powerful instrument for effecting change. The most common complaint against Truman was that despite his progressive stands, he had not, as Loeb explained, "succeeded in uniting the Democrats or the liberals of the country." As Hubert Humphrey had declared in early 1947, the great "tragedy of our movement is that we have everything except a dramatic and appealing symbol on the national level."[14]

Unable to support either Wallace or Truman, many ADA liberals were in a bind. Chester Bowles confided to Humphrey that "under no circumstances" could he support Henry Wallace, whom Bowles believed to be "dominated by Communist influence." He had no alternative "except to follow Truman and hope that somehow he [could] be influenced to free himself of his present militaristic influences and to act as well as talk in liberal terms." Even Humphrey concurred: "I know that a Republican victory would be another blow to progressive government. I know what a Wallace victory would be even worse. We seem to have a gun pointed at us and are being told to accept what we have, for fear that it might be worse." That, Humphrey admitted, "is a bad alternative in these days."[15]

Liberals not only distrusted Truman's commitment to the New Deal but also feared that if he was at the head of the ticket, Wallace and the Republicans would make major gains at the polls. Bowles was afraid that he would lose his own bid for the Connecticut governorship if Truman headed the ticket. He reasoned, "If Truman runs I would have very little chance of splitting off enough votes to come through." But Wallace would have no excuse for running if the Democrats nominated a real liberal like the Chicago economist Paul Douglas. "If he did continue, it would become gradually clear to everyone that he was actually being run by the Communists and his non-Communist support would disappear rapidly."[16]

Humphrey, seeking a Minnesota Senate seat, was, like Bowles, especially sensitive to the political climate and worried about a Truman disaster at the polls. Humphrey had written Henderson in March 1947 that there was "no enthusiasm for Truman out here." He suggested either General Dwight Eisenhower or Supreme Court Justice William O. Douglas for the nomination. Liberals have to do something, he warned, "because we not only face defeat in November—we face a possible disintegration of the whole social Democratic bloc in this country. If we are going to lose, we ought to lose with a good candidate who can help us hold our forces together and, particularly, help us on the Congressional level." Although he claimed to "have a soft spot" in his heart for Truman, he suggested that "for the good of the country, for the good of the party, and for the good of progressive government, a select group of prominent individuals must pay Mr. Truman a visit and ask him to step aside."[17]

Unwilling to accept Truman as the liberal standard-bearer, yet unable to find an alternative, the ADA National Convention meeting in Philadelphia in February 1948 decided to withhold endorsement of any presidential candidate until the parties held their conventions and nominated their candidates. There was certainly no enthusiasm for Truman, but no one knew a way out of the dilemma. Liberals simply had few alternatives. "It's hard to believe that the ADA will support any imaginable Republican presidential candidate," the *New Republic* reported, but it also "doesn't trust President Truman's capacity to appeal convincingly to liberals." Although some members wanted the convention to give Truman "terms" for their support, until the ADA was in a position to deliver a large number of votes at the polls, it was in no position to do so. "In short," the *New Republic* concluded, "it seems the ADA will be for Truman in the end, unless—as one spokesman remarked was not impossible—some miracle should provide a new Democratic nominee at the convention." An observer at the convention remarked on the "palpable restlessness" of the delegates. Most participants "had little hope that either of the candidates, Truman or the GOP nominee, and either of the platforms would hold any more concrete promise of true liberalism next summer than now." Most members felt that only the National Board, scheduled to meet in Pittsburgh in April, had authority to make such an important policy change. In the meantime, the ADA decided to put its efforts into drafting Hubert Humphrey for vice-president, working on a civil rights platform for the convention, and co-ordinating a "plan of action" against Wallace.[18]

Paradoxically, the platform that the convention adopted was almost identical with Truman's program, though, as *Newsweek* reported, "written in sharper, more insistent language." The platform called for the reinstitution of price controls, denounced racial discrimination, and warmly embraced the Marshall Plan. When Senator Francis J. Myers of Pennsylvania called for support of Truman in the 1948 campaign, not one delegate applauded. According to one report, all sat "in glum silence." Delegate after delegate angrily declared that Truman's "actions belied his New Deal words." They denounced the president for appointing Wall Streeters to administration posts even while attacking Wall Street, and for abandoning Wyatt's housing program "under pressure from real estate interests." Berle cited the long and growing list of New Dealers ousted from government posts under the Truman administration. "The President," he said, "takes his orders from the rotten, corrupt, reactionary Democratic machines." Others assailed the embargo against the shipment of arms to Palestine. While opposing Truman's candidacy, the ADA showed no enthusiasm for either Senator Robert Taft of Ohio or for Henry Wallace's third party. Delegates cheered loudly when Wyatt denounced the "dismal 80th Congress" and again when he branded Wallace's candidacy as "dangerous and irresponsible." The ADA was much closer to Truman than it was at the time willing to admit.[19]

The convention reluctantly accepted Truman's inevitable nomination, but the idea of a civil rights fight did strike a responsive chord. Loeb saw it as a way to assert liberal power at the Democratic convention: "If any serious compromises are made on this issue, the position of the Northern and Western liberals would be impossible. Furthermore, in the event that HST is the candidate, his position and ours, if we endorse him, would be much stronger if the Convention wins a good fight on this issue."[20] The liberals had a long-standing commitment to the issue, but they also found that a civil rights fight served some very practical purposes—it allowed the ADA to be for the Democrats without being for Truman; it gave them the opportunity to score against conservative southerners in the party; and, most important, it would prevent Henry Wallace from making political gains with an issue on which the Democrats were vulnerable.

In announcing his candidacy, Wallace had taken a strong stand on civil rights. Until Wallace's announcement Truman had tried to retain black support through rhetoric and token executive action. He publicly condemned discrimination but refused to sacrifice political capital to take direct action against it. Truman responded to Wallace's challenge by sending on February 2, 1948, a 3,500-word message to Congress asking for enactment of an omnibus civil rights program, including a federal antilynching law and an anti–poll tax statute. Southern Democrats accused Truman of "stabbing the South in the back," of "kissing the feet of the minorities," and of trying to "out-Wallace Wallace." Senator James Eastland of Mississippi warned that the proposals "would destroy the last vestige of the South's social institutions and mongrelize her people." On February 19, 52 out of the 103 southern Democrats in the House of Representatives caucused to consider what action to take. They put the administration on notice that the party would face "serious consequences" if it included a civil rights plank in the platform. The southern reaction seemed to scare Truman from submitting his legislation. Although he remained publicly committed to the principles of his February 2 message, he decided to shelve his omnibus bill. The president was clearly in retreat, protecting his flank against the possibility of a southern bolt.[21]

The *New Republic*'s report on the convention recognized a critical problem about the ADA's role in the election—that it was in no position to organize a broad-based movement against an incumbent president. As of June 1948 the ADA claimed it had members in thirty-seven states and seventeen chapters—2,955 chapter members plus 721 members-at-large. Most of the members were concentrated in a few states; just five states—California, Illinois, Maryland, New York, Pennsylvania—and the District of Columbia accounted for over 80 percent of total membership.[22] Most of its funding came from three sources: labor unions, private donations, and chapter income derived from quotas and membership fees. Through the first two years of its existence, the ADA grew to rely more on labor donations and private contributions for its financial sustenance, and less on chapter income. Consequently, the organization's financial well-being rested upon the support of a few individuals not necessarily responsible to broader chapter opinion. In 1947 four labor unions made contributions of over $1,000 to the ADA. David Dubinsky's ILGWU was by far the largest contributor, with a $13,500 donation. The Hotel and Restaurant Employees added $5,000; the International Association of Machinists, $2,000; and the Upholsterers International, $1,000. Total labor income equaled $22,000, or nearly 22 percent of the total for that year. In the excitement of the 1948 presidential election campaign, however, the ILGWU's $24,000 donation alone surpassed the total union contribution of 1947. The Hotel and Restaurant Employees doubled their contribution to $10,000, and a number of other unions contributed for the first time. The UAW, under Walter Reuther, added $10,000, and the United Steelworkers contributed $5,000, as did the Textile Workers. Altogether union contributions were over $55,000 in 1948, more than double the sum of 1947. These contributions represented 45 percent of the ADA's annual income.

Even with strong labor support the ADA had difficulty balancing its books. Personal contributions from a few influential members constituted the second-largest share of the ADA's income. For both 1947 and 1948 just twenty-two individuals donated over one-third of the organization's budget. While combined labor and individual contributions accounted for the bulk of ADA's income, chapter income never established itself as a major source of revenue. In 1947 six chapters contributed over $1,000 to the national office—Chicago, Detroit, District of Columbia, New York, and Philadelphia. All told, chapter contributions came to almost $17,000, or 17 percent of the total income. In 1948 chapter income dropped by $4,000 and, most important, represented a much smaller percentage of the budget.[23]

Given its precarious finances, the ADA was in a poor position to affect political events in 1948. Short of a miracle at the convention, the ADA could only hope Truman would voluntarily withdraw from the race. Truman laid that notion to rest when he announced his candidacy in March. Loeb wrote that while "Truman's announcement of his candidacy was perhaps expected," it "was a body blow." Loeb called a special Executive Committee meeting on March 18 to discuss the "Truman problem." Realizing the feisty president was not going to step aside, the ADA turned its attention to the question that Humphrey had asked in 1947: "How can we peacefully and effectively get rid of the present incumbent?"[24]

A few days before the Executive Committee meeting, Loeb circulated a memorandum of selected comments about a Truman candidacy. The comments were less than encouraging. Democratic leaders in New York termed Truman's nomination "hopeless"; Al Hayes, vice-president of the Machinists Union and secretary-treasurer of the Machinists' Political League, reported that Truman was "not popular with their membership"; the Santa Barbara ADA Chapter urged support of "any candidate but Truman"; Chester Bowles wrote that Truman "would be unlikely to get anywhere in Connecticut"; and an unnamed PCA staff person suggested "that the liberal and labor people start campaigning for someone else, because a Truman nomination would be disastrous to the whole liberal-labor coalition, to say nothing of the success of the campaign."[25] Although he warned that it was crucial for the ADA to be "an important factor in the election," Loeb was uncertain about how to achieve that goal.

Loeb also met with David Dubinsky and Walter Reuther to discuss strategy for the meeting. Both believed that a Truman candidacy would be a catastrophe for the party, but Dubinsky was less willing to fight Truman's nomination publicly. He feared that if the ADA burned its bridges to the Truman administration and if the president won the nomination, the organization would lose all the influence it had worked so hard to establish. He advocated instead a covert campaign against a Truman nomination. Reuther was so certain that Truman's nomination would be a disaster for liberals that he wanted the ADA to lead a dump-Truman movement in favor of either Eisenhower or Douglas.[26] The Executive Committee leaned closer to the Dubinsky position, refusing to overturn the February convention decision to take "no public position . . . with regard to the nomination of President Truman."[27]

Perhaps most significant about both the February convention and the March Executive Committee meeting was the close working relationship the ADA established with labor. Although Philip Murray did not attend either meeting, the AFL's president, William Green, attended the convention, and a number of CIO dignitaries were present at both. At one point during the convention, Reuther and Green stood together on the dais to pledge a "working partnership" with the ADA in its fight "against reaction of the left and right." Union members also accunted for over half of the twenty-eight at-large seats on the ADA National Board, and Hugo Ernst of the Hotel and Restaurant Workers (AFL) and Emil Rieve of the Textile Workers (CIO) were named vice-chairmen.[28] In the early spring of 1948, it appeared that the Wallace threat was doing more to create a close ADA-labor alliance than anything the ADA had done in the preceding year.

Not even the threat of Wallace, however, could temper the growing friction between the local chapters and the national. This tension between a cautious leadership concerned with preserving influence and a more assertive membership committed to maintaining independence was to be a constant, though underlying, theme throughout the ADA's history. It was not, however, until after 1965, during the debates over the Vietnam War, that this division would become irreconcilable. As nearly autonomous political units, the chapters, especially the larger and more influential branches in Philadelphia, Chicago, and Washington, D.C., attempted to assert greater control over the national. At the convention, the delegates rewrote a number of resolutions on the floor—each time in favor of asserting chapter control. The delegates overturned a constitutional provision that permitted the National Board to choose 30 percent of the participants to the convention, and they insisted that board members devote some of their time to local chapter affairs, despite warnings from the leadership that prominent members did not have time and, if pressed, would leave the organization.

Even though the convention reaffirmed the ADA's neutral position on Truman, many of the chapters were growing restless. Claiming that, without a candidate, they were having difficulty organizing and mobilizing support on issues, they pressured the national to break away from its nonendorsement policy. Several chapters threatened to take independent action because they believed it essential "to an effective appeal to liberal sentiment in their communities—or as an effective counteraction to the Wallace third-party appeal." Several board members and many top labor leaders promised to raise the question at the upcoming board meeting in Pittsburgh. One disgruntled chapter representative declared, "On all sides there has been a growing (and more openly expressed) desire for action, whatever it might be."[29]

In March and April public cries for dumping the president also mounted. The South was incensed by his civil rights programs; Jewish voters, by his about-face on the partition of Palestine. Democratic politicians feared for their political lives with Truman at the head of the ticket. "No New York Democrat feels safe with a ticket headed by Truman," the *Nation* reported. In New York both Boss Flynn and Mayor O'Dwyer were talking openly of dumping Truman. The Chicago machine leader Jacob Arvey told the Democratic national chairman, J. Howard McGrath, that he could not support Truman's nomination. Louis Hollander, the leader of the CIO's Political Action Committee in New York said, "I hope the President will not be a spite candidate, like Wallace." A *Newsweek* survey of forty-five Democratic senators showed thirteen definitely committed against Mr. Truman's candidacy, twenty-six uncommitted, and only six publicly for him. In March, of the fourteen

Democratic senators up for reelection, only three considered themselves pro-Truman. Two party stalwarts, John Sprakman, onetime Democratic whip of the Senate, and Lister Hill of Alabama, former Democratic whip of the Senate, opposed Truman. Sparkman warned, "[The] party will be cut to ribbons in November if President Truman is nominated." In Brooklyn three Democratic district leaders came out in opposition to Truman's candidacy. Truman partisans feared that their opposition would spread to other New York City districts where the Palestine problem was a red-hot issue.[30]

The National Board felt mounting pressure publicly to abandon Truman, but no one seemed willing to take that step. A sense of relief and excitement greeted the news that Franklin Roosevelt, Jr., with one bold statement on March 26, shattered the ADA's neutral public posture. Roosevelt called upon Democrats to organize a draft-Eisenhower movement. To some liberals—and to many other people, for that matter—the general seemed the ideal candidate. The supreme commander of American, British, and Canadian forces fighting in Western Europe, Eisenhower arrived home in 1945 a national hero. Although his political leanings remained uncertain, the general had made vague references to "freedom of worship" and "equality before law" in a speech at the Guildhall in London in June 1945. His affability and boyish grin gained him wide acceptance not only as a great patriot but also as a warm and decent man. Political leaders of both parties were keenly aware of his immense public appeal. "Ever since VJ Day," *Time* magazine wrote, "professional politicians had been padding softly behind General Dwight D. Eisenhower." He had an added attraction for liberals trying desperately to sever any ties with communism: his unparalleled record of fighting against fascism and communism promised to put them beyond reproach. His vagueness on most of the vexing issues of the day—Senator Richard Russell was sure Eisenhower was a "states' rights man"—was of little concern. However, Eisenhower seemed to show scant interest in politics, turning down an attempted Republican presidential draft earlier that year and accepting instead a position as president of Columbia University in February 1948.[31]

Although Franklin Roosevelt, Jr., claimed to speak as a private citizen, his position as vice-chairman of the ADA and his name appeal made his cause a rallying point for disaffected liberals. Leon Henderson, a strong Eisenhower supporter, followed up Roosevelt's statement by calling a press conference of his own and announcing that the ADA would reevaluate its neutral position at an expanded National Board meeting in April.[32] The restlessness within the ADA worried Clark Clifford, who instructed members of his political staff to work with administration supporters in the ADA to prevent an outright endorsement of Eisenhower or Supreme Court Justice Douglas at the April board meeting. Clifford, however, underestimated the depth of feeling against Truman. Although the president retained some support among labor representatives at the meeting, especially Boris Shishkin of the AFL and Ben McLaurin of the Brotherhood of Sleeping Car Porters, he got much less backing from the general membership of the ADA. A poll of forty-seven chapters indicated that sixteen were for Douglas, fourteen for Eisenhower, and only two for Truman, the remainder taking no position.[33]

The statement on political policy adopted at the April National Board meeting in Pittsburgh became the basis of the ADA position through the Democratic convention in July. "Our political crisis," the statement read, "is essentially a crisis of leadership. As never before, we need greatness in the Presidency of the United States." While congratulating Truman on his European Recovery Program and commending him for his domestic economic policy, the statement went on, "liberals cannot overlook the fact that poor appointments and faltering support of his aides have resulted in a failure to rally the people behind policies which in large measure we wholeheartedly support." The ADA called for an open Democratic convention and publicly endorsed Eisenhower and Justice Douglas: "With Eisenhower or Douglas in the White House, the free peoples of the world will receive a new infusion of faith and hope, and the USSR cannot but hesitate in its policy of headlong expansion and aggrandizement."[34]

The Eisenhower draft went into full swing following the Pittsburgh meeting. The Executive Committee, unwilling to go beyond the call of the board, decided that board members were free to announce publicly for Eisenhower or Douglas and to join committees but that there would be no direct or formal association of the ADA with any such committee. Despite Ike's public reticence, unofficial optimism was growing that Eisenhower would accept a draft. A confidential memo concerning the "availability of General Eisenhower" circulated at the end of April stated that, "in the right circumstances, General Eisenhower could be drafted for the Democratic nomination."[35] The memo argued that Eisenhower had actually been an unannounced candidate for the Republican nomination months before he withdrew. That he waited so long indicated he was at least somewhat interested in public office. In his letter of refusal Eisenhower also left the door open by stating that he would refuse any draft "in the absence of some obvious and overruling reasons." Liberals mistook Eisenhower's patriotism for political calculation. To them the most convincing evidence of Eisenhower's political inclinations was his telegram to James Roosevelt, chairman of the Democratic State Committee of California, on the third anniversary of FDR's death. "While the text of the telegram was non-political," Henderson observed, "the very fact that General Eisenhower sent it to such a political figure and on such a political occasion . . . is a proof of the General's political interests and convictions."[36] Liberals were obviously stretching their logic to the limit; yet, at the time, an Eisenhower candidacy, no matter how unlikely, appeared to be the only alternative to political disaster at the polls.

The national staff sought various ways to implement the decision to support an open convention and work toward the election of liberal congressmen. On May 20 it released a study of delegates to the convention; the study indicated that Truman had only 176 instructed or pledged votes of the 802 delegates selected at the time. The release received wide radio and press coverage and appeared to douse Truman's hopes for an easy nomination, while fanning the flames of the Eisenhower prairie fire. In a memorandum to all ADA chapters, Henderson declared, "It is now unmistakably clear that the majority of the members of the Democratic Party who have voted to elect delegates to the National Convention . . . want an open convention."[37]

Not everyone in the ADA was convinced that Truman was a weak candidate or that the ADA should actively try to undermine his campaign efforts. Reinhold Niebuhr, for instance, told Loeb, "I am dead set against this Eisenhower boom among liberals." Niebuhr not only was concerned about Eisenhower's liberal credentials but also questioned whether his military background was appropriate training for the presidency. The American foreign policy establishment had enough military men in important places, he said, and it did not need one in the White House. A chapter spokesman summarized well the feeling of those opposed to an Eisenhower endorsement: "We don't want to abandon the allegedly sinking Truman ship for the sheer joy of getting into the water."[38]

Andrew Biemiller, a former liberal congressman from Wisconsin, serving as a lobbyist for the AFL, and an ADA National Board member, was perhaps the most forceful Truman supporter in the ADA. Like most of the other labor representatives on the board, Biemiller wanted liberals to work against the election of a Republican candidate. As bad as Truman was, he was at least against Taft-Hartley, which for labor was the single most important issue in the election. In two memoranda, one written as early as August 1947 and the second in June 1948, Biemiller presented a cogent argument in favor of ADA support for Truman, and of the political isolation of Wallace.

It was Henry Wallace, he said, not Truman or the Republicans, who presented the real challenge to liberals. Accordingly, Biemiller suggested that the ADA work closely with the Democratic National Committee and try to out-organize the PCA. "With the exception of Palestine," Biemiller argued, referring to Truman's decision to accept a partitioned Israeli capital, "Truman has not been wrong on a single important issue. Certainly no liberal can desert the Southerners' revolt on the civil rights issue. Surely we can agree with his basic foreign policy and respect his fight for the Marshall Plan without political strings. He has been right on taxes, social security, labor, inflation control." "If there is any reason to ditch Truman," Biemiller stated, "it should be done by convincing the President he should retire for the good of the nation, his party and the liberal movement. Open talk of ditching him simply strengthens his stubborn streak and makes him more determined than ever that he will run." Dumping Truman would damage party morale and give their enemies a powerful weapon.[39]

Despite such articulate voices in opposition, the draft-Eisenhower juggernaut rolled ahead until the general himself stopped it with a statement released a few days before the opening of the Democratic convention in July. In his statement Eisenhower said he planned to abide by his January refusal of the party's nomination; a few days later, he released a letter, originally written in January, reaffirming his decision not to accept nomination for any political office. With Eisenhower out of the race, some ADA members turned to Supreme Court Justice Douglas to stop Truman. Many liberals actually preferred Douglas over Eisenhower. Yet, for most ADA members, Douglas's candidacy was too risky. As the convention opened, an ADA delegation headed by Leon Henderson informed the Supreme Court justice that the organization would not support his nomination. Reluctantly, Douglas released a statement saying, "I am not a candidate, have not been a candidate and do not plan to resign from the Supreme Court."[40]

When the Democrats assembled in the sultry July heat in Philadelphia for their first national convention since Roosevelt's death, sounds of discord echoed everywhere. "Arriving delegates found an atmosphere of gloom and despondency and encountered a spirit of defeatism among the party leaders," the *New York Times* reported, "that amounted to a confession that President Truman seemed to have little chance of election." Rumors were already circulating that the southern delegation planned to walk out of the convention and form its own states' rights party if Truman did not back away from his recent support of strong civil rights measures. Liberals were just as eager to see Truman's campaign rhetoric incorporated into the party platform. All Truman hoped for was a united party for his fall campaign. "Not since the South rebelled against Stephen Douglas in 1860," *Time* reported, "has the party seemed so hopelessly torn and divided."[41]

As the convention opened on July 13, a group of 75 or 80 ADA members, still unwilling to endorse Truman but realizing they had nowhere to turn, gathered at the ADA convention headquarters, a rented fraternity house on the University of Pennsylvania campus, to discuss options. Humphrey suggested that it was "ridiculous" for the ADA "to delay making a commitment, that Truman was the incumbent President, and that no convention was going to reject him." Since the ADA was represented by only 120 delegates from twenty-three states and had no candidate to support, Humphrey was simply accepting political realities. Others concurred. But Humphrey remembered that much of the support for Truman "was not highly enthusiastic but was based on the inevitability of his nomination." It was not until the ADA delegation was certain of Truman's nomination that "the issue of the civil rights plank took over our thoughts."[42]

At first the ADA thought Truman would support its fight for a strong civil rights platform. After all, Truman's Civil Rights Committee had endorsed the establishment of a permanent civil rights division within the Department of Justice, advocated passage of federal antilynching laws, abolished the poll tax, and called for an end to segregation in the armed forces; and Truman publicly endorsed the committee's recommendations in his 1948 State of the Union Message. Support of civil rights was also a key ingredient in Clifford's recipe for winning the black and labor vote in the North. Yet, already in 1947, Clifford realized he had miscalculated the southern reaction to Truman's civil rights platform. Led by J. Strom Thurmond of South Carolina and Fielding Wright of Mississippi, the states' rights advocates remonstrated against the usurpation of state power and demanded the elimination of any reference to the recommendations of the Civil Rights Committee. As rumors of a state's rights bolt from the party began circulating before the convention, Clifford advised Truman to back away from his stronger civil rights appeal.

Following Clifford's advice, Truman supported an innocuous, one-paragraph civil rights plank that stated in very equivocal language, "We favor legislation, recommended by President Truman, by which the Federal Government will exercise its full constitutional power to assure that due process, the right to vote, the right to live and the right to work shall not turn on any consideration of race, religion, color or national origin." The plank made no mention of legislation to coerce state governments to enforce the laws.[43] This draft sailed through the small domestic policy subcommittee and went to the full platform committee. The 108-member resolution committee, after ten hours of continuous labor marked by stretches of unity and hot interludes of sectional conflict, turned out a document that in spirit was very similar to Clifford's draft. It called upon Congress "to exercise full authority to the limits of its constitutional powers to protect these rights."

The compromise satisfied neither northern liberals nor southerners on the committee. The southerners submitted a draft charging that the Democratic party and the federal government "shall not encroach upon the reserved powers of the states by the centralization of the government or otherwise." They wanted the states to have complete authority to enforce the Fourteenth and Fifteenth Amendments. Dissatisfied with the administration's proposal, liberals, including the ADA, submitted an alternative plank, which repeated the recommendations of the president's own committee—anti–poll tax and anti-lynching legislation, the creation of a permanent FEPC, and an end to discrimination in the armed forces. When the subcommittee rejected the ADA proposal, Humphrey and Biemiller took their case to the full platform committee. In four attempts they failed to win over the committee on the single issue of ending discrimination in the armed forces. Committee leaders, including Chairman Francis J. Myers and Senator Scott Lucas of Illinois, favored the administration's platform. After twelve hours the platform committee broke up, and the convention chairman, Sam Rayburn, gave both the ADA and the southern dissidents permission to file their minority planks on the following day, Wednesday, July 14.

That night the ADA reconvened at its rented fraternity house. Humphrey now had second thoughts about waging a floor fight. The mayor of Minneapolis, a candidate for the Senate, feared that a public demonstration against Truman would split the party and jeopardize his own election in November. Humphrey's position on the ADA plank was crucial since he was closely identified with the fight. His withdrawal, at this late stage, would demoralize the liberal forces. Throughout the night fellow ADA members tried with little luck to persuade him to support the plank. Joseph Rauh reminded Humphrey that voters backed him because of his close public identification with liberal causes. Only if he compromised his liberal values by not supporting a strong civil rights plank could he lose the election. Humphrey remained unconvinced. Finally, at 5 A.M. on Wednesday, just a few hours before the convention was to reconvene, Eugenie Anderson, ADA chairman from Minnesota, proposed adding a short phrase commending the president "for his courageous stand on the issue of civil rights," thus removing much of the anti-Truman sting from the plank and allowing Humphrey to be for civil rights without being against the administration. Humphrey agreed.[44]

With just a few hours' sleep, Rauh rose to orchestrate the liberal forces on the convention floor. ADA members lobbied furiously to convince delegates that Truman might lose the election in November, no matter what happened at the convention, but that congressional and state candidates could be saved by pulling in blacks who would otherwise vote for Wallace. Truman's forces countered that the failure to enact a moderate civil rights platform would alienate the South and ensure defeat in November. Although the ADA proposal contained nothing that Truman had not publicly endorsed himself, it was apparent from the beginning of the fight that the ADA was going to get no help from the president. The Missouri delegation, as well as Senator Alben Barkley's Kentucky and the party chairman J. Howard McGrath's Rhode Island delegations, voted solidly against the plank. In later years Truman took credit for having masterminded the civil rights fight, but his contemporary diary entry revealed his true attitude toward the ADA's efforts. Using one of his favorite derogatory words, he called the plank a "crackpot amendment" by the "crackpot Biemiller from Wisconsin." "The crackpots," he fumed, "hope the South will bolt."[45]

The ADA made some unusual friends during its fight. A number of urban political bosses, desperately in need of black votes to retain both power and patronage, agreed to help pass the ADA resolution when it came to a roll call. Rauh received personal assurances from Ed Flynn of New York, Jacob Arvey of Illinois, David Lawrence of Pennsylvania, and Frank Hague and Archibald Alexander of New Jersey. With many liberals, labor leaders, and political bosses now solidly behind the resolution, there was little doubt that it would pass. Following the administration-backed majority report and three southern-sponsored resolutions, Biemiller presented the ADA's four-point program to the convention.

Humphrey followed Biemiller's presentation with an impassioned plea for adoption of the resolution, which he had hesitated over less than twelve hours earlier. In one of the most memorable speeches of his career, Humphrey electrified the convention hall with his call for the party to enact a "new emancipation proclamation." In response to the resolution's critics, Humphrey charged, "To those who say that we are rushing this issue of civil rights, I say to them, we are 172 years too late. To those who say that this civil rights program is an infringement of states rights [deafening applause], the time has arrived in America for the Democratic party to get out of the shadow of states rights and walk forthrightly into the sunshine of human rights."[46] As Humphrey spoke, ADA delegates bearing banners stepped into the aisles and started marching. While the spectacle did not develop into a general demonstration, the *New York Times* reported that it showed that Humphrey's amendment "was taking hold." All three southern resolutions were handily defeated, only one needing a roll call. Demanding and receiving a crucial roll call, the ADA-backed resolution passed, 651½ to 581½. Rejected by the national party, many of the southern delegates marched out of the convention hall.

The ADA had scored its first important political victory. It received much needed public recognition for its role in the civil rights fight, as *Time, Newsweek,* the *New York Times,* and other major newspapers gave the ADA kudos for its actions. *Newsweek* said it best when it wrote, "For ADA, which has lost its battle for Eisenhower, then its fight for Douglas, it was a lifesaving victory."[47]

A few hours after the bitter civil rights fight, Truman ascended the podium to accept his party's nomination. Following a long and boisterous demonstration of support, Truman launched into his attack on the reactionary Congress, announced he was calling Congress back into session on July 26—Turnip Day in Missouri—and pleaded for labor and liberal support. Jack Kroll, the head of the CIO-PAC, reported that there "was great enthusiasm over Truman's acceptance speech and great enthusiasm among liberals over the Convention proceedings as a whole." Even Truman's selection of the seventy-five-year-old stalwart Alben Barkley as his running mate could not dampen liberal spirits. It was generally believed, Kroll worte, "that labor and liberals could now go to their members and their constituents back home and in good faith ask for their support of the Democratic platform and the candidates running on it."[48]

Many liberals still showed little enthusiasm for the Truman-Barkley ticket after the convention. The *Progressive* endorsed Norman Thomas for president. The *Nation* refused to endorse anyone; the *New Republic* accepted Truman as the lesser of two evils. There was little doubt, however, about what the ADA would do. As Loeb had hoped, the successful fight for a civil rights platform gave it reason to support the president in his uphill battle with Governor Thomas E. Dewey of New York. The ADA's support for Truman, though, proved less than wholehearted. A poll of the New York City chapter found forty-nine members in favor of a Truman endorsement and fifty opposed. If the National Board decided to endorse Truman, twenty-eight favored a token endorsement, while forty-seven called for an active campaign. The question that confronted the National Board as it assembled in Chicago in late August was not whether to endorse Truman—most members felt they had no other choice—but how strong the statement should be. Anticipating a Truman defeat, some suggested that the organization provide only nominal support and focus its efforts instead on restructuring the party after November. Labor led the fight at the meeting for a strongly worded statement of support. Rauh felt that a strong statement would be dishonest, since most ADA members supported Truman only because they saw no alternative.

Agreeing with Rauh, the board issued a lukewarm endorsement praising him for the Marshall Plan, his veto of Taft-Hartley, and his strong stand on civil rights. At the same time the statement warned that the ADA would continue to criticize Truman's record on apointments: "It is our hope that the Chief Executive, in exercising his appointive rights, will in the future choose men who conform to his aggressive campaign statements and stated liberal views."[49]

In the meantime, in late July, the Progressive Citizens of America held their convention. Their platform vehemently denounced the European Recovery Program and the Truman Doctrine and blamed the latter for the Soviet invasion of Czechoslovakia. It demanded an end to all anti-Communist governments, including those of China, Greece, and Turkey, and urged repeal of the draft. Domestically, it advocated public ownership of "the largest banks, the railroads, the merchant marine, the electric power and gas industry, and industries primarily dependent on government funds or government purchases."[50]

Wallace's Progressive platform could not distract attention from the question of Communist influence, a question he never successfully answered at the convention or during the campaign. Wallace, refusing to recognize the subversive nature of the Communist party, believed that it would work for his campaign while asking for nothing in return. As liberal attacks on Wallace increased and as many of his Progressive followers fled the campaign, the Communists assumed increased responsibility. Bruce Bliven, a *New Republic* editor and longtime Wallace friend, admitted that though the Progressive party included "many thousands of honest liberals" the "direction of the party was certainly in the hands of Communist and fellow travelers."[51] He never renounced his Communist support, but Wallace did become frustrated with both their antics and with the volume of criticism they insipred. "If the Communists would have a ticket of their own, the New Party would lose 100,000 votes but gain four million," he complained at one point. It was not until years later, in March 1951, that Wallace would admit the extent of Communist influence on the campaign. "You know," he said, "I didn't actually realize how strong the Communists were in the Progressive Party. I think now that they were out to knife me." In an oral history he later admitted, "I was too much convinced of my own rightness (*sic*) to be as aware as I ought to have been."[52]

Over the next three months the ADA focused most of its attention on preventing Henry Wallace from making serious inroads into liberal support and on working for liberal congressional candidates who would provide the foundation of a new Democratic party after Truman's expected defeat in November. Financial and organizational problems, however, hampered its efforts. Leon Henderson warned, at a National Board meeting in Chicago on September 20, 1948, that he would not continue as chairman of the Executive Committee if the deficit continued. Henderson called a meeting of himself, Loeb, Rauh, and Louis Harris, the treasurer, on October 14. The four Executive Board members agreed to a compromise package that included some staff cuts along with new fund-raising affairs. Reluctantly, Loeb took a salary cut, gave some people immediate notice, and let others know they could be affected in the immediate future. Even the small cuts wreaked hardship on the already understaffed and underpaid organization. Loeb claimed, "The proposed cuts would involve the release of one of the two highly competent members of our overworked publicity staff and the Director of Organization. This would be in addition to the temporary cuts already made in the Legislative Department and to the salary cuts." Morale was one of the casualties of the ADA's financial woes. "Almost every other week," Loeb confessed in a private comment, "I just get the feeling that I can't take any more."[53]

Despite these problems, the ADA found its niche in the campaign. Johannes Hoeber, a member of the research committee and also an ADA National Board member, claimed there was an agreement between the ADA and the national Democratic party that the ADA would focus its resources on Wallace and let the Democrats go after Dewey. They arrived at this decision mutually, agreeing that the ADA had more experience fighting the Wallace wing of the party and would be more successful in appealing to the independent voter.[54] Hoeber later said,

> But there was an agreement very early in the campaign, I do not recall how and when it was negotiated . . . that the job that ADA would take on would be the fight against Henry Wallace. And the ADA published a very extensive book on the role of Henry Wallace, as a campaign document. And by mutual agreement, the Research Division stayed out of that area entirely; this was the speciality that ADA took on. In hindsight, I think, it was a very wise tactical decision to let what you might call the left wing of the liberal movement supporting Truman take on the fight against Wallace rather than the official organization.[55]

As a member of both the ADA National Board and the research staff, Hoeber was in a position to know of any secret deals. However, both William Batt and Joseph Rauh have emphatically denied the existence of a formal collusion between the two groups. Whether a formal agreement existed or not, the ADA did in fact devote most of its campaign activities to isolating Henry Wallace, while the research committee spent its limited resources attacking Truman's Republican opponent.

The ADA continued its close working relationship with organized labor through the final months of the campaign. The liberal-labor alliance was not difficult to understand. Both groups had learned in the preceding two years the importance of coordinating efforts to defeat Republican candidates. Loeb made repeated reference to ADA-CIO cooperation in Biemiller's unsuccessful campaign in the Wisconsin congressional election in 1946. Their efforts, he claimed, won Biemiller 49 percent of the vote in a supposedly safe conservative district. The CIO learned similar lessons. Looking back over their efforts in the congressional racees of 1946, labor leaders felt that a better coordinated effort would produce more successes.[56]

The ADA and the CIO were natural allies. By working as part of a larger coalition, labor could reduce public concern that unions were a special interest group solely concerned with repealing Taft-Hartley.[57] The ADA, for its part, considered labor support essential to its attempt to create a viable liberal movement in America. Of course, in 1948 the CIO and the ADA also had similar political objectives. They agreed that Democrats, at least on the congressional level, had to stay in power and that Henry Wallace threatened that goal. These labor spokesmen feared Wallace because, if he gained enough popular support, he could give the electoral prize to the party of Taft-Hartley. According to Jack Kroll, the CIO-PAC director, CIO strategy "was formulated from the beginning upon the premise of ADA-CIO co-operation."[58]

The ADA strategy was to remind voters that a liberal split would serve the interests only of conservatives, and at the same time to link Wallace to the international Communist movement. The ADA published a pamphlet, entitled "Henry Wallace: The First Three Months of His Campaign," and a sequel, "Henry Wallace: The Last Seven Months of His Campaign," which received wide media coverage. Both painted Wallace as a dupe of a conniving, clandestine Communist movement, which was attempting to subvert American institutions. After establishing the roots of the third party in Communist soil, the pamphlets criticized Wallace for his naive foreign policy positions. They attacked him for blaming the Communist coup in Czechoslovakia on the Truman Doctrine and for making charges about British and American imperialism. The ADA even questioned Wallace's commitment to civil rights. "During his regime as Commerce Secretary," the ADA charged, "Wallace insisted that the segregation policy in the National Airport restaurant, which was under his jurisdiction, could not be changed." Wallace also had an "unearned reputation as 'friend of labor.'" The pamphlets also contained the obligatory statements from members of the Roosevelt family protesting that the ADA, and not Henry Wallace, was the true heir to the FDR tradition.[59]

The ADA also dogged Wallace every step of the campaign. On July 22 Loeb went to the Progressive party convention in Philadelphia and characterized it as "a dangerous adventure undertaken by cynical men in whose hands Henry A. Wallace placed his political fortunes."[60] When, in September, Wallace traveled south to attack Jim Crow laws, bravely withstanding tomato and egg peltings, the ADA accused him of running from the real issue of the campaign—his Communist support. The ADA quoted the NAACP's secretary, Walter White, who claimed Wallace had never cared about racial issues when he served as a cabinet member.

With the ADA covering his left flank, Truman was free to stage a frontal assault on his Republican opponent. Truman went on a whirlwind, transcontinental railroad trip in which he gave 351 speeches to an estimated twelve million people. He blamed the "do-nothing, good-for nothing Eightieth Congress" for everything, from high prices to poor health care. "If you send another Republican to Washington," he told his audiences, "you're a bigger bunch of suckers than I think you are." Dewey, cool and confident, conducted

a leisurely campaign while he made plans for his inauguration and new administration, displaying "the humorless calculation of a Certified Public Ac-
countant in pursuit of the Holy Grail." He discarded old GOP platitudes
against government spending and bureaucracy. "Dewey," *Time* wrote one
week before the election, "bore the air, and the reputation, of a proved
executive and a good administrator, a man who would clear out the dead
wood in Washington but would not rock the boat."[61]

The day before the election the Gallup poll gave Dewey 49.5 percent
of the total vote and Truman 44.5 percent. Elmo Roper predicted a Dewey
landslide comparable only to Roosevelt's over Landon. Fifty Washington
correspondents, most of them bureau chiefs, unanimously predicted a Dewey
victory. On election night the *Chicago Tribune* ran the headline: "DEWEY
DEFEATS TRUMAN." A preelection photograph of Dewey in *Life* was
captioned, "The Next President."

Truman stunned almost everyone, ADA members included, by winning
in November. The *New York Times* called his victory "a miracle of elec-
tioneering for which there are few if any parallels." While Wallace's campaign disintegrated, and Dewey failed to excite voters, Truman's fiesty attacks on the "do-nothing" Eightieth Congress helped reassemble the coalition
that had four times elected Roosevelt. Truman's 24.1 million votes to Dewey's
22.0 million helped him pile up the substantial margin of 304 to 189 in the
electoral college. Wallace's turnout at the polls was an unmitigated disaster.
He received under 1.2 million votes, no electoral votes, and 2.3 percent of
total ballots; and his expectation of 4.0 million voters turned into fewer than
the Dixiecrat candidate Strom Thurmond got. The *New York Times* editorialized, "The abysmal fate of Henry A. Wallace in Tuesday's election proves
once and for all time that this country has no room for a third party allied
with those whose roots are in foreign soil."[62]

Truman's victory hardly represented a mandate for liberalism. With Wallace on his left and the States' Rights candidate Strom Thurmond on the
right, Truman captured the all-important center of the political spectrum.
The president ran behind the national party, and though liberals made gains
in both houses of Congress, the conservative coalition of southern Democrats
and Republicans still held the balance of power. The election did, however,
extinguish Communist hopes of becoming an important force in American
politics. "From that point on," Joseph Starobin has written, "the American
Communist Party became at least a case in civil liberties, at best an object
of sympathy, but no longer a power." Party membership, which leaped to
nearly 73,000 in 1946, declined dramatically, to only 54,174 members in
1949.[63]

Truman's surprise victory and Wallace's poor showing came as welcome
news to the ADA. While few liberals went so far as to claim credit for Truman's victory, they were quick to accept responsibility for Wallace's collapse. James Wechsler later said the ADA was "a leading factor in the rout
of the U.S. Communist movement in the 1948 campaign. . . . Probably

ADA did more than any other single agency to expose the frauds and the fallacies, the double think and double standards through which the Communists tried to entrap American liberals in the late 1940s as they had in the mid-1930s." Many Wallace supporters confirmed Wechsler's account. Curtis McDougall, the PCA's foremost historian and a former Progressive party member, wrote that Harry Truman's and Philip Murray's attacks on the organization "were pretty nasty; but for sustained effort, the ADA exceeded all others. Neither the CIO hierarchy nor the Democratic party was as vehement in their efforts to defeat the Progressive party." Other scholars, such as Athan Theoharis and Allen Yarnell, have taken the argument a step further, saying that the ADA's campaign against Wallace planted the seeds of the McCarthy hysteria of the 1950s. "The ADA," wrote Yarnell, "by focusing on Communism and equating anti-Communism with American liberalism, even for the most sincere reasons, showed how effectively the issue could be used in postwar politics."[64]

These critics overlook a number of important considerations. First, the ADA did not introduce red-baiting into the contemporary political debate. The Republicans had discovered the issue in the 1944 campaign against Roosevelt. Second, there was considerable truth to the ADA's charges against Wallace. Communists did play a major role in his 1948 campaign, as Wallace later admitted. Wallace's view of the Soviet Union was naive, and he did seriously miscalculate Soviet military intentions, especially in Eastern Europe. Also, as John Haynes has pointed out, real issues—ones that concerned the health of a democratic society and the future of the Democratic party—were at stake in the clash between the ADA and Wallace.[65]

Despite this evidence serious questions remain about the ADA's role in the campaign. No matter how Communist-controlled Wallace's campaign or how unsophisticated his view of the Soviet Union, Wallace raised fundamental questions about American foreign policy that liberals would have done well to consider. Wallace's criticisms of the Truman Doctrine, his outcry against the administration's preoccupation with military containment, and his bipolar worldview were certainly worthy of public debate. Yet, the ADA's excessive anticommunism and its yearning to be involved in the political fight—in this case as part of the Democratic party—prevented it from recognizing the relevance of Wallace's criticisms. By linking Wallace to an international Communist movement, the ADA and other anti-Communist liberals effectively dismissed his ideas as alien and worthless. Ironically, the ADA would become the subject of similar tactics during the 1950s.

The ADA was also satisfied with its efforts in congressional and gubernatorial elections. Liberals saw two prominent ADA members, Hubert Humphrey of Minnesota and Paul Douglas of Illinois, elected to the U.S. Senate; three members, Hugh Mitchell and Henry Jackson of Washington and Richard Bolling of Missouri, elected to the House; and two, Adlai Stevenson of Illinois and Chester Bowles, elected governor. Chapters bragged of even greater success on the local level. Detroit claimed that thirty of the thirty-five candidates endorsed were elected, and ten of them were ADA members. In Chicago all but two of the ADA's fourteen endorsed candidates won their races.[66]

In many ways Wallace's campaign fell victim to the emerging Cold War consensus. Most Americans accepted the granting of military aid to Greece and Turkey and economic aid under the Marshall Plan as appropriate responses to Soviet power. The bipartisan approach to foreign policy, endorsed by both Truman and Dewey, limited the range of acceptable debate and left Wallace wandering outside the boundaries of acceptable policies. Soviet intransigence in the months before the election—in Czechoslovakia and West Berlin—seemed to prove all the things Truman was saying about them, and Truman adeptly undercut Wallace's Jewish support by promising, and later providing, federal aid and recognition for the new state of Israel.

Studies of the 1948 election, however, indicate that economic issues, not questions of communism and the Cold War, determined how people voted.[67] Third-party candidates have a history of faring poorly at the polls, especially of fading late in the race, as voters decide not to waste their votes on a protest candidate. What is significant about the 1948 campaign is that fear of a Republican victory persuaded important Democratic constituencies to work together. While the ADA was able to win some Wallace sympathizers over to its cause, it is unlikely its campaign had much to do with his failure at the polls.[68]

The ADA's hopes of leading the fight for a revitalized New Deal soared after the election. Liberals mistakenly interpreted the election as a mandate to extend the New Deal, and many shared James Loeb's belief that liberalism had evolved into a broad movement that no longer depended on the personality of one charismatic individual. Even the *New Republic* wrote begrudgingly that, for the first time in its short history, the ADA could "now speak with . . . authority for the country's liberals and independents." Organizationally, the ADA had ravaged its Progressive rival. Although the ADA had scored the desired victory, many of its problems persisted. It was still relatively small (18,000 members) and geographically limited (primarily Northeast and Midwest) for a national political organization, and its financial weakness prevented any rapid expansion. To these familiar problems, now came a new one. Having helped secure Truman's reelection, the ADA expected to reap the spoils of victory. However, power brought new responsibilities that the organization was not prepared to handle.

3

The Dilemma of Power: The ADA and National Politics, 1948–1952

Despite hopes that its role in the 1948 election would bring the recognition and influence it was seeking, the ADA was repeatedly frustrated in the next few years in its attempts to expand its base of support and solidify its relationship with liberal labor unions. The central problem was that the ADA had not decided what type of organization it was to be. While claiming to be an independent voice for liberalism, the ADA also prided itself on being an effective political pressure group. During the Truman years it found that the two roles often overlapped. On most of the major issues of the day— domestic legislation, foreign policy in Asia and Europe, and civil liberties— the ADA found itself in general agreement with Truman's proposals. When it did disagree, especially on civil liberties questions, ADA leaders were usually unwilling to pay the political price for the advocacy of unpopular ideas. In both cases the result was the same: the ADA's fortunes were closely intertwined with those of the national Democratic party and the Truman administration.

Buoyed by the liberal gains in the 1948 election, the ADA set out on an ambitious campaign to organize new chapters and strengthen its relationship with labor. In the fall of 1949 the ADA appointed a full-time national director, Charles La Follette, a liberal Indiana Republican, and added five new field organizers. It also established regional organizing committees to coordinate communication among chapters and between chapters and the National Board, and members of the national staff traveled around the country to build public interest and support. Loeb went on a three-week tour of chapters on the West Coast, covering Chicago and Minnesota en route, while La Follette visited the Michigan ADA, the state convention of the Illinois and Connecticut Federaton of Labor, and the Philadelphia chapter of ADA.[1]

For all its high hopes and hard work, the organization was unable appreciably to increase its membership. Indeed, ADA spokesmen frequently exaggerated the organization's size. In an appearance before the House Select Committee on Lobbying Activities in 1950, the ADA's national chairman declared that the organization had "123 local chapters in 30 states, and a membership of almost 35,000." *The Story of ADA,* a publicity brochure published in 1953, claimed that the organization had "almost 40,000 members who pay dues of three dollars or more to 125 chapters and organizing committees in 40 states." Actually, both estimates were high. Records indicate that the organization had only 18,000 members and forty chapters in fourteen states.

A number of formidable obstacles blocked the ADA's effort to expand. For one thing, most of the labor representatives, who had worked so hard to minimize Wallace's influence in the liberal community during the campaign, began pulling away from the organization shortly after the election. Union support, which most members considered essential to the ADA's survival, dropped steadily after 1948. Unions contributed less than 20 percent of the ADA's $240,000 budget between 1949 and 1952, less than half of their contribution in 1948. Declining labor contributions forced the ADA to operate, with a crippling organizational debt that climbed as high as $30,-000 by the early 1950s.[2]

Labor's partial separation was, at least in retrospect, not hard to understand. In many ways the close liberal-labor association of the 1940s and 1950s was an anomaly. Most liberals sought broad social reforms and maintained their enthusiasm and support for the labor movement only so long as it seemed to move closer to their own grand vision of the national welfare and the good society. Unions had a more functional view of their role in American life. Their vision focused on the range of issues that directly affected the working man—Taft-Hartley repeal, communism in unions, unemployment, inadequate wages, excessive hours of labor, degrading working conditions. Labor leaders believed that liberals could never succeed in remaking society without their support. Many labor leaders were suspicious, the *New Republic* reported, "that ADA intellectuals have some sinister design on them or their fat bankrolls." Aside from David Dubinsky and Walter Reuther, few important union leaders relied heavily upon the ADA after 1948.[3] As long as labor refused to treat the ADA as an equal partner in liberalism, the ADA's role in the nation's political life remained uncertain.

Many labor leaders, suspicious about liberal motives, wanted to build up their own political action committees so they would not have to rely on independent organizations like the ADA. "Once our own houses are in order," Emil Rieve remarked in 1951, "then we can devote time to other groups." Differences over tactical questions did not help relations between liberals and labor leaders. Rieve withdrew from the ADA because on a number of occasions he found himself in the "embarrassing position of having ADA take a position in elections directly contrary to that of CIO-PAC." He cited the example of the New York mayoralty race in 1948, when the CIO-PAC along with most of the AFL endorsed O'Dwyer for reelection, while the ADA, in spite of labor's "wishes and suggestions" to the contrary, endorsed and campaigned for O'Dwyer's opponent, Newbold Morris. Recognizing that the ADA had a right to choose candidates independently, Rieve "had to therefore choose to work exclusively within either CIO-PAC or

ADA" if the CIO-PAC "was to avoid the embarrassment of political differences that might arise between ADA and CIO-PAC."[4]

The organizations uncertain relationship with the national Democratic party, and specifically the Truman administration, posed another obstacle for the ADA. By 1949 most liberals had abandoned their prewar pleas for economic justice and had instead accepted the Truman administration's moderate reform agenda. Arthur Schlesinger, Jr., articulated the liberals' new philosophy in his book *The Vital Center,* published in 1949. Infused with Niebuhr's pessimism, Schlesinger called for a "new radicalism" that would discard progressive sentimentality and utopian schemes in favor of a sober recognition of the inevitability of social conflict and human weakness and the necessity of political compromise. Schlesinger identified with "the politicians, the administrators, the doers," as opposed to "the sentimentalists, the utopians, the wailers." Consequently, Schlesinger accepted that "the limited state can resolve the basic social questions which were supposed to compel a resort to the unlimited state." Most ADA members subscribed wholeheartedly to the philosophy of the "new radicalism." Yet, in many ways, Schlesinger's vision of the Vital Center only compounded the ADA's dilemma, for although the organization remained committed to "pragmatic" liberalism—which frequently required making compromises for the sake of preserving unity—it also needed to maintain an independent voice, and this usually demanded standing on principle regardless of the political consequences.[5]

At the 1949 convention the debate over the organization's relationship to the party dominated discussion. Some labor leaders and elected officials who supported a proposal calling on the organization to work within the Democratic party pointed out that the ADA's self-declared nonpartisanship was "universally regarded as a fiction." As a result the ADA received neither the benefits of true nonpartisanship nor the reins of power in the party with which it was universally identified. Joseph Lash used a humorous anecdote to express his frustration with the organization's tenuous relationship with the party: "Every time you call up the girl and want to date her, you have the problem: Will she be there? Will she go out with me tonight? What will I have to give her in order to get her to go out with me? It is about time that the liberal groups and labor groups married the girl. They have been going out with the Democratic Party long enough!"[6]

Those opposed to abandoning the ADA's declared nonpartisanship represented several different points of view. A small group wished to retain a nonpartisan position in the hope of eventually forming a third party. Another faction believed it could help achieve a liberalization of the Democratic party by exerting pressure as an outside force. This group saw the Democratic party adopting liberal positions in an effort to win the ADA's support. Still others, like Joseph Rauh, argued for flexibility so that the ADA could work both within and outside the party structure, depending upon local conditions. "In areas where the Party is controlled by liberal elements the ADA could work within the party," he said. "Where machines and reactionary elements predominate, the ADA is most effective as an independent political group." Rauh recognized that the ADA's claims of nonpartisanship and bipartisanship were fictitious, but he did cherish its independence. While he believed that the organization had to work with the Democratic party, he thought it essential that it retain its ability to dissent on principle. Rauh remained faithful to this view, but the organization did not.[7]

These differences in opinion were both ideological and tactical and went to the very heart of the dilemma confronting the ADA. David Lloyd, the organization's director of research before he joined the Truman White House staff in 1948, admitted, "The ADA has something of a split personality. A portion of the people whom it attracts think of it as a sort of Fabian Society, a group for popular education along liberal lines. Another, and larger group think of it as a political organization seeking to achieve liberal aims through political power." The "independent-minded group" that the organization tends to attract, Lloyd claimed, "rebels against party discipline and refuses to seize the fruits of political power which are within its grasp if it would work long and hard within the party framework." The journalist Robert Bendiner noticed a similar ideological and tactical split in the organization. He wrote in the *Nation* that the issue of the ADA's association with the Democratic party tended "to divide those who lean toward the long-range, the ideological, the educational aspects of A.D.A., from those whose thoughts run to the politically immediate—legislation, elections, and all the problems of power." This division, Bendiner remarked, is the dilemma of the liberal and labor forces: "if they surrender their independence, they may be swallowed up; but if they intend to mold the Democratic Party from the outside, that may make more resentment than progress." Gus Tyler's comment on the 1950 convention put the problem in the proper perspective: "In all these debates, ADA was wrestling with its soul—as is all American liberalism: how to formulate a long-range program yet how to avoid the political sterility of the pure visionary."[8]

The organization's inability to define clearly its relationship with the Democratic party created a serious dilemma that plagued the ADA throughout its history and was especially acute during Democratic administrations. The organization was frequently torn between its commitment to broad ideas of social justice and its desire to work within the Democratic party. The contradiction is clear. If committed to work with the Democratic party, the organization was forced to accept the party's limited agenda and compromise not only its independence but many of its values as well. The radical columnist I. F. Stone remarked that while the ADA "was strong enough to force a declaration of independence" for the administration on paper, "it was not strong enough to achieve independence in molding" its own position on many issues. Stone, who wanted to push the Truman administration to the left, protested that though the ADA avoided any legal tie with the party, its fortunes were so closely tied to the administration that it was unwilling to stray too far from Truman's foreign and domestic policy. In a memorandum to the president following the ADA's 1949 convention, David Lloyd tended to confirm Stone's sense that the ADA would be made into a wing of the Democratic party. He pointed out that the "policy statements adopted by the convention were essentially re-statements of the President's legislative program with some long-range embellishments. Nothing very new made its way into the documents." He recommended that the administration cultivate the organization, which will, he predicted, "remain a vigorous political force and will probably increase in influence over the next year." The ADA he concluded, "will be a very valuable ally for the Administration on practically all issues of policy."[9]

Lloyd seriously overestimated the ADA's influence and stature during these years. Instead of capitalizing on its 1948 victory and establishing itself as an influential and forceful advocate of independent liberalism, the ADA floundered. In confronting the difficult issues of the Truman administration, the ADA was torn between its desire to be an independent voice for liberalism and its need to be "responsible" and work for gradual change through established political institutions. This conflict lay at the root of its response to issues in Truman's second term.

Most liberals were excited about the prospects for the congressional session of 1949. To liberals the Eighty-first Congress, which was to assemble in January 1949, was a considerable improvement over the Eightieth. The *New Republic* commented that "many young crusaders were nominated in 1948 because party bosses, certain of Democratic defeat, had put forward liberals." The ADA was also hopeful. The House, it calculated, had seventy-seven ADA-endorsed members, thirty-seven of them new and forty returning. As one columnist wrote, the ADA was certain "that all those Republicans swept out were antiliberal, in ADA terms, while practically all the Democrats who replaced them are liberals or lean in that direction."[10]

In his 1949 State of the Union Message, Truman made clear that he planned to work for the progressive measures that had helped him get elected. Claiming it was government's responsibility to see "that every American has a chance to obtain his fair share of our increasing abundance," Truman called for repeal of Taft-Hartley, an increase in the minimum wage to seventy-five cents per hour, stronger antitrust laws, farm price supports, rural electrification, an increase in benefits and coverage for Social Security, increased health care and aid to schools, and a new housing program. Calling the fulfillment of "the promise of equal rights and equal opportunities . . . among the highest purposes of government," Truman repeated the civil rights proposals he had made to the Eightieth Congress. He promised to introduce legislation outlawing the poll tax, making lynching a federal crime, prohibiting segregation and discrimination in interstate commerce, establishing a permanent FEPC with enforcement powers, and protecting the right of suffrage.[11]

Most liberals found Truman's rhetoric uplifting and generally agreed with the objectives of the Fair Deal. There was certainly little disagreement among liberals about the significance of Truman's victory and the general direction of his program. "There is no longer reason to doubt," the *Nation* assured its readers, "that the unsophisticated politician from Missouri is determined to push on with an extension of Roosevelt's domestic policies, that he regards himself under obligation to the voters to do so, and that 'economic royalists' will find him every bit as tough a customer as his more urbane predecessor." Truman's Fair Deal, the *New Republic* editorialized, is "one of the boldest reform programs ever presented by an American President." It "points toward a social-welfare state and amounts to the most leftward-leaning program ever sent by an American President to Congress." The former Wallace supporter Michael Straight claimed, "[If] he accomplishes a significant part of his present objectives Truman will be remembered as one of the major figures of American liberalism."[12]

Despite his inspiring rhetoric, Truman's Fair Deal had little chance of passage. The president, and most liberals, had seriously overestimated the willingness of the new Congress to accept new or expanded domestic spending. "The young bloods of the 81st Congress had not come to Washington, cheering and defiant, to start a revolution," *Time* commented. "They had come to consolidate one. . . . [W]hat the people really said last November was that they wanted not new highways but a widening of the roads that Franklin Roosevelt had built."[13] Truman's civil rights proposals were the first casualty of the new legislative season. The fate of the civil rights fight depended on Truman's ability to challenge the Senate's cloture rule and thus curb the effectiveness of southern filibusters. Debate opened on February 28 with Truman demanding cloture by a simple majority. But after two weeks of complicated maneuvering, the Senate voted against the administration's position. Civil rights became a dead issue. Most observers believed that Truman gave only halfhearted support to the cloture fight. Fearing that a divisive cloture fight could sabotage the rest of his legislative program, Truman did only what was necessary to demonstrate his concern for the issue. The *New York Times* columnist Arthur Krock remarked, "It is obvious that everybody wants civil rights as a campaign issue but not as a law and that goes for Harry Truman, the Democratic party and the Republican party."[14]

Despite Truman's reluctance to push for strong civil rights legislation, the ADA National Board intentionally toned down criticism of the administration, focusing its ire on the conservative Congress. At its National Board meeting in December 1949, the ADA considered a draft of a civil rights statement that denounced Congress and the president for failure to enact civil rights legislation. The members agreed to delete the section attacking the president and release only the part criticizing Congress.[15]

Here, as on other issues during these years, the organization was torn between its Fabian desire to advocate bold ideas, no matter what the political consequences, and its commitment to practical politics, which required that it stay close to the political mainstream. The organization was unflinching in its support of Truman's civil rights legislation; it had led the fight at the 1948 convention to have most of the measures Truman proposed written into the Democratic platform. Yet, once Truman was elected, the organization needed to consider the potential political consequences of its action. That calculation inevitably led toward moderation. Schlesinger, in a visit to Chattanooga to look into establishing ADA chapters in the South, found that though the ADA people were "perfectly clear in their own thinking on civil rights," the issue was "the main obstacle in recruiting and organizing." Southern liberals did not "want ADA to modify its stand in the slightest," but life was made more difficult for them by anything that made the ADA "seem exclusively or largely concerned with the civil rights issue." Schlesinger suggested, "It might help our organizing in the South if something could be done to make ADA seem something else than another Yankee liberal outfit." It was especially important that the "ADA seem in the South much less a personal machine for the civil rights program of Hubert Humphrey."[16]

Truman was little more successful on other aspects of the Fair Deal program. On March 30 he signed the Housing and Rent Control Act, which extended rent controls until June 30, 1950. It provided less than Truman had requested. He had pressed for 810,000 public housing units over a period of six years, while the legislation authorized construction of only 156,000 units. Other legislation, including his request for a federal health care program, outmatched by an effective lobbying campaign by the American Medical Association, went down to defeat. Also, in May 1949 the House defeated the administration's attempt to repeal the Taft-Hartley Act. Truman vowed to fight on for repeal, although the Senate, disturbed by labor disruptions, was not interested in taking action.

"On November 3 last," James Loeb told a radio audience in March, "the free peoples of the world read in the newspapers that a great liberal victory had been won in the American Presidential and Congressional election. Today, less than two and a half months after the beginning of the Congress which was elected in November, the entire legislative program is a shambles." Loeb realized he and other liberals had overestimated the power of the liberal bloc in Congress. "The majority role of the Democrats has been demonstrated to be a meaningless myth in the face of the combined strength of the Dixiecrats and the Republicans." At its Second Annual Convention in April 1949, Vi Gunther complained, "Any illusion that the liberal Democrats dominate either the House or the Senate has been completely blasted." Humphrey told liberals that the 1948 election was "not so much a victory as a reprieve."[17]

Although the ADA supported the Fair Deal and usually refrained from publicly criticizing Truman, it did express mild reservations about the president's economic policy. Truman relied heavily on his Council of Economic Advisers, especially on Leon Keyserling, a former aide to Senator Robert Wagner who joined the council in 1946 at the age of thirty-eight and became its chairman in 1950. When a mild recession in 1948–49 raised fears of a depression, Keyserling remained cautiously optimistic that continued economic growth without cumbersome controls would help the recovery. Many ADA economists were not as optimistic. Robert Nathan charged that because Keyserling was "chiefly concerned with the maintenance of a high level of economic activity without further inflation," he gave too little attention to "the problem of avoiding a depression." Although Nathan confirmed "there was no immediate threat of a major deflation," he wanted the president to act quickly "to undertake corrective measures that would prevent a bust." Leon

Henderson predicted "a sharp recession," criticized Truman for an obsession with inflation, and characterized the president as "a budget balancer at heart." On June 12 the ADA National Board released a statement asserting that the nation was "on the thin ice of a recession" and, in the absence of quick and effective action, might "plunge through into disaster."[18]

Most ADA economists expressed concern about an impending depression, but on the broad contours of economic policy the organization's position was nearly identical to Truman's. In July the ADA sponsored a "Full Employment Conference," attended by representatives of thirty-four national organizations. In this day-long conference, over one hundred persons heard addresses by political, labor, and liberal leaders, discussed proposals for a full-employment economy, and urged passage of the Murray economic expansion bill of 1949. Keyserling set the tone of the conference by calling for an "enormous reorientation in the thinking of industry, labor, agriculture and government" toward acceptance of the goal of lifting the national output to $300 billion within a few years. Senator James Murray, sponsor of the Economic Expansion Act of 1949, explained the purposes and provisions of the legislation. He denounced "those wild-eyed, hare-brained reactionaries who propagate the philosophy of corrective recessions," and called for similar conferences throughout the country to tell the people about his bill and other measures "essential to the prosperity and well-being of the American people." Chester Bowles admonished liberals to "face up honestly to the fact that all the New Deal achievements, while great, never succeeded in eliminating large-scale unemployment." Emil Rieve, in a statement read by George Weaver, criticized the description of unemployment as "merely a healthy readjustment." "Don't let anybody tell me," Rieve said, "that when as many as 200,000 textile workers are unemployed and thousands of others are working short hours there is something healthy about the present situation." Unemployment, he warned, is a "wonderful breeding ground for communism."[19]

Despite some of the bluster in the speeches, the conference resolutions were nearly identical to Truman's Fair Deal policies. The resolutions urged nine immediate steps: greater unemployment compensation and a higher minimum wage, overhaul and equalization of Social Security, enactment of the liberal Brannan farm program, wage increases, repeal of Taft-Hartley, FEPC, emphasis on government public works and purchasing in areas where unemployment was critical, repeal of wartime excise taxes, adequate funds for the new housing program, help for American firms doing business abroad, and reduction of excise prices to reasonable levels.[20] Because the administration was already publicly supporting most of these measures, the ADA, rather than advocating bold new initiatives found itself affirming the Fair Deal legislative agenda. This merging of interests was due in part to Truman's basic liberalism, but it also had much to do with the ADA's desire to work with the national Democratic party.

Truman's foreign policy evoked a more positive response from most of the ADA's national leadership. Standing in the frigid Washington air for his first inaugural, Truman had reaffirmed his strong opposition to Communist aggression. The "false philosophy of Communism," he said, replaces freedom and justice with "deceit and mockery, poverty and tyranny." "The actions resulting from the Communist philosophy are a threat to the efforts of free nations to bring about world recovery and lasting peace." He outlined four guiding principles to his foreign policy: "unfaltering support to the United Nations and related agencies"; continued support of the Marshall Plan and reduced trade barriers to maintain economic recovery in Europe; negotiation of a North Atlantic mutual defense treaty to "strengthen freedom-loving nations against the dangers of aggression"; and, "Point Four," "a bold new program for making the benefits of our scientific advances and industrial programs available for the improvement and growth of underdeveloped areas."[21]

Truman's proposals touched on the central question confronting postwar liberal foreign policy: How could America prevent Soviet military expansion, especially into countries on its borders, without giving aid to repressive regimes? The president's new call for military assistance to Europe was bound to cause alarm among liberals, who had accepted the Truman Doctrine only reluctantly. Those who opposed the North Atlantic pact feared that it would undermine the United Nations, bolster undemocratic governments, and be interpreted by Moscow as an unfriendly move. Supporters compared the pact to the Monroe Doctrine and criticized opponents for ignoring "the fact that the policy which it represents has been forced upon us" by Soviet aggression.[22]

The delegates to the ADA's 1949 national convention, Niebuhr remarked, "tore their souls" before deciding to support the treaty. ADA leaders, however, were firm in their support of the proposal. In testimony before congressional committees, Charles La Follette argued that economic and political aid had to be America's "first line of defense" but that sometimes military force was needed to form a protective shield so reforms could take root. Many ADA leaders sought to identify the treaty with FDR's prewar advocacy of quarantining the aggressor. James Loeb supported it because he felt it would reassure the democratic forces of Europe. "Most of our European friends feel safer now," he declared. "This is certainly true of our friends in liberal and labor circles in Europe. And it seems to me that should be the touchstone of judgment for most American liberals."[23]

According to David Lloyd, Schlesinger and Niebuhr, as supporters of the administration's foreign policy, maintained strong control of the foreign policy discussion and prevented any serious challenge to the administration's position at the 1949 convention. In dealing with the Marshall Plan, for example, the Washington chapter objected to the Truman administration's licensing system, which, it charged, subordinated economic aid to military concerns. The convention's foreign policy commission omitted the chapter's innocuous, one-sentence resolution—"We condemn those who would use the ERP as a means of preventing necessary social change." The same thing happened with the Washington chapter's proposal on Point Four. The commission refused to consider the chapter's resolution, which called for the program to be given public rather than private funding and distributed "as far as possible through international agencies in order to avoid both the charge and the fact of imperialism." The same problem occurred on issues ranging from Spain to German rearmament and to Israel.[24]

While the national leadership was able to unite behind Truman's European foreign policy, it found itself divided on how to deal with events in Asia. Were events there simply an Asian version of the problem America faced in Europe? Could America prevent Communist advances everywhere, or would it have to choose between Asia and Europe? Should the United States support a corrupt regime just because it was anti-Communist? The debate over American policy in Asia revealed deep cracks in the Vital Center armor. ADA members were divided over the wisdom of applying to Asia the lessons learned from Europe.

Problems arose after the war in East Asia and especially in China, where the anti-Communist forces of Chiang Kai-shek were losing an internal struggle against Mao Tse-tung's Communist forces. "All in all, China was the most momentous, the most explosive, the most damaging issue that Harry Truman confronted as president," Robert Donovan has reflected. Since assuming office, Truman had tried to carry out Roosevelt's policy of establishing a coalition government in China in the hope that it would become one of Roosevelt's "Four Policemen." By 1947 repeated American attempts at mediation, the most recent by General George C. Marshall, had proved unsuccessful, and the administration tried bracing the United States for the ultimate Communist victory. Dean Acheson wrote later that when he took office as secretary of state in 1949, Chiang's regime was on the verge of collapse: "I arrived just in time to have him collapse on me."[25]

Truman believed that when it finally became evident that diplomatic relations with Mao's government were in the interest of the United States, Washington would reluctantly recognize the new Communist government. In the summer of 1949, as the Communists defeated Kuomintang forces on the mainland of China, Washington debated heatedly the question of what to do about Formosa, to which Chiang's forces were fleeing. Truman attempted to clarify his policy by releasing, on August 5, 1949, a 1,054-page white paper on China that explained his dissatisfaction with Chiang, pointed out the differences between Soviet and Chinese communism, and tried to convince a skeptical public that events in China were out of America's control. On January 5, 1950, Truman issued a statement declaring that the United States was determined to stay out of the Chinese civil war, had no interest in Formosa, and would offer no military aid or advice to Chiang. This prudent policy came under heavy partisan attack from a well-organized China lobby and a ferocious Republican minority, who tried to rally public sentiment in favor of Chiang Kai-shek.[26]

Chiang's supporters were able to trap Truman in the logic of his own containment rhetoric. If communism was a monolithic, Soviet-inspired movement, which endangered the security of the free world, how could the United States sit by and allow a landmass as large as China to fall? After all, if communism was to be contained in Greece and Turkey and in Western Europe, why not in China? they asked. Truman's ambiguous policy of recognizing the Nationalist regime as the legitimate government of China, aiding it through 1949, yet not helping it enough to survive, was difficult for the public to grasp and seemed to contradict his earlier warnings about Communist expansion.[27]

Responding to these criticisms, most liberals went to great lengths to point out the differences between Chinese and Soviet communism. They charged that, unlike the Soviet satellite states of Eastern Europe, China did not share linguistic and cultural links with the Soviets. The Marxism of the Chinese was one, they argued, "whose tactics and timing have been conditioned by their quarter-century of work in the Chinese countryside." China experts like John K. Fairbank of Harvard and Edgar Snow, the author of *Red Star over China,* confirmed the differences between the Chinese and Russian experience. The revolution in China, Snow wrote, was actually a "revolt of the peasant against the authority of the landlord." A great social revolution sweeping through Asia, unrelated to and independent of the USSR, was the cause of unrest in China. Fairbank confirmed, "In China, to a more obvious degree than in Eastern Europe, we are confronted by a genuine national and social revolution, not just a made-in-Moscow drive for the seizure of power." While these liberals did not expect Communists to be democratic or liberal, they would be better for the Chinese people than Chiang. Moreover, they did not pose an immediate threat to U.S. security.[28]

The ADA, reflecting such views, defended Truman from Republican charges that he was responsible for losing China. The ADA argued that, whereas in Europe American aid through the Marshall Plan and the Truman Doctrine prevented communism from establishing a foothold, in China internal events over which the United States had little control determined the situation. It charged that Republican "harping upon Communist successes in China as a failure of U.S. Policy" was nothing more than a partisan "attempt to create a political issue to use against the present administration." The problem in China, the ADA claimed, "was that Chiang was incompetent and stubborn and no amount of American aid could have prevented his failure unless he was willing to make important changes." While he may have been personally honest, the ADA declared, "Chiang's desire for complete power and his anger at being opposed turned him increasingly to the advice of the extreme rightists who urged him to be uncompromising toward all opposition, both in the party and outside it. . . ." As Chiang became more uncompromising, he lost the ability to crush the Communists because he was no longer sure who would carry out his orders.

The ADA added that the withdrawal of American aid did not cause the collapse of the Nationalist government. Rather, the ADA reasoned, the collapse of Chiang's government rendered the aid ineffective. In defense of Truman's actions, the ADA explained that the United States withdrew its support "only when it was evident that further assistance of the same kind would be of no use, and that any effective aid would involve the U.S. directly in the war." Quoting Fairbank, the ADA concluded, "We did everything for Chiang we could except kill Chinese for him." There is, Niebuhr commented sarcastically, "no political future in Chiang Kai-shek. Should stabilization approach in the Far East, Formosa should be placed under the United Nations, and Chiang Kai-shek should go into honorable retirement at the Waldorf-Astoria."

The ADA also declared that there was nothing inconsistent about the United States refusing to support Chiang in China but standing firm in Europe. The problem was logistical. In China the United States had only two alternatives—"complete intervention, with American troops, or withdrawal." Geography, as well as internal political conditions, determined the course of action. In Greece government armed forces of between 150,000 and 200,000 were fighting about 20,000 guerrillas who held no population centers. In China at the end of 1947, Nationalist armed forces of 2.5 to 3.0 million faced 1.0 to 1.5 million Chinese Communists who controlled one-fourth of China, and the Nationalist advantage in numbers and position was rapidly declining.[29]

Not everyone in the ADA accepted this distinction between Soviet and Chinese communism. Arthur McDowell of the Upholsterers International Union, in a letter to Hubert Humphrey, vented his frustration at the ADA's China position. His grievance was actually much deeper; he resented what he believed was the ADA's softness on communism, its unwillingness to make the defeat of comunism, whether in Europe or in Asia, a strategic priority. Although McDowell represented a distinct minority in the organization, his objections exposed divisions that pitted many labor leaders and elected officials against a larger group of intellectuals and former New Dealers. This division, present though not dominant in 1950, was to fracture the organization during the debates over the Vietnam War in the 1960s. "Western intellectuals," McDowell wrote, "have not yet drawn the full consequences for themselves intellectually or morally from the events of 1939. They refuse to equate the two great forms of totalitarianism and if they go down the line in Europe vis a vis Russia, they in large numbers are still saving up a reservation for communism in Asia or even in the Jugo-Slav corner of Europe."[30]

At a September 1949 National Board meeting, McDowell got nowhere trying to persuade the board to tone down its criticism of Nationalist China. His amendment "insisting on a policy of no appeasement by admission of an aggressive Red China to the United Nations" received only one vote other than his own. He then offered a motion that called on the organization "to revise the policies of ADA which are even more hostile to the Chinese Nationalists regime than our State Department appears to be," and "to strike out their insistent repudiation of any aid for or from the Chinese Nationalists on Formosa and favor at least our present level of aid and extension of support from appropriations actually already made by Congress." This proposal received only ten votes, half of them from labor representatives.

At the end of the meeting, McDowell announced his union's resignation from the board. His differences with the ADA over Asian policy, he said later, were too great to be overcome. He was shocked that good liberals like Walter Reuther and Niebuhr would "make a distinction between world Communism and Russian imperialism." They refused to believe, he complained, "the fact of the fundamental identity of world Communism and the military, political organization for its achievement." He could not accept the "speculation that Mao would separate himself from the Russians and turn out to be a Titoist." When Franklin Roosevelt, Jr., in a speech in New York said that his intuition told him Mao was not a stooge of Stalin but merely a temoprary co-operator for his own purpose and would soon become a Titoist, McDowell wrote Roosevelt asking him "if this intuition was on the same level as his March, 1948, intuition that Eisenhower was a Democrat, available for nomination and probably a liberal." He concluded by saying that he no longer trusted "this whole group in the intransigent fight against the Communists and Communism."[31]

On June 25, 1950, North Korean forces crossed the thirty-eighth parallel in a massive invasion of South Korea. "The attack upon Korea," a stern Truman declared, "makes it plain beyond all doubt that Communism has passed beyond the use of subversion to conquer independent nations and will now use armed invasion and war." In order to meet the challenge, Truman ordered U.S. air and sea forces to give the Korean government troops "cover and support," sent the Seventh Fleet "to prevent any attack on Formosa," strengthened American forces in the Philippines, and increased the delivery of arms to the French in Indochina.[32]

Uncertain about the relation between the Chinese civil war and aggression in Korea, the administration now saw itself preventing the spread of communism in Asia. "No less than their critics," the historian Warren I. Cohen has argued, "Truman and Acheson seemed unconvinced that a difference existed between the extension of Communist power by civil war and the extension of Communist power by an act of aggression." The fighting in Korea forced Truman to end his attempt to reach a détente with China.[33]

Most liberals agreed with Truman that the North Korean invasion required a reaffirmation of American interests in Asia. Eleanor Roosevelt invoked the lessons of Munich to justify American involvement in Korea: "Had the United Nations permitted this to go on their weakness would have been comparable only to the weakness of the League of Nations in its last days." Other liberals used the same analogy. The former PCA leader Frank Kingdon praised Truman for not taking "the road to Munich." The *Nation* compared the Communist invasion to Hitler's aggression. Others shared Eleanor Roosevelt's belief that if the United Nations did not act to repel North Korea, its credibility would be undermined. Willard Shelton wrote in the *Nation* that "the fall of South Korea . . . would deal the international organization a blow from which it might not recover." "This is where we came in," said Elmer Davis, "about 1938, when the pattern of totalitarian aggression had become clear." Walter Reuther told Truman that he had given "renewed hope and strengthened determination to the people of the world." The *New Republic* commented that by "taking a bold stand the United States has undoubtedly gained new prestige among the Western powers." The ADA praised the president for following in the tradition of Roosevelt's "quarantine" speech. Even Henry Wallace supported the decision: "I am on the side of my country and the United Nations." The journalist Eric Sevareid compared the experience to the American revolution: "For the colonies seeking to achieve freedom, the time came in 1776. For the nations seeking to preserve freedom, that time has come now, in our year of 1950."[34]

A simmering clash of wills between Truman and MacArthur then added to the urgency of liberal support for Truman's policy in Asia. MacArthur wanted Truman to blockade mainland China, "unleash" Chiang Kai-shek for raids in Korea or China, and authorize air-sea attacks on Chinese "sanctuaries" in Manchuria. Without such help, MacArthur insisted, America could not win the war. When MacArthur made his grievance known in April 1951 in a letter to the House minority leader, Joseph Martin, Truman had little choice but to fire him. MacArthur raised more troubling questions than simply that of insubordination. How important was Asia to American national interests? Whereas MacArthur believed that Chinese communism in Asia was a greater menace than Soviet communism in Europe, the ADA and the Truman administration held to a Europe-first strategy, fearing that a larger war in Asia would weaken America's European defense. In short, the Korean invasion while leading to ADA support of Truman, did not provoke the organization to formulate a policy of global anticommunism.[35]

Niebuhr argued at a December 1950 board meeting that MacArthur called into question "the strategic center of the world conflict against communism." According to administration policy, the center was Europe; MacArthur claimed it was Asia. "The whole of Europe," Niebuhr charged, "is in potential revolt against our leadership in world affairs, because they have come to fear that our policy has veered from that of the Administration to that of MacArthur." Niebuhr felt that Truman's approach was correct and feared that MacArthur's reckless actions in Asia could jeopardize American interests on the Continent. "We can survive as a free world if we hold Europe though we lose Asia. We cannot survive if we lose Europe though we hold Asia." Since America cannot "follow the MacArthur policy without losing both our European and Asian allies in the United Nations," Niebuhr suggested, the "only possible resolution of this critical situation is acceptance of a *modus vivendi* acceptable to the whole of the free world as represented in the UN. This means coming to some kind of agreement with Communist China."[36]

The ADA National Board supported the spirit of Niebuhr's position and passed a resolution stating that Europe "must be defended with every possible means and held in alliance with the free world." In order to accomplish this goal, the board recommended that U.S. policy in Asia had to be "to hold UN strategic positions yet to avoid unlimited engagements on the Asian mainland." Such engagements, it feared, might well invite Soviet aggression in Europe. The statement also warned that America was simply not capable of fighting full-scale land wars on two continents. "We must not," the resolution warned, "allow ourselves to be maneuvered into fighting on Stalin's terms."[37] The ADA's position was essentially the same as Truman's. Yet the resolution left many questions unanswered. At what point would the United States decide that its interests in Europe were being sacrificed to events in Asia? More immediately, how could the United States prevent Soviet expansionism into Asia, or for that matter, other Third World countries?

In an attempt to define a clear course for the ADA in Asia, Loeb had organized an ADA commission in June 1950 to study the problem and make recommendations to the National Board. It was obvious from the very beginning that the commision was divided between those, like Niebuhr, who wanted to use economic and political reform to lure China toward the West, and those labor representatives who considered China at least as great a threat as the Soviet Union. When the commission submitted to the 1951 convention a resolution that called for diplomatic recognition of China, discontinuation of aid to Chiang Kai-shek, and permission for China to regain control of Formosa, some labor leaders on the committee objected. Gus Tyler, David Dubinsky's representative in the ADA, wrote an angry letter on February 16, 1951, complaining that the "compromise draft" was "heavily weighted in tone and content toward finding a solution of the Chinese problem by heavy concessions to Mao." The draft, Tyler asserted, showed the influence of a number of groups, including the Popular Front, that believed "that Mao is a Tito." This belief, he charged, is a serious delusion that "saps all our strength to resist Chinese aggression, to undermine Chinese Communism, or even impose a stalemate." It is the ADA's job, he said, to "combat the idea that Chinese Communism isn't Communism at all and the additional idea that Chinese Communism is not part of Russian imperialism."[38]

Tyler threatened to bring his grievances to the ADA's convention in April 1951. The ADA *World* expected a "full-dress debate" on America's China policy to be the "highlight" of its Fourth Annual Convention. Yet, ADA leaders did not want to appear divided over such an important policy issue. With one labor representative already gone, and Tyler near the breaking point, the ADA leadership was eager to reach a compromise. The foreign policy commission decided to accept most of Tyler's suggestions in order to prevent a potentially divisive floor debate. The resolution passed by the commission and accepted without amendment from the floor was much more anti-Mao than the position the Far East committee had recommended. Condemning the Korean invasion as "one facet of Communist world aggression," it supported the UN decision to intervene, added that the United States should not use negotiations as a way to "reward aggression," and concluded by delaying indefinitely—"so long as the Peking regime continues to defy the principles of the United Nations Charter"—China's admission to the United Nations. The debate was thus stopped short of serious division—in a way that kept anti-Communist labor spokesmen from rebelling. Still, it proved a little hard for the Asia commission to handle. Later, on October 5, 1951, its chairman, Andrew Rice, asked the National Board to disband the ADA Asia policy commission. "The extremely controversial nature of United States Far Eastern policy," he claimed, "has made it practically impossible to reach agreements in the Commission meetings which became too often debating forums."[39]

The debate over American policy concerning communism in Asia foreshadowed more serious divisions that were to develop in later years, especially during the Vietnam War. For the time being, though, the organization found that its foreign policy position, like its position on the Fair Deal, was in essential agreement with the Truman administration's.

A little over a month after taking office in 1945, Truman was informed of the presence of classified American documents discovered in the office of the magazine *Amerasia,* which was under the control of Communist supporters. The president ordered that the six persons arrested be prosecuted for conspiracy to violate the Espionage Act. In June of 1946 the disclosure of a Soviet spy ring in Canada induced Truman to strengthen the federal security program. Confronted with mounting public criticism that the government was lax in weeding Communists from important government positions, Truman in November 1946 appointed the Commission on Employee Loyalty. The commission recommended that the president bar from government service anyone with "membership in, affiliation with or sympathetic association with any foreign or domestic organization . . . designated by the Attorney General as totalitarian, fascist, communist or subversive." Truman accepted the commission's recommendations and on March 21, 1947, issued Executive Order 9835, establishing a loyalty program for all civilian employees in the executive branch.[40]

The loyalty program was vast in mandate and execution, calling for the FBI to make a "name check" on each of the more than two million persons already on the federal payroll, and on all future applicants for federal positions. If authorities found any "derogatory information," they would commence a "full field investigation" into the individual's background. Results of the investigation would be handed over to a loyalty board that determined whether the evidence justified dismissal. The procedure did not require that the accused be confronted by his accuser or be entitled to substantive proof of the charges against him. One historian has commented as follows on the position of the accused in these procedures: "It was up to him to prove his innocence of charges that were usually vague and unspecific, made by persons whom he did not know, whom he could not confront, and whose credibility he could not challenge."[41]

The ADA was torn between approval of the loyalty program's objectives and concern about its procedures. The ADA statement supported excluding from government "persons who adhere to foreign governments or totalitarian political philosophies where such adherence may endanger the best interest of the United States." It warned, however, that proper procedures needed to be applied. The accused should have a fair hearing, based on specific written charges, with opportunity to examine witnesses and ask for appeal. Although the ADA judged that the president's program did not "meet these tests," it did not question the assumptions guiding the program. Schlesinger, who helped draft the organization's position on loyalty questions, provided insight into the liberal view of the issue in a November 1947 *New York Times Magazine* article. He wrote that a "fanatical group which rejects all American interests in favor of those of the Soviet Union" did present a serious threat to American security. America had to respond swiftly and effectively to extinguish the threat while also recognizing that "Americanism is not a totalitarian faith, which can impose a single economic or political dogma or require a uniformity in observance from all its devotees." The solution to this dilemma, Schlesinger claimed, is "to construct some means of ridding the security agencies of questionable characters, while at the same time retaining enough safeguards to insure against indiscriminate purges." Schlesinger found some of the safeguards established under the president's program flawed not because they violated civil liberties but because they were ineffective. Most of Schlesinger's—and the ADA's—differences with the president's program were over minor points. He had little difficulty with some of the most objectionable aspects of the program, including the right to discharge on suspicion and to deny the accused the right to confront the accuser. While discharge in advance of an overt act may seem "a rough policy," Schlesinger claimed, "the failure to discharge suspicious persons may well imperil national security." Consequently, the ADA recommended the creation of a government review board that would "acquaint the accused with the charges and permit him the protection of counsel." Yet, the accused would be permitted to confront the informant only when evidence was tenuous and some doubt remained. "Espionage breeds counter-espionage," Schlesinger declared, "and government counter-espionage agencies simply cannot unveil their agents to every demand of a defense attorney."[42]

As abuses developed, the ADA became less certain of its earlier technocratic solution to the larger issues presented by the loyalty program. For James Wechsler the case of William Walter Remington proved instructive about the inherent abuses of the system. A Commerce Department employee with an impeccable record, Remington was suspended from his sensitive position and brought before the local loyalty board, found guilty, but later acquitted by a federal loyalty board. Shortly afterward the House Un-American Activities Committee (HUAC) reopened the case and presented witnesses charging that Remington had indeed been a Communist. Acting on the new evidence, a grand jury indicted and later convicted him on perjury charges. Wechsler believed that the case exposed "the program's most glaring injustices." Wechsler originally supported the loyalty program because he believed "that Communists have no 'right' to smuggle themselves into responsible posts inside Democratic government." But by February 1949 the government had screened millions of employees and found 99.9 percent to be loyal. There was "little justification for perpetuating the program in those agencies clearly unrelated to national security," he claimed nearly two years after his original support for the program.

Ironically, even Wechsler's reformed program would have done little to protect those like Remington who worked in sensitive positions and were still subject to loyalty checks. The ADA *World* argued in February 1949 that the Remington case dramatized "one of the most appalling injustices in the Government program: the failure to permit the accused to confront his accuser." The *World* announced that, in light of the Remington case, the ADA would undertake a "re-examination of the entire Government loyalty program." The review, it said, will be "made in the light of many disheartening and disquieting episodes which have occurred in the Federal Loyalty proceedings." Yet, it will also keep in mind "that Communists, while they are tolerated in our society, are full-fledged agents of a foreign power whose interests are clearly inimical to those of every democracy."[43]

The reevaluation that the *World* spoke of took place a few months later. The organization's 1949 domestic policy platform passed at the convention, while "recognizing the right of the government to require loyalty to free institutions as a qualification of public employment," criticized "the crude and indiscriminate methods" of loyalty investigations during the preceding year as having done "more harm than good." The ADA now demanded that loyalty tests in security agencies and jobs "guarantee every individual the full right and opportunity to defend himself" through fair hearings, specific written charges, disclosed evidence, the confrontation of accusers, the right to cross-examination, and full appeal.[44] The ADA's response to the loyalty issue was instructive of how the organization planned to deal with other sensitive civil liberties issues. The organization tried to be in favor of both anticommunism and civil liberties. It pointed out the real dangers of Communist subversion, denied that Communists had any civil rights, but also raised some minor objections to the procedures though not the spirit of the administration's measures. For a short time the ADA could have it both ways. However, as public anxiety grew with the Korean invasion and as conservative demagogues made it politically riskier to defend civil liberties, the ADA found it difficult to straddle the fence.

The ADA took a similar approach on the question of the civil liberties of Communists. In 1948 eleven Communist leaders were indicted, tried, and sentenced to prison under the Smith Act of 1940 for "conspiracy to advocate" the violent overthrow of the government. By introducing the question of "conspiracy," the court, as the political historian David Caute has argued, "opened the door to dragnet trials based on sympathetic association and obviated the hard task of proving the case against each defendant at the same level of rigor."[45] Liberals watched anxiously as the case made its way through the Federal District Court in New York, where in June 1949 Judge Harold Medina not only confirmed the lower-court finding but even denied the suspects bail. Although most liberals, the ADA included, publicly opposed the Smith Act, they were reluctant to stand up for Communists being tried under the act. On October 21, 1949, Charles M. La Follette, national director of the ADA, in a statement not cleared by the board, condemned Judge Medina's decision as "unnecessarily vindictive." He charged that the men were convicted "under a law whose constitutionality is greatly in doubt" and were denied bail, "which even murderers and traitors are allowed." Chester Bowles, articulating the reluctance of public figures in the organization to get too far ahead of public opinion, said that he thought it a "very unwise move and a mistake in judgment on the part of the National Office" to release the statement. He stressed "that individuals such as himself and Governor Stevenson have to work hard on clear-cut issues to be good liberals, and there is no sense in the liberals making it harder for them to be elected."[46] The National Board at its next regularly scheduled meeting, in Baltimore on December 17 and 18, 1949, discussed whether La Follette had overextended his authority by issuing the statement. While the board ruled that La Follette acted within his authority, it recommended that on such controversial questions the director clear his statements with as many board members as possible.

Joseph Rauh prepared, in the event the Circuit Court of Appeals reversed Judge Medina in the Communist trial, a public statement praising such a decision. He called Executive Committee members in New York, Philadelphia, and Baltimore to get their reaction to the proposed release. There was not enough time to poll the entire board; so he contacted those who were involved in political campaigns, assuming they would be most sensitive to the possible political ramifications. Whereas New York and Baltimore had no problems with the statement, Johannes Hoeber of the Philadelphia chapter "opposed the issuance of the statement on the ground that it would adversely affect the Philadelphia election." Rauh called Richardson Dilworth, the ADA-supported candidate for mayor, who "stated that the issuance of the statement would definitiely injure chances of success in Philadelphia." Although Dilworth agreed with the content of the statement, he felt "that the sentiment against bail was so strong in Philadelphia . . . that the issuance of the statement would be a bad blow to their chances in the election." Rauh conceded, "[It] was a hard choice to make between the general needs of our organization and the particular needs of Philadelphia. In view of the strength and vitality of the Philadelphia Chapter and the importance of their election, we decided that the issuance of the statement would not be in the best interests of the ADA."[47]

The rights of suspected Communists proved a troubling problem for an organization attempting at once to safeguard civil liberties and to wield political influence. Many ADA members feared a political backlash against the organization if it appeared too "soft" on the Communist question. Daniel O'Keefe, a member of the New Haven chapter, probably captured the feeling of many ADA members. While he recognized that in some abstract sense a case could be made for defending the rights of Communists, O'Keefe thought it better that liberals "not 'stick their necks out' and jeopardize the position of their party or organization." Very much aware of the political climate, he warned, "The ADA will never be an effective organization if it gets nailed as a 'Pink' or 'Red-tinged' organization and will completely lose its effectiveness." The issue of whether Communists deserved bail, he concluded, is not "worth making a fight over. . . . [A]ren't there some other violations of civil rights that we could protect against?"[48] For O'Keefe and for the ADA, the political risks of defending the civil liberties of Communists outweighed the moral commitment to some abstract notion of civility.

Despite Truman's moves to defuse the Communist issue, the House Un-American Activities Committee had refused to let the issue go. The committee used the sensationalist testimony of Elizabeth Bentley, a confessed wartime Communist spy, to identify a number of New Dealers close to Roosevelt who had allegedly furnished information to Soviet agents. The most troubling was the charge of Whittaker Chambers, a onetime Communist, that Alger Hiss, formerly the director of special political affairs in the State Department, was part of an underground Communist group in Washington. Hiss's first trial for perjury resulted in a hung jury on July 8, 1949. His second trial brought a conviction on January 21, 1950.

The Hiss trial was only one of a series of shocks in 1949–50 that Eric Goldman claimed "loosed within American life a vast impatience, a turbulent bitterness, a rancor akin to revolt." The first shock occurred in March 1949, when the FBI arrested Judith Coplon, a Justice Department employee, for providing the Russians with confidential information. In August, Truman released the China white paper warning that the world's largest country was about to fall into Communist hands. On September 23 Truman announced in a terse statement to the press the most ominous news of all: "We have evidence an atomic explosion occurred in the USSR." Most of the public seemed to believe that the conservatives' fear about Communist subversion was justified.

The shocks grew in 1950. In January, Truman said that he would not only refuse to defend Chiang Kai-shek in the event of a Communist assault but also not spend the $75 million that Congress had already mandated for Formosa. "I've still got [the money] locked up in the drawer of my desk," the defiant president exclaimed, "and it is going to stay there." In February a British scientist was arrested for passing secrets to the Russians. While Americans received a steady diet of congressional testimony about Communist influence in the State Department, Julius and Ethel Rosenberg became national celebrities. Most devastating of all the events was the news in June of the North Korean invasion. The war exacerbated the red scare by convincing Americans that a beleaguered Communist party still presented a serious threat to U.S. security. Public opinion polls revealed overwhelming sentiment in favor of registering Communists and outlawing the party.

The identity of the spooks had long been evident to conservative Republicans who charged, "In our government household, Communists and their New Deal fellow travelers are being harbored in key positions where they can sabotage our nation's policies." The most sensationalist charges came from Wheeling, West Virginia, where a junior senator from the state of Wisconsin was making a routine campaign stop to drum up support for the local GOP. The senator's name was McCarthy, and the speech turned out to be far from routine.[49] A brawny, unkept man, with ever-present five o'clock shadow and a compulsive desire to appear tough, McCarthy came to the Senate in 1947. He was undistinguished and largely anonymous until, in February 1950, he hoisted himself to sudden fame on the Communist issue. Perhaps Richard Rovere's description of McCarthy is still the most accurate.

He was, Rovere wrote, "in many ways the most gifted demagogue ever bred on these shores. No bolder seditionist ever moved among us—nor any politician with a surer, swifter access to the dark places of the American mind."[50]

McCarthy's speech that day was simple in theme and similar to the pompous and unsophisticated campaign oratory that characterizes most elections. "The reason why we find ourselves in a position of impotency," the disheveled Senator explained, "is not because the enemy has sent men to invade our shores, but rather because of the traitorous actions of those . . . who have had all the benefits that the wealthiest nation on earth has had to offer. . . ." Building to a dramatic climax, McCarthy claimed to have in his hand "a list of 205" known Communists "still working and shaping the policy of the State Department." The red scare, already fanned by HUAC and political oratory since World War II, now became a central concern.[51]

This red scare must have seemed ironic to members of the anti-Communist Left. The ADA spent much of its early existence warning the American public about the dangers of an international Communist conspiracy. During its 1948 campaign against Henry Wallace, the ADA drove the point home in stark and strident language. Less than twelve months later, liberals and the ADA found themselves the object of attacks from frustrated conservative Republicans desperately searching for an issue with which to embarrass the New Deal–Fair Deal heritage of the majority party. The *Chicago Daily Tribune,* commenting on the ADA's 1949 convention, said that the organization consisted of the "extreme left wing of the New Deal" and that it "issued a series of solemn pronouncements as to how the country can be carried in a hand basket best and quickest." In late 1949 John Flynn, a member of the Committee for Constitutional Government, a right-wing political group, published *The Road Ahead,* which referred to the ADA as "the spearhead and central planning and propaganda machine of the National Socialist Economic Planners in this country." In October, Westbrook Pegler, while admitting the ADA "is not yet frankly a Communist force," charged that it "advocates nothing which a Communist would oppose except the North Atlantic Pact and a strong American war machine." In February 1950 Senator Homer Capehart of Indiana told the Senate that the ADA was part of "an international conspiracy to socialize America."

In February 1950, when *Reader's Digest* printed a condensed version of *The Road Ahead,* Hubert Humphrey wrote the editors that the book seriously misrepresented the ADA. The editors refused to publish Humphrey's rebuttal. "Any article," they explained, "which would have to deal so largely with interpretations and implications could hardly have that simple, down-to-the-ground reader interest which a mass-circulation magazine must continually strive for." The conservative attacks on the ADA were becoming so frequent that the ADA *World* began publishing a regular column called "What They're Saying." The pastor of the First Presbyterian Church in Nashville, Tennessee, informed his flock that the ADA was "about as Democratic as Stalin." Fulton Lewis, Jr., in a broadcast referred to the "OPA long-haired, left-wing, stargazing, mouth-hanging-open, fair-haired boys, who, when they were bounced out of the government, formed the Americans for Democratic Action." The *Troy* (N.Y.) *Morning Record* wrote, "Socialist planning in this country now seems centered in the Americans for Democratic Action." Westbrook Pegler called the ADA "an insidious, non-partisan advance symptom of the British version of Marx." The *Boston Herald* referred to the ADA as a "group of left-wingers hitch-hiking along with the national administration."[52]

The ADA became a target in a number of races in the 1950 campaign. William F. Meade, Republican city chairman in Philadelphia, attacked Mayor Richardson Dilworth and other ADA members for alleged Communist leanings. "When Dilworth tied himself in with the Communist-infiltrated ADA, he joined the company not only of sinister, and dangerous crackpots," Meade said, "but still worse, of the associates of convicted subversive criminals." In Detroit, Guy George Gabrielson, chairman of the Republican National Committee, charged in an October 3 speech that the "left-wingers" of the CIO-PAC and the ADA had gained control of the Democratic party in Detroit by using "the Communist techniques of beating down opposition by violence." As a good measure of public apprehension, concerned citizens who had heard of or, in some cases, were thinking of joining the ADA, but were unsure of its loyalties, flooded the FBI with letters. Congressman Thomas Lane of Massachusetts called the Washington FBI after receiving an invitation to join the ADA. He wanted to know if the organization "was on the up and up."[53]

At first the ADA tried to counter the charges by showing that it was actually more anti-Communist than many of its critics. In October 1950 the National Board tried turning the tables on conservative Republicans by charging, "Congressional reactionaries . . . have wittingly or unwittingly helped the cause of communism here and throughout the world." The real issue, they charged, was this: "What program and politics are best to combat communism here and abroad, and who favors or opposes them?" The board asked voters to consider "whether economic and military assistance to foreign countries, full appropriations for the Marshall Plan, economic aid to Korea, passage of the civil rights program and other welfare legislation helps or hinders democracy in its fight against communism."[54]

The results of the 1950 congressional elections indicated that the public believed McCarthy had the stronger case. "The fact might as well be faced frankly," Schlesinger admitted in November, "the election of 1950 was a victory for McCarthyism." Schlesinger and other liberals saw little reason for optimism. In California, Richard M. Nixon, whom Schlesinger called "the West's streamlined McCarthy," defeated the liberal Helen Gahagan Douglas. In Colorado "an extreme reactionary Republican" named Eugene Milikin defeated John Carroll. In New York, Herbert Lehman won, but by only a small margin, against a "feeble and pathetic" candidate. In Wisconsin, Andrew Biemiller, an ADA member and strong opponent of McCarthy, lost his congressional seat to a conservative Republican. The most dramatic result was the defeat of Millard Tydings of Maryland, a veteran conservative Democrat whom Roosevelt had once tried to purge in 1938. The biggest reason for

Tydings's defeat, William Boucher, chairman of the Baltimore chapter of ADA told the National Board, was McCarthyism.[55]

The ADA took a strong stand against McCarthy. In October 1951 it expressed "full and active" support for attempts to expel McCarthy from the Senate and asked Truman to issue a "declaration of war against McCarthyism." It saluted Senator Benton "for his courageous action in focusing the spotlight on Senator McCarthy's chronic and systematic distortions and deceit," and it hoped that "the tide has begun to turn against McCarthyism." Throughout the year it issued press releases, and many of the organization's leading members gave public speeches condemning McCarthy's ruthless tactics. In the fall of 1952 the Students for Democratic Action (SDA) organized its own campaign against McCarthy, called Operation Freethought. Most of the thirty SDA chapters active in the campaign held well-attended speaker meetings and circulated a new SDA civil liberties pamphlet affirming "that McCarthy has never discovered a single Communist, or anything resembling an espionage agent; that he has never produced evidence of any kind to substantiate his charges against individuals; and that he had nothing to do with the the the trial of Alger Hiss, or with the prosecution of anyone else ever tried for any connection with Communism."[56]

Yet, direct confrontation with McCarthy was not the best way to measure liberal success in combating the red scare. Perhaps the most damaging consequence of McCarthyism was that it made liberals less able to deal with the more subtle, though important, aspects of the red scare. While favoring a broad definition civil liberties, the ADA could not ignore the political consequences of jumping too far ahead of public opinion. By tempering its commitment to civil liberties with a clear recognition of political possibilities, the ADA's response to many of the abuses of the period never rose above the level of calculated ambiguity. When forced to choose between its morality and its politics, the organization chose the latter. Lawrence Smith, the chairman of the Philadelphia chapter of the ADA, in a series of political recommendations to the National Board, summed up the dilemma liberals faced in the red scare:

> The record is perfectly clear for all who would look at it that ADA has vigorously opposed Communism, both at home and abroad. Yet, it seems to me that our greatest weakness in this field at home has always been that we seem to be consistently defending people who are being charged with Communism. . . . We have, it seems to me, been put in the position whereby we have permitted the enemies of Democracy to become the destroyers of Communists. We ourselves should have that position. . . .[57]

On June 4, 1951, the Supreme Court in *Dennis et al. v. the United States* upheld the constitutionality of the Smith Act—and the conviction of the Communist leaders—by invoking the clear-and-present-danger doctrine of the Schenck case of 1919. By declaring the Communist party itself a conspiracy the Court upheld the lower-court ruling that all members of the party were guilty by association. "On June 4, 1951," the *New Republic* editorialized, "the Supreme Court of the US paid tyranny the tribute of imitation."[58] Over the next few years the government tried, convicted, and imprisoned nearly a hundred state and regional Communist leaders under the Smith Act for allegedly advocating the violent overthrow of the government, not for any criminal acts.

Rauh and Wechsler prepared a statement contesting the Supreme Court's decision, claiming that the prosecution was directed against the advocacy of ideas, which was not covered by the clear-and-present-danger clause. "Freedom of speech," they charged, "ought never be made a political football." Since Rauh did not want to wait until the next board meeting to release the statement, he polled the National Board by wire and phone. He found more opposition than he had expected. Schlesinger "strongly" opposed issuing the statement, claiming "This would kill us here." Senator Lehman advised that "such statements accomplish no purpose and put ADA and its Board in unenviable light." William Muehl of New Haven argued that issuing the statement would make the organization "sitting ducks by coming out with these dramatic protests in situations in which we accomplish nothing more than to convince a few more bewildered people that what 'they say' about us is true." The most strenuous objections came from the national chairman, Francis Biddle, who had served as attorney general under Roosevelt. Biddle admitted that the law was "unwise and foolish" but did not consider it unconstitutional. He only objected to the statement in principle; he believed that it would do the ADA "infinite harm, and would cause a great many resignations to no purpose."[59]

According to Loeb's notes, Biddle prevailed, as the members of the board voted somewhat less than two to one against issuance of the statement. Loeb stated that some members "merely indicated disapproval and gave no reasons"; that some "disagreed seriously with the particular text of the statement without disagreeing with its principles"; and that still others "felt that a decision of the Supreme Court should not be publicly opposed." Decisive, perhaps, were those who, "while expressing general agreement with the ideas expressed, nevertheless, felt that no institutional or other advantage could be gained by the issuance of the statement."[60]

The matter did not die there. On June 20 Arthur Schlesinger, Jr., met with Wechsler to iron out differences so the organization could make a statement on it. Schlesinger offered Wechsler a "compromise platform" demanding repeal of the provisions of the Smith Act that penalized advocacy, denouncing further prosecutions under the act, and calling for "a new law outlawing the Communist Party as a criminal conspiracy systematically utilizing perjury and espionage in the interests of a foreign totalitarian power." This position, Schlesinger concluded, "serves the double purpose of repelling a dangerous attack on our traditional sphere of civil freedom and at the same time providing a specific legal basis for protecting our society against a conspiracy determined to destroy it."[61] Schlesinger's compromise became the basis of a new ADA proposal written by David Lloyd. The statement did not criticize the Supreme Court decision, but it did express liberal opposition to the "use of the decision by the Department of Justice as the basis for new and large-scale prosecutions." The statement held that the best place to fight Communists was in "the market place of American opinion" and that no benefit could be had from "new prosecutions directed against the advocacy of ideas." "Freedom of speech," it repeated from the original statement, "should never be made a political football."[62]

Once again, Biddle led the fight against the new, watered-down statement. He felt it was unjustified in calling for the repeal of the Smith Act because the ADA had approved "by a substantial majority" the first prosecution under the act. Liberals, the new ADA statement said, "are overwhelmingly united in their opposition to the use of the decision by the Department of Justice as the basis for new and large-scale prosecutions," but, Biddle argued, "there have been no large-scale prosecutions." The *Dennis* case was tried fairly, and the "second indictment is of the same nature, and we cannot assume that it will not receive the same treatment."

According to Biddle, the statement that "freedom of speech ought never to be made a political football" was "unwarranted" and "unfair." The Communists, he said, were not convicted for "propaganda" but for "revolutionary techniques which constituted a danger to the country." The Communists were were not engaged in "open propaganda in the market place of ideas, but secret and organized efforts—not to persuade—but to act violently when the time comes." Furthermore, the ADA statement said the "real Communist threat is the threat of sabotage and espionage." "Why then," Biddle asked, "should the Government take no steps to punish the secret teaching of a preparation for sabotage and espionage?" Moreover, Biddle feared that whether justified or not, release of the statement would have a negative impact on the political well-being of the ADA: "Whatever may be our views on the damage of the Communist revolutionary movement within the United States, I am convinced that such a statement would do the ADA infinite harm."[63]

Supporters of the new statement criticized Biddle for being too concerned with political consequences. "If in the present climate of opinion harm will come to ADA," retorted Harry Girvetz of the California chapter, "is this not an eloquent reason for dedicating ourselves to changing the climate?" Since the Communist party no longer poses a threat to American security, then it "must follow that the Smith Act is a product of hysteria and who, if not ADAers, should point this out?" Yet Girvetz's logic did not convince many of his colleagues on the National Board, which remained divided. As of July 25 the vote was twenty-six in favor and twenty-two against. Almost all of the public figures in the ADA, including Hubert Humphrey, Franklin D. Roosevelt, Jr., Herbert Lehman, and Chester Bowles, along with most labor representatives, including Gus Tyler, A. J. Hays, Hugo Ernst, Marx Lewis, and Ben McLaurin, opposed issuing the statement. Most of the support for the statement came from intellectuals and chapter representatives. Unable to reach a consensus, the National Board decided to remain silent on the question of prosecutions and instead reemphasize its original opposition to the Smith Act—something on which everyone in the organization could agree.[64]

Although most ADA leaders were sincerely committed to speaking out against violations of civil liberties during the red scare, they were equally concerned with maintaining some influence on the political process. The ADA spoke out against McCarthy, but when it came to the more subtle and sometimes more pernicious manifestations of the red scare, the organization's response was timid. In most of the difficult civil liberties problems it faced in 1949, the ADA aligned itself with Truman and the Democratic party. Once again the organization was unwilling to pay the political price of advocating unpopular ideas.

By the end of the Truman years, many ADA members were frustrated and demoralized. Its membership remained small and was confined to just a few states. The hopes of making the organization a home for intellectuals and progressive labor leaders, which had seemed so realistic in 1948, were greatly diminished by 1952. Most labor leaders gradually withdrew financial support from the organization, and those who remained, like Dubinsky and Reuther, provided only nominal aid. Also, signs of tension were appearing between labor and political figures on the one side and intellectuals and former New Dealers on the other. More important, however, the organization was unable to move beyond the Truman program, thus revealing how beleaguered American liberalism was in the years 1949–52.

4

The ADA, Adlai Stevenson, and Civil Rights, 1952–1956

In 1948 the ADA had led a vicotrious drive for a strong civil rights plank in the platform. But the walkout that followed and the bolt of four southern states from the Democratic side in November came as a shock to party leaders. In the four years after the walkout, many southern congressmen made Fair Deal Democrats pay a price for their action: they voted with conservative Republicans in complete disregard for the Democratic platform and the president's wishes. As the 1952 election approached, the South posed the dominant problem. Faced with the formidable opposition ticket of Eisenhower and Nixon, Democratic party leaders preached the need for unity. The call for unity put the ADA in a difficult position. While still committed to a strong civil rights plank, the ADA also understood the political consequences of another confrontation with the South. Both national elections of the decade raised a classic question for the ADA: Should it stand firmly on principle and risk sacrificing its political influence, or should it compromise its principles for political gain?

If there was one man liberals believed could lead the Democratic party to victory in 1952, it was Adlai E. Stevenson, the incumbent governor of Illinois. Stevenson was a man of subtle contradictions: gregarious, he fancied himself a loner; called an intellectual by many, he rarely read; hailed by liberals, he was respected by many conservatives; considered the champion of the "common man," he was, at heart, an elitist. As Galbraith has noted, "He ran for President not to rescue the downtrodden but to assume the responsibilities properly belonging to the privileged."[1]

Stevenson endeared himself to liberals during his four years as governor of Illinois, from 1949 to 1953. Although he devoted much of his time to good-government issues—streamlining the state government, cutting out waste, holding the line against pork-barreling—Stevenson also took a strong stand for the Illinois FEPC, and he increased spending for welfare services and doubled state aid to public schools. His decisive response to the Cicero race riot—in 1951 Stevenson sent the National Guard to the Chicago suburb of Cicero when its largely East European workingmen population rioted against a black family trying to move into town—increased his stature as a defender of black rights. The conservative Republican majority in the state senate, which fought him every step of the way, served only to make Stevenson appear, by comparison, a fighting liberal.

Perhaps what liberals found most impressive was Stevenson's courage in confronting the anti-Communist hysteria. He vetoed the Broyles bill, a state version of the Internal Security Act, with the comment "We must not burn down the house to kill the rats." He also gave a deposition attesting to the good reputation of Alger Hiss when he was on trial for perjury. Despite intense public criticism, Stevenson refused to retract his statement in support of Hiss. "It seems to me that it will be a very sad day for Anglo-Saxon justice," the governor declared, "when any man, and especially a lawyer, will refuse to give honest evidence in a criminal trial for fear the defendant in an action may eventually be found guilty."[2] In 1952 many liberals were prepared to accept Stevenson solely because of his forthright stance on the Communist issue, regardless of his moderate position on other problems, including civil rights.

Stevenson also impressed liberals with his style. Max Ascoli, editor of the liberal *Reporter* magazine, wrote, "Adlai Stevenson is a politician with a sense of style. This sense of style shows itself in the language he uses, in the honest dignity of his behavior." He had a quick mind, a sharp wit, and he spoke with charm and intelligence. Stevenson raised political discourse to a new level, standing apart from many of his political contemporaries. Many admirers compared his oratorical skills to Lincoln's and FDR's. "What he lacked in commitment, especially in commitment to liberal programs," the historian John Frederick Martin has written, "Stevenson made up for in words."[3]

Ill at ease with social reformers of any stripe, Stevenson was especially uncomfortable with liberals intransigent on civil rights issues. He always considered himself a conciliator, not an ideologue. Like most of his contemporaries, Stevenson "simply did not understand the civil rights issue."[4] His insensitivity was due partly to his conciliatory temperament, partly to his upbringing. Although Stevenson had an intellectual aversion to racism and discrimination, his upbringing in a small, rural midwestern town, and his wealth and comfortable lifestyle insulated him from the plight of blacks. Stevenson never developed the visceral attachment to civil rights as a moral issue that required immediate and drastic action.

On a number of occasions Stevenson referred to himself as a "moderate" and expressed his dissatisfaction with the liberal wing of the party. During one meeting with Loeb, in March 1952, Stevenson defiantly outlined his differences with the Fair Deal program. "What do you want me for?" he asked repeatedly. "I don't agree with your programs." He said he opposed the principle of public housing; favored amending, not repealing, Taft-Hartley; did not support federal aid to education; and opposed "socialized medicine" and the Brannan Plan for agriculture. On civil rights he felt that it was the states' responsibility to act and that the federal government should not "put the

South completely over a barrel." "You know, I've got southern blood in me," he blustered. He considered himself orthodox on economic matters and could not ignore the rising national debt. Only in foreign policy did he express support of Truman's position. After the meeting, Loeb briefly considered reporting to his ADA colleagues that the ADA should prevent, not promote, Stevenson's nomination.[5]

During the 1952 campaign, liberals were not blind to Stevenson's conservative views. Most, however, felt not only that he was the best candidate available but also that he was genuinely liberal at heart and that with better advice and information he could be led away from some of his more conservative views. The problem, according to Donald Montgomery, a political aide to Walter Reuther, was that, although Stevenson was "the most able politician" of his generation, "his views on key issues [were] stated here and there in haphazard fashion." Montgomery worried about the governor's position on civil rights. Stevenson's claim that he was looking for unity between the northern and southern branches of the party, and his expressed hope that "the civil rights plank can be mutually satisfactory to both sections," did little to allay liberal suspicions. Stevenson sought "to have conservative support in addition to liberal support," Montgomery assumed, warning that the governor was against "socialized medicine and the Brannan Plan" and that his position on Taft-Hartley was inadequate. The evidence, Montgomery concluded, "does not make a good case for the man." But Montgomery considered Stevenson an "openminded, intelligent man," and, since Stevenson had the best chance of winning the nomination and the election, he recommended that Reuther and other liberals try to work within his organization to influence the direction of his campaign.[6]

A number of prominent ADA members, including Arthur Schlesinger, Jr., Reinhold Niebuhr, Violet Gunther, and James Loeb, agreed with Montgomery, arguing that the ADA should play an active role in recruiting Stevenson for the nomination and in assuring his victory over the other Democratic challengers. "Prompted by a great concern for the future of our country," Niebuhr pleaded with Stevenson to seek the nomination. Schlesinger agreed, informing Stevenson, "You appear the only solution." The Chicago affiliate of the ADA, the Independent Voters of Illinois, complemented the efforts of Stevenson partisans on the National Board. The IVI was the first group in the nation to endorse Stevenson for the nomination; in January it formed the Illinois Committee for Stevenson and later merged with the Stevenson committee to begin work on a nationwide network of Stevenson for President Clubs.[7]

None of the other prominent contenders—Senators Robert Kerr of Oklahoma and Estes Kefauver of Tennessee and Governor Averell Harriman of New York—inspired liberal passions. Kerr, the Senate's millionaire oilman from Oklahoma, was the least acceptable of the three, since he was too closely identified with corporate special interest. Liberal indifference to Kefauver's candidacy is more difficult to explain. Raised in the New Deal tradition, he was a forceful proponent of both the New Deal and the Fair Deal agendas.

Yet, Kefauver's folksy, neopopulist southern style made him anathema to the ADA's brand of urbane liberalism. He also alienated many of the big-city Democratic leaders by uncovering close ties between political bosses and organized crime during the nationally televised hearings of his Senate Crime Investigatory Committee. Also, persistent rumors about Kefauver's personal life, including charges of a chronic alcohol problem, made many liberals question whether he was suited to be president.

More important, Kefauver was caught in the peculiar sectional split that plagued the post–New Deal Democratic party. In trying to walk the narrow path between his segregationist colleagues in the South and his liberal supporters in the North, Kefauver ended by pleasing no one. Violet Gunther said, "He is too good for the South and not good enough for the North." According to Gunther, there was considerable discussion at ADA Executive Committee meetings about presidential possibilities. "Stevenson certainly has much greater support among our people," she commented, "despite the fact that many of our Board members are personally friendly to Kefauver." Most members believe "that his candidacy is a hopeless one, doomed first by his bad civil rights record which rules him out in the important northern industrial states, and secondly because of President Truman's total opposition to him." Besides, she concluded, he "has practically no important Democratic Party support, and has a great many unsavory characters rallying round."[8]

Harriman had no such liabilities. A man of impeccable liberal credentials, he made few compromises and showed little willingness to moderate any of his liberal views to appease southern opinion. Harriman readily displayed his New Deal pedigree and directed his appeal to northern urban liberals, who formed the backbone of the ADA. Although Harriman did entice some liberals to get down from the Stevenson bandwagon, most refused to jump. They praised Harriman's progressive stand on the issues but questioned whether his colorless personality and spiritless speaking style would prevent him from rallying public support for his positions. Most of all, they doubted his chances of defeating Eisenhower in the general election.

Selecting a suitable nominee was not the only problem worrying liberals in 1952. They knew that two southern states, Mississippi and Texas, still smarting from their bruising at the 1948 convention, were sending rival delegations to the Democratic convention scheduled for Chicago. The establishment of a Fair Employment Practices Commission (FEPC) also promised to be a contentious issue. Some in the South showed a willingness to accept an "educational" FEPC that would be limited to making recommendations without having any enforcement powers. Other progressive southerners expressed support for local FEPCs rather than for one, central agency. According to this proposal, a federal FEPC would have authority to issue subpoenas, hold hearings, and make recommendations but not to enforce its recommendations.

Democratic party strategists eager to avoid a fight at the 1952 convention on either of these issues presented another formidable obstacle for liberals to overcome. The Republican nomination of Eisenhower, over the sentimental favorite Robert Taft a few weeks earlier, made it even more necessary to prevent a southern walkout. Many believed that, against a popular candidate like Eisenhower, the party could not afford to lose the four southern states that had given their electoral votes to the States' Rights Democratic party in 1948. Governor Paul A. Dever of Massachusetts was the first to extend the olive branch to the South. In a nationwide television address in May 1952, he claimed there was little difference between the milder 1944 civil rights plank and the contentious 1948 plank and suggested that liberals accept the 1944 plank as a compromise.[9]

In the weeks before the convention opened, the ADA appeared in no mood to compromise on either the loyalty pledge or FEPC. In response to Dever's peace offer, Francis Biddle said the question confronting the country today "is not whether the Democratic Party can effect a strategic retreat, or even stand the ground it has gained during the two New Deal-Fair Deal decades." The first priority, he argued, is that "there must be no compromise on the Civil Rights issue." Civil rights stands "before the world as the symbol of the sincerity of our dedication to freedom." Liberals, he warned, "will not support unprincipled compromisers." At the same time the National Board issued a warning to party leaders not to take liberal support for granted. "The margin of victory," it claimed, "will be the gap between passive indifference and enthusiastic support. The liberal-labor coalition would not provide that enthusiasm if the candidates were not uncompromising in their devotion to the liberalism of the New and Fair Deals."[10]

Many liberals doubted that the South was important to Democratic victory in 1952. The southern bolt in 1948, they argued, proved that the party could win without southern votes. Truman lost thirty-nine electoral votes in the South to J. Strom Thurmond, the States' Rights Democratic party candidate. If Henry Wallace had not won three northern cities, the Democrats could have won the election without the southern states. Biddle summed up liberal opinion on the subject in a Fourth of July letter to the delegates at the Democratic convention: "The Democratic Party has won when it had offered a concrete liberal program. It is inconceivable that it can mortgage this program at the Convention and thus insure victory next November." Calling anything less "surrender by the majority to the Southern minority," Biddle claimed, "Twenty years of Democratic administration has done more to strengthen the economy of the southern states than the seventy years of Republicanism before it."[11] At a press conference on the Friday before the convention, the ADA, as part of the Leadership Conference on Civil Rights, repeated its claim that the South had played no decisive part in the Democratic victories since 1932.

As the convention opened, most of ADA's leadership favored a strong civil rights plank but was also committed to seeing that Stevenson became the party's nominee. If Stevenson decided to run, however, it was going to be as the head of a united party. He had no intention of forcing a civil rights plank that the South would find offensive. By closely identifying itself with Stevenson's candidacy, the ADA limited its leverage in pushing for civil rights. Most leaders preferred Stevenson running on a weak platform to a weaker candidate on a strong platform. While publicly committed to a strong Democratic statement on both FEPC and the loyalty pledge, many ADA leaders concerned with the organization's political influence refused to challenge the conciliatory mood prevalent at the convention. Hubert Humphrey was perhaps representative. Humphrey assured party leaders that he would not repeat his performance of 1948 and wage a floor fight that could precipitate a southern walkout. Although personally in favor of a statement on FEPC, Humphrey was politically committed to Stevenson, who was quietly working to unite the party behind a moderate plank that omitted FEPC. Since Humphrey felt that Stevenson had the best chance of defeating the formidable Republican challenger, Eisenhower, he was reluctant to do anything that would hurt Stevenson's chances of nomination. Humphrey was also aware that Harriman was waiting anxiously in the wings orchestrating a platform fight for a stronger civil rights plank. A North-South split would swing liberal votes to his candidacy and away from Stevenson.

Not all ADA members agreed with Humphrey. James Loeb, Franklin D. Roosevelt, Jr., Walter Reuther, and Joseph Rauh were all committed to Harriman's candidacy and to a strong civil rights plank. They lobbied tirelessly in support of the minority plank Harriman was advocating. Their efforts proved fruitless; they were overwhelmed by the Stevenson tide and the division within liberal ranks. In the end the moderates prevailed. The platform omitted the adjective "enforceable" in describing the FEPC law and substituted a promise that measures should be "effective." At the urging of Senator Sparkman, all mention of the filibuster rule was removed from the civil rights section and transferred to a section on "strengthening Democratic government." Congress should, the plank said, "improve Congressional procedures so that majority rule prevails and decisions can be made after reasonable debate without being blocked by a minority of either house." Loeb perceptively observed that the liberal civil rights plank failed because Stevenson's supporters tempered their commitment to principle with their loyalty to a candidate. Although Stevenson's supporters were intellectually tied to the more forceful plank, they were "never willing to risk the disunity which would endanger their candidate's chances." Adlai Stevenson, he said, "was the candidate of unity." Franklin Roosevelt, Jr., agreed with Loeb's assessment, calling Stevenson the "Northern Dixiecrat."[12]

Most of the Democrats who gathered in Chicago did not share Roosevelt's reservations. Stevenson won the hearts of delegates with his wit and seriousness in his welcoming remarks. Promising no "superficial solutions"—"Words are not deeds and there are no cheap and painless solutions to war, hunger, ignorance, fear and imperialistic communism"—Stevenson warned that only hard work, sacrifice, patience, and reason could effect the "transition from an age that has died to an age struggling to be born." Although Kefauver led on the first two ballots, the animosity of many party leaders and the defections of favorite-son candidates moved the nomination in Stevenson's direction. The Illinois governor was nominated on the third ballot.

Stevenson's selection of Sparkman as his running mate did little to assuage liberal concerns about Stevenson's civil rights position. On civil rights, the *Nation* said, "Sparkman has a record which is not to be distinguished from that of Senators Eastland, Byrd, Ellender, or any of the Dixiecrats." Although the ADA National Board unanimously endorsed the Democratic ticket, there was some debate over the wording of the endorsement, especially as it concerned Sparkman's civil rights record. A draft statement mentioned "the default on the civil rights program which marred the voting record of Senator Sparkman." But the statement went on to "recognize him . . . as the standard-bearer of the emerging liberal movement in the New South." Not everyone accepted this position. Leon Shull, then executive director of the Philadelphia chapter, considered the section about Sparkman too weak. "After all," he said, "there is a need for ADA to differentiate itself from the ordinary political hacks who will take anything that their party puts up. . . ." Shull wanted Sparkman to make clear his poor civil rights position so the ADA could "point out how unimportant the Vice-President is in determining policy." For the appearance of unity, the drafting committee did not accept Shull's comments, and the endorsement made only minor changes in language and none in tone or substance.[13]

The significance of the Democratic show of unity did not escape the purview of a skeptical press. The *Wall Street Journal* declared, "Last week there came . . . the end of a revolution. The Democratic Party itself called a halt to the militant movement that for 20 years has been known as the Fair Deal or New Deal." Edwin A. Lahey of the Washington bureau of the Knight newspapers summed up events in the *New Republic:* "The Democrats beat back their own left-wing and nominated a middle-of-the-road candidate who is probably the most conservative man to head the ticket since John W. Davis."[14] There was also little confusion about the direction in which Stevenson planned to move the country. "Right or wrong, wisely or not," wrote William White, "the Democratic party has now gone slightly to the right— enough to the right to satisfy the center, but not far enough mortally to offend the left or to please the right. . . ." It "is obvious now that the Roosevelt-Truman philosophy of government is nearing the end of an era," wrote the *New York Times* correspondent Anthony Leviero. "This philosophy, essentially the welfare state, seems to be destined to undergo a marked change, no matter whether Gov. Adlai E. Stevenson or Gen. Dwight D. Eisenhower wins the election. . . . Both are definitely to the right of Mr. Truman, though General Eisenhower is more so."[15]

Once nominated, Stevenson embarked on a campaign that would "talk sense to the American people." To assist in his effort, he recruited ADA supporters Wilson Wyatt, who served as campaign chairman, and speechwriters Arthur Schlesinger, Jr., and John Kenneth Galbraith. Even while surrounded by liberals, however, Stevenson could not be inspired to shed his conservative skin. He continued to express his suspicion of unions, his sympathy with Taft-Hartley, and his belief that Keynesian economics amounted to little more than a rationalization for poor management.[16] Many of his liberal staff members worked feverishly, if not always successfully, to tone down some of his more illiberal statements. "In the end," Galbraith said, "he could be persuaded, although only on occasion, to elaborate ambiguity."[17]

Stevenson also tried to put distance between himself and his liberal advisers. He feared that the public would perceive him as too dogmatic, as merely a captive of the liberal faction of the part. Stevenson's conservatism frustrated many of these advisers, yet, convinced of the governor's liberal instincts and pleased to be near the center of power, they continued their faithful support. The strain between Stevenson and his liberal-labor supporters over the sensitive issue of civil rights also persisted during the election campaign. Stevenson's penchant for making uninformed statements caused considerable consternation among his liberal backers. He frequently hedged on controversial issues—for example, telling southern groups he opposed FEPC and telling liberal groups he favored it. His statements "appear to have been based upon incomplete information" and "created deep and widespread apprehension, and for very good reason," an aide informed Reuther. Fortunately, Stevenson's staff eased liberal distemper by being "receptive to their concerns and willing to meet and discuss the situation."[18]

The ADA not only accepted the weaker civil rights plank and the balanced Democratic ticket; during the campaign it also worked through the Volunteers for Stevenson rather than as an independent political group. The national ADA warned its locals not "to publicly dominate or exclusively direct the policies and activities of the committees." The object was to work with groups that did not necessarily subscribe to all ADA programs and policies but that were "not appealed to by regular political party organization." Stevenson's liberal advisers believed that the ADA could be an important political ally. Leo Lerner, a member of Stevenson's national campaign staff, suggested in a "personal and confidential" memorandum that the governor "extend the handclasp of friendship to ADA'ers in the East, especially those who were active in the Kefauver and Harriman campaigns." He also hoped to "obtain in writing all pertinent facts from ADA files for use at organizing level of national headquarters in Chicago."[19]

This relationship did not work out as planned. Widespead Republican attacks against the ADA, the decidedly more liberal positions of the ADA staff people, and the inevitable tension between ADA partisans and loyal campaign staff created serious problems. The ADA had grown accustomed to attacks from the conservative press. George Sokolsky, Fulton Lewis, Jr., and Westbrook Pegler were among the ADA's most acerbic critics. In his syndicated column "These Days," Sokolsky repeatedly referred to the ADA as the "principal vehicle for go-slow socialism." ADA members, he claimed, are actually a greater menace than known Communists because "they masquerade as gentle folk who wish to do good, while, in reality, they are Socialists." Fulton Lewis used the same tactic, calling the ADA "a group of Socialist thinkers who felt a distaste for the Communist label." While the ADA claimed to be anti-Communist, he said, it was soft on all issues concerning communism. Westbrook Pegler, a columnist for the *Washington Times-Herald,* repeatedly charged that the ADA was attempting to "substitute the Master State under a discipline similar to Hitler's or Stalin's." It was, he blustered, "a Marxist-Socialist organization" founded "to cause the disintegration of the two big political parties and reduce our politics to continental European confusion."[20]

The ADA could handle being a "whipping boy" for the fringe Right, since these writers were mostly singing to the choir. The ADA was not prepared, though, for the pernicious campaign of the Republican National Committee to discredit Democratic candidates by tying them to the "Marxist-Socialist" ADA. The committee, exploiting public anxiety about domestic communism, produced a lengthy booklet full of juicy quotations for Republican candidates to use against their opponents. The ADA, the report claimed, "has its roots deeply embedded in the Communist inspired 'Popular Front' movement that united both factions of Marxism, i.e. Communists and Socialists." Having planted the ADA's roots in subversive soil, the report went on to accuse the organization of promoting "Marxist-Socialism," attempting to undermine the democratic process, and being soft on communism. It then made the vital link between the ADA and the Democratic party. The ADA people not only control that party, it said, "but have this year a candidate of their choice for the Presidency of the United States and for the Vice-Presidency, and are backing a large number of candidates for the United States Senate and House of Representatives."[21]

In August 1952 a House Republican newsletter called the ADA "a leading front organization for Marxist Socialism in the United States." Prominent Republicans took the message on the road. The day before the 1952 election, Pat McCarran responded to Stevenson's charge that he "used to be a Democrat" by saying that Stevenson had "been consorting so long with the Americans for Democratic Action that he wouldn't know a Democrat if he saw one." Never one to be shown up, Joseph McCarthy had some specious accusations of his own to level against Stevenson. His favorite target was Arthur Schlesinger, Jr., Stevenson's most cherished speechwriter. McCarthy accused Schlesinger of writing in praise of Russia, of disparaging religion, and of speaking in favor of allowing Communists to teach in universities. Besides, he claimed, Schlesinger was a member of the ADA, which, on sundry issues, supported Communist causes.[22]

The Republican smear tactics had an effect. "ADA was so frozen out" of the Stevenson campaign, one report from Washington indicated, that "we practically have to use spies to find out what they are doing." Although the situation in Washington was worse than in other states, every active chapter confronted the problem of being isolated by Stevenson's conservative supporters. The Kansas City chapter of the ADA, for example, reported that it was working independent of the Stevenson campaign because the Republican attacks "heightened the ordinary and usual suspicion of and hostility toward the ADA."[23]

Part of the problem was that many of Stevenson's campaign staff distrusted his liberal advisers. Mrs. Edison Dick, cochairperson of the Volunteers for Stevenson, wrote that many of his supporters worried that Wilson Wyatt and Arthur Schlesinger, Jr., were too liberal and too influential. Stevenson, irate at spending so much time defending the patriotism and personal loyalty of his liberal staff members, stressed his independence from both Wyatt and Schlesinger. But Stevenson was never able to allay the fears, even of his own staff, that he was being influenced by his ADA advisers.[24]

It was public fear of Korea, inflation, and taxes, however, that dominated Stevenson's attention during the campaign. Eisenhower kept Stevenson on the defensive throughout the campaign. By accepting the general principles of the New Deal—"Social security, housing, workman's compensation, unemployment insurance, and the preservation of the value of savings," Eisenhower declared, "are the things that must be kept above and beyond politics and campaigns"—the general successfully focused the campaign on Republican issues. Although Eisenhower frequently contradicted himself on the war, at times expressing support of MacArthur's plans to cross the thirty-eighth parallel and at other times criticizing the administration for squandering American resources, he capitalized on his enormous stature as a military leader by promising to go to Korea. He promised to end the war on "honorable terms"—whatever that meant—and then return the country to a peacetime economy of lower taxes, smaller budgets, and less inflation. In the meantime his vice-presidential running mate, Richard Nixon, assumed the anti-Communist charge, calling Stevenson "Adlai the appeaser" and a "Ph.D. graduate of Dean Acheson's cowardly College of Communist Containment." "Can such a man as Stevenson," Nixon asked, "be trusted to lead our crusade against Communism?"

Stevenson, burdened by the need to attract Truman's support while escaping the administration's liabilities, attempted to answer his opponent's charges. Whereas Eisenhower was free to speak in vague terms about ending the war, lowering taxes, and easing inflation, Stevenson needed to defend the Democratic record. High taxes, inflation, and a budget deficit, he argued, were the price America had to pay to maintain freedom around the world. Korea, he declared, "was the testing point for freedom throughout the world. . . . Everyone of us knows in his heart why we had to stand up and fight in Korea." Stevenson also forcefully defended himself against charges of being soft on communism and continued his strong opposition to redbaiting at home. At one point he appeared before the American Legion to condemn those who for "political or personal reasons" attacked the loyalty of faithful government servants.

Despite a gallant effort, Stevenson failed. Charges of internal communism, corruption in the Truman administration, and, most of all, anxiety over Korea played into GOP hands. The war issue, concluded Louis Harris, was "the Achilles heel of the Democratic campaign." Eisenhower won a landslide victory in November. Stevenson carried only nine states, all in the South or border areas. Eisenhower polled almost 34 million votes to Stevenson's 27 million; the electoral college returns were 442 to 89. Stevenson's conservatism on civil rights notwithstanding, the Democrats lost such traditional Democratic states as Texas, Oklahoma, Florida, Virginia, and Tennessee. Some concerned Democrats blamed the ADA. One disgruntled Democrat informed Stevenson that the governor's close association with the ADA influenced him greatly to vote for Eisenhower. "You see, Mr. Stevenson," he wrote, "we folks at the grass roots want our President 100% for America, with no reservation." Foreshadowing perhaps another confrontation between North and South at the next Democratic convention, Texas's Democratic governor, Allan Shivers, who had backed Eisenhower, said after the election that Ike's victory was "an expression of independence that ought to strengthen the Democratic party and help those promoting the liberal-pinko type of party to their senses."[25]

Shortly after the 1952 Democratic convention, James Doyle submitted recommendations to the National Board concerning the ADA's political program. While claiming not to overlook the "non-partisan quality of ADA's political program," he assumed "general agreement . . . that for the present on the national level, ADA political activity will center within the Democratic Party." Although differences exist between Democrats and ADA members, he said, "for some time the ADA has been identified within the Democratic Party more and more sharply and exclusively, by its position on civil rights and by its position on intra-party developments reflecting the basic North-South division within the Democratic Party on the issue of civil rights."

Since the ADA's future was closely tied to the party's, Doyle said, "ADA should pursue a course which will lessen the tendency to identify it exclusively with North-South divisions in the Democratic Party" and should "re-define and shift the emphasis of that part of ADA political activity which does bear on these North-South divisions." Many Democratic liberals, he feared, "are reluctant to work actively and openly with ADA on intra-party questions," because the ADA is "unnecessarily rigid on north-south issues." Doyle recommended that by concentrating "on fronts other than the extremely tender north-south divisions within the Democratic Party," the ADA would reassure "organization Democrats" that liberals could "be close working allies." The ADA's overriding political objective, Doyle concluded, "is the election of a liberal president in 1956." To accomplish this goal, "ADA will be required to accept the limitations of an imperfect vehicle [the Democratic party], and to cooperate with ADA's friends, warm and lukewarm, to obtain maximum performance from the vehicle in 1956."[26]

James Loeb agreed with Doyle's assessment. Although a strategy of confrontation had worked well in 1948, he said, moderation would be a more appropriate stance for the ADA in 1956. In 1948 the organization was "interested in glorious defeat rather than an inglorious defeat." It did not have "the slightest hope or belief that Harry Truman could be re-elected," so its goal was to influence the direction of the Democratic party. In 1956 the Democrats had a very good chance of coming to power. "Consequently, in our own interest," Loeb said, "we want to be more responsible in terms of the election itself than we felt we had to be in 1948." The ADA, he argued, had a "vital interest" in helping Stevenson's election.[27]

Loeb feared that Harriman supporters would try to force a strong civil rights plank on the 1956 convention, one that Stevenson would be unable to accept. "The result would be either that Stevenson would be denied the nomination, or that he would have to repudiate the platform he was running on." Loeb, finding himself in the awkward position of supporting a moderate candidate against a strong civil rights plank, urged caution and suggested that the ADA coordinate its strategy with Stevenson to prevent Harriman from succeeding.[28] Eleanor Roosevelt had similar feelings. While she did not question Harriman's liberalism, she interpreted his militancy as a tactical maneuver that would force Stevenson to the left and cause him to lose following in the South.

Support for Stevenson was more than a matter of political expediency. A number of prominent ADA leaders accepted his moderate approach on civil rights questions. Calling Stevenson's position "statesman-like," Niebuhr took a veiled shot at Harriman by claiming that "the other candidate's position" was "governed purely by political considerations." Like many other liberals, Niebuhr believed that the South and the whole nation had made "steady progress in racial justice," and warned it would "be a calamity if this progress were arrested by heedless action." Previous experience with "Federal police action against recalcitrant communities in the prohibition era," Niebuhr claimed, "taught us that the power of force is limited against communities and that it tends to stiffen the resistance to the law." The federal government should leave it to the communities to adjust their practices to the law, and Americans had to do all they could "to give these organic processes of persuasion a chance to close the hiatus between the standard of equal justice and the mores of the community."[29] Eleanor Roosevelt, who had developed a close friendship with Stevenson, shared a similar commitment to maintaining party unity. "I think," she said, "understanding and sympathy for the white people in the South is as important as understanding and sympathy for the colored people."[30]

Caution was in order for other reasons. Although questions of civil rights and civil liberties had dominated the ADA agenda since 1948, the organization had by the end of the Korean conflict in 1953 begun turning its attention more to the life-threatening issues of war and peace. It was on the issues that liberals felt Eisenhower was most vulnerable. Niebuhr called Eisenhower the "Chamberlain of our day." "Let it not be said by future historians," Chester Bowles warned, in criticizing Eisenhower's fiscal restraint, "that in the second decade after World War II freedom throughout the world died of a balanced budget." Rauh claimed that with Eisenhower in power America had a foreign policy of "drift, confusion, bluff and blunder."[31] Stevenson spoke, often eloquently, about those issues that concerned liberals most. On world interdependence he said that the world was "like a drum"—"strike it anywhere and it resounds everywhere." Regarding the dangers of massive retaliation, he asked a 1954 conference of Democrats meeting in Miami, "Are we leaving ourselves the grim choice of inaction or a thermonuclear holocaust?"

He spoke of "collective strength and security," advocated "pushing steadily forward in developing the economic and moral strength of the non-communist world," and warned of the revolution of "rising expectations" and "revolutionary nationalism" in the world.[32]

The ADA's compromising attitude toward civil rights also demonstrated a recognition of political realities. In the years between 1952 and 1956, its influence in the Democratic party reached a new low. Republican attacks during and after the 1952 campaign convinced many moderate Democrats that the party needed to put distance between itself and the ADA. The most serious incident occurred in December 1953, at the Massachusetts chapter's annual convention. The keynote speaker, Foster Furcolo, the state treasurer and a leading candidate for governor, told the stunned audience that ADA "ceased to enjoy the confidence of the public because its record makes such confidence impossible." The ADA's "wishy-washy line of softness toward Communism and leftist causes" made it "a killing burden, weakening or defeating Democratic candidates." "The fact is," he said, "the public is apt to oppose immediately whatever you support." What shocked many ADA members as much as the speech were the strong words of support from many prominent Democrats. John Carr, state chairman of the party, said "it was a strong speech and had to be delivered." Approval also came from State Senator John Powers, who said it "was an inspirational speech to all Democrats." Massachusetts was only the most dramatic case; similar incidents occurred in Ohio, where the conservative Democratic governor, Frank Lausche, suggested that the ADA should go out of business. In Newark, the ADA was becoming such an issue in the election that a group started a "Citizens Committee against the ADA."[33]

Furcolo was not about to get an argument from the new Democratic National Committee chairman, Stephen Mitchell, who had replaced Frank McKinney in 1952. The new chairman was intent upon mending fences with the South and was angry with some ADA leaders for attacking the Democratic congressional leadership. Mitchell expressed some of his reservations in a televised talk show in Chicago in December 1953. In trying to minimize the ADA's significance, he said he had never seen a "live" member and would be glad to meet one "in the flesh." Two weeks later, before a radio audience in Philadelphia when Lawrence Smith, head of the Philadelphia ADA, asked whether an ADA endorsement would help or hurt candidates, Mitchell retorted, "We can get along without it all right."[34]

The timing of Mitchell's remarks was unfortunate because they followed, by just a few days, the Foster Furcolo incident. An angry exchange of letters ensued between Mitchell and ADA supporters. Mitchell's statements were also the main topic of discussion at the ADA's annual National Board meeting in January 1954. Gus Tyler described the mood of the meeting as belligerent. Although many members wanted to redress the damage inflicted by Mitchell's verbal assault, they knew that liberal fortunes depended upon Democratic success at the polls. Creating an open rift with the party would only help the Republicans. Rather than confronting the real differences between the two groups, they decided to heal the wounds and demonstrate their unity.[35]

As a step in their reconciliation, Mitchell met first with Schlesinger in Chicago and later with James Doyle and Joseph Rauh, and they came to an understanding. They agreed the Democratic party should maintain its distance from the ADA in public, while working with it behind the scenes. To redress the public damage from Mitchell's remarks, the ADA and the national leaders of the Democratic party organized a unity dinner in Chicago.[36] Despite the public display of harmony, the tension between the two groups continued unabated in private. Mitchell remained personally hostile to the ADA. In January he scribbled a brief note to Stevenson complaining about the governor's name appearing on an ADA Roosevelt Day pamphlet. "This is the type of publicity effort that accounts in part for the newspaper 'tie in' of your name and ADA," he blustered. In a memorandum to his assistant Harry Barnard, Mitchell made his position especially clear. He said that he "was nettled" by Smith's attempt to associate the ADA with the Democratic party before millions of listeners. Mitchell feared that these incidents "might be taken as a 'plant' " by "political opponents who were forever claiming that the Democratic party is run by the 'ADA wing.' " It was necessary, he said, to "somehow disassociate the Democratic Party with the ADA since they are not related, in fact, and to make clear that the ADA is an independent organization and not a wing of the Democratic Party." Afterward he expressed satisfaction that his comments "slowed down the criticism from Republican speakers and editors."[37]

Mitchell also confided to his aide that he was not very impressed with the ADA as a political organization. He said he never saw any ADA members and was rarely consulted about ADA proposals to the Congress. The ADA people, he said, are "so quick to claim credit and so very noisy in any of their activities," yet they are "not only ineffective in usual problems of political organization," they have "been a real millstone to the Democratic Party in seeking popular favor." Mitchell was so concerned about appearing to be under the influence of the ADA that he rejected its proposals even when he agreed with them. Although many ADA "proposals were quite appealing and would in the normal course have been supported by the National Committee," Mitchell confessed that "on at least two or three occasions," he rejected the ideas "because they had been offered by the ADA and [his] support of them might be seized upon as 'proof' of the Republican charge of ADA influence in the Democratic Party."[38]

Stevenson agreed with Mitchell that Republican attacks against the ADA may have diminished its "political utility," but he also recognized that he needed liberal support to secure both the nomination and the election. As usual, when caught between the two extremes, Stevenson chose to equivocate. "I should like not to get involved in all of this," Stevenson wrote one of his liberal supporters in response to the ADA-Mitchell affair. He successfully extricated himself from that imbroglio, but he could not escape the larger problem raised by the dispute—the growing gap within his own party over the civil rights issue.[39]

Equivocating on civil rights became even more difficult after 1954. On May 17, 1954—a day known in parts of the South as Black Monday—the Supreme Court ruled to outlaw segregation in the nation's public schools. "Separate educational facilities," the Court declared in reversing *Plessy* v. *Ferguson* (1896), "are inherently unequal. . . . [S]egregation is a denial of the equal protection of the laws."[40] In protest nineteen southern senators and seventy-seven representatives signed a manifesto in 1956 that bound them to "use all lawful means to bring about a reversal of this decision." Eisenhower, privately opposed to the decision, assumed a public posture of neutrality. "I don't believe you can change the hearts of men with laws or decisions," he said. Eisenhower's reticence infuriated liberals, who charged that the president had abdicated responsibility and actually encouraged segregationists to resist the Court's decision. "There is only one man in the country who can summon up, not just the legal, but the moral resources of the nation and bring to people a sober realization of the terrible crisis toward which we are fast moving," wrote Arthur Schlesinger, Jr. "But thus far the President has displayed no interest at all in what is surely the most ominous domestic situation we have seen for many years."[41]

Many blacks, their expectations raised by the Supreme Court's decision, expressed anger with the federal government's failure to act. Some impatient blacks decided to force the issue. In December 1955 Rosa Parks, a black seamstress, boarded a Montgomery, Alabama, bus after work. Rather than move to the rear of the bus as required by Montgomery law, Parks sat quietly in a section reserved for whites. In response to this open defiance, Montgomery police arrested Parks for violating the city's segregation laws. Montgomery blacks rallied around Parks by organizing a boycott of the city bus system that would last for 381 days. "There comes a time," a young black leader named Martin Luther King, Jr., told five thousand blacks on the first night of the boycott, "when people get tired." Blacks, King warned, were "tired of being segregated and humiliated, tired of being kicked about by the brutal forces of oppression." Demonstrating that they were willing to sacrifice comfort and security to ensure their dignity, black leaders looked to the national Democratic party, and to liberals in particular, to assist their cause.

Despite overwhelming liberal support for the Supreme Court decision, Stevenson, more fearful of losing the votes of white southerners than those of blacks, avoided taking a stand. Actually, Stevenson was aggressively seeking détente with the South. Harry Ashmore, one of the governor's closest advisers, summed up the campaign strategy in a March 1956 "personal and confidential" memorandum. Convinced that "the nomination and quite possibly the election, will once again turn on the civil right issues," Ashmore warned that if the southern delegates did not get an acceptable ticket, they would organize "a bolt of considerably greater magnitude than that faced by President Truman in 1948." Compounding the problem was a new militancy among many black leaders"; "seeing their ancient goal within reach," they were "insistent and sometimes arrogant." Given this explosive situation, Ashmore recommended that Stevenson take great care "not to inflame passions on either side." Advocacy of either new federal legislation or even strict enforcement of existing laws, Ashmore reasoned, would only exacerbate tensions and deepen divisions. Reminding Stevenson that his nomination depended largely on their "ability to hold together the substantial southern support" Stevenson and Mitchell had built since 1952, Ashmore recommended that Stevenson continue to walk the middle ground between "the Madison Avenue abolitionists" and "the Southern racists." He suggested that the governor convey the image of a "Great Conciliator" who could bring together moderate black and white leaders in the South. Stevenson, he said, "must emerge as the only candidate who can unite the national Democratic Party and hold it together in the years ahead."[42]

Stevenson's conciliatory approach simply reflected the desire of the Democratic party's national leadership, which was committed to making peace with the South. Paul Butler, who had assumed the party chairmanship following Mitchell's resignation in 1954, expressed complete agreement with Stevenson's strategy. Butler, like his predecessor, was a moderate bent on preserving party unity. A year before the 1956 convention, he predicted that it would approve a mild civil rights plank and proclaimed that the loyalty oath was "out the window." The ADA organized a meeting with the former Indiana state chairman to make him aware of its dissatisfaction with his predecessor and to ask for his cooperation. Rauh wrote after the meeting that Butler dissociated himself from Mitchell's position on the ADA. "He recognized," Rauh said, "the usefulness of criticism from the left in terms of his own job of trying to keep all the elements of the party together." Rauh and Gunther felt not only that Butler understood the role of the ADA in the Democratic party, "but that he welcomed the existence of ADA."[43]

If some ADA members found Butler personally more receptive, they did not find him prepared to make major changes in the party program. Butler made that clear in a meeting with civil rights leaders organized by the ADA. In attendance were Butler, the NAACP's Roy Wilkins, Arnold Aaronson, representing a coalition of Jewish civil rights groups, Rauh, and Edward Hollander. After brief pleasantries, they listed their grievances with the Democratic party: its widespread opposition to implementing the Supreme Court decision on school integration; its failure to make the slightest move in Congress toward enactment of any civil rights legislation; and Butler's statements minimizing civil rights as an issue. Butler responded by denying that he was trying to engineer a retreat from the party's position on civil rights. He emphasized his responsibility to bring together the widest possible range of views in the party and said, "I have to make some decisions on the basis of expediency when you fellows can stand on principle."[44]

While trying to convince party leaders that they were responsible, the ADA also had to confront rumblings among the general members about its leaders' close association with Stevenson. Some chapter representatives publicly questioned the governor's commitment to the ADA's brand of liberalism. Those opposed to him favored a break with the southern wing of the party and felt that the nomination of Kefauver or Harriman would be more likely to bring that about. "It is Stevenson's announced purpose to unify the Democratic party. A party which includes Eastland and Mrs. Roosevelt is not united, and cannot be united," complained Alfred Lewis Baker. "The nomination of Kefauver or Harriman or some other more truly liberal candidate would be more likely to have the effect of causing the Southern reactionaries to bolt as they did in 1948."[45] Others opposed Stevenson on more practical grounds, concluding that a moderate candidate and a campaign based on moderation had no chance of defeating Eisenhower. The president owed his political success, they argued, not to his conservative ideas but to his personal following. The Democrats could not counter Eisenhower's personal following, so they had to present a platform that gave voters a clear choice. The last thing the public needed, they held, was two Republican parties.

If liberals were to sever their ties with Stevenson, the 1956 campaign offered the same alternatives as before. In the four years since the last campaign, Kefauver had increased his stock with liberal brokers. He continued to support New Deal programs but found a new cause in consumer rights. Also, his refusal to sign the "Southern Manifesto," written in protest of the *Brown* decision, helped his image with northern civil rights advocates. Yet, with sectional tensions running high in the party, liberals could not accept a southerner to lead what they felt was clearly a northern cause. And while some ADA members continued to praise Harriman for his progressive stand on the issues, most still doubted his ability to rally public support behind his candidacy. His defeat in the primaries in 1952 and his narrow New York gubernatorial victory in 1954 only confirmed liberal suspicions about his lack of public appeal.

"There is an air of unreality about this week's blowout," James Reston reported as the Democrats assembled for their convention in August 1956. "Everybody assumes it will be Adlai E. Stevenson for President again." Before the coronation, however, the convention needed to develop a platform. On August 10 a number of liberal groups testified before a platform committee dominated by moderates bent on preserving party unity. Roy Wilkins spoke for the NAACP and the Leadership Conference. Yet it was Rauh, testifying on behalf of the ADA, who presented the strongest case for a strong civil rights plank. Rauh demanded that the party champion civil rights. "Once and for all, the Democratic Party must set to rest the notion that the geographical division of the Party requires compromise," he thundered; "once and for all the Party must surmount this geographical division and put itself wholeheartedly on the side of civil rights." Governor George Bell Timmerman of South Carolina followed Rauh to the committee room. "We in the South," he said, "know from generations of experience that segregation is best both for the Negro and the white. For this Party to approve the desegregation decision would be to ask us to support what we know is wrong."[46]

To members of the platform committee, Timmerman seemed to have the better case. The committee presented an innocuous civil rights draft. The Democratic party, it stated, "recognizes the Supreme Court of the United States as one of the three constitutional and co-ordinate branches of the Federal Government, whose decisions are part of the law of the land." After this brief civics lesson, the draft said nothing about the Court's decision in the *Brown* case, except that it had "brought consequences of vast importance." As for enforcement, it said the party rejected "all proposals for the use of force to interfere with the orderly determination of these matters by the courts." The full platform committee went into executive session, approved the plank, and also issued a minority report that would have restored to the platform the wording of the 1952 plank. More important, it pledged the party to "carry out" the Court's antisegregation decisions, though again without force.

A number of liberals—Harriman, Governor Lehman of New York, Governor G. Mennen Williams of Michigan, Senator Paul Douglas of Illinois, Rauh, and representatives of the AFL-CIO and the NAACP—banded together, on behalf of the ADA, to gain a substantially stronger plank. Their only hope was for the large states—Michigan, Minnesota, and New York—to force the platform chairman, Sam Rayburn, to ask for a roll call on their plank.

Rauh led the fight against the drafting committee's plank. He said that it lacked a pledge of federal legislation, including FEPC, and that it needed to show support for the Supreme Court's decisions by inserting the statement "We pledge to carry out these decisions." "This," he said, "is the absolute minimum pledge." Rauh knew what he was going to be up against. He told the ADA Executive Board on August 11 what to expect. The drafting committee was stacked with people who opposed a strong statement. "Therefore, if the fight is to be won it will have to come from the bottom of the Convention. The leadership has not made civil rights an issue." The only alternative, he said, is a floor fight. "No candidate can afford at this point to champion the issue and run for office, therefore it will have to be delegates and a floor fight."[47]

The ADA convened a meeting in Walter Reuther's suite at the Morrison Hotel at noon on Wednesday, August 15. There Reuther, James Carey, and Wilkins, along with Robert Nathan and Rauh, debated how adamant they should be on the civil rights issue. Should they bring a resolution to the floor and risk embarrassing Stevenson? Could the Democrats keep the black vote with a weakened civil rights platform? They decided to test the waters to see how much support they could muster for a challenge to the platform committee's statement. They called on the committee to add the final paragraph of the 1952 platform, which was omitted, and include the sentence "We support the carrying out of these decisions," in reference to the Supreme Court's antisegregation decisions.[48]

Reuther and Rauh, with Roy Wilkins, lobbied for their position among the caucuses that afternoon, while Governor Lehman informed members of the platform committee that unless they changed their position, the ADA and other liberal groups would bring the fight to the floor. There was an element of bluff to the liberals' demands; they wanted to avoid a floor fight as much as party leaders did. Most of them, Reuther and Rauh being the most vocal exceptions, sought a way out of the jam. They wanted the convention to adopt a forceful civil rights position, but they also wanted to assure Stevenson's victory and a unified party.

At the same time when Rauh was lobbying for support for a floor fight, other prominent ADA members appealed for moderation. Eleanor Roosevelt called a press conference to counter Truman's endorsement of Harriman and his criticisms of Stevenson's civil rights record. The former first lady asked liberals not to fight for the one point resisted by the South—specific endorsement of the Supreme Court's decision against racial discrimination in public schools. The word "moderate" does not mean "stand still," she claimed, "it means going ahead one step at a time in accordance with the realities, and the priority of importance." She repeatedly defended Stevenson from attacks from both Harriman and Truman, claiming, "Mr. Stevenson supports the basic principles underlying the general attitude of the Democratic Party, and they are the general approach of my husband and Mr. Truman."[49] Hubert Humphrey joined Mrs. Roosevelt in calling on the convention for moderation. In an August 12 appearance on "Face the Nation," Humphrey said "patience" was important to wiping out discrimination. In an attempt to make his personal bid for the vice-presidency more attractive to the South, he said he was thinking more in terms of "observance" than of "enforcement" of the Supreme Court's decision. "We're going to have a strong plank on civil rights," he held, but it will be one that is acceptable to the South.[50]

Sympathetic members of the platform committee offered the ADA a way out of its quandary. They suggested a compromise whereby liberals would drop their insistence on a statement supporting the Court's decisions in exchange for southern acceptance of the final paragraph of the 1952 plank. The platform committee members assured Nathan they could persuade the South to accept the compromise. Rauh, representing the ADA, rejected the compromise and began planning for a showdown on the floor. Paul Douglas, Herbert Lehman, and G. Mennen Williams implored delegates to accept the more liberal minority plank. Chairman Rayburn, however, summarily ruled the minority plank defeated by voice vote. Anticipating Rayburn's response, Rauh had organized a "spontaneous" rally on the floor to force the convention to make a roll call. But most liberals, ADA members included, afraid a floor fight would hurt Stevenson, refused to follow through on their threat.[51] Passage of the moderate platform assured Stevenson's nomination.

For many liberals the 1956 general campaign lacked the drama and excitement of the preceding presidential race. Most commentators had difficulty even pretending the race would be close. "The Republican mood," wrote the columnist Marquis Childs in September, "is one of supreme conviction of victory." The columnist David Lawrence thought that even before the campaign commenced, "a preponderant number of citizens ha[d] already made up their minds how they [were] going to vote." Professional gamblers were giving four-to-one odds in favor of Ike. Throughout the long and arduous campaign, Stevenson spoke of his vision of a "New America." The central issue of the election, he said, is "whether America wants to stay on dead center, mired in complacency and cynicism; or whether it wants once more now to move forward—to meet our human needs, to make our abundance serve all of us and to make the world safer." Yet, fatigue and repetition made the speeches read better than they sounded. Eric Goldman wrote of the campaign, "Adlai Stevenson, the lilt gone from his voice, ran with all the zest and decisiveness of a man taking the final steps to the gas chamber."[52]

The commentators were right; the Eisenhower-Nixon ticket won with the largest popular vote in U.S. history up to that time. Stevenson's 1952 electoral count fell by sixteen. Eisenhower's support of 57.4 percent of the voters had been exceeded only by FDR's in 1936. The popular president carried such Democratic strongholds as Chicago and Jersey City, along with other urban areas like Baltimore, Milwaukee, Los Angeles, and San Francisco. He carried a majority of the Catholic vote and did well among blacks. Eisenhower even ate into the "solid South," despite the Democrats' attempt to diffuse the civil rights issue. The election results were especially disappointing for the ADA. Not only did the organization fail to gain power, but it also miscalculated the dynamics of the civil rights movement. The ADA, which had compromised principle for the sake of power, was left with neither.

In May 1957 Arthur Schlesinger, Jr., reflecting on the first ten years of the ADA's history, commented that as a political organization the ADA had "functioned not only in the field of policy but in the field of politics." At times these two programs conflicted, he confessed "sometimes a sense of practical possibility has kept us from pushing issues as hard as a more strictly intellectual ('Fabian') organization might have done." Nevertheless, Schlesinger believed that the organization succeeded in maintaining the delicate balance between politics and commitment.[53]

Whether the organization was as successful as Schlesinger claimed is questionable, but he was certainly correct in pointing out the tension between the ADA's concern with political action and its commitment to particular issues. The ADA never resolved the question of exactly what role it was to play in the political process. Some leaders, seeing the Democratic party as the only hope for liberal reform, wanted the ADA to work as a liberal caucus within the party and—as it did from 1949 to 1952—attempt to influence national policy from within. They wanted to purge the party of its conservative elements and realign the two-party system on ideological lines. After 1956 some argued that the ADA should combine with Volunteers for Stevenson and become a "loyal opposition" within the party. A larger group, however, wanted the ADA to retain its independent status—to be a nonpartisan group working outside of the two-party system and attempting to rally liberals of both parties. The ADA, they believed, could better attract new members as an independent organization than as a faction in the party.[54]

The elections of 1952–56 exposed the difficulties of working from inside. While claiming to be nonpartisan, the ADA was actively involved with the fortunes of the national Democratic party. In most cases it worked within the party's structure and accepted its agenda. The organization compromised its status as an independent political group by working with the Volunteers for Stevenson, and it compromised many of its liberal positions for Democratic electoral success.

But though the ADA worked with the party, it was never accepted by most Democratic pols as a key part of it. Even if the ADA had wanted to merge, leading Democrats would probably not have accepted the offer. The fear of Republican charges of creeping socialism, as well as the need to maintain southern support, led Democrats to distance themselves from the ADA. The ADA appeared caught between two conflicting goals. On the one hand it wanted to develop an aggressive liberal philosophy that would serve as a blueprint for the future; on the other it wished to be an active liberal lobby.[55] Members found that in order to retain any influence in the Democratic party, they needed to temper their liberal program to suit the needs of party regulars. The ADA was unwilling to abstain from political action and follow its Fabian instincts; yet it was largely frustrated, in the conservative 1950s, in its efforts to move the party in the desired direction.

5

The ADA, Eisenhower, and
Liberalism in the 1950s

After the Democrats were turned out of power in the Eisenhower landslide of 1952, the ADA, for the first time in its brief history, confronted an administration openly hostile to its existence. The pervasive political conservatism that dominated both the public mood and the administration's policies limited the ADA's political influence in Washington during the rest of the decade. Although the organization continued to deal with sensitive civil liberties questions, after 1954 it turned its main attention to economic and foreign policy issues. Leon Keyserling, former chairman of the Council of Economic Advisers, became the leading spokesman on economic matters for the ADA, as the organization moved squarely behind his philosophy of growth economics. Keyserling's ideas about economic growth also influenced the ADA's position on foreign policy. Because of their faith in Keyserling's economics, ADA leaders were convinced that America could increase significantly the amount of money spent on defense without neglecting needed social programs. Despite near unanimity in the ADA about the need for economic growth at home and competitive coexistence with the Soviets, clear divisions among liberals were emerging on central issues.

Dwight Eisenhower made a strong appeal to the middle-income, middle-of-the-road voter. In a press conference on December 8, 1954, he described his followers as "progressive moderates," and several months later he talked of his program as one of "dynamic conservatism." Eisenhower's bland personality—amiable, modest, indecisive, and intellectually limited—reinforced his nonideological image. Many of the men who surrounded the president reflected the needs and values of the giant corporate interests that dominated the Republican party. Secretary of the Treasury George Humphrey, an arch-conservative, had directed a business empire worth $120 million. Secretary of Health, Education, and Welfare Oveta Culp Hobby had been a millionaire Texas newspaper publisher and head of the Women's Army Corps. Secretary of Commerce Sinclair Weeks was a wealthy New England banker and manufacturer whose view of government-business relations, wrote the journalist Marquis Childs, came "straight from Calvin Coolidge." Millionaire businessmen or corporate lawyers held every cabinet office except that of secretary of labor, which was reserved for Martin Durkin of the plumbers' union. Liberals accused Eisenhower of appointing a cabinet of "eight millionaires and a plumber."[1]

Many of the president's men had not only similar social standing but also a common perception that the government that regulated least, regulated best. At the dawn of his administration, the new president ended all price and wage controls imposed during the Korean War. He allowed the Reconstruction Finance Corporation, which had lent about $40 billion since its founding by Herbert Hoover in 1932, go out of business. In April 1953 Eisenhower received authority from Congress to sell to private industry government-owned and government-operated synthetic-rubber-manufacturing plants capable of producing some 800,000 tons per year. And in August 1954 Eisenhower obtained an amendment to the Atomic Energy Act of 1946 that permitted private industry to participate more widely in the development of atomic materials and facilities. When a business recession, which threatened to turn into a full-fledged depression in 1958, confronted Eisenhower with the highest unemployment rate of the postwar period, he and the Council of Economic Advisers were convinced that drastic action was not necessary. He stood firmly behind a more limited program of increased credit, encouragement to home construction, a 7 percent increase in Social Security benefits, extension of unemployment insurance payments, and some expansion of federal spending for highways, hospitals, housing, and schools.

Eisenhower did not, however, attempt to dismantle the social welfare programs of the New Deal. In 1954 and again in 1956, he agreed to increase Social Security benefits and broaden the system to include an estimated ten million new workers. In 1955 he agreed to a new minimum wage law that increased the minimum wage from seventy-five cents to one dollar an hour. Between 1953 and 1961 the federal government spent some $1.3 billion for slum clearance and public housing. In health and medical welfare, too, Eisenhower carried forward existing programs. On April 1, 1953, he signed a bill that raised the Federal Security Agency to cabinet rank as the Department of Health, Education, and Welfare. Although he opposed Truman's plan for national health insurance, Eisenhower did ask for, but Congress refused to provide, federal support for nonprofit health insurance plans, which had been growing rapidly since the 1940s.[2]

Liberals had always looked to the executive branch of government to provide inspiration and leadership for political reform. Despite its sometimes stormy relationship with Truman, the ADA had found his administration sympathetic to liberal ideas. That was not true of the Eisenhower administration. For the first time in the ADA's short history, Republicans controlled the White House, and not since 1947 had liberals been treated with such contempt in Washington. Arthur Schlesinger, Jr., immersed in writing his *Age of Roosevelt,* complained "Switching back and forth between the presidency of Roosevelt and the presidency of Eisenhower makes me wonder at times whether I am living in the same country!" "For two decades," Galbraith recalled, "Washington had seemed an accessible and friendly place," but "it would now be a closed, forbidden city. . . . I had come, without ever realizing it, to think of myself as part of a permanent government. I too was now out of office."[3]

Liberals not only were distant from the sources of power in Washington but also had to contend with a repressive political atmosphere that allowed Joseph McCarthy to thrive. Eisenhower's victory propelled McCarthy to the chairmanship of the Senate Committee on Government Operations, and he used his new power to rampage through the foreign affairs agencies of the Republican administration. Although Eisenhower had been critical of McCarthy's attacks on government, he did not stand in his way. Despite the general's genuine dislike for McCarthy's methods, he had refused to criticize McCarthy publicly during the 1952 campaign and even appeared on the same platform with him. Once in office, Eisenhower decided to avoid a confrontation with McCarthy. "I had made up my mind how I was going to handle McCarthy," he said later. "This was to ignore him. . . . I would give him no satisfaction. I'd never defend anything. I don't care what he called me, or mentioned, or put in the papers. I'd just ignore him."[4]

A liberal organization like the ADA did not have the luxury of ignoring the Wisconsin senator. Yet, it had also not discovered an effective way of exposing him for the charlatan that he was. The organization's criticisms glanced off McCarthy's thick armor, while his own attacks on the ADA had more serious consequences. In April 1953 the ADA's national chairman, Francis Biddle, called upon Attorney General Herbert Brownell to "institute a thorough investigation" into Senator McCarthy's "personal affairs." The same month the ADA printed the suppressed 400-page report on the financial affairs of Senator McCarthy by the Senate Subcomittee on Privileges and Elections and informed McCarthy that it would waive its immunity if he would bring a libel suit "to test out the basic truth of the subcommittee report." McCarthy never accepted the challenge, and the ADA sold over four thousand copies of the report.[5]

In November 1953 the ADA released a statement urging the appointment of "a non-partisan, non-political committee of outstanding citizens . . . to study and report on the whole problem of security and civil liberties." Also in November, Rauh, representing the ADA, debated Roy Cohn, the McCarthy committee's prosecutor, on the NBC radio and television program "American Forum of the Air." Rauh charged that the senator's Fort Monmouth investigation was a "hoax on the public" and predicted that it would fail to uncover "any present espionage." In the course of the debate, Rauh accused McCarthy of conducting a "kangaroo court." He pointed out that as a result of the investigation, the army suspended thirty-three persons on such incredible charges as being a member of the American Veterans Committee or the Federation of American Scientists, or favoring the "leftist writings of Max Lerner." "Almost without exception," Rauh insisted, "it was a question of guilt by association of the worst kind." In June 1954, some two thousand people gathered at Hunter College in New York to hear an ADA-sponsored presentation of "The People vs. McCarthy." Cosponsored by the

American Jewish Congress, the American Veterans Committee, the NAACP, the Jewish Labor Committee, the Liberal party, and the New York Young Democratic Club, the group passed a "sense of the meeting" resolution that asked the Senate to censure McCarthy and move to consider his fitness to hold office.[6]

Usually, McCarthy responded to the ADA's attacks with unrestrained bluster. "It should be recalled," he said, "that the ADA of which Biddle is national chairman, has viciously attacked the FBI, has attacked the Smith Act, has urged the recognition of Communist China, and in many other respects has followed the Communist party line." Put on the defensive by these attacks, the ADA found it difficult to recruit new members. In June 1954 Edward Hollander informed the National Board, "There is some reason to believe that in the present political atmosphere the attacks have made it rather more difficult to recruit new members among the kindred but timid spirits." Membership, which stood at approximately 11,500 in 1954, was not much higher than it had been in 1947, when the ADA was still in its infancy, and it was significantly lower than its peak figure of 18,000, in 1948. Membership not only declined but was restricted to a few large northeasten states. Just four states—New York, Pennsylvania, New Jersey, and Massachusetts—accounted for nearly three-quarters of the organization's forty chapters and over 90 percent of the total membership. The largest chapters were still in Chicago (741 members), Philadelphia (602 members), Baltimore (327 members), Washington, D.C. (324 members), and Detroit (250 members).[7]

As usual, although the ADA publicly opposed McCarthy, it had difficulty confronting other aspects of the red scare. After a heated floor debate, delegates at the ADA's 1954 convention approved a policy upholding the firing of teachers found to be Communists or fascists. The debate revolved around two resolutions. The first, proposed by LaRue Brown, Boston state chairman of the Massachusetts ADA, and Reuben Cohen, vice-president of the Philadelphia chapter, supported excluding "from teaching positions all persons who have surrendered their freedom of thought to Communist or Fascist control." Opponents presented an alternative proposal declaring that membership in a fascist or Communist party, or refusal to testify under the Fifth Amendment, "should not be automatic grounds to disqualify a teacher, but should be given only such weight as full inquiry shows to be warranted in determining the competence of the teacher, which is the primary consideration." For nearly two hours the six hundred delegates gathered at the Shoreham Hotel in Washington debated the two motions. Those wishing to bar members of the Communist party from teaching positions maintained that party members were unfit to teach because they were "bound irrevocably to follow Communist dictates." Opponents charged that, as a liberal organization, the ADA could not in good conscience deny Communists the same rights enjoyed by other political groups. When the debate was over, the hardliners had won by a close margin.[8]

The Communist Control Act introduced in the Senate by the ADA founding father Hubert Humphrey, on the morning of August 12, 1954, was perhaps the most striking example of how some liberals attempted to deal with the pervasive mood of anticommunism. The measure declared the Communist party "the agency of a hostile foreign power, an instrumentality of a conspiracy to overthrow the Government of the U.S.," and "a clear, present, and continuing danger to the security of the United States." The bill provided penalties for membership under the Internal Security Act of 1950: fines of up to $10,000 or imprisonment for five years, or both.[9]

Humphrey's action outraged many liberals. The *New Republic* charged Democrats with "running after a wraith called public opinion, no longer leading as they were elected to lead, but blindly following the election returns of two years before." The *Nation* commented, "Here, once again, the Democratic 'liberals' have outsmarted themselves in their neurotic, election-year anxiety to escape the charge of being 'soft on communism' at the expense of sacrificing constitutional rights."[10] Most ADA mmbers expressed displeasure at Humphrey's action but tended to be sympathetic to his political situation. Marvin Rosenberg wrote Humphrey that while he thought the bill was "a violation of our civil liberties," he understood the political pressure he was under. The ADA must recognize, he added, "that there are times when its leaders who hold public office must take a position because of political realities which is not completely in accord with the ADA's stated principle." Seeing nothing wrong with these conflicting interests, Rosenberg said that with "mutual trust and understanding the two groups could work together "very comfortably."[11]

Schlesinger, writing in his *New York Post* column, "History of the Week," called Humphrey's action "hasty and reckless" and "infected by pre-election fever." After a brief trip to Central America, Schlesinger returned to find a pile of correspondence provoked by his column on the Communist Control Act. The Harvard historian was "shocked" that his column had given rise to such hostile criticism of Humphrey's action. Admitting that the column "was written in haste and under stress," Schlesinger apologized for "certain regrettable phrases" that "may have piled fuel on the anti-Humphrey fire."[12]

Humphrey sent a short memo to Max Kampelman, his chief legislative aide and author of the Communist Control Act, in which he let off some steam over the whole affair. "Well, Max," he fumed, "I have always felt that most of these top people in ADA never really had much time for me anyway. They wanted me as their mouthpiece but they preferred to do all the thinking and anyone who deviated was to be censured." While admitting that the ADA had "done a wonderful service in American politics," he had no intention of being "browbeaten by any of them": "I have just about had a belly full of their intellectual paternalism as it relates to their acceptance of me."[13]

The debate over the Communist Control Act exposed once again the gap between those, like Humphrey, who were primarily interested in practical politics and those, like Schlesinger, who though not against the ADA's playing a role in politics were also concerned with its Fabian role. Through the fall and winter, as the bill made its way to passage, the ADA refused to criticize the Humphrey-drafted section of the legislation and instead focused its ire on a part of the bill that would have restricted unions. One ADA member, Frank Serri, objected to the organization's position, claiming that it had "criticized the bill because of the provisions about unions, but it was silent on the major evil: the unconstitutional outlawing of a political party, the nullification of the 1st Amendment rights." Its criticism was similar, he declared, "to objecting to a lynching party because the rope used was too roughly woven."[14]

At its convention in 1955, held just a few weeks after passage of the bill, the ADA could not reach agreement on whether to oppose Humphrey's bill. While most members felt the legislation was unnecessary at best and unconstitutional at worst, they feared that public criticism of their most celebrated political member would create undue hardship for the organization and the senator. Humphrey's displeasure with liberal criticism of his bill was well known; as delegates gathered for the convention, many feared that if they came down too hard on the Minnesota senator he would leave the organization. At a time when the ADA's relationship with the Democratic party was already seriously strained, it could ill afford losing someone of Humphrey's stature. Irving Howe, an observer at the convention, understood the ADA's precarious political situation perfectly. Since it had already committed itself to the Democratic party and ruled out the possibility of forming a new party, the ADA was "now frozen in its familiar political course." Prominent Democratic politicians like Humphrey, Howe commented, "have the ADA over a barrel: they know they can do or say almost anything and still be sure of its support."[15]

The delegates skirted the problem by not ruling on Humphrey's clause to outlaw the Communist party and by instead urging the president to veto the legislation because of other problems. Hollander explained to Humphrey that the convention decision by no means reflected disapproval of his position. "I hope you do not misunderstand the action of the Executive Committee in urging the veto of the Communist Control Act." Because the organization had never "taken a position on the question of outlawing the Communist Party, and because of the differences of opinion among the officers and members, our action in opposition to the bill was addressed specifically to the provisions of the Butler Bill which was appended." There was no reason, he assured Humphrey, "to construe this decision as an expression of fundamental disagreement with you and your colleagues."[16]

By this time McCarthy's influence had already begun to wane. He had overstepped himself when he challenged the army in a series of televised hearings that ran from April 22 to June 17. Democrats who had long been silent in regard to McCarthy found after the Army-McCarthy hearings that they could speak without fear of reprisal. Most would have agreed with Senator McClellan of Arkansas, who confided to a friend, "I'm fond of Joe McCarthy, but he's getting out of hand, and we have to do something to control him." In September, just six weeks before the midterm elections, a committee chosen by the president recommended that McCarthy be censured.[17]

McCarthy, who had been active in the 1950 and 1952 elections, was a liability to his party in 1954 and consequently took no part in the campaign. However, Vice-President Richard Nixon kept the Communist issue alive. Nixon spearheaded the campaign by visiting ninety-five cities in thirty states. He attempted to frighten voters with the specter of a Democratic Congress "dominated by its Truman-Stevenson-ADA left wing." In New Jersey, Nixon attacked Senator Clifford Case as the candidate of "the Communist *Daily Worker* and the equally red ADA." In May, speaking at a GOP centennial dinner in San Francisco, Nixon stated, "The Democratic Party, unfortunately, is controlled in California and nationally by the ADA left wing, a group of men honestly, but I believe mistakenly, dedicated to the socialization of basic institutions in this country." In New York a few weeks later he warned, "[The ADA] is selling socialism under the guise of liberalism. It is practicing the greatest deception of the century."[18]

On election day the Democrats won control of both the House and the Senate, liberal incumbents did well, and a number of Republican red-hunters went down to defeat. The election, a historian has noted, seemed "to signal the end of the political dynamic which had supported McCarthy and the Communist issue." According to the ADA *World,* the election results demonstrated the "tough resiliency of liberal political strength." Not a single ADA-endorsed congressional candidate was defeated. The Massachusetts chapter reported that most such candidates won easily and that although some of the state candidates lost, they did so by small margins. A number of ADA-supported candidates won in highly visible contests, including Senator Paul Douglas in Illinois, Averell Harriman in the New York gubernatorial race, and George Leader in the Pennsylvania gubernatorial race.[19]

The following month, on December 2, 1954, the Senate voted, sixty-seven to twenty-two to condemn McCarthy for sundry affronts to the dignity of the Senate. While the ADA applauded passage of the censure resolution, it expressed concern that most senators condemned him not because of the "fundamental immorality of McCarthyism as a political *modus operandi* but because of McCarthy's personal misconduct." McCarthyism would continue to be a force in American political life, it charged, until the American people recognized "that McCarthyism meant not only the abandonment of rationality and decency of means, but also the corruption of ends."[20]

Even though McCarthy was gone from the political scene, the poisoned air remained. At the 1955 ADA convention, delegates considered proposals dealing with Communist espionage and sabotage as well as with academic freedom. On both issues the organization took a strong anti-Communist position. The domestic policy commission recommended to the convention that the ADA adopt a resolution that wholeheartedly supported "energetic enforcement of laws against espionage and sabotage" yet opposed "limiting the right to advocate unpopular political proposals, including communist ideas." The commission reasoned that the Communist party was not a conspiracy and actually had "a legitimate function as well." However, when the resolution came to the floor for a vote, the delegates, by a vote of ninety to sixty, deleted the words "including communist ideas." The final statement declared that the Communist party was a "conspiracy" whose objective was "espionage and sabotage" and that these constituted the "most immediate threat to our internal security."

Delegates also considered possible changes in their statement on academic freedom. David Robinson of the Cambridge, Massachusetts, chapter wanted to change the 1953 resolution making membership in the Communist party cause for dismissal. He submitted a proposal that would have made teacher competence the decisive factor in judging qualifications to teach. George Eaton, representing City College of New York, said that guilt by association ultimately led to loyalty oaths, which in turn led to informers. Alfred Lewis of Connecticut headed the assault against the proposed change. Recalling Soviet duplicity at the time of the Nazi-Soviet pact, he charged that liberals should not be fooled again. Another member, in the heat of emotion, declared, "Every member of the Communist party is a member of Soviet intelligence."

The convention hall quickly divided into two camps, each of which sent a long parade of speakers to the microphone to either defend or criticize Robinson's proposal. As the debate went well past the alloted time, Chairman Robert Nathan ordered each side to call its final speakers. When the organization's leading civil rights attorney, Joseph Rauh, rose to speak against the amendment, the result was all but decided. In his "unabashed appeal" for defeat of the amendment, Rauh argued that the issue was dead: there were no more Communists left in the schools, and the ADA should not waste valuable resources on a no-win resolution. After Rauh's speech, Nathan ordered the delegates to cast votes. They defeated the amendment 131 to 117. The *New Republic* congratulated the ADA for recognizing "a maximum [amount] of freedom without any illusions as to the fundamentally conspiratorial character of the Communist Party."[21]

The debate, however, did not end there. In order to appease the large minority of delegates who opposed the anti-Communist positions, Rauh, the newly elected national chairman, told a press conference, "Civil liberties shall be one of our main purposes in the coming year. We intend to fight for the expression of all ideas, including Communist ideas." Rauh's statement brought immediate criticism from conservative Republicans and concerned Democrats alike. Senator Butler of Maryland claimed that Rauh's statement proved that the ADA was "infected by a hard core of Communist sympathizers." Truman's former special assistant Charles Murphy wrote Rauh, "Your statement gives me considerable concern as I am inclined to the view that supporting the right to advocate communist ideas is something like supporting the right to advocate rape, arson, and murder—which I do not regard as being required by a due regard for freedom of speech."[22]

McCarthy's demise allowed the ADA to move on to the more comfortable and politically less sensitive ground of economic policy. The end of active fighting in Korea led to a mild recession beginning in midsummer 1953. Unemployment rose through the winter and reached 5.8 percent of the labor force in February 1954, when there were two million more persons unem-

ployed than there had been a year earlier. Eisenhower's reluctance to authorize decisive antirecession measures left him open to criticism from Democrats and liberals.

The ADA hoped to gain much needed momentum with the recession
issue. The organization owed much of its forceful critique of Eisenhower's
economic policy to Leon Keyserling, who joined the ADA after leaving the
Council of Economic Advisers in 1953. The Keyserling-ADA relationship
was mutually advantageous: the ADA provided Keyserling a forum for his
theories on economic growth; Keyserling gave the ADA a Fair Deal economist of national stature. He also supplied the ADA with a broad and com-
prehensible economic program. Other ADA economists were able to expound
on specific parts of Keyserling's theories in the 1950s, but he was the person
who fashioned the grand design.

The organization wasted little time putting Keyserling on display and
presenting his theory of economic growth as an alternative to Eisenhower's
conservative fiscal and monetary policies. In preparation for the 1954 congressional campaign, the ADA published a collection of essays by prominent
ADA members entitled *Guide to Politics, 1954,* edited by Arthur Schlesinger,
Jr., and Quincy Howe. Mayor Joseph Clark of Philadelphia set the tone of
the book in his introduction, assuring readers that the authors wanted "to hold
on to the best of the past." "They are not radicals," he wrote. "They do not
wish to tear out the roots."[23]

In the spirit of Clark's introduction, Keyserling outlined the ADA's policy
of full employment. The United States, he asserted, needs "to raise the annual
rate of our total economic activity—our total production of goods and services—
by about 40 billion dollars between now and early 1955." This goal can be
accomplished, Keyserling argued, only by increasing by "a few billion dollars"
the "level of federal spending." He called for a $4 billion to $5 billion reduction
in the taxes imposed upon middle- and low-income families. It is foolish to
worry about the federal deficit, he held, because "the Federal deficit would
be smaller at a full economy level of national production and income than
it is now, or might even disappear." Among the other specific measures he
advocated were a liberal credit policy, a higher-minimum-wage law, a massive
program designed to build two million houses a year, and a liberalized international trade policy. If the government adopted these measures designed
to increase consumption, especially that of middle- and low-income families,
Keyserling predicted that by 1960 the United States would have a $500
billion or $600 billion economy and "at least a one-third increase in the
average standard of living." Moreover, he concluded, "we can have a much
higher level of business profits and farm incomes, because in the long run
we must all sink or swim together."[24]

In response to Eisenhower's fiscal restraint, Keyserling developed a "national prosperity budget" designed to create an economy large enough to
pay for all necessary social services without sacrifice. With full economic
growth, he claimed, the United States can increase total educational outlays
from "$22 billion in the school year 1958–1959 to about $38 billion by the

school year 1964–1965"; double the "average social security payments to individuals by 1964"; increase federal assistance to publicly financed health services from $4.50 per capita in 1960 to more than $17.00 per capita by 1964; raise "federal outlays for housing from about $3 per capita to about $11.5 per capita over the same period"; and "lift our outlays for economic and technical development overseas from about $1.7 billion to close to $4 billion." The dramatic increase in the GNP will mean that social spending will not encroach upon national security needs. The United States can, he insisted, "increase national security expenditures by the amounts urged by those experts who are not tailoring our defense outlays to the public revenues yielded by a stagnating economy."[25]

The ADA remained pledged to the idea of full employment. Its convention platform, passed without significant debate throughout the decade, was undiluted Keyserling: "We subscribe to the concept of full employment in an expanding economy as the cornerstone of American economic policy." With continuous full employment, the statement continued, "we can year by year gain mightily in domestic strength and world security." The statement lifted, without change, figures from Keyserling's "national prosperity budget," calling for a GNP by 1960 of $500 billion, which would, in turn, provide about four million new jobs and raise the American standard of living by about 25 percent. The ADA expected a GNP of $600 billion by 1965, creating between seven and eight million jobs and lifting the American standard of living by about 50 percent. "If public and private economic policies are directed toward these attainable goals," the ADA declared, "we can greatly reduce poverty in a land of plenty, pay for costs of an expanding level of necessary welfare services without excessive taxation and with a balanced budget, and do our full part in making the free world more prosperous, hopeful, and secure."[26]

The ADA blamed the Republican tight money policy for the slow rate of economic growth. The restricted money supply made it harder for Americans to buy a home and receive consumer credit, although large business had no problem buying equipment, thanks to tax benefits that allowed unnecessarily high depreciation allowances. "What we find is not an effective policy to fight inflation, but rather a program designed to enrich the bankers, to hurt the farmer and homeowner and consumer, and to bring about a greater concentration of American business into the hands of big corporations," wrote Robert Nathan.[27]

The ADA supported most of the important liberal social welfare legislation proposed in Congress during the decade, including area redevelopment, housing, extended coverage of unemployment benefits, increases in the minimum wage, and expanded Social Security coverage. It also called for a "substantial temporary cut in taxes" designed to increase consumption, which was lagging behind production. The tax cuts, Robert Nathan told the Subcommittee on Fiscal Policy of the Joint Economic Committee in April 1958, "should accrue principally to middle- and low-income consumers, through reductions in income taxes in the lower brackets and through cuts in excise taxes." A tax cut, he warned, "should not preclude programs of essential public works which are useful in themselves and which must be carried forward under any circumstances short of total defense mobilization." The combination of public spending and tax cuts would inevitably lead to a temporary deficit, yet Nathan, like a true Keynesian, believed that a large deficit would help end the recession and pave the road to full employment.[28]

Although the ADA supported all these programs, it spent most of its time dealing with the question of full employment and economic growth and gave little attention to problems of poverty. Not once, in the period 1952–60, did an ADA platform passed every spring by the organization's convention contain a statement on poverty. The ADA's public statements made no mention of income redistribution or guaranteed national income. Most ADA members held firmly to the Keyserling faith in economic growth as a means of solving the problems of poverty. They believed that increased consumption through deficit spending, tax cuts geared to lower-income Americans, and slightly expanded social welfare measures would create a general growth that would benefit all groups in society.

The budget-conscious policies of the Eisenhower administration influenced its foreign policy as well. Eisenhower chose as his secretary of state John Foster Dulles, a skilled lawyer who was the nephew of Robert Lansing, Woodrow Wilson's secretary of state, and the grandson of John Foster, secretary of state under Benjamin Harrison. A stern Presbyterian, Dulles took a moralistic approach to foreign policy. The "world Communist movement" was to him "an unholy alliance of Marx's communism and Russia's imperialism." His tirades against the "negative, futile, and immoral" policy of containment helped keep conservative Republicans behind the president's policy, but they also frightened America's allies and confused its opponents.

Despite Dulles's bombastic rhetoric, Eisenhower believed that the Korean War taught that neither the American people nor the American economy would support a series of limited, conventional wars. Eisenhower's strategy called for America to maintain "a strong military posture, with emphasis on the capability of inflicting massive retaliatory damage by offensive striking power." It stated, "In the event of hostility, the United States will consider nuclear weapons to be available for use as other munitions." By relying on strategic power, Eisenhower could make a significant reduction both in force levels and in defense spending. Termed the New Look, it allowed the president to cut back the army from its post–Korean War high of twenty divisions to a 1957 goal of fourteen and to make similar, though smaller, reductions in the navy budget. As Samuel Huntington has noted, "The basic military fact of the New Look was the overwhelming American superiority in nuclear weapons and the means of delivering them."[29]

The Eisenhower administration's strategy of massive retaliation could not prevent Communist gains in Asia, a loss of prestige in the Middle East, or the Soviet occupation of Hungary. In Vietnam, Eisenhower, like Truman, acquiesced in France's return to Vietnam and actively supported its effort to suppress Ho Chi Minh's revolution. Yet the French, destined for defeat in 1954, agreed to sign the Geneva accords that neutralized two states, Laos and Cambodia; temporarily partitioned Vietnam at the seventeenth parallel; granted to Ho Chi Minh control of North Vietnam and to France rule over the South until the free elections scheduled for 1956. Eisenhower refused to sign the accords and instead worked to undermine them by committing American prestige to the fragile South Vietnamese government of Ngo Dinh Diem. The new leader lacked Ho Chi Minh's personal appeal, but a lack of charm was the least of his problems. A devout Catholic in a Buddhist country, Diem was also corrupt, provincial, and repressive.[30]

While dealing with this crisis in the Far East, Eisenhower was trying to thaw the Cold War. As part of his plan to foster peaceful relations between the United States and the Soviet Union, Eisenhower in the spring of 1955 agreed to a summit with the Soviets in July at Geneva. In a dramatic gesture Eisenhower unveiled his "open skies" concept. The United States, he said, was prepared to exchange military blueprints of all its armed forces for those of the Soviet Union and to permit regular and frequent aerial inspections of its territory in return for similar concessions on the part of the Russians.

A new crisis in the Middle East, however, threatened not only to disrupt the U.S.-Soviet détente but also to undermine Western unity. In 1956 Lieutenant Colonel Gamal Abdel Nasser, who had come to power in Egypt preaching "neutralism," attempted to assert his independence from the West by recognizing Communist China and negotiating an arms deal with Czechoslovakia. At the same time he was negotiating with the United States to finance a large hydroelectric plant, the Aswan Dam. The United States promptly responded by withdrawing its offer to help build the dam. Nasser, refusing to knuckle under to American pressure, nationalized the Suez Canal Company and closed it to Israeli shipping. On October 29, 1956, without American knowledge or approval, Israel attacked Egyptian forces in the Gaza Strip and the Sinai Desert, while Britain and France intervened to "protect" the Suez Canal. Eisenhower, outraged at the allies' duplicity, sent an American cease-fire resolution to the UN General Assembly, which overwhelmingly approved it. The incident only enhanced Nasser's image in the region, increased Soviet influence there, and divided the Western allies. The Suez crisis also helped the Soviet Union in another way—it distracted attention from its brutal repression of the Hungarian revolution on November 1.[31]

During the 1950s the ADA articulated foreign policy alternatives that in tone and emphasis were strikingly different from Eisenhower's approach. Eisenhower, consumed by a sense of fiscal responsibility, was unwilling to spend large amounts of money to defend America's overseas commitments. The ADA, on the other hand, captivated by Keyserling's growth economics, believed that a thriving American economy could maintain American power and influence throughout the world. Most ADA members believed that, in the years ahead, superpower competition was going to take place in the Third World. More than the Eisenhower administration, they recognized how the decline of colonial powers and the rise of nationalism were transforming the underdeveloped world. Also, unlike the administration, which relied heavily upon bombast and the threat of nuclear retaliation to assert American power in the world, the ADA insisted upon a flexible response to international problems, one that relied more on nonmilitary solutions. Believing that international prestige was just as important as military might, the ADA opposed unilateral military action and demanded that the United States rely upon international agencies like the United Nations.

Yet, despite these important differences, certain common assumptions and political circumstance linked the ADA and the Eisenhower administration. Like the administration, most liberals remained remarkably bipolar in their view of the world. With all its subtle recognition of the importance of international cooperation and the rise of nationalism, the ADA remained wedded to the bogeyman theory of history that placed the Soviet Union near the heart of all postwar international disturbances. Even more, liberals and the administration alike were captive to the pervasive mood of anticommunism that poisoned the political dialogue during the 1950s. The ADA's need to appear "tough" on communism and its essentially bipolar worldview clashed with its more nuanced appreciation of both the limits of military force and the important changes occurring in the underdeveloped world. Because the organization was never able to resolve this tension, it could not present a compelling alternative to Eisenhower's foreign policy. Instead, it advocated a type of situational ethic, sometimes condemning the administration for being too soft on Communist expansion, at other times criticizing it for being insensitive to Third World nationalism.

Because of their faith in Keyserling's economics, liberals believed that America could afford to spend nearly limitless amounts of money on defense. "It is transparent and dangerous nonsense," the National Board declared in October 1953, "to say that this country, with its great riches and enormous productive capacity, 'cannot afford' the kind of national defense that is most likely to protect us against Communist aggression." The "over-riding issue before the American people today is whether the national defense is to be determined by the demands of the world situation or sacrificed to the worship of tax reductions and a balanced budget."[32]

Many in the ADA felt that increased spending on the military was not only possible but even necessary because of a change in Soviet tactics following Stalin's death on March 5, 1953, and the end of the Korean War. In August 1953 Robert Nathan polled the Executive Committee to see whether the members believed that these changes required the ADA to change its foreign policy priorities for the future. Responses to Nathan's inquiry indicate that many members were convinced that, while Truman's successful European policy had forced a change in Soviet tactics, it had not altered their ultimate objective. Gus Tyler felt that "the new Soviet line" was "another zig in the continuous zig-zag policy to win the entire world for Communism." Tyler rejected the argument that Stalin's death marked the end of militant communism. There was no more reason to believe this idea, Tyler claimed, "than to have believed the same of Stalin's theory and practice of Socialism-in-one-country (1924–1929); or of the Popular Front policy (1934–1945); or of the World War II coalition (1941–1945)." Each of these "friendly" periods was "abruptly and rudely terminated" by Soviet intransigence. History was repeating itself in 1953, and he suggested, "ADA ought to say this clearly and loudly, because we can not start too soon to dispel the inevitable illusions about the nice new Soviets." Hubert Humphrey was just as skeptical as Tyler. "If Russia's sudden new change can turn us from determination to complacency," Humphrey argued, "bring about curtailment of defense expenditures, and disrupt progress toward unification of the free world's defense efforts, the Kremlin will have won a tremendous victory without firing a shot."[33]

One of Stalin's last decisions, they argued, was to shift from a hard to a soft policy toward the United States. Stalin changed his policy because he realized the United States—under Truman, anyway—planned to stand firm against Soviet aggression. Truman's decisive action in Korea sent a clear message to the Kremlin that the United States would resist Soviet military expansion anywhere on the globe. Although Truman may have frustrated the Soviets' short-term military strategy, there is no reason to hope, the ADA *World* editorialized, "that the Soviet leaders have abandoned their long-term objective of a Communist world." The Soviet change may have been tactical, "an effort, by counterfeiting moderation, to divide the free nations in order to destroy them one by one"; or it may have been strategic, "a decision, now that the opportunities offered by war and its aftermath have been exhausted, to settle down within Communism's new frontiers until 'the inevitable crises of capitalism' offer fresh prospects for further expansion."[34]

The question that confronted liberals in the mid-1950s was how the United States should meet the new challenge. Many ADA members believed that America had to develop a more sophisticated and diverse response to potential Soviet meddling in the Third World. Flexibility, the ADA National Board declared in January 1955, means that the United States "must compete more effectively than it is doing at present, particularly in social and economic fields." Competitive coexistence, it said, "should be a spur to much greater action in the non-military field, not an excuse for doing less than we can and must do. With our unsurpassed productive resources, we have an immense potential advantage in such a competition."[35]

But Eisenhower's preoccupation with balanced budgets, they argued, left the United States unprepared to compete with the Soviets. Eisenhower's so-called New Look, seemed to liberals a rationalization for excessive and dangerous cuts in America's defense program. The ADA feared that both America's economic aid program and its military budget were "being trimmed to the dimensions of small-minded businessmen who concern themselves with cutting taxes rather than with planning for the expansion of the American economy." The only way the United States could persuade the Soviets to agree to a serious negotiation of differences was by showing "its willingness and ability to compete with the Soviets in all aspects of conventional and nuclear armaments." Eisenhower's cutback in both conventional arms and economic aid was especially dangerous because it came at just the time when the Soviet Union was attempting to expand its influence into underdeveloped areas, especially Asia. "The struggle against Communist aggression," wrote Robert Delson, a member of the ADA's foreign policy commission, "must be carried on because Communist success would mean the conquest of the free world, beginning with Asia as the preliminary step to the destruction of the West." The United States can best defend against Communist aggression by helping establish stable nations. These countries, "enjoying the loyalty of their peoples, will be invulnerable to the appeal of Communism because they will be realizing their aspirations within a democratic framework."[36]

Most ADA members believed that the best way to establish and maintain "stable nations" was through Asian versions of the Marshall Plan and the Truman Doctrine. The United States, the argument went, needs to provide a military shield so that social and economic reforms can take root. "Military strength is necessary to defend the free world against communist aggression," commented the ADA's 1955 pamphlet "Partnership for Freedom." Since the "main thrust of communist expansion" is "directed against economically underdeveloped countries," the best way to blunt this thrust is "to help those countries provide the reality of freedom and make an actual start toward economic betterment." In a situation where military forces approach an equilibrium, economic measures, the report concluded, "become very nearly decisive."[37]

Given those assumptions, the ADA recommended that the United States double its economic assistance to underdeveloped countries from $1.5 billion to $3.0 billion. One-third of the money would come from private investment, one-third from public loans, and another third from public grants. The ADA expected that, as the countries became more stable, grant funds would "gradually be superseded by larger loans," and loans would "gradually give way to private investment." Most ADA members were supremely confident that the American economy could outproduce the Russian economy if only Eisenhower had the courage to accept the Soviet challenge. Robert Nathan testified before the Senate Foreign Relations Committee that the United States should challenge the Soviet Union to "competitive co-existence." "The Communists couldn't have put this competition on grounds more favorable to America," he boasted. "When it comes to the know-how and capital for economic growth, the US holds the trumps. Gentlemen, this is our dish."[38]

The French problems in Vietnam provided the ADA with a proving ground for its new strategy. The ADA denounced Eisenhower's policy in Indochina as "improvised, vacillating, and sometimes contradictory." Seeing a ripe opportunity to assert its anticommunism, it warned that the "fall of Indo-China to the Communists would be a disaster, not only to the Indo-Chinese people, but to the whole free world."[39] While claiming to recognize that "there was a single front of Communist aggression stretching from Korea in the north to Indo-China," the administration refused to help the French resist the tide. Instead, the United States disengaged itself "and left Britain and France to cope with the wreckage—an unprecedented abdication of American leadership."[40] Although no admirer of France's role in Indochina, the ADA did believe that the French were trying—if in all the wrong ways—to stem the tide of communism in the area.

Given its dire warnings about the consequences of a Communist victory in the region, and its strident attack on Eisenhower, what did the ADA recommend? The organization returned to its familiar refrain of increased economic aid and more international cooperation in the region. The National Board called on the United States to meet the challenge in Indochina "in the context of a broad, long-range policy aimed not only at checking Communist aggression but also at maintaining and strengthening democracy in free Asia." The board, meeting in Washington in June 1954, asked the administration to recognize that military measures against communism, however important, were "merely holding operations," and it advocated "a large scale economic program of loans and grants to help the free Asian nations help themselves." Only a UN settlement, the ADA insisted, could "assure the people of Viet-Nam, Cambodia and Laos the opportunity to determine their own future, free from military threats from any side, and free to make independent political decisions, including whether or not to remain within the French Union."[41]

It is doubtful that the medicine the ADA prescribed would have been potent enough to cure the problems that plagued Indochina. For a time the ADA could have it both ways: it could be firmly convinced that the United States should never allow a Communist victory in Indochina, and it could recommend a solution that required little sacrifice. This paradox, which trapped policymakers as well, would come back to haunt liberals in the 1960s.

Although the ADA supported Eisenhower's Geneva initiative, it expressed concern that the United States not be lulled into a sense of complacency by Soviet pleas for peace. The Geneva conference, the ADA National Board said, "inspired the world with fresh hope that war is not inevitable and broadened the conviction of America's dedication to peace." However, the ADA added, "unless the United States takes steps to maintain the momentum of Geneva and fulfills its responsibility for leadership, this great (and perhaps final) opportunity for peace may be lost."[42] While hopeful about the "spirit of Geneva," and critical of Eisenhower's limited proposals, the ADA also feared that the prospect of arms control would make the West complacent. In November 1955 the National Board accepted without change a memorandum written by Reinhold Niebuhr and warning that the Soviets had become more formidable "at the precise time when the summit meetings at Geneva tended to lull the Western nations into promoting complacency." The danger, it noted, "has been heightened not only by the greater flexibility of Russian policy and its greater guile, but by the continued weight of the inheritance of 'colonialism' of the past against our moral prestige in Asia or in Africa." Here the Soviet ability to exploit the revolutionary yearnings of formerly enslaved peoples, and American inexperience with this area of the world, created an explosive situation.[43]

The ADA, whose membership was largely Jewish, had little problem with Eisenhower's policy toward Egypt. Edward Hollander, in a September memorandum to Schlesinger and Nathan, gave a glimpse of how many ADA members viewed the situation in the Suez. "Without over-straining the analogy," which he admitted was "fragile at many points," Hollander suggested that the United States "should agree in general with the British position that Nasser should be restrained as Hitler should have been restrained, for the sake of checking an aggressive and truculent nationalism before it becomes powerful enough to do further harm to the peace and to Western alliance." The objectives of American policy, he claimed, are to keep the Canal open, to restrain Nasser, to strengthen the Western alliance, to safeguard the European oil supplies, and "to do this by providing leadership and resources that will make it possible to accomplish these ends without the use of military force."

Hollander's recognition that the ADA's objectives did not "differ greatly from those of the Administration" did not prevent the organization from chastising the president.[44] However, since Eisenhower's response was similar to its own, the ADA was left with little to say. The ADA urged the administration to "move promptly within the UN toward a permanent settlement, including the negotiation of peace between Israel and her Arab neighbors and assurances that the Suez Canal will be open unconditionally to the ships of all nations—including those of Israel." Yet, again seeing an opportunity to flex its anti-Communist muscle, the ADA compared unfavorably the administration's quick condemnation of America's allies in the Middle East with its slow response to Soviet repression in Hungary. "In contrast to the self-righteous haste of the Administration to condemn Israel, Britain and France," the National Board said, the president was moving "with leaden feet during the crucial hours when Hungarian freedom hung in balance." Despite its criticism of Eisenhower's handling of the Hungarian crisis and its suggestion that the United States could somehow have prevented the Soviet invasion, the ADA offered no alternative policy.[45]

The launching of Sputnik, in October 1957, confirmed for liberals everything they believed about the new Soviet threat and Eisenhower's vacillation. Americans suddenly realized that, if the Russians had rockets powerful enough to launch satellites, they also possessed rockets with which to bombard the United States with nuclear weapons. Liberals tried to use the Soviet satellite as a rallying cry, not just to support larger defense appropriations but also to push for greater government involvement in all aspects of life. "Beyond the immediate and awful dangers to our military defenses and international policy," Robert Nathan claimed, Sputnik symbolized "the Soviet challenge to the free society in all its aspects: our educational system, our technology, our economy and the very basis of our political and social system." It seemed to prove to the underdeveloped countries of the world Soviet charges that Western democracy was "soft and flaccid with riches, incapable of purpose or direction or the discipline to meet the tests of the Twentieth Century." Rauh argued that Soviet advances should spur America on to new heights of activity in every field. It should have "triggered gigantic educational efforts here at home," brought "whirring machines and full employment," and encouraged a "massive foreign aid and foreign trade program."[46]

Other Soviet scientific advances at the end of the decade seemed to deepen liberal concern about Soviet technological progress. The Soviet launching of Lunik in 1959, Niebuhr wrote, "proved that, though Russia may be inferior to us in general productive capacity, it has gained superiority over us in many technical fields, particularly in the conquest of outer space." It will, he feared, "prove to the non-industrial nations of Asia and Africa that there is a path to technical competence which does not require the difficult achievement of an 'open society.' " Equally important, the Soviet demonstration of superiority widened "the dangerous gap in the 'balance of terror' upon which the peace of the world depends." With that advantage the Soviets will be even more intransigent in their dealings with the United States. "[If] someone does not awaken the nation," Niebuhr predicted, "we might have the same destiny which many soft and effete nations and empires had before us, when they failed to meet the challenge of a political force which had been disciplined by poverty and privation to a tough and hardy stance in the competitions of life."[47]

Sputnik dealt a serious blow to Eisenhower's bland, though accurate, assurances that the United States was holding its own in the arms race. Within a few months of Sputnik, a number of other events contributed to public unease about Eisenhower's leadership. His indecisive response to the sharpest postwar recession, which began in August 1957 and lasted through April 1958, exposed the limits of his commitment to fiscal responsibility. Also, just five days after signing the 1957 Civil Rights Act, Eisenhower was forced to send troops to carry out court-ordered desegregation of Central High School in Little Rock, Arkansas. The incident not only hurt Republican attempts to make inroads into the Democratic South; the image of military escorts for black students also appeared to confirm liberal complaints about America's declining prestige abroad. The president's faltering health (he suffered a stroke in November 1957) and recurring charges of corruption in his administration (the presidential assistant Sherman Adams was accused of dubious financial relations with a New England textile manufacturer) added grist to the political mill.

Public unease translated into electoral success for the Democrats in the 1958 congressional elections—their biggest triumph since FDR's victory in 1936. Nine incumbent Republican senators were defeated, and twenty-six of thirty-four Democrats were elected or reelected. Democrats increased their majority in the House from 235 to 282. Democratic victories on the state level gave them control of thirty-four governorships, including those in traditional Republican strongholds like South Dakota, Wisconsin, and Nebraska. Most observers interpreted the election as a harbinger of a liberal resurgence. "Manifestly we are in for a liberal swing," commented the *New York Times.*

For liberals who had spent a large portion of the decade defending themselves from conservative Republican attacks, the year 1958 seemed to mark a brief reprieve, a lessening of the oppressive weight of public suspicion. Even the Democratic congressional leadership, which had languished in moderation for most of the decade, was now eager to take the offensive.[48]

Inspired by the election results, the ADA called on Congress to enact a "New New Deal." Although the organization proposed nothing new, the tone of its statements was more confident. It demanded responsible action "adequate to meet the urgent economic and social needs that have been so long neglected . . . carried out in such ways as to use the country's vast resources fully and efficiently to meet those needs without causing inflation." Included among the specific recommendations were $4 billion a year for school construction and teachers' salaries; a ten-year, $10 billion urban renewal program; an increase of 20 percent in old-age payments, along with increases in public assistance payments and unemployment compensation; medical and hospital insurance for Social Security recipients; and more active government enforcement of civil rights legislation.[49]

While in domestic policy the ADA changed only the tenor of its program, in foreign policy it offered two dramatic initiatives—it called for nuclear disarmament and advocated China's admission to the United Nations. In January 1958 Hubert Humphrey informed the board that liberals had to abandon a number of assumptions that had guided them in the immediate postwar period. First, liberals believed that because America had "superior power" there was no need "to talk openly about negotiation" with the Soviets. Second, liberals felt that if America kept "the pressure on the Soviet Union," the latter would collapse. Humphrey argued that the recent past proved both assumptions false. If the Communists want peaceful competition we should welcome it," he declared. While claiming not to "minimize the difficulties of negotiating even living on the same planet with the Soviet Union," Humphrey contended that "there is no other planet to live on." The opposite of "co-existence" is "no existence." When, he asked, "are we going to face up to the dreadful threat of nuclear catastrophe?"[50]

In the spirit of Humphrey's speech, the ADA's 1958 convention recommended an end to all nuclear testing and the establishment of a UN inspection system as a first step toward the ultimate goal of "eliminating the manufacture of nuclear weapons, disarmament, and a UN force displacing national armed forces." It also, for the first time since the Korean War, called for China's admission to the United Nations. It recommended recognition "not as a gesture of moral approval—which the Chinese Communists obviously do not merit—but as a means of establishing the normal channels of international communication between the two nations." The decision was hotly debated, and a number of prominent members protested. A few wrote to the ADA *World* criticizing the decision as "an assault on the basic tenets of human dignity." At a time when American foreign policy should be "levelled against recognition and appeasement of totalitarian regimes," the letter continued, "the ADA resolution is ill-timed and ill-advised." It failed "to recognize the historic truth that Red China remains a source of actual and potential aggression against democratic regimes and causes in Asia."[51]

The debates over China policy revealed deeper divisions in the organization that were emerging at the end of the decade. Many members believed that the ADA, and liberals in general, needed to rethink many of the assumptions that had guided them in the immediate postwar era. The political climate, they argued, had changed dramatically since the ADA's founding convention in January 1947. As William V. Shannon, a columnist for the *New York Post,* pointed out in May 1958, the problems the ADA confronted in the 1950s were quite different from those it had faced in 1947. In the winter of 1947 liberalism was menaced by Truman's apparent ineptitude, a reactionary Republican Congress, and a domestic Communist movement. "What," he asked, "has happened in the intervening 11 years?" Liberals routed domestic communism; Senator Taft, the able leader of the conservative forces in Congress, died, making a genuine Old Guard return to power unlikely; and Truman's upset victory in 1948 "closed the gap between the liberal community. and the orthodox Democratic organization."[52] Shannon was not suggesting that the ADA no longer served an important role, only that it had to redefine its puprpose.

While the ADA had fulfilled part of its short-term political agenda, its dream of a revitalized liberal-labor alliance that actively influenced the events in Washington was fading rapidly. That alliance, never very close after the 1948 election, received a further shock in 1955 with the unification of the AFL and the CIO. Under the leadership of George Meany, the new sixteen-million-member association reflected the conservative, craft-oriented approach of the AFL, while the CIO, despite the efforts of Walter Reuther, seemed to have lost much of its militant fire. Generational change explains much of labor's growing complacency during these years. Many of the class-conscious unionists who had led the great strikes at Flint and River Rouge during the 1930s were now middle-aged and middle-class. James Wechsler, who in 1948 had had great hopes for a progressive labor movement, in 1959 lamented that though once "the catalyst of the strongest idealistic emotions in our society," labor leaders were "as dedicated to business as usual as the men they meet across the bargaining table, and as hostile to innovation." That the AFL-CIO would continue to pull away from liberal groups like the ADA in favor of its own political action committee was evident in labor contributions, which fell from 26 percent of ADA income in 1954 to less than 10 percent by 1959.[53]

By the end of the decade, many critics also began to challenge the central tenets of the ADA's brand of Vital Center liberalism. Radical scholars like Paul Goodman, C. Wright Mills, and Herbert Marcuse questioned the excessive optimism of modern liberalism, its blind devotion to pragmatism and gradualism as means of social change, and its belief that economic growth would melt away class differences in America and produce a satiated middle-class society.

Some liberals agreed that liberalism appeared tired and worn from years of battle with reactionary Republicans and conspiratorial Communists. Reflecting on the hopes of liberals attempting to construct a Vital Center at the end of the war, Wechsler lamented in 1960, "The center has proved less than vital and the left is often indistinguishable from the center."[54] For many liberals the greatest disappointment was their failure to push the Democratic party in a more liberal direction. They believed that the Democratic congressional leadership had jettisoned its New Deal heritage. The party, they charged, was hopelessly backward, controlled by conservative southern interests, and out of touch with public opinion.

When a number of liberals were defeated in Democratic primaries in 1958—including Chester Bowles in the Senate race in Connecticut and Richardson Dilworth and Thomas Finletter in the races for the governorship of Pennsylvania and New York respectively—Arthur Schlesinger, Jr., wrote a bitter article for the *New Republic* entitled "Death Wish of the Democrats." Schlesinger criticized the "Know-Nothing" revolt "of the low-level professional within the party organization against the New Deal and post–New Deal leadership of the Democratic Party." The essence of the revolt, he said, "is to wipe out the transformation wrought in the Democratic Party by Franklin Roosevelt and the New Deal and to recreate something like the Democratic Party of the twenties." Schlesinger defended the role of intellectuals in politics, claiming that while they could not command an army of voters, they provided inspiration and ideas that kept the party alive and active. He concluded with a warning: "A party which seeks to qualify itself for responsibility in an age of national and international crisis is not well advised to begin to do so by blowing out its own brains."[55]

Schlesinger was disenchanted with the Democrats and, in a series of articles written throughout the decade, tried to articulate an alternative vision for both the party and liberals. He argued that the liberalism born during the depression needed to be superseded by a liberalism adapted to the new age of abundance. Liberals, he contended, had to readjust their priorities and find a new political constituency to sustain them in the future. Instead of a quantitative liberalism "dedicated to the struggle to secure the economic basis of life," Schlesinger called for a "qualitative liberalism dedicated to bettering the quality of people's lives and opportunities." Since most Americans had already secured the necessities of living—a job, a square meal, a suit of clothes, and a roof—Schlesinger encouraged liberals "to count that fight won and move on to the more subtle and complicated problems of fighting for individual dignity, identity, and fulfillment in a mass society." Qualitative liberalism, Schlesinger cautioned, was neither cheap nor painless. It required just as much governmental initiative, taxation, and spending as quantitative liberalism.

According to Schlesinger, liberals sowed the seeds of their own demise by creating a satiated middle-class society. The years of prosperity and full employment "gave millions of people new economic and social status and enabled them to become 'respectable.'" Consequently, "they moved out of the cities into the suburbs, abandoned tenements for bungalows, bought automobiles, and became Republicans. . . ." The new enemy, he said, "is not a conspiracy of wealth seeking to grind the faces of the poor" but a "conspiracy of blandness, seeking to bury all tension and conflict in American life under a mess of platitude and piety—not the hard-faced men, but the faceless men." The new issues like civil rights and liberties, the environment, and foreign policy were not economic but cultural and personal, concerned with opportunity for moral growth and self-fulfillment.[56]

Schlesinger was joined by his friend and Harvard colleague John Kenneth Galbraith, who in 1958 published the ground-breaking book *The Affluent Society*. Galbraith wrote in his memoirs that what motivated him to write it was "the conviction that, in starving our public services and in placing so much faith in the general curative powers of increased production, we were inviting grave social ills." The thrust of the book, he wrote, "is that increased production is not the final test of social achievement, the solvent for all social ills."[57]

Galbraith challenged the notion that "any action which increases production from given resources is good and implicitly important; [that] anything which inhibits or reduces output is, *pro tanto,* wrong." He questioned the "conventional wisdom"—a favorite Galbraithian term—that economic growth, underwritten by Keynesian fiscal policy, would sustain full employment, abolish poverty, and improve the standard of living for everyone. Liberals, Galbraith asserted, were stubbornly clinging to the rules and assumptions of a poorer age. Galbraith admonished liberals to turn their attention to the twin dangers of an age of affluence: inflation and consumer debt. He also advocated a radical shift in liberal values, calling for wage and price controls, a national sales tax, cuts in military spending, and a guaranteed annual income. Needs in an affluent society were no longer the basic ones of food, shelter, or clothing; rather they were the product of salesmanship, advertising, and fashion. As production and consumption increased, it became possible to consider the effect of increased output on physical surroundings. "Is the added production or the added efficiency in production worth its effect on ambient air, water and space—the countryside?" he asked. To help answer his own question, Galbraith created the term "social balance," which referred to an equilibrium between the production and consumption of private goods and outlays for public services.[58]

Schlesinger and Galbraith attracted attention in liberal circles and, not surprisingly, incurred the wrath of Leon Keyserling. Reflecting a view shared by many liberals and labor leaders, Keyserling complained about Galbraith's "pigheadedness" and accused him of being careless, of being "highly presumptuous if not offensive," and of misrepresenting Keyserling's views.[59] While he agreed that civil rights and civil liberties were important issues for liberals to address, the two other "prime political problems" of the time were still "the vast impoverishment of millions of our citizens" and "the vast impoverishment of public services." About these problems, and especially the former, he charged, Galbraith said little. He chided Galbraith for claiming that poverty was "no longer a massive affliction," that most poverty was of the "case" or "insular" variety, attributable mostly to individual shortcomings or the lack of geographic mobility. Almost a quarter of all multiple-person families in America lived below the poverty line, he claimed in taking issue with Galbraith's dismissal of the problem. "These people may be living in 'affluence' compared with the people in India, or compared with an even larger number of people in the U.S. a generation or two ago. But they are certainly living in poverty by any standard that should have meaning for us today." "Evidently," Keyserling added sarcastically, "the problem of poverty is not 'massive' in the Widener Library." Keyserling charged, "It is perfectly clear that an expansion of public services such as education and health, while urgently desirable, cannot—in the absence of economic growth—remedy the truly massive problem of private poverty." In the final analysis, the incomes of the poor "can rise significantly . . . only through the expansion of those parts of the economy which provide private employment and pay wages and salaries."

Keyserling also challenged a number of the Harvard economist's specific proposals for raising taxes to pay for enlarged social services. On Galbraith's proposal to increase sales taxes, Keyserling commented, "We can find better ways to expand our domestic public services than to take more pennies in sales taxes from the depleted pockets of the poor." Keyserling charged that Galbraith's claim that social security was "finished or largely finished business" neglected "the incomes and living conditions of an aged population." He also condemned as "ethically and morally wrong" Galbraith's suggestion that inflation, and not unemployment, was the bane of the affluent society.

Keyserling aimed most of his attack at Galbraith, but he did have comments to make about Schlesinger's new agenda for political reform. Accusing Schlesinger of taking "a temporary holiday from his discipline," Keyserling refused to accept Schlesinger's assertion that liberals had made the great strides in solving the basic economic problems of modern society. Keyserling refuted Schlesinger's charge that qualitative issues were at the heart of American liberalism, perhaps even more than was the fight against poverty. "I beg to differ," he wrote Schlesinger; "it seems to me that these movements, and Woodrow Wilson's New Freedom as well, were directed toward the improvement of the relative and absolute economic and social status of the common man; they were not interested in what he read."[60] When it came to politics, Keyserling felt that the Harvard historian was out of his element. We cannot tell the American people, he wrote Schlesinger, "that they are wallowing in a sea of private plenty, and that we propose to throw them a lifesaver in the form of higher taxes to support more public spending."[61] Keyserling did not feel that the intellectual's role was to get involved in questions of political strategy. While conceding that "intellectual innovators" could "successfully combine their intellectual activity with embroilment in more proximate political maneuvers," Keyserling charged that this combination was not "their most likely forte."[62]

The *New Republic,* the *New Leader,* and major newspapers like the *New York Times* and the *Christian Science Monitor* carried the debate between Keyserling, Galbraith, and Schlesinger. According to Robert Lekachman, the differences between them amounted "to the revival of an old, old debate between those who want to improve the world by making it richer so that men can afford to live largely morally and aesthetically, and those who wish to alter men's hearts so that they will value the right and spurn the wrong, in consumer goods as in moral choices." Since it is always easier to change "men's incomes than their tastes," Lekachman remarked, "Keyserling's line of analysis has a considerable attraction." Lekachman pointed out, and properly so, that, Schlesinger's protestations to the contrary, Keyserling was much more in line with the reform impulse of the New Deal–Fair Deal. Like his liberal predecessors, he accepted the basic structure of American life, its central values and institutions, and wished only to enlarge its capacity. On the other hand, Galbraith's approach implied "more disturbance of existing arrangements," demanding reallocation of existing resources and not just the channeling of the proceeds of growth.[63]

The debates between Schlesinger, Galbraith, and Keyserling centered on domestic issues but had an important foreign policy dimension as well. Schlesinger, like Chester Bowles and a small band of other liberal intellectuals, maintained that the mellowing of Soviet international behavior meant that U.S.-Soviet competition in the future would be nonmilitary and directed at capturing the loyalty of nonaligned Third World nations. In order to be successful in this new arena, Schlesinger believed, the United States needed to practice freedom and opportunity at home before it could preach it abroad. "Until we have a moral and political revival in our national community," he argued, "our foreign policy is likely to continue impotent or to depend exclusively on armed strength." Keyserling rejected claims that Soviet international strategy had changed or that the military competition between the two superpowers had been altered. He thought that Schlesinger's attempt to hold essential international commitments hostage to progress on social causes at home smacked of isolationism. While liberals were making America "a shining example for the world to follow," Keyserling feared, the Soviets would make significant strategic gains.[64]

In late 1959 the ADA National Board arranged a debate on this issue. At the meeting Schlesinger cautiously suggested there had taken place slight changes in the Soviet worldview that opened the possibility of the negotiation of important differences. The changes, Schlesinger argued, were great enough to lead to the conclusion that "a foreign policy designed for the age of Stalin is not necessarily perfect for the age of Khrushchev." While the difference was not "great enough to justify any relaxation of strength or vigilance," it was "great enough to justify new efforts at the settlement of issues and the establishment of forms of international order." Three considerations made Schlesinger believe that the Soviets were changing: Khrushchev had reduced the level of internal terror in the Soviet Union and was therefore less dependent on international tension to maintain domestic control; a new fascination with consumer products would lead Soviets to spend more of their scarce resources on consumer goods than on massive armaments; and a growing split between China and Russia would force Russia to be more cautious in dealing with the West. Schlesinger was not sure, however, how these changes would translate into policy.[65]

David Lloyd, formerly the ADA's chief legislative officer, who had joined the Truman White House in 1949, took an opposing position. "Domestic changes inside the Soviet Union are of interest to the sociologist and the historian," he said, "but they have no relevance in this discussion unless they produce real changes in the foreign policy of the Soviet Union." The mere fact that Russian citizens enjoyed more consumer goods and that Soviet leaders indulged "in amicable gestures" did not mean they had "changed their international strategy." The Soviets had on many occasions, he charged, changed tactics, but their objective of world conquest remained the same: "The united front policy initiated in 1934 did not betoken any real change in the Soviet attitude toward the Western democracies, nor did the Soviet-Nazi Pact of 1939 alter the fundamental hostility between the Soviet Union and Nazi Germany. The summit meeting of 1955 in Geneva likewise signified no moderation of the basically aggressive Soviet policy toward the West." In short, Lloyd did not "see much hope of trust and mutual confidence with the Soviet Union."[66]

When the floor opened for discussion, Lloyd found himself on the defensive. Robert Schwartz, the New York representative, read a statement agreeing in essence with Schlesinger's position. The United States, it declared, should "support negotiations with the Soviet Union and other powers designed to end nuclear tests and to achieve controlled disarmament with inspection as quickly as possible." The United States should "assume a posture which will indicate to the world our sincere and abiding determination to achieve broad international agreements which will contribute to the reduction of tensions." One participant scribbled on his copy of the resolution, "This resolution suggests that U.S. is primarily at fault for not having achieved agreements with S.U." Lloyd was obviously thinking the same thing. He objected to the resolution, charging, "[It] is a grave mistake to assume that the intransigence of the Russians is the fault of the West." The ADA's role, he argued, is "to get clearly before the American people the real degree of Soviet aggression and Communist and totalitarian methods."

Lloyd found little support among those who spoke at the meeting. One member complained, "Why shouldn't this statement call for something more radical?" Another member implored the board to deal with more significant issues like "World Law" and "World Court." Marvin Rosenberg believed that the ADA needed to "refer to the abolition of war," and not just to peace, as an objective of liberal foreign policy. The Harvard professor Samuel Beer, however, came to Lloyd's defense. He questioned any suggestion of a "change in Soviet intentions." "They are no less aggressive than they were," Beer charged, "but they are aggressive in a more sophisticated way." Their aggression was more subtle, directed against "developing countries" rather than Europe. It was aggression nevertheless, and Beer warned that unless the United States responded to the challenge, the Soviets could win the war of "prestige politics" in the Third World. The discussion ended with the board deciding by voice vote to write a statement "and to make the statement conform in general to the Schlesinger memo."[67]

The dispute that pitted Galbraith and Schlesinger against Keyserling, Lloyd, and many of the labor leaders in the organization marked a hardening of divisions that had existed since the organization's founding convention. The differences, sometimes subtle, centered on very fundamental issues that liberals needed to confront. Those like Keyserling, perhaps properly referred to as traditionalists, wanted to reaffirm New Deal values, for their vision was still firmly rooted in the image of economic scarcity of the Great Depression. They wanted liberals to renew their commitment to the New Deal and reforge the old coalition of labor, farmers, and intellectuals. Most of these traditionalists wanted the ADA to content itself with serving as a source of ideas for the Democratic party and not get heavily involved in partisan politics itself. Also, fearful of Soviet intentions and confident that a growing economy could provide for expanded social services and increased armaments, traditionalists bristled at suggestions of détente with the Soviets. In 1959, traditionalists controlled between 30 and 35 votes on the 110-member National Board but had considerably less support among the general membership.

Another group consisting of many intellectuals and former New Dealers, and represented most visibly by Schlesinger and Galbraith, differed with these traditionalists on all four points. They believed that the problems that had inspired the New Deal had been solved and that liberals needed to find new issues that would broaden the coalition. Perhaps best referred to as moderates, the members of this group also hoped to preserve the old New Deal coalition, including labor. But they wanted to reach out to new constituencies as well. They believed that the intellectual had an important role to play in electoral politics and wanted the ADA to be both a source of liberal ideas for the Democratic party and an effective political pressure group. While not rejecting the Cold War, moderates hoped for an accommodation with the Soviets that would help end the arms race and allow the United States to address urgent Third World issues. Moderates lacked the cohesiveness and sense of solidarity that characterized the traditionalists. They could, however, usually count on the support of between fifty and seventy members of the National Board.

In many ways, moderate and traditionalist reform ideas had different roots. Moderates traced theirs to the Progressive period. They believed that just as Progressives had adopted an agenda appropriate for a time of prosperity, so reformers in the 1960s and beyond would have to abandon the rhetoric and substance of class antagonism and address social questions. Moderates also shared with the Progressives a faith in social engineering, a passion for efficiency and rationalization, and a commitment to bureaucratic and technocratic solutions. The only difference was that moderates were more willing than Progressives to use state power to rationalize society. Traditionalists, by contrast, traced their roots to the class struggles of the New

Deal. They never lost their sense of moral outrage at the existence of economic injustice. They rejected the moderates' emphasis on social cohesion, believing instead that workers could protect their interest only by organizing in opposition to business.

As the 1950s came to a close, the ADA still presented a mostly united commitment to economic growth at home and to an expanded and diversified American presence abroad. Yet, by 1960 there was growing ferment in the organization—ferment that raised fundamental questions about the direction in which liberalism should move, the coalition that should sustain it, and the role the ADA should play in the nation's political life.

6

The ADA and the Kennedy Administration

The ADA hoped to follow through on the gains made in the 1958 congressional races by electing a Democrat president in 1960. While most of the ADA's leaders favored Hubert Humphrey for the Democratic nomination, they realized that the organization would have to accept whomever the party nominated. Once Senator John F. Kennedy of Massachusetts established himself as the clear front-runner, the organization, reluctantly yet inevitably, supported his candidacy. The Kennedy administration put the organization in the same dilemma it had been in during the Truman years: How could an independent liberal organization maintain a proper balance between its need to stand for liberal values and its desire to play politics? In other words, how could it prod a sympathetic yet unconvinced Democratic president to move in a more liberal direction without alienating itself from the source of power? For a time, most ADA members, captivated by the Kennedy style and satisfied with having access to the White House, were willing to overlook his flaws. Yet, as evidence mounted that Kennedy was not living up to his campaign promises, ADA criticism grew louder. While moderates and traditionalists bickered over the proper tone that criticism should take, a new generation of members began flexing their organizational muscle.

Of the four contenders for the Democratic nomination in 1960, only two were making a serious bid for liberal affection—the ADA founding father and former cochairman, Hubert Humphrey, and the young senator from Massachusetts, John F. Kennedy. For obvious reasons, liberals found Humphrey the more appealing candidate. Although the ADA did not endorse anyone before the Democratic convention, Robert Nathan recalled, "there was no question, the whole tenor of the ADA . . . was to go all out for Humphrey." Liberals had a number of reservations about Kennedy. They were concerned, most notably, about his relatively limited exposure to issues, his failure to vote for McCarthy's censure, and the influence of his isolationist father. Nathan agreed with James Burns's observation that Kennedy lacked the tragic quality, that his was a "liberalism without tears." While "liberals are emotional" and "excitable," Nathan remembered Kennedy as cold and reserved. "He smiled, he was charming, but there was no outgoing affection, or warmth, or even indignation. He was master of what he was saying and he

131

could say it vigorously, but there wasn't the passion that Hubert put into it." Rauh agreed with Nathan's assessment. "Kennedy," he said later, became a liberal "by intellectual persuasion," unlike Humphrey, who was "a liberal by guts, by insides, by just emotion, by immediate reaction."[1]

Realizing that liberals favored Humphrey for the nomination, Kennedy tried to make himself acceptable as a second choice. Once Humphrey was eliminated—and Kennedy believed he surely would be when the liberal albatross weighed him down—then progressives would turn to him as an alternative to Lyndon Johnson. Kennedy did not believe that liberal support would be crucial in the primaries, but he wanted to start early to gain acceptance for the general election, in which that support would be crucial. "These people," one adviser informed the Kennedy political strategist Theodore Sorensen, "can influence few voters at the nominating convention," but "their attitudes affect the thinking of many thousands of independent voters. While I do not believe their support can help Kennedy get the nomination, I feel certain it could help win the election, if nominated."[2]

Wisconsin presented the first head-to-head confrontation between Humphrey and Kennedy. Although Kennedy won the primary decisively—getting 478,901 votes, compared with Humphrey's 372,034—he lost the Protestant vote and was therefore unable to put the religious issue behind him.[3] In May the campaign moved from the fields of Wisconsin to the hills of West Virginia, where each candidate tried to trace his roots to the New Deal. While Humphrey scurried around the state in his Scenicruiser bus draped with a banner reading "Over the Hump with Humphrey," Kennedy purchased nightly television time and flew around the state in his private Convair plane. Humphrey reminded audiences of his youth during the Great Depression and of his New Deal credentials, and he steadily fired at Kennedy's early Senate record of voting against farm supports. When the returns showed Kennedy sweeping the state by 220,000 votes to Humphrey's 142,000, Humphrey recognized that his candidacy had come to an end. In a simple statement he announced, "I am no longer a candidate for the Democratic nomination."[4]

Kennedy's strategy for winning liberal support appeared to be working. Eleanor Roosevelt conceded that after Humphrey's withdrawal Kennedy would "be considered the candidate of the liberals." Schlesinger wrote that "though Humphrey was an old friend and a man we greatly admired," he and others were attracted to Kennedy "by increasingly strong ties of affection and respect." Nathan said that the primaries "made him into a national figure" and helped him create a "national image and stature" that appealed to liberals eager to work for a winner.[5] Despite these endorsements many liberals remained cold to Kennedy's candidacy. Kennedy feared that liberals would turn to their sentimental favorite Adlai Stevenson in a last-ditch attempt to derail his candidacy. Concerned that Stevenson could just take enough liberal votes to open the door to Johnson, Kennedy changed tactics and began actively seeking liberal support.

In order to demonstrate that Stevenson did not have a monopoly on liberal support, Kennedy asked a number of prominent liberals to sign a petition entitled "An Important Message of Intent to All Liberals," shortly before the Democratic convention. Signed by the ADA members Galbraith, Rauh, and Schlesinger, it was designed to convince progressives of Kennedy's liberal credentials. The statement even said that Kennedy had "shown his willingness to sacrifice short term political gain to advance the cause of liberal idealism." Of course, Kennedy could not win all liberals to his cause. James Loeb, believing that Kennedy was still a cold and ruthless politician, refused to sign the statement. "He seems to me," Loeb said, "to have ice-water in his veins and something very mechanical where his heart ought to be." In particular, Loeb objected to "the part about admiring the way he conducted his primary campaigns and that other part about sacrificing political gain for principle." "If and when he ever did that," Loeb added, "I must have been someplace else."[6]

In his efforts to head off any rush toward Stevenson, Kennedy also set out to reassure liberals by appointing Chester Bowles to head the platform committee and by promising that he would support the Supreme Court's desegregation decision.[7] The platform that Kennedy supported was the most liberal in the party's history and echoed much of the ADA's program. "The time has come," it declared, "to assure equal access for all Americans to all areas of community life, including voting booths, schoolhouses, jobs, housing, and public facilities." It called on school districts to comply with the Supreme Court's desegregation decision, called on the president to empower "the Attorney General to file civil injunction suits in federal courts to prevent the denial of any civil rights on grounds of race, creed or color," and called for a Fair Employment Practices Commission "to secure for everyone the right to equal opportunity for employment." The civil rights plank testified to the new, more liberal mood concerning civil rights—a mood stemming from growing dissatisfaction with the Eisenhower administration and from impatience at noncompliance with the *Brown* decision.

Kennedy's new strategy worked. Neither Stevenson nor Lyndon Johnson could prevent the Kennedy juggernaut from winning the Democratic nomination on the first ballot. In an attempt to consolidate support for his candidacy, Kennedy chose Johnson, his former unannounced opponent for the nomination, as his running mate. Kennedy's choice revealed once again his political cunning. Having appealed to the left to secure the nomination, he now veered quickly to the right in order to win the election. The move infuriated liberals, who were just beginning to believe that maybe they had sold Kennedy short and that he was one of them after all.

When the ADA National Board assembled for its first meeting after the convention to decide whether to endorse Kennedy and, if so, with what degree of enthusiasm, it found considerable indifference to his candidacy. Gunther wrote Rauh that she was unable to draft any endorsement language in preparation for the meeting, because there seemed to be "such a sharp division opinion among Board members."[8] At first the board decided to endorse the Democratic platform but to postpone a decision on endorsement of the candidates until October. According to its proponents this action would put

Kennedy on warning that he could not take liberals for granted, and it would also give them an opportunity to see how he and Johnson behaved during the campaign. Opponents of the motion, however, carried the day. They argued that to postpone the decision to October 15 would fatally handicap the Democrats, that Nixon had already secured the support of the conservative Democrats, that the city machines were putting most of their energies in local elections, and that Kennedy needed and deserved the support of liberals.

Of the twenty-five ADA chapters that responded to the National Board's inquiry on candidate endorsement in 1960, fourteen favored endorsement of the Democratic ticket, six opposed it, and five had no clear preference.[9] Those who opposed endorsement reflected doubts about Kennedy's "liberal sentiments" and concerns about his choice of Lyndon Johnson as the vice-presidential candidate. The ADA, the Dallas chapter suggested, should "maintain a consistent policy and, in view of past opposition to Johnson, should endorse only the Democratic platform and not the candidates." The Essex County, New Jersey, chapter claimed there was a "general sentiment that ADA should wait and see what happened as the campaigns progressed."

Most of the chapters that favored endorsement accepted the wisdom of the West Side, New York City, chapter, which "favored Kennedy as lesser of two evils." Others pointed out that he was running on the most progressive platform in history, that Nixon was simply unacceptable, and that America's national problems were just too great for the ADA not to participate. Only a few expressed unreserved support for Kennedy's candidacy. "We must not allow our disappointment over the failure of Humphrey or Stevenson to win the nomination," argued one of the few Kennedy partisans, "to ignore the fact that liberals still have a real choice to make between a candidate who is liberal and one who is not."

Whereas the local chapters were split on the idea of a Kennedy endorsement, most National Board members were more supportive. Fourteen of the eighteen members who expressed an opinion at the meeting spoke in Kennedy's favor. John Roche, a National Board member from Brandeis University, summed up the ADA's ambivalent feeling toward Kennedy: "He is chilly and ruthless" and "believes in nothing but ambition"; he "is a man without conviction even though he has a good voting record." But it was not Kennedy's voting record that troubled liberals; it was his political style. Stevenson, Roche argued, "was a Greek figure which liberals identify with; Kennedy was a Roman." Despite Kennedy's limitations, Roche called Kennedy a good candidate. "We must permit him to grow up," he added. The board defeated the motion to postpone by a vote of twenty-nine to ten and instead endorsed the ticket.

With the question of endorsement out of the way, board members turned their attention to the exact language to be used. Carl Auerbach of the Wisconsin School of Law wanted to couple the ADA's endorsement of the ticket with an open letter to Johnson calling on him to accept the charge of the

Democratic platform and champion the cause of civil rights. Rauh rejected the idea, claiming that it would probably rub Johnson the wrong way.[10]

Samuel Beer, a Harvard professor and strong Kennedy supporter recently elected national chairman, rushed to put the ADA squarely behind Kennedy's candidacy. He, Rauh, Schlesinger, and much of the organization's national leadership pushed for a strong endorsement statement. Their proposed endorsement letter stressed that "in the critical fields of humane concern—foreign affairs, economic and social policy, civil rights"—Kennedy had "shown himself an aggressive champion of creative liberalism." Most chapter representatives, while reluctantly agreeing to support Kennedy, refused to accept such a strongly worded endorsement. "The majority," Schlesinger later informed Kennedy, "simply refused to believe these things about you." Instead, after more debate, the group decided to issue a more "subdued" letter of support.[11]

After the National Board meeting, Schlesinger wrote Kennedy a candid letter informing him of the organization's decision. "The main discernible emotion" in support of his candidacy, Schlesinger told Kennedy, "was opposition to Nixon." As one chapter representative said, "We don't trust Kennedy and we don't like Johnson; but Nixon is so terrible that we have to endorse the Democrats." The endorsement, Schlesinger emphasized, "was put over by the national leadership, and if the mood persists among chapter representatives, they will not lift a hand for the ticket." He also warned Kennedy not to attribute the ADA's coolness to religious differences: "Eugene McCarthy, also a Catholic, would have won endorsement easily." One statement, Schlesinger said, captured the problem: "It isn't what Kennedy believes that worries me. It's whether he believes anything." Samuel Beer expressed shock at the depth of the opposition and warned Kennedy, "[Among] a good many liberals . . . there is still a sort of indifference, or worse, to your candidacy."[12]

Following his nomination Kennedy set out against his seasoned opponent, Vice-President Richard Nixon. Kennedy attacked the Republicans for America's weakness and declining prestige abroad; Nixon scoffed at the charge that the United States was second best and maintained that the nation needed a strong leader who could deal with Khrushchev. Nixon called Kennedy "naive and inexperienced" and the "spokesman for national disparagement." "All this yakking about America with no sense of purpose," Nixon said, "all of this talk about American being second-rate—I'm tired of it and I don't want to hear any more talk about it."

The ADA participated in its usual events for a presidential campaign. The New York chapter organized an October 19 rally billed "Kennedy or Nixon: It Does Make a Difference," where Schlesinger and Wechsler addressed an audience of about six hundred. Most chapters took part in registration campaigns and worked with local Kennedy for President committees making phone calls, canvassing, and performing clerical work. Prominent members, like Galbraith and Schlesinger, spent much of the fall explaining to Jewish audiences that Kennedy "was not a new Torquemada—that the Holy Father would not be a presence in the Oval Office."[13]

The turning point in the campaign may have come when the candidates clashed in two television debates between September 26 and October 24. Especially in the first debate, Kennedy seemed alert, aggressive, and cool while Nixon appeared nervous and perspired profusely. After the first debate Kennedy's crowds grew in size and intensity. The momentum from the debates carried Kennedy to victory—but just barely. Kennedy received no clear mandate in 1960: he won a mere 49.7 percent of the vote and carried only twenty-two states. Of the nearly 68,500,000 popular votes cast, Kennedy won 34,227,000 and Nixon 34,108,000. Kennedy's popular margin of two-tenths of one percent was the smallest in a presidential election since 1880. The vote in the electoral college was 303 to 219. Although the country gave little indication that it supported Kennedy's call to action, some liberals nonetheless expected Kennedy to launch a domestic program embodying the ideals of the Fair Deal, a commitment to a strong presidency, and a redefinition of the national purpose. They were to be disappointed.

On January 14, 1960, less than two weeks after declaring his presidential candidacy, Kennedy quoted to the National Press Club from *King Lear:* "I will do such things,—What they are yet I know not,—but they shall be The wonders [*sic*] of the earth." He claimed that the problems of the coming decade required "a real fighting mood in the White House," which "must be the center of moral leadership." "We will need in the sixties a President who is willing and able to summon his national constituency to its final hour—to alert the people to our dangers and our opportunities—to demand of them the sacrifices that will be necessary."[14]

Everything about the new president seemed to confirm the promise that he would lead the nation to new heights. His reign was to be, as Robert Frost said at the inaugural, an Augustan age "of poetry and power." His youthful vigor, sharp wit, and keen intelligence contrasted with the staid and stodgy Eisenhower style. The oldest president in history was transferring the reins of power to the youngest. "It seems long ago now," David Halberstam wrote years later, "that excitement which swept through the country, or at least the intellectual reaches of it, that feeling that America was going to change, that the government had been handed down from the tired, flabby, chamber-of-commerce mentality of the Eisenhower years to the best and brightest of a generation." The political columnist Rowland Evans, Jr., commented that the Kennedy administration was "a restless government, fascinated by the art of politics and the meaning of power, zestful for experimentation." "Our faith in him and in what he was trying to do was absolute," Press Secretary Pierre Salinger reflected, "and he could impart to our work together a sense of challenge and adventure—a feeling that he was moving, and the world with him, toward a better time."[15]

Not surprisingly, a number of ADA members were included among the

Kennedy appointments. There were three White House aides, three cabinet members, and thirty-one key administrators in sundry other important government posts who were either active or past members of the ADA. Heading the list was Arthur Schlesinger, Jr., whom Kennedy appointed as a special assistant. Joining Schlesinger was Theodore Sorensen, who had been a member of the SDA during his student days at the University of Nebraska. Harris Wofford, special assistant to the president on civil rights, was a former ADA member. Cabinet members who at one time associated with the ADA included Secretary of Labor Arthur Goldberg, Secretary of Health, Education and Welfare Abraham Ribicoff, Secretary of Agriculture Orville Freeman. Other prominent members were Governor G. Mennen Williams and Philip H. Coombs, both assistant secretaries of state; Frank W. McCulloch, chairman of the Labor Relations Board, Treasury Under Secretary Henry Fowler, and Solicitor General Archibald Cox.[16]

This placement record did very little to increase the organization's influence in making policy. Most appointees, like Sorenson, Wofford, and Bowles, had either left the organization many years earlier or were only nominal members to begin with. Others, like Schlesinger and Galbraith, who were more visible ADA members had little input in policy decisions at the White House. "It was one thing to have an aroused intellect, but quite another to misperceive the world," the historian Herbert Parmet has said of Kennedy's attitude toward liberals and intellectuals. They tended to be idealistic, audacious, and visionary; Kennedy, by contrast, admired pragmatism, coolness, and hardheadedness.

Despite his rhetoric about getting America moving again, and his declarations about the need for presidential leadership, Kennedy was not inclined to fight losing battles. "There is no sense in raising hell and then not being successful," he said. A pragmatic politician, Kennedy shied away from moral crusades. As the Kennedy biographer Parmet has written, "Kennedy had struggled to reach the top. Once there he paused, looked at the barriers to further progress, and, rather than press forward with his momentum, accommodated himself to the new realities."[17] The "new realities" included a number of formidable obstacles. For one thing, Kennedy did not receive a clear mandate in his 1960 victory. The vote itself was ambiguous, reflecting no commitment to a particular issue. If anything, it is likely that the rising fortunes of the Democratic party, which made successive gains after 1956, carried Kennedy into office. A recalcitrant and conservative southern leadership in Congress presented Kennedy with his greatest obstacle. The southern conservative Democrats who occupied most of the key committee chairmanships had little sympathy for the urban, liberal northern orientation of the Kennedy administration.

In dealing with most of the major problems he faced during the first year of his presidency—civil rights, economic policy, and foreign policy—Kennedy inclined more to caution and moderation than to bold advocacy of liberal ideas. Kennedy's approach to civil rights problems, for example, was a case study in caution. Both John and Robert Kennedy had a vague intellectual aversion to discrimination, but they lacked the personal experience to develop a real passion on the subject. Kennedy's personal feelings on civil rights combined with institutional forces—his lack of a clear mandate, a conservative Congress, and his political philosophy of balance—to create a politically safe approach to the problem.[18] During the first year of his presidency, Kennedy limited his actions on behalf of civil rights to symbolic acts—choosing blacks for high-level government employment, desegregating the press corps, and inviting black leaders to the White House, and granting rhetorical support to the civil rights cause. There was, however, a major flaw in Kennedy's strategy. His policy of moderation may have been appropriate to the congressional mood of 1961, but it miscalculated the dynamism of a powerful movement.[19]

Many blacks already realized that symbolic acts would not assure them social justice. In February 1960 a group of young protesters organized a dramatic sit-in demonstration at a segregated lunch counter in the South. This marked the first shot in the new war for civil rights. By May 1961 CORE (Congress of Racial Equality) workers were staging "freedom rides" into the South to desegregate bus terminals. The freedom riders wanted to test the Supreme Court decision forbidding racial discrimination in terminals serving interstate travelers. In Rock Hill, South Carolina, and in three Alabama cities—Anniston, Birmingham, and Montgomery—first CORE and then SNCC (Student Nonviolent Coordinating Committee) took up the challenge. While Kennedy recognized his constitutional responsibility to assure the riders safe passage, he hoped to use personal persuasion rather than federal force, in order not to lose the support of the white South.

Civil rights was not the only policy area in which Kennedy worried ADA liberals; Kennedy was also an unwilling convert to Keynesian economics. When he was inaugurated, the fourth postwar recession had not yet ended. In February and March more men and women were out of work than at any other time since the Second World War. Although Kennedy spoke throughout the campaign about "getting the country moving again," his course of action was more cautious than dramatic. A number of Kennedy appointments, especially Douglas Dillon as secretary of the treasury, confirmed suspicions about Kennedy's fiscal conservatism.[20] Like Roosevelt, Truman, and Eisenhower, Kennedy pledged his allegiance to the idea of a balanced budget. Despite a number of initiatives—a $5.6 billion federal aid-to-education bill, a $4.9 billion urban renewal proposal, as well as legislation for housing, area redevelopment, and an increase in the minimum wage—Kennedy assured Congress that the programs he was proposing would "not by themselves unbalance the budget." As with civil rights, politics determined Kennedy's course of action. Republicans had been depicting the Democratic party as the party of reckless spending and inflation, and throughout the campaign Kennedy had done his best to neutralize that issue by speaking of fiscal soundness. Also, lacking a clear mandate, he wanted to demonstrate to the American people his sense of fiscal responsibility. Having spoken of sacrifice in his inaugural address, he believed he could not then turn around and give a handout.[21]

In areas like foreign policy the administration showed no such caution. Kennedy believed, as did many liberals, that the United States was not doing all it could to win the Cold War. "Are we doing as much as we can do?" he had asked repeatedly during the campaign. Kennedy believed that Eisenhower's New Look had limited America's ability to respond to Soviet advances in Third World areas. To rectify this problem, Kennedy embarked on a massive military buildup of conventional and nuclear forces, one that would provide a "flexible response" to threats, both large and small, anywhere on the globe. Kennedy's instinctive activism led him to commit one of the greatest blunders of his administration—the attempt in April 1961 to overthrow the Cuban leader Fidel Castro.[22] Kennedy and the men around him were wedded to the assumptions of the Cold War. "Our greatest obstacle," Kennedy said, "is still our relations with the Soviet Union and China. We must never be lulled into believing that either power has yielded its ambitions for world domination." Despite his strident rhetoric, Kennedy hoped to negotiate differences with his Soviet counterpart. In June 1961 Kennedy traveled to Vienna to reach a settlement on the German question and to discuss arms control. It proved a sobering experience for the young president. Khrushchev threatened to sign a separate pact with East Germany that would allow them to control access to Berlin. Khrushchev's deadline passed without incident, but only after the Soviets had begun construction of the Berlin wall and American and Soviet tanks had faced each other across the boundary dividing East and West Berlin. At Vienna, Khrushchev also promised that he would not act unilaterally to break the moratorium on atmospheric nuclear bomb testing. Yet, at the end of August he announced that the Soviet Union would resume testing its nuclear weapons. Two days later the Soviets ended a three-year moratorium on nuclear testing by exploding a medium-sized bomb in Central Asia. Kennedy, after waiting a full year, reluctantly ordered the renewal of American testing. On March 2, 1962, he told a nationwide audience that America needed to "maintain an effective quantity and quality of nuclear weapons."[23]

Many liberals believed that Kennedy's actions in office did not live up to the promises made during the campaign. Walter Lippmann declared that the Kennedy administration was "like the Eisenhower Administration 30 years younger." Oscar Gass, writing in *Commentary,* claimed Kennedy "projected little and accomplished almost nothing." While the president "thrilled his American audiences with the call to sacrifice," he "confronted them by not asking for any." Some liberals, however, felt that Kennedy was sincerely committed to liberal legislation. TRB, a *New Republic* editorialist, thought that Kennedy actually wanted to run a larger deficit but that practical considerations, most notably a conservative Congress, prevented him from doing so. "Why doesn't Kennedy move faster?" he asked rhetorically. Because, TRB said, the seniority system, rules of procedure, rural domination of state legislatures and one-party control in the South all made Congress more conservative than the nation itself.[24]

During the early months of the new administration most ADA members appreciated the restraints Kennedy faced. He had won a narrow election and confronted a conservative Congress. Most members were uplifted by his rhetoric, moved by his style, and encouraged by his appointments. Kennedy's style and cultivation attracted many liberals. Like Stevenson, Kennedy appeared urbane, sophisticated, and charming. Unlike Stevenson, though, Kennedy possessed a mental toughness and physical presence that made him a potent national figure. "Adlai Stevenson . . . spent his adult life in a persuasive effort to present himself as he was not," Galbraith recalled some years later. "Kennedy gained grace by precisely the opposite trait, by being himself."[25]

Nonetheless, Kennedy's lack of accomplishment disappointed many liberals. For the first time since Truman had left the Oval Office eight years earlier, the ADA was working with a friendly administration. It had every reason to expect a harmonious relationship. The organization had endorsed and campaigned hard for Kennedy's election; some of its members, Schlesinger and Galbraith among them, had developed personal ties with the new president. Yet, with the new opportunity came old risks. The ADA always had more difficulty working with a Democratic administration than with a Republican incumbent. When Eisenhower was in office, the ADA had one obvious role—that of liberal critic. With a sympathetic Democratic president, the organization was frequently torn, as it had been during the Truman years, between its commitment to criticize and to prod the administration to move in a more liberal direction and its pragmatic need to accept what was politically feasible and support what it considered to be mediocre programs. Samuel Beer expressed the dilemma well. The ADA's "commitment to practical politics," he reasoned, means that it has to build strength for the administration, while its stature as an independent organization "means that we cannot simply become a political arm of the Administration."[26]

In the afterglow of Kennedy's victory and his appointment of prominent ADA members, the organization was hardly in a mood to criticize him if he did not live up to his billing. National Chairman Samuel Beer set the tone for the ADA's relationship with Kennedy during the first year in office. Once the administration had assumed power, the Harvard professor intentionally tried to steer the ADA toward a close and uncritical alliance with it. He believed that the ADA had two objectives: to sell the president's program and build support for it and to make constructive criticisms that pushed him further. "Yet," he noted, "I feel that we have spent more time on criticism than on trying to build support and attacking his conservative critics." He thought it unrealistic to criticize Kennedy for being less than 100 percent in favor of the ADA program. Such an approach left Kennedy vulnerable to attack by both conservatives and liberals. Rather than criticizing Kennedy for not doing enough, the ADA should help "him get from Congress what he asks for and in building up support for his requests." Marvin Rosenberg agreed with Beer's analysis. "If he were to take the most extreme liberal point of view," Rosenberg reasoned, "his position would be untenable and, in fact, could only result in more conservative legislation." While in the past the organization "could merely press and criticize," it usually ended up "tilting at windmills."[27]

When Samuel Beer, Robert Nathan, Joe Rauh, and Marvin Rosenberg met with Kennedy in February 1961 to talk about civil rights and economic policy, the president appeared charming and witty but made no concessions. To Nathan's explanation that the type of full-employment measures the president supported entailed a rise in the deficit to $50 billion, Kennedy reacted warily. "I don't believe that, right or wrong, there's any possibility of doing that kind of all-out economic operation that you want. But, I want you to keep this up. It's very helpful now for you to keep pushing me this way." Kennedy's tone changed when the topic switched to civil rights. According to Nathan's recollection, Kennedy "didn't want ADA to push him very hard on civil rights. He felt that this was an issue that needed some calm, unemotional and unpressured attention." Rauh had a more vivid impression. "I've never seen a man's expression turn so fast," Rauh said of Kennedy, when he suggested they wanted him to do more for civil rights. "Absolutely not," Kennedy snapped. "It's a totally different thing. Your criticism of civil rights is quite wrong." Kennedy conceded nothing in his meeting with ADA officials, who reported to the National Board, "We felt that in both fields [economics and civil rights] the President's objectives were ours, and that he was attempting and would consider to attempt to pursue them just as fast and as far as he thought he politically could."[28]

At a press conference just before the annual convention in May, Chairman Beer characterized the administration as "able and progressive," adding, "I like pretty much all that it is doing, but there is much more to be done." Its "tone and temper," he proclaimed, "is like the tone and temper of ADA: not ideological, not hysterical, not perfectionist, but rather steady, rational, realistic and at the same time vigorous, unrelenting and basically optimistic." Schlesinger felt the same way. "I can personally testify," he informed delegates in his banquet speech, "that we have a brilliant President who has a lofty vision of American resources and leadership." He reminded them that "no President can go faster in formulating new policies than public opinion allows him."[29]

The *New York Post* editor James Wechsler disagreed with Beer's and Schlesinger's assessments of Kennedy's presidency. The question the ADA needs to address, Wechsler said in his keynote speech, is "why we are the girls who are always invited to the autumn proms and so often forgotten in winter and spring." Although many of his liberal colleagues asserted "Any critical appraisal of the president at this juncture is ill-advised and ill-considered, a liberal luxury that the country cannot afford," Wechsler charged that Kennedy had become captive to "the ancient alliance between Southern Democrats and conservative Republicans" and that it was the ADA's responsibility to tell him so. The ADA's function, Wechsler declared, is to be "the conscience of the political community," to say what it believes regardless of political consequences, "to debate the issues that are too often muted, to fight the battles that men in political life are too often reluctant to wage." Failure to stand as an independent voice for liberalism, Wechsler reasoned, would alienate an army of young potential supporters who are "uninspired by the chatter and clatter of our conventional political discourse."[30]

Convention delegates, believing accommodation with Kennedy still possible, rejected Wechler's challenge. It would take the emotion of the Vietnam War to convince them of the wisdom of Wechsler's advice. According to the ADA *World,* the convention "registered solid satisfaction with many aspects of the New Frontier but pressed for more far-reaching action in the areas of civil rights and economic growth." The civil rights resolution called on Kennedy to fulfill the promises of the Democratic platform. On economic policy it charged the administration with "drifting into the worst mistakes of the Eisenhower years" by not taking measures designed to bring full employment and economic growth. After a long debate the organization opposed unilateral American intervention in Cuba but left open the possibility of American involvement as part of hemispheric action; it also adopted a strong resolution on disarmament.[31]

ADA criticism upset Kennedy, who called Schlesinger into his office to complain about the organization's assault on his policies. Flustered, Schlesinger fired off a letter to Rauh accusing the organization of being insensitive to Kennedy's political situation. Rauh angrily responded that the convention actually went out of its way to mute real differences with the administration. The rank-and-file delegates, Rauh noted, "are disturbed at the meager economic proposals to date," at "the slow progress on civil rights," and at the "Cuban invasion." Given the deep feelings on these matters, Rauh thought "the Convention acted in a very responsible and constructive manner towards the Administration and without any bitter criticism whatever." Liberals were "appreciative," Rauh claimed, that Kennedy no longer swept problems under the rug, but they were also "dreadfully concerned by the gap between these problems and the solutions that are being proposed."[32]

The ADA's patience, however, was not eternal. Through the spring and summer, as Kennedy appeared unwilling to use his political capital for a civil rights bill or public expression of support for Keynesian economics, many prominent ADA members, especially traditionalists, began publicly to criticize him. Unlike moderates, traditionalists did not believe that the ADA's most important function was to influence the administration or to rally public support behind his programs. Most believed, as they had since 1947, that the ADA could be most effective by working to change public attitudes, thereby laying a foundation for broad political reform. These differences were not always obvious in 1961, as even most traditionalists gave Kennedy a chance to feel his way around the office. By the fall of 1961, however, some began expressing doubts about Kennedy's commitment to liberalism and about the ADA's commitment to Kennedy.

Leon Keyserling emerged as Kennedy's harshest critic in the ADA. In the fall of 1961 Keyserling debated his fellow economist and ADA National Board member Seymour Harris in the pages of the *New Republic* about how political an organization like the ADA should be in dealing with Kennedy. Harris, like most moderates, accepted Kennedy's quiet commitment to liberal economics and placed the blame for his moderation on a conservative congressional opposition and an uneducated public. "Should the President move too far ahead of the Congress in his espousal of deficit financing, his program could be in jeopardy," Harris asserted. Keyserling argued that liberals should not be so political in their judgments of the administration. "If liberal economists like Harris lower the flag on our essential public needs, in order to provide a short-sighted political rationalization for inadequate national policies, who is to raise it again?" he asked. The fact is, Keyserling insisted, Kennedy's actions fall "short of the courageous national . . . leadership evinced in his campaign."[33]

Other prominent ADA members also began voicing complaints. Rauh, the organization's unrelenting spokesman for civil rights, told *Newsweek* in April 1962, "Compared to Ike or Nixon, Kennedy is O.K. But compared to the high hopes we had, he's a bitter disappointment." The ADA's 1962 convention resolutions reflected Rauh's criticisms. The delegates stated in the economic policy resolution that they strongly objected to the administration's "lack of vigor" in pursuing full employment. They accused the administration of being in "fundamental error in placing undue emphasis on the principle of a balanced budget." They attacked it for not giving "all-out support to a comprehensive civil rights program" that included provisions for immediate school desegregation, for the establishment of an FEPC, and for the guarantee of voting rights.[34]

The convention also elected John Roche to succeed Samuel Beer as chairman. Roche, Morris Hillquit Professor of Labor and Social Thought at Brandeis University and chairman of the political science department, had served as vice-chairman of the ADA's Massachusetts chapter and board member of the Philadelphia chapter. Although an intellectual, Roche identified with the traditionalist wing in the ADA and, like Keyserling, was openly dissatisfied with Kennedy. Roche found Kennedy's brand of "technocratic liberalism" inadequate to America's needs in the 1960s. "Kennedy's got the words," Roche quipped, "but he'll never learn the music." The fact is, Roche wrote, "that the New Frontier, for all its remarkable achievements in many areas, has little political vitality." Kennedy's brand of liberalism, which traced its roots to the Progressive Era and the gospel of efficiency, was too elitist and too dispassionate. The Kennedy administration, Roche concluded, "needs an infusion of liberal enthusiasm . . . of good old-fashioned crusading zeal."[35]

If the ADA hoped that by moving away from the administration it could apply political leverage, it was mistaken. The ADA simply lacked the influence to command serious attention in the White House. "If an organization is large enough," commented one Kennedy aide, "the President may feel that he has to explain an action to it, or even consult it. The ADA is not one of those organizations." The ADA saw just how tenuous its political situation was during the 1962 congressional elections, when it came under heavy fire from Republicans trying to discredit Kennedy by tying him to the ADA. The Republican National Committee produced a twenty-five minute film entitled "The ADA: Seed-bed for Socialism." Barry Goldwater, the conservative senator from Arizona, served as the point man in the Republican assault. "The right-wingers may make speeches and write letters to the editor," Goldwater declared, "but the ADAers in government can make decisions, institute policy and enforce their desires with the full power of the Federal machinery." Goldwater promised on "Meet the Press" that, as chairman of the Senate GOP Campaign Committee, he would pin the ADA label on the Democratic party. The Republican congressman Robert Wilson of California told a Sioux Falls, South Dakota, audience in September 1962 that President Kennedy "made more mistakes in one and a half years than Harry Truman made in seven and a half years because he surrounded himself with liberals from the Americans for Democratic Action." The ADA's old nemesis Fulton Lewis, Jr., refused to pass up an opportunity to rap the organization. The "top echelons" of the Kennedy administration, he claimed, "are honeycombed with members of the ultra-liberal organization and they exert a strong influence on his policies." The ADA, the *Freedom Press* announced, is "virtually in control of the entire United States government, even though its membership is a paltry 50,000!"[36]

Events in Cuba frustrated Republican attempts to make the ADA an important campaign issue. In the summer of 1962 the Soviets placed a large number of ballistic missiles in Cuba. On October 15, American U-2 reconnaissance flights over the western part of the island disclosed the clandestine construction of the missile launchers. Early the next morning Kennedy viewed the pictures and immediately summoned an ad hoc group consisting of key members from the State and Defense Departments and from the military, intelligence, and public information sectors. The committee's mandate, Robert Kennedy recalled, was to "make a recommendation which would affect the future of all mankind, a recommendation which, if wrong and if accepted, could mean the destruction of the human race." The committee listed a number of possible options, ranging from diplomatic protests to a surgical air strike, but eventually agreed upon a naval blockade. On Monday, October 22, Kennedy revealed the situation to the American public in a television address. "The 1930's," he said, "taught us a clear lesson: aggressive conduct, if allowed to go unchecked and unchallenged, ultimately leads to war." For two anxious days the two superpowers stood "eyeball to eyeball." On October 24, sixteen ships stopped dead in the water and began their voyage back to Russian ports. Two days later Khrushchev and Kennedy agreed that the missiles would be withdrawn if the United States ended its blockade and pledged not to invade Cuba.[37]

The ADA supported Kennedy during the crisis, charging that the president "was compelled to respond" to the Soviet action. It refrained from sanctioning the blockade but did applaud him for taking the issue to the United Nations and the Organization of American States—although it would have "preferred that he had placed it before these international forums immediately, rather than present them with what amounted to a *fait accompli*." It also suggested that the U.S. bases in Turkey weakened America's bargaining position.[38]

This head-on clash with Khrushchev marked Kennedy's greatest political triumph. "If the President was running for office in this campaign," commented a Capitol Hill veteran, "he'd even carry Maine and Vermont." Kennedy's personal triumph did not hurt Democratic candidates running in the election. Democrats gained four seats in the Senate (for a balance of 68 to 32) and lost four in the House (for a balance of 259 to 176). For the first time since 1934, the incumbent party held even in the off year.

The missile crisis had another unanticipated effect as well—it gave momentum to an already growing student peace movement, which rejected many tenets of postwar American foreign policy. Although many ADA leaders grew frustrated with Kennedy's caution, they still identified with his goals and aspirations and shared little with the disillusioned young. In May 1962, however, the National Board directed the organization to intensify its contact with peace groups and attempt to find ground for agreement. The ADA sent a liaison to peace meetings and participated in a postmortem on the missile crisis. Serious obstacles, though, divided the ADA from the peace movement. The peace movement, one ADA member warned, represented "a crossroads for the liberal movement as a whole" and could change the course of liberalism "as much as events of 1948 did." It was, he declared, "less optimistic than the recent liberal tradition," less sure of the "benefit of moderate change," "less anti-communist," and "less elitist than ADA or other liberal traditions." What these differences mean, he predicted, is that "if ADA is to be close to and related to the peace movement, the word 'liberal' is going to have to change a great deal. . . ."[39]

Most of the ADA's leadership rejected this counsel, believing instead that the peace movement represented the naive yearnings of a younger, untested generation. In January 1962 a Harvard University student asked Beer to support an initiative entitled "Student Action for a Turn Toward Peace," which criticized American foreign policy as "essentially military" and called on the United States to take unilateral actions in order to reduce tensions with the Soviet Union. Beer chastised the student for "misleading" himself by terming " 'essentially military' this policy of negotiation which the Administration pursued in good faith and to which it gave perhaps highest priority in foreign affairs." He also reminded the student of the lessons of his generation—that the Soviet Union did have aggressive tendencies and that the United States needed to maintain a strong military presence. "The more the balance of military power tilts against us," Beer argued, "the more the Communist world may be tempted to seek its purposes through pressure and blackmail, and the less likely it is that negotiation will produce just or lasting results." Arthur Schlesinger, Jr., also took delight in chiding young radicals for their naive and unsophisticated view of the world. "The cold war is long, slow and agonizing," he admonished. "It is unbearable for those who seek simple answers and final solutions in a complex and ambiguous world." National Chairman John Roche joined in the attacks in an October 1962 article that appeared in the *New York Times Magazine*. Roche wrote that young radicals had deluded themselves into believing a number of myths about American society. First, they possessed a romantic longing for the radicals of the thirties, who Roche thought "seem to be preserved, like flies in amber, in the militant postures of their youth." The second myth concerned the nature of the Communist party, which young radicals perceived as a "pathetic, persecuted group."[40]

By the middle of 1962 the civil rights movement had moved into a more active stage, and many black leaders were dispirited with Kennedy's lack of leadership. In the fall of 1962, after an angry crowd became violent, Kennedy reluctantly and belatedly called in the federal troops to protect James Meredith's attempt to enroll in the all-white University of Mississippi. The first confrontation of 1963 occurred in Birmingham, Alabama. The problem began when Martin Luther King, Jr., and his Southern Christion Leadership Conference decided to target the city in April to end discrimination in department stores and at lunch counters. In response, the police commissioner, Eugene ("just call me 'Bull' ") Connor, set upon the marchers with dogs, clubs, and fire hoses, making martyrs of his victims and assuring their triumph. "Let those people come to the corner, Sergeant," shouted Connor to a group of whites gathered to watch the spectacle. "I want 'em to see the dogs work. Look at those niggers run." Shortly after the events in Birmingham, Kennedy faced another challenge from George Wallace, the newly elected governor of Alabama. Wallace, who campaigned promising to block the doorway of any building under court order to admit blacks, was given the opportunity when the University of Alabama at Tuscaloosa announced it was admitting two black students. Kennedy tried negotiating with Wallace to avoid a confrontation, but to no avail. On June 11 the deputy attorney general, as television cameras recorded the event, confronted Wallace on the steps of the registration building. Wallace backed down, but the events provided Kennedy with an excellent opportunity to address the nation on civil rights.[41]

Kennedy requested time from the networks for an eight o'clock address to the nation. That night he gave one of the most moving and eloquent speeches of his presidency. For the first time he referred to civil rights as a moral issue—one that was, he said, "as old as the scriptures and as clear as the American Constitution." Eight days after addressing the nation, Kennedy sent his specific legislative proposal to Congress. In it he requested legislation to buttress voting rights, to provide technical and financial assistance to school districts that were desegregating, and to extend and revise the Civil Rights Commission. He also proposed a broad new law banning segregation of public facilities and sought authority for the attorney general to initiate proceedings against the segregation of schools. He renewed and expanded earlier requests for education and training programs. Although it was the boldest and most comprehensive civil rights program ever proposed by any president, Kennedy's legislation could not calm the rising storm of black protest.

Kennedy's economic policy underwent a similar transformation. The Keynesian faithful, led by Walter Heller and the Council of Economic Advisers, persistently and patiently tried to educate the president about the benefits of deficit financing. The twin shocks of the stock market collapse and the steel crisis in the spring of 1962 shook Kennedy from his complacency and gave the Keynesians their opportunity to win him over to their position. In August, Kennedy went before a nationwide television audience to announce his new tax-cutting scheme. Although tax reduction would temporarily enlarge the deficit, he assured his listeners, it "would prevent the even greater budget deficit that a lagging economy would otherwise surely produce." In January 1963, with the congressional elections out of the way, Kennedy submitted to Congress legislation calling for an increase in spending of $4.0 billion and a tax reduction of $11.4 billion.[42]

Kennedy also took halting steps toward a détente with the Soviets. The missile crisis left both sides more aware of the dangers of the arms race and inspired Kennedy and Khrushchev to get more personally involved in seeking an arms control agreement. In June 1963 Kennedy delivered an eloquent speech at American University that called on the superpowers to control the arms race. Shortly afterward Kennedy succeeded in negotiating a Russian-American ban on nuclear testing on land, on the seas, and in the atmosphere (the measure did not permit on-site inspection, nor did it prohibit underground testing, which continued virtually unchecked).

In other ways, though, Kennedy remained wedded to his Cold War mentality. He showed, for example, no desire to change the pattern of American policy in Vietnam. "Inheriting from Eisenhower an increasingly dangerous if still limited commitment," the historian George Herring has observed, Kennedy "plunged deeper into the morass." When Kennedy took office, about two thousand American "advisors" were in Vietnam. By the end of 1963 that number had increased to sixteen thousand. Cautious and hesitant, Kennedy in his improvised policy unwillingly expanded America's role while trying to keep it limited. Kennedy, to his credit, tried to make American aid contingent on Diem's making necessary social reforms at home. However, each time Diem accepted the aid but refused to make changes, Kennedy backed down. By deferring to Diem, the United States only encouraged his intransigence. When, in October 1963, a group of generals informed the American ambassador, Henry Cabot Lodge, that they were planning a coup, the Kennedy administration acquiesced. The coup was successful but not peaceful—Diem was brutally executed. Three weeks later, Kennedy was assassinated, and it was President Lyndon Johnson's turn to address the problem.[43]

Kennedy's actions during the last year of his presidency did little to alleviate liberal suspicion about his commitment to liberalism. The ADA still criticized him for proposing halfhearted measures and for being too cautious. Nevertheless, Kennedy's civil rights legislation and his economic policy, while not nearly what the ADA wanted, went beyond what any other president had proposed. In dealing with Kennedy's tax cut, even Keyserling could agree with his arch-rival Galbraith's assessment that "we are going to have to have a large amount of revenue for both domestic and overseas purposes and that the cutting of taxes in this situation is not the best form of economic policy." Edward Hollander said at a September 1962 National Board meeting that the ADA had two alternatives: "supporting the bill as more good than bad" or "opposing it." Although it called the bill "a great disappointment"—"neither as bold as the economic situation calls for, nor as realistically related to the needs of the country as President Kennedy's campaign promises"—it feared continued unemployment so much that it accepted tax reduction to stimulate growth.[44]

The ADA also complained that Kennedy's civil rights legislation did not go far enough. Working as part of the Leadership Conference on Civil Rights, the ADA lobbied unsuccessfully for FEPC, authority for the attorney general to initiate suits protecting the constitutional rights of individual citizens, deadlines for total school integration, and stronger voting rights provisions. In the end, however, members recognized, in Rauh's words, that "even without FEPC . . . President Kennedy's bill was the most comprehensive civil rights proposal ever made in Congress." It "contained the administration's best estimates of what could be enacted, rather than what was needed." The ADA, Rauh, concluded, would give its "wholehearted support" to the administration bill while lobbying for more.[45]

While the organization had no difficulty supporting the nuclear test ban treaty, it worried about the course of events in Southeast Asia. The ADA expressed alarm that the United States was spending $700 million a year and that some twelve thousand soldiers served as "instructors" in Vietnam. It called on Kennedy to pressure Diem to make much needed reforms, to consult with other friendly Asian nations to develop a mutual guarantee system based on the Charter of the United Nations, and to avoid unilateral action in the region. Again, however, despite its criticism of events in Vietnam, the organization shared with the administration the central premise that the United States needed to prevent a Communist victory in that country.

In May 1963 the ADA displayed its new, contentious mood in a meeting with the president. The ADA delegation's assertiveness contrasted sharply with the earlier group's visit in May 1961. More aggressive than Beer, Roche took the offensive by telling Kennedy that his administration had failed to propose bold programs that would inspire liberals. Kennedy responded by reciting the political facts of life—he had only 180 secure House votes for liberal legislation, he needed to propose new programs one at a time, and he wanted to lay the foundation through public education before proposing broad programs. After the meeting Wechsler commented that Kennedy's "rendition would have been an almost total success" a few years earlier because "liberals are perhaps too easily captivated by the prose of pragmatism." But this was "the time of horror in Alabama, which overshadowed everything else." Wechsler conceded that Kennedy "won great goodwill, with wit, charm and intelligence," but the politics of personality were just about exhausted by "the great Southern crisis."[46]

The irony of the ADA's relationship with Kennedy in 1963 was striking. Just when Kennedy was showing signs of moving in a more liberal direction by proposing a strong civil rights bill and accepting deficit financing, liberals became more strident in their criticism. Kennedy inched to the left, but that was not quick enough for the liberals. Why were liberals becoming so impatient? Part of the reason was that Kennedy's activist style and his eloquence raised expectations. Also, the public mood in the early 1960s seemed more receptive to reform than at any other time in the postwar period. Within the organization, too, other pressures were pushing the leadership to be more critical of the administration.

Beginning in the early 1960s a vocal group of reform liberals began raising basic questions about American foreign policy and the ADA's commitment to the Cold War. These reformers tended to represent a younger generation of liberals. Born between the depression and the Second World War, they had experienced neither the suffering of the depression nor the sense of betrayal that liberals felt when Stalin occupied Eastern Europe at the end of World War II. Coming to political maturity during the 1950s, they had also been spared the bitter struggles between anti-Communists and Communists in labor unions and other Popular Front organizations. Whereas older liberals had been nurtured on the beneficence of the New Deal, and still emphasized bread-and-butter issues, the younger reformers witnessed a cautious government's slow and halfhearted response to the plight of blacks in the South in the late 1950s and early 1960s. This generational experience helps explain the young reformers' peculiar brand of liberalism. On the whole this group tended to be more activist more independent of the Democratic party, and more moralistic in its view of politics than most older liberals were.

Reform liberals also had little in common with the growing legions of New Left radicals who nurtured on the ideas of Paul Goodman, C. Wright Mills, and Herbert Marcuse, joined the Students for a Democratic Society (SDS), the student arm of the old League for Industrial Democracy. Reform liberals, like older liberals, were still nonideological and saw politics as a means of solving problems; most radicals wanted politics to be the collective expression of a moral society. Reform liberals also placed their faith in the vast institutions of government; radicals were committed to "participatory democracy."

Although it is impossible to know their exact numbers—the ADA never kept very precise membership statistics—one can conclude from correspondence and other references that the emerging reform movement in the ADA was centered in many of the large and influential chapters—those of Philadelphia, Chicago, New York, and Boston—by as early as 1963.

Curtis Gans, who joined the organization in 1964, was the first visible member of this reform group. Gans explained that he had an orientation different from that of most ADA members. He "cut his teeth" on the civil rights movement in the South at the end of the 1950s, was active in the sit-in demonstrations in 1960–61, and, inspired by Kennedy's rhetoric, became a domestic recruiter for the Peace Corps in 1961. Younger than most ADA members, he confessed, "Hitler and Stalin were not central to my experience." Consequently, he disapproved of Kennedy's Cold War rhetoric, viewed the Cuban missile crisis as "dangerous brinkmanship," and criticized the president's slow and halfhearted response to the plight of blacks in the South. Gans was no radical; he was a self-proclaimed anti-communist who felt no empathy for the New Left—"I was concerned with organizing majorities, not confrontational minorities," he recalled. Yet, with the exception of Kennedy's American University speech, Gans saw little difference between Kennedy and Dulles. What infuriated him even more was that most liberals tried to rationalize Kennedy's conservatism. "John Kenneth Galbraith was the only prominent ADA intellectual who was not bought by the Kennedy family," he remembered with some bitterness.[47]

An amorphorus and leaderless group, these reform liberals had little or no representation on the National Board, although they were influential in many of the larger chapters. They did, however, exert some influence on the ADA's deliberations. The former national chairman Beer blamed the reformers for dividing the organization and minimizing its influence in the political debate. Even though the organization is in "a position today to be listened to by a considerable public," Beer acknowledged, it still exists on the periphery. The reason, he explained, is "that on the really burning issue of the time—defense policy and relations with Russia—we can't really make up our collective mind." While many members, Beer thought, "would go along with the Administration on these questions," "a large minority" identified with the pacifist position. This division, he warned, "makes it impossible for us to take a clear-cut position and to give it a strong lead."[48]

The split that Beer identified went much deeper than just foreign policy. In part it was generational—brought on by the influx into the organization of younger members nurtured in the reform movements in the major cities. In part it was organizational—the result of an effervescence among new members, many of them reform liberals, who believed that the national leadership had grown old and tired and needed to be replaced. In part, finally, it was philosophical—representing a basic difference in liberal ranks concerning the direction that liberalism should take and the coalition that should sustain it.

These reform liberals believed that the ADA, and liberals in general, suffered from a moral hardening of the arteries. The liberal preoccupation with pragmatic politics, the reformers charged, led them to exorcise from politics the moral dimension of issues. The ADA's economic philosophy, reformers said, was too piecemeal and too closely associated with Keyserling's theory of economic growth. Its foreign policy was too anti-Soviet, too reliant on military containment, and too insensitive to the national aspirations of many Third World countries. Part of the reformers' difference with the New Deal coalition was a matter of culture and style. That coalition was ethnic, built on personal loyalty and family ties, bound by patronage, and led, on the local level, by machine bosses. The reformers believed that politics should be based on moral codes and principles of conduct, rewarded by merit not patronage, and concerned with community values rather than private interest.[49]

Many of the reform members of the ADA took a very different approach to the major foreign policy questions of the day. David Williams, for example, had suggested, in an article published in the October 1961 issue of the *Progressive,* that American policymakers and, inadvertently, many of his fellow liberals had "grossly" exaggerated the importance of Communists in many of the social revolutions sweeping through the Third World. Robert Delson, chairman of the foreign policy commission, boldly suggested that the United States abandon its defensive and military containment policy abroad and its moderate welfare state at home in favor of an undefined "dramatic, sweeping, powerful conception which would stir the imagination and enlist the support, not only of the American people, but of those aspiring to participate in the age of welfare for all throughout the world." Other members made even more radical proposals. One ADA member from New Jersey proposed "universal total disarmament down to the police force required in each nation for maintaining internal law and order, and a world system adequate to maintain international peace in the disarmed world." He proposed a "World Security Organization" that would have a police force large enough to overcome any national police force. Arthur Waskow suggested to the 1963 convention that the ADA's foreign policy was "not protecting or advancing liberty in the world and [was] even endangering liberty at home." He called upon the ADA to condemn current American policy as "wasteful, useless, and extremely dangerous."[50]

The only issue that aroused the passion of reformers more than disarmament was Cuba. As early as the fall of 1960, David Williams had met with a number of critics of American policy toward Cuba, including C. Wright Mills. Williams and Mills agreed that although "Castro considers himself a Marxist [he] is certainly not a Communist. He turned to the Russians only when he had been cold-shouldered by the U.S. and Yugoslavia. . . ." Williams felt that domestic political pressures forced Castro to identify with the Communists. Williams, after the disastrous Bay of Pigs invasion, raised a number of objections about American policy toward Castro. In April 1961 he informed the National Board that the "Castro government was probably as ephemeral as other Latin American governments, and of no present danger to us." He regarded American aid to the rebels as "contrary to both national and international law" and damaging to America's relations with other Latin American republics. The board's reaction to Williams's complaints was less than overwhelming. Williams and Joseph Rauh were alone "in deploring what the U.S. had done."[51]

A rigid and ossified organizational leadership compounded these differences over substantive foreign policy issues. The problem the ADA faced was, as one chapter representative informed the board in January 1963, that "many young people" considered the organization "old-hat, stale, and somewhat conservative." Ralph Mansfield of the Independent Voters of Illinois echoed those sentiments. The ADA, he said, must be the leader of a "dynamic and attractive political liberalism that will win to the cause of ADA the college students, the teachers, the workers, the professionals of all callings." James Wechsler also understood the need for change in the organization. "ADA has become primarily a mating ground for those with sentimental ties to the liberal and radical past, a sort of Alumni Association that recruits too few of its members from more recent classes," he lamented. Sheldon Pollack of California informed Beer as early as July 1961 that his chapter was ignoring the "old issues" of labor, unemployment, and workmen's compensation and was instead addressing quality-of-life issues like "planning, metropolitan government, open spaces, recreation, consumer problems, housing, [and] government structure." Another chapter representative told Hollander that the ADA's close identification with issues like domestic communism, and its enthusiasm for Kennedy, was keeping many potential members at arm's length.[52]

Despite a growing membership and a sympathetic administration in Washington, a general feeling of discontent existed in the ADA, especially in many of the larger chapters. According to ADA officials, its total membership had grown to 50,000 in 1961, housed in approximately one hundred ADA chapters in sixteen states, and a campus division of twenty-two chapters with almost 2,000 members. These figures are probably exaggerated. The Post Office circulation statement of the ADA *World,* which went to every dues-paying member, indicated only 18,600. Although membership did increase during these years, a more accurate figure would be the 30,000 names on the ADA mailing list given to the Kennedy campaign in March 1960.[53]

Many members complained that the national leadership was seriously out of touch with the needs and the concerns of the local chapters, and alienated from the emerging reform movements in many of the nation's urban centers. Many of the chapters believed that the national office had insulated itself from the local chapters for so long that it had become insensitive to changes taking place under its feet. Dick Lambert wrote Violet Gunther in April 1963 that the midwestern chapters, in particular, felt "that too much of the leadership and decision making in the ADA revolve[d] around a few individuals." A representative from the New Jersey chapter criticized the organization and its leadership for being "too elitist, too money-conscious, and too Washington-oriented." "As it is," he concluded, "there is absolutely no correlation between what goes on in Washington at the national office and what goes on in the chapters."[54]

They had a point. Robert Hartman, in researching his 1961 series on the ADA for the *Los Angeles Times,* observed a great deal of organizational stagnation in the ADA. "The formal organization and key policy-making officials of ADA have remained remarkably the same throughout its 14-year history," he wrote. "Its national officers are virtually all founders or early members and alternate in musical chairmanships and vice-chairmanships." Despite the ADA's self-professed philosophy of flexibility and change, "its latest policy platform is strikingly like the first. With a few exceptions, the resolutions were approved by a voice vote of the Convention exactly as they came from drafting committees of top ADA founders and perennial officers, also little altered over the years."[55] Although unnoticed at the time, structurally the organization was depending more upon the chapters for support and income. Throughout the 1960s, union contributions fell off significantly. In 1960, unions contributed $14,075 to the ADA's income of $126,292, or about 11 percent. By 1962, labor contributed only 2 percent of ADA's total income, while chapter income from quotas and per capita rose to 13 percent. The declining union contribution took its toll on the organization, which by August 1963 was running a deficit of $30,000.

At least one member of the national staff, Violet Gunther, the director of organization, worried about the problem. In her last memorandum before leaving the ADA, after fifteen years of service, she said that the biggest change she saw take place was the concentration of decision making in the national office, leaving the local chapters isolated. "For a whole multiplicity of reasons," she warned, "the generating of creative ideas which used to spring from the non-staff leadership of ADA has in the past years devolved upon the staff." If the trend continued, Gunther predicted, the ADA would be nothing but "a constantly diminishing voice in public affairs."[56]

In an internal study of the organization, ADA leaders found that the most successful chapters (in Philadelphia, Massachusetts, and Chicago) existed "in situations where local government was inept or corrupt" and where the ADA could build its reputation on "good government" issues. These chapters tended to be in varying degrees self-sufficient in leadership and finance, and therefore less dependent on the national organization. In areas where there were "good government" movements independent of the ADA, the organization had difficulty establishing a firm foothold and was usually "absorbed by the reform movement or exist[ed] on the fringe of it." In either case, the vitality of the local chapters depended heavily on the emerging reform movement, which was popular in many of the nation's largest cities.

One of the most common complaints chapters made against the national office was that it toned down their criticisms of the Kennedy administration. The chairman of the Baltimore chapter charged that the national officers did not permit any direct or implied criticism of the administration at the 1962 convention. She accused Beer of closing the Saturday session early to prevent passage of a resolution critical of the administration's position on nuclear testing, and of keeping other resolutions—that on civil defense, for example— from ever reaching the floor. In the same year a delegate complained that the domestic policy committee smothered a proposal that accused the administration of crippling the economy and draining off resources from needed social services with its "wasteful, useless, and extremely dangerous" military expansion program. In the preceding year, the Washington, D.C., chapter submitted a policy resolution charging that despite "our claim to the highest standard of living in the history of the world, American life is characterized by an alarming and increasing poverty of public services," and calling on Kennedy to double spending on public services over the next two decades. The revenue for this, it claimed, should come from increased national growth or, if that was not sufficient, from higher tax rates. The proposal never came to a vote.[57]

Reform liberals wanted the ADA to put itself back in the forefront of the liberal reform movement. M. A. Myerson of the Massachusetts chapter asked a question that troubled many ADA members in the early 1960s: "What have we done in recent years which was sufficiently colorful, effective, or unique to make a good brag?" There was a general feeling in the organization, Edward Hollander noted in 1963, that the ADA should "chart a new course for action, with some specific accomplishments as our goal. . . . The program should be much more concentrated, particularly on a few domestic issues. . . ." The ADA should not spend its time "for those causes which are part of the President's program or which are being carried on by other groups much larger or more influential than ADA." Instead, "each year ADA should assign top rank to one substantial matter, or two, ADA's issue or issues of the year. . . . Mainly, they should be our own babies and deal with important and gutsy issues."[58]

By the time the Kennedy administration came to a tragic end in November 1963, the ADA was experiencing an effervescence that had not existed since its founding days. This development, like the rise of more radical movements at the same time among students, reflected the rise of a revolution in expectations, which in turn owed something to postwar affluence and to Kennedy rhetoric. The increased militancy of the civil rights movement as well as the generational change in the organization was leading many ADA members to reevaluate their liberal faith. Ironically, just when the ADA was about to be called on to propose and support bold domestic initiatives, it found itself uncertain and divided.

7

The ADA, Lyndon Johnson, and the Great Society

The dread cadence of muffled drums, the flag-draped coffin, the drummers and military marching units, the tolling bells from St. John's Episcopal Church, the caisson and its six gray horses, the mourners' tears—aspects of a sorrowful yet serene autumn day when America buried its young president. It was a day of pain and grief for a widow and two children, a day of nostalgia for the tragic promise of the New Frontier, and a time of uncertainty as the nation turned its attention to the man who assumed the office of president.

Many liberals believed that Lyndon Johnson was an insecure yet overbearing politician who reveled in manipulation, sought power for the sake of power, and consciously tried to outdo his illustrious predecessor. They charged that he was too provincial, too southern, too flamboyant, and too much the servant of the special gas and oil interests of Texas. For someone who had been a master of the Washington power structure for so long, Johnson was surprisingly insecure. "Why don't people like me?" Johnson asked in a rare moment of introspection. "Because, Mr. President," one aide responded, "you are not a very likable man." His apparent insecurity was obvious to those who watched the Johnson White House. "Dubious whether people liked him," Eric Goldman observed, "he pleaded, clawed, and maneuvered to have them love him." His insecurity was driven at least partly by the inevitable comparison between himself and Kennedy. Johnson lacked Kennedy's wit and charm; he replaced Kennedy's Cambridge savvy with a Texas drawl. Kennedy was urbane and sophisticated; Johnson was rural and provincial. "Detachment, understatement, irony, sophistication, coolness—those were the qualities that were seen in the manner of John F. Kennedy," observed the columnist Anthony Lewis. "The trademarks of Lyndon B. Johnson are emotion, flamboyance, folksiness."[1]

Many liberals were never able to accept either Johnson's provincialism or his enormous vanity. Also, liberals since the days of FDR had come to see the presidency as a pulpit for moral leadership. They expected the president to be able to arouse the passion of the American people against the parochial special interests that were so powerful in Congress. Johnson lacked the ability to excite that type of passion. In many ways Johnson was a victim of the television age. The same medium that had exalted his predecessor seemed to diminish him. In twisting arms in the back room of the Senate, Johnson had no equal; in appealing to millions of people on a television screen, he had much to learn. No matter what he did—whether he wore glasses or not, toned down his distinctive southern drawl or not—he had trouble establishing himself. "Every time I appear on television," he lamented at one point, "I lose money."[2]

Johnson felt especially uncomfortable with liberals and "in-tel-lec-shuls." Educated at Southwest Texas State Teachers' College, Johnson was convinced that professional liberals with an Ivy League education conspired against him. "I've got their legislation passed, bills that haven't been passed for decades," Johnson later told Humphrey, "and they *still* won't accept me. . . . I don't understand it. . . . I don't have the right eau de cologne for them." Despite his disdain for most liberals, Johnson's guide to action in the period immediately after Kennedy's death was to establish himself as a broad liberal leader and to get rid of the tag of wheeler-dealer. In the post-Kennedy days, the historian Eric Goldman noted, Johnson's major political problem was "whether Northern Democrats and independent voters [would] look on him as an authentic liberal in the FDR, Truman, Stevenson and JFK tradition." To help paint the proper picture, Johnson set out to win the confidence and affection of groups that had long been leery of him: labor, Negroes, intellectuals, and "those whose minds fell into the general Northeastern pattern of thinking."[3]

For the ADA, Johnson's accession to the presidency nonetheless imposed a brief moratorium on internal bickering among moderates, reformers, and traditionalists. Despite doubts about his personality and his commitment to liberal programs, many ADA members were optimistic about Johnson's presidency. While the moderates Schlesinger and Galbraith felt a personal sense of loss over Kennedy's death, others had been frustrated by Kennedy's ineffectiveness. Although they agreed that Kennedy grew while in office, he still, at the time of his death, fell far short of their expectations. They hoped that Johnson would use his legendary legislative skills to push through and make improvements in Kennedy's logjammed domestic program. "Like everyone else I was shattered by the bullet," Allard Lowenstein wrote Johnson in November. "Your speech to Congress today started the long pull back together, for me and for countless others."[4] The ADA was prepared to judge Johnson on the two issues that concerned it most in the mid-1960s: civil rights and economic policy.

"For Lyndon Johnson as for John Kennedy," Anthony Lewis wrote in the *New York Times,* "the great challenge from within this country is the cry for justice in race relations. History will judge the Johnson Administration, domestically, by its success in answering that cry." Johnson inherited a difficult civil rights situation from his predecessor. The discontent of blacks had been rising, their demands were becoming more strident, and their mood was more militant. In August 1963 nearly a quarter of a million people had attended a march on Washington to demonstrate support for the civil rights legislation before Congress. Underneath the outward unity, however, were clear signs of discord. Dissatisfied with the slow progress under two "liberal" Democratic administrations, many blacks, by the fall and early winter of 1963, were beginning to doubt whether the national coalition of labor-liberals and Democrats would ever redress their grievances. More black children attended segregated schools in the South in 1964 than in 1954. Blacks were still denied the vote in most states, and Jim Crow laws flourished. "The liberal," a disillusioned black wrote, "must be forced to choose between the Negro's support and that of the Dixiecrats; he must not be permitted to support the fence-straddling of the Kennedys and Johnsons."[5]

Convinced there was a direct correlation between disfranchisement and indigence, CORE and SNCC had returned to the South after the August 1963 march to work on voter registration. CORE concentrated its efforts in Florida, Louisiana, and South Carolina; SNCC operated in Alabama and Mississippi. Robert Moses, working through a revitalized Council of Federated Organizations, a coalition of civil rights groups founded in 1962 to organize poor black communities in the South, organized a Mississippi summer project to register blacks in massive numbers. The June 1964 slaying of three freedom fighters—two Jewish students, Andrew Goodman and Michael Schwerner, and one black, James Chaney—just outside of Philadelphia, Mississippi, widened the cleavage between whites and blacks in the movement, diminished faith in nonviolence, and increased distrust of government institutions and antagonism toward liberals.[6]

Most ADA leaders were northern white liberals, and they were unsure about how to respond to the increased militancy of the civil rights movement. While they supported stronger legislation and federal involvement to protect the civil rights of blacks in the South, they were also committed to achieving their vision of the just society by working through the established institutions of government. Although frustrated by the lack of progress, they were not prepared to countenance acts of violence born of despair. They could understand black discontent but could not accept radical solutions. Their strategy was to intensify their efforts to get civil rights legislation passed, while at the same time trying to keep frustrated blacks from committing acts of indiscriminate violence and to get them to work with the Democratic party.

In dealing with the question of civil disobedience, for example, Edward Hollander, chairman of the Executive Committee, warned John Roche that it was "unthinkable" that the ADA could approve of what "the student" meant by civil disobedience—"combatting the power structure with chaos." On the other hand, he said, "I do not know that we can take a categorical position against any and all acts of civil disobedience, as such, under all circumstances." Roche decided the issue was too controversial for the Executive Committee and deferred consideration until the May 1964 convention.

At the convention, the domestic policy commission, controlled by moderates and traditionalists, called for ADA support of peaceful and legal sit-ins. A number of reformers in the local chapters objected, claiming the ADA needed not only to support but also to participate in acts of civil disobedience. Howard Wachtel of the Washington chapter submitted a substitute resolution that, while supporting only peaceful demonstrations, argued that the ADA had to "protest against the way in which laws [were] being administered." ADA members, he said, should "lie down in front of trucks in order to eliminate civil wrongs." In the long discussion that followed, those advocating the minority plank suggested that the issue was the intensity of the ADA's commitment to the civil rights movement. One member said "that the essence of the Minority Report [was] the willingness of ADAers to go to jail." Everyone was anticipating Rauh's position. As the organization's leading spokesman on questions of civil liberties and civil rights, he could swing the debate in either direction. Rauh spoke in support of the majority plank, claiming that "as a serious political organization, ADA must base its policy on the United States Constitution." With his supoprt the majority plank passed by a wide margin.[7]

Many ADA members feared that black discontent with liberalism would lead to more radical solutions, which would only polarize the debate and make progress impossible. The organization was so concerned with events in the South that in November 1964 it sent Curtis Gans to Atlanta for meetings with civil rights leaders. The question the ADA had to confront, Gans wrote National Director Leon Shull in his first report, "concerns the nature of the 'new' movement in civil rights and the relationship of the older organizations to it." The ADA should do its "best to offer all aid and assistance to them and then, at the same time, do everything [it] can to point out the dangers of association with politically undesirable elements." SNCC was the one organization Gans called "politically undesirable." The organization is not democratic, he held, and "a small elite close to the top controls all the decisions." This "small elite is politically unorthodox and is thus using SNCC as a political base for its purposes." SNCC's executive director, James Forman, Gans charged, is "allied with unhealthy organizations," and Ella Baker "has been thought suspect for a number of years." He recommended that the ADA "have no formal relations" with the Southern Student Organizing Committee (SSOC), a SNCC-organized attempt to bring together campus liberals and blacks in the South. While Gans agreed "that some type of organizing and communications effort on campuses would be a good thing," he did not feel that "a SNCC inspired effort offered the best opportunity." If the ADA and other moderate groups were unable to talk SNCC out of its radical schemes, Gans recommended, the ADA should "seek to discourage participation in that group through either membership or financial support." He added, "There was considerable feeling in Atlanta that it would be just as well if this particular group did not get off the ground. I share this view." Gans thought it important that they do all of this work quietly, without drawing public attention. Public repudiation, he feared, "would immeasurably harm the total effort and give conservatives what they have been asking for in the way of documentation that subversives were running the movement."[8]

Directing the civil rights movement in the South into constructive channels was only half of the ADA's program. It also planned to prod the federal government to pass strong civil rights legislation. The organization found that the Johnson administration did not need much coaxing. Johnson was committed to enacting and strengthening the civil rights legislation Kennedy had submitted to Congress the preceding summer. On November 27, 1963, when he appeared before a joint session of Congress to urge completion of urgent unfinished legislative business, Johnson singled out civil rights. "We would be untrue to the tasks he relinquished when God summoned him," Johnson said, if we did not pass the civil rights bill. In his 1964 State of the Union Message, Johnson reiterated his commitment to civil rights. "It is a moral issue," he declared. "Today, Americans of all races stand side by side in Berlin and in Vietnam. They died side by side in Korea. Surely they can work and eat and travel side by side in their own country."[9]

On January 31 Johnson expressed support for the new civil rights bill reported by the House Judiciary Committee. The new legislation was stronger than the original Kennedy bill in two important ways: first, it included a "Part III," which empowered the federal government to intervene in cases where a person's civil rights were threatened; second, it provided for a FEPC, which the Kennedy staff had declared "politically impossible." The ADA believed that Johnson's legislation could be strengthened by making the public-accommodations section all-inclusive, by having Part III permit the attorney general to initiate, not just intervene, in civil rights suits and by changing the FEPC provision to allow administrative rather than judicial enforcement.

The ADA, working through the Leadership Conference on Civil Rights, had to make a decision as the bill made its way to the House floor: Should it accept the bill as it was, or should it risk defeat by pressing for strengthening amendments? Johnson informed Rauh on January 21 that he opposed any changes in the House bill. Agreeing that any strengthening amendments from the floor were unlikely, the ADA modified its position from support for strengthening amendments to "opposition to all weakening amendments."[10] In this effort, as in many others, the ADA's emphasis was on practicable legislation, not on utopian schemes that had little chance of success.

The ADA mobilized support for the congressional battle by sending delegations to contact friendly congressmen to make sure they would be on the floor to vote against any weakening amendments. Local chapters organized letter-writing campaigns to influence undecided legislators. A working coalition of northern Democrats and moderate Republicans made passage of the legislation almost certain. Some of the credit in the House went to the Republican leader, Charles Halleck of Indiana, who helped bring the GOP into the coalition. The debate on the House floor was surprisingly moderate and restrained. Only Virginia's segregationist representative Howard Smith tried to strain the decorum by noting that a chiropodist in a hotel would be covered by the public-accommodations section. "If I were cutting corns," he said, "I would want to know whose feet I would have to be monkeying around with. I would want to know whether they smelled good or bad." Despite Smith's colorful metaphor, the bill passed the full House on February 10, by a vote of 290 to 130.

The question civil rights supporters faced as the bill made its way to the Senate, Rauh claimed, "was whether the Senate fiilibuster could defeat the House-passed bill or gut it as had been done in 1957." In order not to repeat the previous experience, the civil rights forces, working with their floor leader Hubert Humphrey, planned to outorganize the southerners. One of the big advantages was that Johnson had told Rauh at his January 21 meeting that "he would not care if the Senate did not do another thing for three months until the civil rights bill was enacted." Johnson effectively removed the opposition's most potent weapon—that it could hold up other needed legislation that would require the Senate to put aside the civil rights bill. The ADA and other civil rights organizations believed that the greatest danger was "the possibility of an early and unsuccessful cloture vote which would force a compromise to obtain the missing votes for cloture." As the debate rolled through April and May, the lobbying efforts of the ADA and other liberals began paying off. A number of senators reported that their mail was changing from opposition to support. This change was reflected in overall public opinion, which showed a 7 percent increase (from 63 percent to 70 percent) in favor of the legislation and an even wider margin against the filibuster.[11]

In May, Humphrey and Minority Leader Everett Dirksen entered into negotiations. Dirksen demanded a number of weakening amendments. In the fair-employment and public-accommodations section, he wanted to eliminate the attorney general's right to initiate court action in individual cases of discrimination, to have complaints about public accommodations and fair employment referred to state agencies before the federal government stepped in. The ADA "strongly urged Senator Humphrey to hold fast" and not give in to Dirksen's demands. Humphrey, knowing that the minority leader's support was essential to passage, agreed to all of Dirksen's demands. Rauh, speaking on behalf of both the ADA and the Leaderhip Conference on Civil Rights, recognized that while "concessions had been made to Senator Dirksen in language and on occasion in substance . . . the basic structure of the House-passed bill remained intact." Rauh feared that if the ADA declared victory, Dirksen would be encouraged to ask for more concessions, but that to say the bill had been weakened would lower the morale of civil rights workers and possibly "intensify racial tensions." The ADA decided to do both. It issued a statement that, while supporting the bill, complained that some of the amendments weakened the measure and resulted "in unnecessary delays in enforcement."[12]

With a compromise agreed upon, Humphrey was ready to bring the filibuster to an end. Angry exchanges marked the debate over cloture, but the

Democratic leadership held firm. When the clerk read the tally, it stood seventy-one for cloture, twenty-nine against. With four votes more than necessary, the Senate, for the first time in its history, had invoked cloture against a civil rights filibuster.[13]

ADA liberals were overjoyed about the passage, for they had long been at the forefront of the fight for civil rights. The law, they thought, provided elementary and long-overdue justice. But more conservative feelings also affected the ADA's reaction. More than anything else, they hoped that the bill would send an important signal to the black community that the federal government was willing to deal with their demands—that violence and extremism were not necessary. "Specifically, the legislation will provide a framework of achievable goals within which agitation, demonstrations and picketing will tend to take place," commented the *Nation*. "Insetad of spreading all over the lot, this activity can be directed along the lines of the legislation, which will channel and concentrate the energy of the movement." The ADA also hoped that passage of the bill would help placate blacks. While no one expected that the civil rights movement would stop dead in its tracks or that the bill would suddenly bring an end to years of indifference, the ADA did see it as "an effective tool to end much of the shameful discrimination that has scarred the American scene."[14]

Most liberals, ADA members included, overestimated the impact the law would have on the daily lives of most blacks. No legislation could have satisfied the fervor of the civil rights revolution. The ADA may have been ahead of its time for advocating strong civil rights measures, but the gap between its moderate goals and the demands of civil rights groups was rapidly becoming insurmountable. That fact became strikingly evident at the 1964 Democratic convention. During the summer of 1964, SNCC leaders organized the Mississippi Freedom Democratic party (MFDP), an extralegal political party for disfranchised blacks who demanded the right to represent the Democratic party at its convention. They planned to replace the racist, lily-white delegation, which threatened not to support the national ticket.

In keeping with their desire to channel black energies into the national Democratic party, most ADA members were leery of the MFDP. Rauh, who later became legal counsel to the group, first heard of the idea while chairing a panel of the Civil Liberties Clearing House on March 20, 1964. Assuming that the Republican candidate would be fighting for the black vote, Rauh believed that "it would not be difficult to persuade the Democratic National Convention to give strong support to the Freedom Party." Curtis Gans, however, saw the potential dangers in the movement. "Clearly," he said, it will "be the President's inclination to incorporate the Negroes into the national Democratic Party." Therefore the ADA should use "whatever influence it has to urge SNCC to abandon the Freedom Democratic orientation of its black belt party as being harmful to the freedom and representation the Negroes seek." If the ADA fails to persuade SNCC, it "should seek to get President Johnson's and the Justice Department's support on a systematic approach to voter registration—following the movement to where it is organizing so that the Black Belt Project will have no basis of long-term ostracization to feed upon." Quick granting of voting rights, he argued, will mean "quick recruitment by the Democratic Party, which will in turn mean quick scuttling of Freedom Democratic parties and SNCC control." The ADA, he concluded, "should assess SNCC's program on a project by project basis and assist in a quiet freeze of funds on those projects which do have a Freedom Democratic party orientation."[15]

As the Democratic National Convention opened near the tawdry Atlantic City boardwalk in August, the MFDP's hopes rested on members of the credentials committee's bringing a minority report to the floor of the convention, where liberal supporters would be able to carry the issue. On August 22 the credentials committee listened to the appeal of the MFDP. "I have only one hour," Rauh told the committee, "to tell you a story of moral agony that could take years." Witnesses, led by MFDP's chairman, Aaron Henry, followed Rauh, telling of the brutality and terror blacks experienced in the South. Fannie Lou Hamer gave a moving account of her "woesome times." "Is this America, the land of the free and the home of the brave, where we are threatened daily because we want to live as decent human beings?" Rauh concluded with a passionate appeal: "Are you going to throw out of here the people who want to work for Lyndon Johnson, who are willing to be beaten and shot and thrown in jail to work for Lyndon Johnson? Are we for the oppressor or the oppressed?"[16]

Johnson, however, wanted to prevent a Dixie walkout at the convention that would hurt his chances of election in the South. "If you seat those black buggers," Governor John Connally of Texas told him, "the whole South will walk out."[17] With the civil rights act to his credit, Johnson did not feel disposed to risk the complete alienation of the no-longer-solid South. "The only way Lyndon Johnson can lose this election," one Democrat said, "is for voters to cast their ballots on the question of whether or not they like Negroes." Along with the threat of a southern bolt from the party went the fear of a "white backlash" in the North among working-class Democrats. Also, looking beyond November, Johnson, like Kennedy, needed the support of powerful southern committee chairmen to enact his domestic legislation. Following Hamer's impassioned speech, Johnson called for a compromise. On August 23 Rauh was told that the Johnson backers were prepared to offer the MFDP delegates the right to serve as "honored guests" of the convention, but not to participate or vote. All major MFDP backers rejected this compromise.

As the pressure mounted, Johnson began twisting arms, effectively dangling the vice-presidency in front of Humphrey to lure his liberal friends away from the MFDP. Humphrey begged Martin Luther King, Jr., and other MFDP leaders to accept Johnson's plan. "Negroes want Negroes to represent them," Moses responded. But Johnson did not stop there. Rauh claimed that a black California supporter was told "that her husband wouldn't get a judgeship if she didn't leave us [MFDP], and the Secretary of the Army told the guy from the Canal Zone that he would lose his job if he didn't leave us." Johnson imported Walter Reuther to aid Humphrey in his efforts to woo liberals away from the MFDP. Reuther let Rauh and others know that if Humphrey did not get the nomination, the blame would rest on their shoulders. Swayed by Johnson's power play, several liberal committee members shifted their support from the MFDP to a new compromise backed by Johnson, which would give Aaron Henry and Edwin King at-large seats at the convention and accept the other delegates as "guests." In addition, the convention required a loyalty oath of regulars, established a civil rights commission to ensure future integrated delegations, and barred from future conventions any state delegations that discriminated against blacks. By August 25, liberals eager to assure Humphrey the vice-presidential nomination and Johnson the nomination on a united platform had forced the compromise on a reluctant MFDP delegation.[18]

The ADA took no official position on the compromise that Johnson offered the MFDP at the convention, but its approach to civil rights questions in general and the actions of members like Humphrey, Reuther, and Rauh who were present at the convention leave little doubt that the organization would have accepted it. In this situation, as often in its history, it inclined toward political effectiveness rather than impractical idealism. While the ADA opposed the lily-white delegation and supported black involvement in national politics, many members were not willing to sacrifice party unity for moral principle. As at the 1956 Democratic convention, at which the organization abandoned its insistence on a strong civil rights plank for the sake of party unity, the ADA in 1964 realized that its fortunes were closely aligned with the national Democratic party. Beyond the political calculation, many members, most notably Reuther and Humphrey, believed that the ADA had worked out a "reasonable" compromise between the president and the MFDP.

The MFDP's response to the compromise showed just how far apart liberal and black approaches had grown. It was the experience of the MFDP in 1964 that gave momentum to the drive within SNCC for racially separate and militant politics. Before that, as Julian Bond, a black Georgia political leader remarked, the staff was still "operating on the theory that here was a problem, you expose it to the world, the world says 'How Horrible!' and moves to correct it." John Lewis said the lesson of Atlantic City was "When you play the games and go by the rules, you still can lose, if you don't have the resources, if you're going to disrupt the natural order of things." Stokely Carmichael believed that the defeat of the MFDP challenge indicated the need for racial power. The experience showed "not merely that the national conscience was generally unreliable but that, very specifically, black people in Mississippi and throughout this country could not rely on their so-called allies." The militant leaders of COFO labeled the compromise a "back-of-the-bus" agreement. "Things could never be the same," SNCC's Cleveland Sellers wrote. "Never again were we lulled into believing that our task was exposing injustice so that the 'good' people of America could eliminate them. We left Atlantic City with the knowledge that the movement had turned into something else. After Atlantic City, our struggle was not for civil rights, but for liberation."[19]

In addition to dealing with civil rights, Johnson proposed a wide range of new social legislation. His program was a mixture of rural populist revulsion from the eastern "establishment," the conservatism of a self-made Texas businessman, and the liberalism of the poverty-haunted New Deal politician. While including new spending requests for health, education, and poverty programs adding up to an increase of $3.6 billion, Johnson's budget for 1964–65 advocated a tax cut and anticipated only a small deficit. Johnson knew he would not be able to get the tax bill through the Senate if the budget was over $100 billion. When his budget director Kermit Gordon protested that it would be impossible to meet the president's budget ceiling, Johnson snapped, "Unless you get that budget down around $100 billion, you won't pee one drop." Johnson accomplished this fiscal sleight of hand by cutting $300 million from military spending as well as $2.1 billion from domestic programs, including veterans' benefits and agricultural price supports. Above all, Johnson was counting on continued economic growth to sustain productivity and increase government revenue.[20]

Johnson's strategy paid off. In March he persuaded Congress to pass Kennedy's tax cut legislation, which called for a reduction of $9.1 billion in individual income taxes and a drop of $2.4 billion in corporate taxes, with two-thirds of the cuts taking effect in fiscal 1964 and the rest in 1965. Treasury Secretary Douglas Dillon claimed that the tax bill would "help launch a brilliant new chapter in the economic history of the United States." Johnson boasted to a nationwide audience after the signing that it was "the single most important step that we have taken to strengthen our economy since World War II." The skeptical House minority whip, Les Arends, was perhaps closer to the truth when he commented that Johnson promised "to give everyone more of everything—at less cost."[21]

While the ADA applauded Johnson for realizing the Keynesian proposition that a government deficit was a principal means of attaining full employment, it questioned his reliance on tax cuts rather than increases in expenditures. By "choosing to cut income taxes, and to restrain public expenditures," Johnson was favoring private affluence over urgent social needs—in education, welfare, health, housing, transportation, and conservation.[22] All factions in the ADA criticized the tax cut. "Tax reduction that curtails or limits public services has a double effect in comforting the comfortable and afflicting the poor," admonished John Kenneth Galbraith. He called the specific provisions of the 1964 tax bill that allowed a more generous capital gains exemption "a remarkably frank form of free-loading for high-bracket taxpayers." Keyserling complained that the "orgy of tax reduction" was misplaced because it aggravated an already inequitable distribution of income. "Relatively too much income and other incentives," he said, "have flowed to those who invest privately in the plant and equipment which add to our productive capabilities, and relatively too little . . . has flowed toward the expansion of demand for ultimate products."[23]

Johnson's next goal was to secure passage of a "War on Poverty" program first broached under Kennedy. The core of the program was an amorphous

concept of community action that would allow the poor to organize themselves. Daniel Moynihan remembered that "the resulting program sent to
Congress March 16, 1964, thus represented not a choice among policies so
much as a collection of them." Trying to keep costs down, Congress funded
the program with $962.5 million in its first year and established the Office of
Economic Opportunity (OEO) to administer it. The architects of the War on
Poverty designed the community action programs to provide opportunity, not
to provide quantitative relief through the provision of money and jobs. The
other parts of the program—the Job Corps, grants for low income college
students, loans for small business, a domestic Peace Corps, as well as a job-
training program for low-income adults and the Youth Conservation Corps—
were self-help programs that provided training as the opportunity of employment but stopped far short of providing jobs. Only the Youth Conservation
Corps promised immediate employment.[24] Johnson had hoped that liberals
would rally around his new poverty program; after all, it went beyond the
original ideas discussed during the Kennedy years. What he did not realize
was that liberals themselves were seriously divided over how to wage the War
on Poverty. While all were uplifted by the president's commitment to the
struggle, they disagreed on how to win it.

Most moderates and reformers tended to accept, with varying degrees of
enthusiasm, the ideas of John Kenneth Galbraith, who believed that an assault on poverty needed to deal with both the structural causes of poverty
and the personal and cultural characteristics of the poor. "The problem of
poverty in the United States is the problem of people who for reasons of lo-
cation, education, health, environment in youth or mental deficiency, or race
are not able to participate effectively—or at all—in the economic life of the
nation," he wrote in *Harper's* in 1964. The only way to address these deeply
rooted institutional problems, Galbraith argued, was through large expenditures of public funds, outlays that by their very nature redistribute income.
He did not believe that the problem of poverty could be solved through economic growth alone. "It won't be accomplished simply by stepping up the
growth rate any more than it will be accomplished by incantation or ritualis-
tic washing of the feet. Growth is only for those who can take advantage of
it." Poverty, he maintained, needed to be addressed directly through a wide
range of government programs—investment to conserve and develop resources,
assistance to new industries, vastly improved education, training and retraining, medical and mental care, youth employment, housing, slum abatement,
and the assurance of full civic equality.[25]

Leon Keyserling, still the ADA's most dominant voice on economic matters, was a disciple of the economic-growth or full-employment approach to
eradicating poverty. Reflecting on Johnson's poverty programs, Keyserling
commented, "Jobs are the big thing. How did the president's economic advisors forget it? How did the economic reports forget it? How did the war
against poverty forget it?"[26] Keyserling perceptively pointed out that "large
inroads against poverty and deprivation without high economic growth would
imply redistributive programs so immense that politically they would be en-

tirely unattainable." Yet, Keyserling did not accept the argument that economic growth alone would wipe out poverty. "A bigger and better pie is not feasible if too much sugar and not enough flour are used," he said. Keyserling believed that sustained and increased rates of economic growth could finance larger outlays of public funds for Social Security and other programs designed for specific groups. The answer to the problem of poverty, he claimed, lies not in the creation of a single agency like the OEO but rather in the "deficiencies of the nation-wide economic and social policies under which the poor must live." Ten poor people could be "helped immediately by improvements in these policies . . . for every one who could be helped immediately or even in the long run by highly personalized treatment." Keyserling objected to the conservative structural approach to poverty that the Johnson administration employed. The "wars against poverty and low economic growth and unemployment are really one," he believed, and manpower training, retraining, and education, though desirable, were not the way to fight poverty. Economic growth, which creates a high enough level of aggregate demand, can reduce "unemployment to minimum levels, educate many people on the job, and tell us what to train others for." Keyserling warned, "The anti-poverty war under the Economic Opportunity Act attributes far too much poverty to personal characteristics of the poor requiring corrective treatment, rather than to systemic defaults in our general economic performance and programs." From his macro perspective, Keyserling saw only three ways to transfer income to the poor: reduce unemployment to minimum levels; enlarge the incomes of those employed but receiving substandard pay; and allocate larger shares of the national income to those who cannot be employed, like older people and women with small children but without a husband.[27] What it all "really boils down to," he concluded, "is that the kind of war against poverty we should be waging requires much more planning and coordination at the national level than we have thus far been equipped or willing to undertake."[28]

At its Seventeenth Annual Convention in May 1964, the ADA tried to reconcile Galbraith's and Keyserling's criticisms of the War on Poverty. While it "wholeheartedly" applauded and welcomed Johnson's "declaration of unconditional war on poverty," it charged that the president's proposals did not go far enough to "adequately deal with the awesome economical and motivational problems raised by the plight of the unemployed, underemployed, underpaid and unemployable." It claimed there was no need for the president to choose between the social welfare and the employment approaches to poverty. "The poor are poor," the convention resolved, "because their incomes are low, and the war against poverty must include action to raise substandard incomes, whether by employment or otherwise." Showing Keyserling's strong influence, the convention stated, "Full employment alone will not win the war against poverty, but everything we do will be easier if it is done in a full employment economy. And raising the standards of productivity and consumption of the poor will be a major step toward a totally employed economy." While the ADA said the importance of the Economic Opportunity Act "can not be over-estimated," it also declared "that the war against poverty must be fought on a broad front." Basic changes needed to be made in benefits and coverage of government transfer payment programs. Unemployment compensation had to be increased and extended and restrictive eligibility requirements eliminated. It advocated raising the minimum wage for $1.25 per hour to $2.00 per hour and expanding its coverage to the estimated fifteen million Americans who were uncovered. It also advocated substantial improvements in the Social Security and old-age assistance programs.[29]

In deference to Galbraith's supporters, the resolution also addressed the cultural aspects of poverty. It said that any program to fight poverty needed to attack "ignorance, squalor, despair, discrimination, and the alienation of the impoverished from our society and its values." Because the ADA believed that the War on Poverty had to attack the lack of mobility that mired the poor in impoverishment from generation to generation, it "wholeheartedly" supported the emphasis on jobs, training, education, and services for young people. "In our view," it said, "the community action program . . . and the experimental projects for training and employment of unemployed fathers . . . would inevitably be focused on providing the environment and the means for building the competence of young people and restoring their opportunities and motivations."[30]

Having come to the presidency by the whim of an assassin's bullet and having spent his first year in office successfully implementing his predecessor's legislative program, Johnson saw the 1964 election as an opportunity to win the office in his own right. Humphrey's efforts in resolving the credentials fight helped earn the Minnesotan the second spot on the Democratic ticket. He was a logical choice for Johnson. With the South prevented from bolting, Johnson had to increase his hold on the North and West. When Johnson asked Humphrey why he would want such a "thankless" job, Humphrey reasoned, "I thought I could be of help with liberals, blacks, and the labor movement, areas in which Johnson could use help if he needed it at all. My greatest strength lay then in the northern industrial states." Johnson demanded complete loyalty from his vice-president, warning Humphrey, "This is like a marriage with no chance of divorce. I need complete and unswerving loyalty." It was an agreement Humphrey was later to regret.[31]

Johnson had the good fortune to oppose Barry Goldwater, an Arizona senator who combined laissez-faire economics with a militant anticommunism. At his party's July convention in San Francisco, Goldwater chose an obscure conservative congressman from New York named William Miller as his running mate. Politics for Goldwater was an expression of personal conscience, not an exercise in social consensus. In his acceptance speech in San Francisco's cavernous Cow Palace, Goldwater spoke about "law and order," "the sanctity of private property," "violence in our streets," and the "growing menace . . . to life, to limb, and property . . . particularly in our great cities." He made a deliberate effort to taunt his moderate foes: "I would remind you that extremism in defense of liberty is no vice. And let me remind you also that moderation in pursuit of justice is no virtue." The root of the problem, he said, is the welfare state. "If it is entirely proper for government to take from some to give to others, then won't some be led to believe that they can rightfully take from anyone who has more than they?" Goldwater's call to arms was the slogan "In your heart you know he's right." Some critics developed a substitute slogan, "In your guts you know he's nuts." A more irreverent version also appeared: "In your heart you know he's right, but in your ass you know it's just gas."[32]

As in the past, Republicans hoped to discredit the Democratic ticket by tying Humphrey to the ADA. On hearing that the Democrats had nominated Humphrey, Goldwater responded, "It destroys the myth that the Johnson Administration is conservative." Humphrey's philosophy, he said, "is that of the Americans for Democratic Action, which proposes bigger and bigger government programs and more and more government control."[33] Goldwater left most of the dirty work to his running mate, Miller. In his first campaign address, in Lockport, New York, Miller charged that Humphrey "was a founder of the Americans for Democratic Action, unquestionably the most influential organization in our nation's capital attempting to subvert and transform our government into a foreign socialistic totalitarianism." "Do we want a Vice President from the Americans for Democratic Action," he asked in his standard campaign speech, repeated time and again, "which advocates diplomatic recognition of Red China . . . which advocates the admission of Red China into the United Nations . . . which advocates removal of the travel ban so that Chinese Communists can come travel through this country?"[34]

The Republican National Committee used the same tactic in congressional races to defeat liberal Democrats. The Republican candidate, according to a prepared script, would ask the audience, "Just how close is America to Socialism?" Answering his own question, the candidate would say, "Just as close as the ADA can get it." The problem, of course, is that "rubber stamp Congressmen who blindly follow the ADA line are pushing the ADA legislative proposals" and "helping to bring about the ADA dream of a socialized welfare state in America." Claiming that the Democratic challenger was on the "ADA Honor Roll," the Republican candidate warned, "You can vote against the ADA on November 6th. Vote against your rubber stamp congressman. Vote 'Nay' on the ADA—Vote Republican all the way."[35]

The Republican attempts to use the ADA to convince the public that Johnson was a closet socialist were bound to fail. Not only had Johnson already cultivated the image of a reformer safely in the American mainstream, but he also raised troubling questions about Goldwater's stability. Johnson's victory turned out to be staggering. He won every one of the East's 142 electoral votes and made a clean sweep of the Midwest, the Mountain and Border states, and the West. Only in the South did Goldwater salvage some victories, capturing Alabama, Georgia, Louisiana, Mississippi, and South Carolina, as well as his home state of Arizona. LBJ's electoral margin of 486 to 52 was second only to Roosevelt's 523-to-8 margin over Alf Landon in 1936. His 61 percent of the vote and 15-million plurality were the largest in history. Democrats captured huge majorities in Congress, 68 to 32 in the Senate and 295 to 140 in the House.

In many ways the ADA did not mind its new notoriety. While it had grown accustomed to bearing the brunt of conservative attacks, this was the first time it had been inserted as a major issue in a presidential race. Many ADA members, and apparently much of the public, perceived Goldwater's attacks as what John Roche called "the death rattle of a politically bankrupt" candidate. It was especially heartening that the attacks did not work. Leon Shull bragged that identification with the ADA was a "kiss of victory" in the election. "Every candidate for the Senate who had a liberal quotient of 75% or more on the ADA voting record," with one exception, won reelection.[36]

A strong current of optimism ran through the ADA in the months following the election. Most ADA members would have accepted Schlesinger's declaration at the organization's Eighteenth Annual Convention that 1965 offered "the greatest opportunity for constructive liberalism in a generation."[37] The organization had reason to be optimistic. Since its founding convention in the winter of 1947, the ADA had advocated expanded welfare benefits, federal aid to education and housing, and programs designed to alleviate poverty and guarantee the rights of blacks to participate in American society. While Truman's Fair Deal and Kennedy's New Frontier were sympathetic to the ADA's agenda and, at times, able to push through small items, neither was able to muster the political will or support to wage an all-out offensive for liberal programs. But 1964–65 was different. Not only was most of the ADA agenda written into the Democratic party's platform, but Johnson's triumph at the polls also seemed to indicate that the country was at last ready to accept a greater government role.

Still, there was also reason for caution. Most liberals knew that public attitudes could be fickle and that the opportunity for reform would be all too brief. Leon Shull told the convention, "Nineteen sixty-five will be a year of challenge to American liberalism. . . . We must realize that the consensus that exists today will not exist forever and that the programs that have thus far been proposed for America's future fall far short of what is needed." John Roche, who saw "no reason why a full liberal program [could] not be won in the 89th Congress," admonished the ADA "to prevent a repetition of 1936 when FDR's great electoral victory resulted in very little substance."[38]

Lingering doubts still existed about Johnson's character and his commitment to liberal programs. Everything about his background—his long years as a congressional manipulator, his family's accumulation of considerable wealth through a government-regulated television station, his very appearance and mannerisms, which easily suggested the riverboat gambler—all had made the public skeptical about his basic motives as soon as he entered the White House. His association with Bobby Baker, a close aide who managed to amass a $42 million nest egg in his spare time as the $19,600-a-year Democratic Majority Secretary, did little to allay doubts. Even Johnson's landslide election in 1964 and his legislative success with the Great Society programs brought him no surcease from liberal suspicion. Although he appears sincere, the

New Republic commented, the fact is "that he is an unbeliever in absolutes, a highly pragmatic and extremely crafty doer. It will be a great error if people either at home or abroad are lulled by his sermonizing into believing that he would sacrifice all for love or that all he wants is the lowest common denominator of agreement."[39]

Believing that the country was ready for liberal programs, the ADA set its legislative sights high. In so doing, it established the tone for its dealings with the Johnson administration. It warned, "Warmed-over programs from the past will not suffice to build the great society or the kind of world to which the ADA's energies, intelligence, and organization are devoted." "Rhetoric and timid programs will neither conquer poverty nor build that world we are determined to have," it said. "Only bold programs commensurate in scope and range with the challenges and opportunities confronting us will satisfy the need of nations." Two months later, Edward Hollander, in a press conference at the Willard Hotel, set 1967 as a deadline for achieving full employment and 1970 for abolishing poverty and raising every American family above the level of mere economic subsistence. Hollander called for a "realistic and attainable" fiscal 1967 budget of $125 billion, adding that by 1969 the budget should grow to $150 billion. He advised the president to act quickly in order to "make significant inroads on American poverty." He also recommended immediate action to increase Social Security benefits, expand unemployment compensation benefits, upgrade welfare benefits, and raise the minimum wage. Hollander urged passage of a $40 billion, four-year program of federal aid to education as well as of a comprehensive medical care program for the aged.[40]

Johnson had a few reform ideas of his own. Following his landslide victory over Goldwater, Johnson and the massive new majority in both houses launched his Great Society. Exhilarated, LBJ interpreted the election as a mandate for further domestic reform. "Hurry, boys, hurry," he told his aides. "Get that legislation up to the Hill and out. Eighteen months from now ol' Landslide Lyndon will be Lame-Duck Lyndon." Over the next few months Johnson prepared, and Congress willingly approved, an education act that authorized $1.3 billion for direct assistance to public schools. Congress also passed the Higher Education Act of 1965, authorizing $650 million in federal aid to colleges and universities for scholarships to needy students and to strengthen teaching and research; the Appalachina Regional Development Act, earmarking $1.1 billion for highways, health centers, and economic development; a Medicare bill, enlarged to include low-cost insurance against doctor's bills as well as hospital and nursing expenses for all those over sixty-five; and the Housing and Urban Development Act, mandating construction of 240,000 units of low-rent public housing and authorizing $2.9 billion in federal grants for urban renewal over a four-year period. In addition, Congress created the federal Department of Housing and Urban Development of cabinet rank. The administration also set out to control pollution and to give the government authority to set safety standards for automobile manufacturers. "Working in the White House during this period produced on occasion an almost eerie feeling," Eric Goldman has observed. "The legislation rolled through the House and Senate in such profusion and so methodically that you seemed part of some vast, overpowering machinery, oiled to purr."[41]

Despite initiating new domestic programs, Johnson still paid homage to the magical spending ceiling of $100 billion. "The President wanted a budget figure around $99.5 billion," said one White House aide, "and by God, he got it." The fiscal 1966 budget, announced in January 1965, reflects, the president said, "hard decisions and difficult choices . . . what we must do, but not for all we would like to do." The new budget called for an increase in the spending on the War on Poverty to $1.3 billion and on education from $1.5 to $2.6 billion, while defense would see a $300 million reduction. All told, domestic health, labor, and welfare programs increased from $28.9 billion to $34.1 billion.[42]

The National Board called Johnson's proposed budget one of bold aims but "timid numbers." Edward Hollander, chairman of the ADA Executive Committee, praised the administration for having "a policy of compassion" but said the budget would neither promote full employment nor accomplish the president's vision of the Great Society.[43] Hollander, speaking on behalf of the ADA, said that the expenditure side of the budget "appeased the Neo-lithics." The expenditures were "particularly inadequate measured against the brave words about 'economic progress,' 'human compassion,' and 'new challenges and opportunities.'" Nowhere in the expenditure side of the budget, Hollander charged, was "there a reflection of programs which [would] come close to meeting the acknowledged needs" of education or housing. Johnson's so-called "all-out attack on the problem of poverty" was "represented by a slight elevation of $500 million, equivalent to about one half of one percent of the Budget, and one tenth of one percent of the national output." Hollander did not question Johnson's sincerity but did question his intentions "that these brave, well-meant words should be so meagerly supported that there does not appear to be the basis in the 1965 Budget even to make a meaningful start toward mounting an 'all-out attack.'" Hollander concluded by quoting from one disappointed liberal: "He has put the mirrors where the money ought to be."[44]

ADA members flooded Capitol Hill testifying before House and Senate committees in support of the administration's proposals for education, housing, and poverty. In every case the ADA position was the same: while praising the administration's proposals as a good starting point, it criticized them for not going far enough. For most ADA members the War on Poverty was the most disappointing aspect of the new program. The war was actually very feeble, it charged, and was not "grappling with the main factors in the composition of poverty itself." Borrowing directly from Keyserling, the organization claimed that about 50 percent of all poverty related "directly to the mainstream of the employment and unemployment problem." Another 27 percent consisted of people over sixty-five years of age who could be helped by old-age insurance and pension payments. About 29 percent of the poor were single-houhehold families headed by women who could be helped through a guaranteed national income. Finally, about 15 percent consisted of farmers who could be helped by restructuring farm policies.[45]

By the end of 1965, however, Johnson's heart was no longer in the struggle, and he was giving little presidential support to the effort. The community action programs became mired in local power struggles between advocates for the poor and local Democratic leaders. When he recognized that the program was raising trouble with his political allies, Johnson's humanitarian instincts gave way to practical politics. Administration officials also worried about creeping inflation. In its fifth year of expansion, the economy was beginning to show signs of strain. The annual rate of increase in productivity slipped from 3.4 percent to 2.5 percent. Federal expenditures were running well beyond the anticipated $99.7 billion. Many economists began to wonder out loud how to finance a rapidly escalating war in Vietnam, achieve the essential goals of the Great Society, and sustain prosperity without inflation. "We are in danger of too much steam," Johnson's advisers warned on December 4. As Arthur Okun, a member of the President's Council of Economic Advisers, said, "We've been chasing this rabbit for five years. Now we've got to learn what to do with it."[46]

For these reasons, the ADA's hopes for the Great Society were never realized. Many ADA members believed that Johnson's original proposals were too timid and did not adequately deal with the enormous problems he was trying to address. Although Johnson had initiated more domestic legislation than any president since Roosevelt, he could not satisfy the soaring expectations of most liberals.

As his Great Society was being challenged from both the left and the right, Johnson's ephemeral consensus faced another challenge from the civil rights movement. In Selma, Alabama, Martin Luther King, Jr., planned to stage his fight for voting rights. Selma was a city of 29,500 people—14,400 whites, 15,100 blacks. Its voting rolls were 99 percent white. On January 2, 1965, King announced, just a few weeks after accepting the Nobel Peace Prize, that he planned to dramatize injustice in Selma "by marching by the thousands to the places of registration." "We are not asking," he warned, "we are demanding the ballot." Over the next month King tried to provoke Sheriff Jim Clark into a confrontation. Unable to duplicate the moral drama of Birmingham, King on March 6 called on blacks to march from Selma to Montgomery to present a petition of grievances to the governor. When Governor Wallace issued an order proscribing the demonstration, King canceled the march and went to Atlanta, claiming he needed to minister to his congregation. SNCC militants, however, were not about to back down. On the next day, Sunday, March 7, as planned, they led five hundred chanting protesters along U.S. Highway 80 to Montgomery. As they crossed Pettus Bridge, state troopers and sheriff's deputies—known affectionately among white locals as "squirrel shooters"—attacked a peaceful column of six hundred blacks, sending some fifty demonstrators to the hospital. White spectators cheered the police on, while Sheriff

Clark bellowed, "Get those God Damn niggers!" Television cameras once again captured the frightening scenes for a horrified nation.[47]

It appeared that the strategy of massive demonstrations had paid off. Supporters staged marches in Detroit, New York, Chicago, and Los Angeles. Sympathizers in Washington conducted sit-ins at the White House, at the Capitol, and, during rush-hour traffic, on Pennsylvania Avenue. On March 15 President Johnson went before a joint session of Congress to ask for guarantees for voting rights of all Americans. He demanded that Congress enact legislation that would place federal registrars in every county that did not have a representative black voting turnout. Civil rights leaders hailed the message. "A moment at the summit in the life of our nation," Roy Wilkins said in a telegram to the president. James Farmer, national director of CORE, described it as "an eloquent and substantial statement." Bayard Rustin called the speech the "most eloquent and forthright" of President Johnson's career. Martin Luther King, Jr., called it "one of the most eloquent, unequivocal and passionate pleas for human rights ever made by a President of the United States."[48]

The ADA responded to the events in Selma by renewing its call for "legislation establishing Federal registrars as a remedy for illegal denial of the right to register and vote." While it supported the thrust of Johnson's legislation, the ADA worked with the Leadership Conference on Civil Rights to broaden the coverage of Johnson's bill. Among the proposals it supported were elimination of the poll tax; addition of an automatic triggering device of less than 25 percent Negro registration, rather than 50 percent; abolition of the requirement that a prospective registrant had to see a state official before using the services of a federal registrar; and increased protection from intimidation in the registration process.[49] Johnson, however, opposed any changes in his original legislation and fought off attempts by the ADA and the Leadership Conference on Civil Rights to strengthen the bill.

Five months later, on August 6, in the President's Room of the Capitol, just off the Senate Chamber, where 104 years earlier, to the day, Lincoln had signed a bill freeing slaves impressed into the service of the Confederacy, Johnson signed the Voting Rights Act of 1965. With a statue of Abraham Lincoln to his right and the Great Emancipator's bust to his left, and behind him the Trumbull painting of Cornwallis's surrender to George Washington at Yorktown, Johnson recalled when the first blacks came to Jamestown in 1619. "They came in darkness and chains. Today we strike away the last major shackles of those fierce and ancient bonds."[50]

The civil rights movement, however, did not stop with the passage of the act; it simply entered a new, more militant phase. Ironically, just when Johnson was legislating into law the most progressive domestic legislation in history, black discontent reached a new high. "We're only flesh," remarked one SNCC leader. "I could understand people not wanting to be beaten anymore. . . . Black capacity to believe [that a white person] would really open his heart, open his life to nonviolent appeal was running out." James Forman, the executive secretary of SNCC, captured the increased militancy of blacks when he said, "If we can't sit at the table of democracy, then we'll knock the fucking legs off."[51] The cries for black militancy revealed the limits of the liberal faith in gradualism. The question remained: Would militancy serve the black cause any better? In 1965, most liberals, while recognizing the limits of their approach, saw no hope in violence.

On August 11, just five days after Johnson signed the Voting Rights Act, the most destructive race riot in more than two decades began in Watts, a part of the Black Channel, a seventy-two-square-mile area that housed 90 percent of Los Angeles County's 600,000 blacks. For four nights marauding mobs in the black suburb burned and killed, while 500 policemen and 5,000 National Guardsmen struggled to contain the fury. By the end of the week, 35 were dead, 900 injured, and 4,300 arrested, and property damage exceeded $100 million. While the struggle in the South raised the hopes of ghetto blacks in the North, it did nothing to improve their condition. Violence became a means of expressing their rage at the limited pace and scope of racial change and their bitterness over increased white opposition to their minimal advances. Militant blacks did little to reassure whites with their promises that more was to follow. Forman said, "There's going to be a considerable amount of violence if major changes are not made." The author Louis Lomax: "The Negro masses are angry and restless, tired of prolonged legal battles that end in papers decrees." James Baldwin: "To be a Negro in this country and to be relatively conscious is to be in a rage almost all the time."[52]

Like most Americans, ADA members were confused and uncertain about how to respond to the Watts riot. While the ADA called the Voting Rights Act "a charter of freedom implementing, at long last, the great Civil War Amendments to protect Negro rights," less than a week later, after surveying the actual gains blacks had made over the preceding twenty years, it admitted the limits of gradual reform. After all the pain and anguish of two decades of struggling for civil rights, it recognized how little had been done to confront the economic aspects of racism, especially in many northern cities, where discrimination, though more subtle, was no less pernicious. In 1965 the ADA *World* editorialized, "Less than forty percent of the negroes throughout the South are registered to vote and less than twenty percent in the deep South." Black schools are "still two years behind white schools," which in turn are "years behind the rest of the nation." The annual income of the typical black averages "one-half that of his white peer and that is still way below average for the rest of the nation."[53]

The ADA's immediate response to this realization was to broaden the federal efforts for racial justice. Indeed, it openly criticized the administration's civil rights enforcement, calling for better enforcement of existing legislation, urging "a vastly increased program of federal registrars," and insisting that federal agencies like the U.S. Commission on Civil Rights had "to engage in an active, vigorous education campaign to encourage registration." It declared the Johnson administration "timid, weak and vacillating" in enforcing the 1964 and 1965 Civil Rights Acts and supported the creation of a congressional subcommittee to oversee enforcement because of "the failure of the

Administration to come to grips with its responsibility in the civil rights area."
It cited a number of areas of nonenforcement: refusal to cut off funds from
school districts that failed to desegregate, unwillingness to send federal registrars into the South to enforce registration, and lack of resolve in filing suits
against employers who discriminated in hiring. "Words do not make a dream
reality and laws without enforcement do not make the promise of those laws
a fact," the ADA declared. "Only rigorous enforcement of both the 1964 and
1965 Civil Rights Act will bring an end to segregation and enable the Negro
in the South to retain his faith in the federal government and the representative process."[54]

As for the riots, the ADA claimed that at best they were "understand-
able." The organization believed the riots were "to be condemned, not con-
doned," but it said they should be "condemned with an understanding of
what caused them and a rededication to meet the underlying causes and provide a human existence for the people of Watts." The only way to prevent
future riots was to provide the people of Watts, and of all other ghettos, with
jobs.[55]

In the fall of 1965 a sense of frustration settled over the organization. The
Great Society had raised the hopes of liberals but had not fulfilled all their
promises, and the close liberal-black coalition of the preceding two decades
was unraveling. The ADA's frustration with the Great Society and its bewilderment at the increased militancy of the civil rights movement stemmed
from the tension inherent in postwar liberal ideology. ADA liberals believed
that problems like racial discrimination and poverty could be solved through
legislation designed to guarantee minorities equal access to economic and
political opportunities and through carefully managed economic growth. Liberals, in other words, believed they could achieve their ambitious agenda with
only incremental and fairly conservative means. However unrealistic that approach might appear, it was responsible for most of the significant gains made
in social welfare and civil rights during the 1960s. Yet, in another way, it
contributed to its own demise by raising expectations much higher than could
reasonably be satisfied. After years of sustained economic growth, poverty
persisted; despite two significant pieces of civil rights legislation, blacks still
lacked basic opportunities enjoyed by most whites. Moreover, blacks, in particular, were resentful, claiming that liberals oversold a flawed product. In
desperation they turned to more militant means to achieve the equality liberals
had promised for so long, even though militancy offered even less realistic
hope for change.

The ADA criticized Johnson for his halfhearted commitment to the War
on Poverty and lackluster enforcement of voting rights. The real problem with
the Great Society, however, had less to do with Johnson's personal failings
than with the limits of liberal vision. Many reform liberals in the ADA understood that to be true to their ideal liberals would have to advocate structural
solutions—most notably, redistribution of income and federally enforced

quotas—to the problems of poverty and racial discrimination. Older ADA members, especially traditionalists, but also most moderates, resisted such suggestions. If Johnson's program met so much opposition, how could liberals develop public support for programs that went significantly beyond the limited range of the Great Society? In 1965 no one in the ADA was prepared to confront this difficult question.

8

The Agony of Dissent:
Liberals and Vietnam, 1965–1967

Vietnam, Godfrey Hodgson has written, "became the organizing principle around which all the doubts and disillusionments of the years of crisis since 1963, and all the deeper discontents hidden under the glossy surface of the confident years, coalesced into one great rebellion." The ADA faced no issue as explosive as that of the Vietnam War. The journalist David Halberstam remarked, "Nothing mirrors the dilemma of the liberals more than the terrible divisions within the Americans for Democratic Action, a group which had for decades focused the tastes and goals of American liberalism."[1] The war heightened tensions between the traditional, moderate, and reform groups in the organization, making compromise and consensus—key ingredients of the liberal faith—impossible. Despite the heroic efforts of the moderate faction in the organization, the war drove a deep wedge between the reform and traditional groups. As protest against the war grew louder, the ADA found it even more difficult to maintain its role as an independent voice of liberalism while also working with the administration.

For all his experience in national politics, Johnson came to the presidency ill-prepared for the art of international diplomacy. Having had little responsibility for foreign policy during his years as vice-president, and almost none earlier, Johnson was disposed to use in his relations with the leaders of other countries the same techniques that worked so well with recalcitrant senators— some strong words, a little arm-twisting, and, as a last resort, compromise and negotiation. The problem in Asia, he claimed, was that the North Vietnamese believed that the United States lacked the will to stick it out. As he said at one point, "The need now is not for negotiations but to get the message across to them—leave your neighbor alone and we can all have peace and get ahead with our business."[2]

Like others of his generation, Johnson had learned too well the lessons of Munich. Hubert Humphrey commented that his former boss believed "that aggression unchecked was aggression unleashed." Johnson, in a press conference in 1965, explained that America's defeat in South Vietnam "would encourage and spur on those who seek to conquer all free nations within their reach." He went on, "This is the clearest lesson of our time. From Munich until today we have learned that to yield to aggression brings only greater threats." Having remembered the chastising Truman received when China "fell" to the Communists, Johnson told the U.S. ambassador to Vietnam, Henry Cabot Lodge, Jr., "I am not going to be the president who saw Vietnam go the way China went." Granted free rein by the Gulf of Tonkin resolution in August 1964—passed overwhelmingly by Congress in the wake of a purported attack on American destroyers off the North Vietnamese coast, it granted the president wide powers to prosecute the war—Johnson planned to fight a presidential war without congressional interference.[3]

Johnson's closest advisers, the "best and the brightest" left over from the Kennedy administration, confirmed his suspicions. They felt with considerable conviction that they were upholding the containment policies the United States had pursued since the late 1940s. They were, however, frequently vague as to what they were containing: at times they stressed China, at other times communism, and at still other times wars of liberation in general. Whatever or whoever the enemy, they were certain of one thing—U.S. withdrawal from Vietnam would encourage disorder throughout the world and drastically weaken American influence. If the United States pulled out of Vietnam, Johnson warned on one occasion, "it might as well give up everywhere else—pull out of Berlin, Japan, South America." Yet Johnson was also driven by his fear that a Communist victory in Vietnam would undermine support for his Great Society.[4]

The escalation itself began early in 1965 after the Vietcong rebels killed 7 Americans and wounded 109 at Pleiku, a mountain town two hundred miles north of Saigon, where 1,000 American military personnel were stationed. Anticipating such a need, just twelve hours after the attack, the White House organized strikes in response to "provocations ordered and directed by the Hanoi regime." Three days later Johnson authorized regular bombing, again on targets chosen in 1964. In April, after Vietcong attacks had almost succeeded in blowing up the American embassy in Saigon, he stepped up the dispatch of ground troops. While satisfying hawks by expanding America's commitment, Johnson hoped to woo the doves with several dramatic peace initiatives. In a speech at Johns Hopkins University on April 7, Johnson affirmed that the United States was prepared to enter into "unconditional discussions" and even held out the offer of a billion-dollar economic development program for the Mekong River Valley region, a program "on a scale even to dwarf the TVA." In early May the president approved a five-day bombing pause. Despite his offer to participate in "unconditional discussions," his administration had no real desire to begin serious negotiations at a time when America's bargaining position was so weak. His offer was hardly unconditional. Johnson insisted that the United States would cease the bombing only when North Vietnam withdrew its forces from the South, and he refused to accept any peace terms that included the National Liberation Front (NLF) in a coalition government in South Vietnam.[5]

Only a few cautious liberals challenged the official optimism from Washington, and protest against the war was restricted to a few disgruntled voices on the fringe of American politics. The *Nation* and the *New Republic,* along with Democratic senators like South Dakota's George McGovern and Idaho's Frank Church and influential journalists like Walter Lippmann, expressed skepticism about the assumptions guiding Johnson's policy as well as fear of its ultimate consequences. Liberals were also concerned with Vietnam's effect on America's moral leadership in the world. Perhaps most troubling for liberals was Johnson's dishonesty in justifying American involvement in the conflict. "Never has a small coterie conducted a war with more concealment and dishonesty to its people," editorialized the *New Republic,* "than has been practiced, first under John F. Kennedy, now under Lyndon B. Johnson." Many liberals were shocked when Adlai Stevenson revealed in an interview with Eric Sevareid that Johnson had turned aside a number of peace feelers. Stevenson's revelations, according to the *Nation,* "horrified even some of the most experienced manipulators of public opinion." "Official lying works for a time," the *Nation* added, "but when the curtain of secrecy is momentarily pulled aside the revelations are all the more damaging." One newspaper editor said, "I feel as if I have been cuckolded." "It seemed fairly obvious that while the Administration might talk peace for domestic consumption, the arms build-up and intensification of the war were its real objectives. The rest was camouflage."[6]

While a few Republicans hoped to gain political advantage from Johnson's difficulties, most political leaders were confused by the situation. An Associated Press poll showed that of eighty-three senators, only two called for an end to U.S. involvement and only three for escalation. The rest agreed with the Oklahoma Democrat Mike Monroney: "We should do what we are doing, but do it even better." Congress's uncertainty reflected broader public confusion. In February 1965, 66 percent of the American public wanted the United States to continue its present policy; only 19 percent wanted it to withdraw. Americans split on whether the war would expand: 44 percent said it would; 43 percent said it would not. When asked whether they would be less or more inclined to vote for their congressman if he advocated sending more men to Vietnam, 33 percent were more inclined and 38 percent less inclined.[7]

The war was perplexing, especially for a generation nurtured on the Cold War and the Korean War. Many liberals expressed reservations about the tactical decisions in Vietnam and were genuinely concerned about the consequences of America's actions, but none were ready to abandon South Vietnam to the Communists. For all its alarm, the *New Republic* shared many of the same assumptions that guided the administration—that American military power could force the Communists to seek a negotiated settlement that would allow for a free South Vietnam. "The US could of course pick up its marbles and quit right now," wrote the *New Republic.* "But this would mean the Communists getting all they want, on their terms. A better alternative is for the US to participate in terms."[8]

Within the ADA the war increased tensions between the traditionalist, moderate, and reform groups. Each group viewed the war in the context of its larger design for liberalism. Reform liberals, opposing the war on its own terms, saw antiwar agitation as an opportunity for liberals to reach out to dissatisfied young, pull them into the political system, and create a new coalition that would endure for a generation. Moderates also saw the advantage of channeling student fervor into the Democratic party but still refused to give up on the old coalition. Gus Tyler of the ILGWU and his traditional supporters, on the other hand, never accepted the idea of a "new liberalism." Their liberalism, still rooted in the experience of the Great Depression and the early Cold War, held firm to the old coalition and the New Deal agenda, including containment of communism in Asia.

The traditionalists saw the war as another example of international Communist aggression. In Vietnam, John Roche told the ADA National Convention in April 1965, the United States was "fighting a carefully limited war in the effort to attain a perfectly reasonable objective: not the destruction of the Hanoi regime, but the maintenance of the integrity of the Saigon Government from Communist aggression masked as civil war." Traditionalists found Johnson's actions justified and prudent; moreover, convinced of the enormous productive capability of the American economy, they did not believe that the war would drain resources away from the Great Society. More than anything else, they wanted to maintain the New Deal coalition and fulfill its unfinished agenda and to avoid a divisive debate on an issue as seemingly peripheral as that of Vietnam.[9]

For the reform group the war represented everything that was wrong with American foreign policy. Vietnam was not an arena for superpower competition, and America was not, as Johnson claimed, there to save a bastion of democracy from an aggressive worldwide Communist conspiracy. It was a nasty, ugly local war that should have been of little interest to the United States. In keeping with their larger agenda for liberalism, reformers wanted the ADA, by leading the opposition to the war, to attract new younger members and cast aside its more conservative labor support. Ironically, they were very close to the realistic critique of Hans Morgenthau, also an ADA board member, and Walter Lippmann. "Does the U.S. propose to become the monitor of the world," asked Allard Lowenstein, "this country which itself has plenty of monitoring left to do at home?" They called upon the United States to cease the bombing, negotiate with the NLF, and abide by the results of free elections even if the Communists won.[10]

The moderate faction was caught between the conflicting agendas of the reform and traditionalist groups. For a number of reasons, older liberals like Schlesinger and Galbraith were less willing to criticize the original decision to escalate. For one thing, they feared a divisive national debate on Vietnam. "This is the greatest opportunity for constructive liberalism in a generation," Schlesinger told the 1965 ADA convention. It appeared to ADA founding fathers like Rauh, Galbraith, and Schlesinger, who had long worked to give the ADA the recognition they felt it deserved, that they had finally reached their moment in the sun. Johnson had campaigned on a platform calling for the enactment of liberal programs that the ADA had advocated for twenty years, and he chose as his running mate ADA's own Hubert Humphrey. Even repeated Republican attempts to discredit the Democratic ticket by tying it to the ADA—a technique that had worked well in the 1950s—could not prevent the largest popular landslide up to that time. Moderates had every incentive not to alienate the administration.

Also, most of the moderates, imbued with Niebuhrian pessimism, were suspicious of the younger reform group's simplistic critique of the war. "When I hear the confident and glib liberal answers to questions which have baffled the statesmen of the ages, I sometimes recall Oliver Cromwell's appeal to the Church of Scotland," Arthur Schlesinger told the 1965 ADA convention: "I beseech you, in the bowels of Christ, think it possible you may be mistaken." While uncomfortable with the idea of a large troop commitment to Southeast Asia, and critical of the corrupt South Vietnamese government, the moderates were more willing than the reform group to view the conflict in superpower terms, and more likely to believe that American prestige was on the line. They hoped that the ADA, by standing just to the left of the administration, could maintain the support of labor while making the organization attractive to younger, reform liberals.[11]

Niebuhr, for example, believed that the United States had to prevent Communist expansion in Southeast Asia, but he doubted whether Vietnam was the place to draw the line. Although we were "honor-bound to defend our allies in the effort to contain Chinese expansion," he wrote, "we had no particular obligation to Vietnam." He suggested "that it might be wise to persuade Thailand, for instance, to offer asylum to all anti-Communist warriors, and then defend this asylum with massive military power." In a 1965 debate with Hans Morgenthau, Schlesinger argued that, though America's original commitment to Vietnam in 1954 was a mistake, our honor was at stake and we could not withdraw. When Morgenthau stated that the United States should accept the Chinese domination of Southeast Asia, Schlesinger retorted that Chinese domination of Southeast Asia was no more foreordained than Germany's domination of Europe had been three decades earlier. He believed that the United States should expand its ground presence there but not escalate the war through bombing.[12]

Moderates, already the dominant group in the ADA, had increased their influence with the election of Leon Shull, who had for twelve years been executive director of the Southeastern Pennsylvania chapter, as national director in January 1964. An extremely competent executive with an endless reservoir of optimism and energy, Shull would serve the organization for the next twenty-one years with unselfish devotion and unquestioning dedication. Shull began his career in politics working for the Socialist party while a high school student in Philadelphia. America was in the midst of a depression, and he was convinced there was a better solution to it than Roosevelt's New Deal. He went to the library one day "and found out there was something called Socialism." Like many of his generation, however, Shull repudiated his Socialist views at the end of World War II, explaining them away as the "arrogance of youth." Although deeply affected by the experience of the depression and by his struggles with communism after the war, Shull in 1965 was sensitive to the critique of the younger reform members. His main concern, however, was with maintaining the organization's political effectiveness and lobbying for important domestic legislation. Like other moderates, he remembered the lessons of Munich and wanted to prevent Communist aggression in Southeast Asia, but he also did not want to sidetrack the Great Society or disrupt the liberal coalition to do so.[13]

Since the reform group, based in the local chapters, was still not accurately represented in the organization's power structure, the ADA's official position on the war reflected a compromise between the traditional and moderate groups. At its 1964 convention the ADA approved a statement that remained unchanged for the next two years. It approved a resolution on Southeast Asia committing the United States to a policy of strengthening "those countries which seek to maintain their independence from external aggression and internal subversion." "Pacification by military means alone cannot succeed," it felt. U.S. policy in that region of the world, it claimed, "will succeed only within a framework of political, economic, and social policies that win support from the people for the local governments." Despite its call for social, political, and economic reforms, the convention refused to rule out further military assistance by voting down a minority resolution that would have put the organization on record against any further commitment of American military resources. Paul Seabury, the chairman of the foreign policy commission, explained the organization's logic in his defense of the majority resolution. He claimed that only three choices existed for the United States in Vietnam: "One is withdrawal; two, neutralist which, judging by the situation in Laos, is unrealistic; and the third is escalation." For Seabury, and most other liberals, the choice appeared easy.[14] The organization was trapped in the same dilemma that imprisoned American policymakers—it wanted to prevent a Communist takeover in Vietnam but did not want to get tied down in a major war.

The one aspect of American policy on which all groups could agree was opposition to the bombing. The reform group saw the bombing as morally wrong. "The soul of the nation is troubled," Lowenstein told audiences, "by the increasing barbarity of the struggle." For the traditional and moderate groups, it was not a moral problem but a tactical mistake. They charged that the bombing would only infuriate the North Vietnamese and have the same effect on Hanoi that the Japanese bombing of Pearl Harbor had had on the United States. While expressing support for the general goals of Johnson's policy, the ADA nevertheless tried to convince the administration that the bombing was counterproductive. It faced two major obstacles. First, on foreign policy matters, Johnson was much more concerned with appeasing conservatives than with pleasing liberals. "Don't worry about the hippies and the students and the Commies," Johnson warned an aide; "they'll raise a lot of hell but can't do real damage. The terrible beast we have to fear is the right wing."[15] Second, an astute and sensitive politician, Johnson realized liberals were divided over the war and thus were not a political force he needed to reckon much with.

Unfortunately, the ADA did little to dispel Johnson's belief that it was not united on the war. ADA leaders, gathering in Washington for their annual convention in April 1965, pleaded for a meeting with Johnson. Rauh, who organized the meeting, wanted to invite local and national ADA leaders to meet with the president and give him their impressions of how liberals from their respective chapters viewed the war. Johnson, skeptical of their intentions and not very interested in what they had to say anyway, rejected a meeting. Humphrey intervened on behalf of the ADA and persuaded Johnson to reconsider. At the last minute Johnson informed Rauh that he expected the ADA representatives to provide him with concrete alternatives to pursue in Vietnam—something they were not prepared to do. Caught off guard, many of the members resorted to vague references about bringing the dispute to the United Nations. According to David Halberstam's account of the meeting, some of the ADA people "were quite impassioned"; the bombing of the North had to stop. "It was wrong, it was against everything America stood for." As members of the group left the room, they passed through the White House pressroom, where they were questioned about their meeting. Rauh and Roche clashed over wording. Rauh told reporters the exchange had been sharp, that the ADA had expressed its opposition to the bombing in very strong terms. Roche tried to soften Rauh's statements. After the meeting, in the presence of the Joint Chiefs, McNamara, and Rusk, the president, again according to Halberstam, "reached into the wastebasket and scooped up the notes which the ADA people had brought to the meeting and written to each other during it. He then proceeded to mimic his previous guests to perfection taking great pleasure in the one Rauh had written: 'Why doesn't he take the issue of Vietnam to the United Nations?' "[16] The incident only hardened Johnson's conviction that liberals were both naive and divided over the war and did not, for the time being, have to be taken seriously. It was one of a number of miscalculations that Johnson made that alienated him from potential supporters.

Johnson did little that spring to ease liberal disquiet. At the end of April he sent U.S. Marines on a dubious mission to quell an insurrection in the Dominican Republic. He feared that a violent coup on the island would threaten stability in the area and that the republic would go the way of Cuba. There are signs, the president declared in a broadcast on April 30, "that people outside the Dominican Republic are seeking to gain control. . . . The American nations cannot, must not, and will not permit the establishment of another communist government in the Western Hemisphere." In order to justify the use of American troops, Johnson exaggerated the magnitude of the threat. He told stories of fifteen hundred innocent people murdered and beheaded, and claimed that he spoke to the ambassador by phone while the ambassador was hiding under his desk to guard against bullets.

The ADA claimed that the U.S. action was a violation of its treaty obligations with both the United Nations and the Organization of American States, and an "excursion" in "gunboat diplomacy" that would only continue "to raise the spectre of American imperialism in the minds of the Latin American people." No evidence exists, it held, that Communists are leading the revolution; "indeed, indications are that the revolt has the large-scale backing of the majority of the Dominican people who also have expressed their large-scale dissatisfaction with the American intervention."[17]

The ADA's dilemma was thus acute as early as 1965. The organization, while concerned about what it considered to be Johnson's impetuous response to the situation in the Dominican Republic and about the rash bombings of South Vietnam, was committed to working with the administration on various other fronts. The question the ADA had to face was as perplexing as it was simple: How does a liberal political organization committed to gradual reform working through the established institutions of government—and, in this case, the Democratic party—express its dissent over a policy it disagrees with? With the reform group a distinct minority, moderates unwilling to rock the boat, and Johnson indifferent to their concerns, the organization had little leverage. The simple fact was that the ADA needed Johnson much more than he needed the ADA.

So when Johnson dispatched fifty thousand troops in July 1965, the ADA refused to criticize him and instead chastized the Republican party. "We can only decry the irresponsibility of the House Republican leadership," the ADA stated, "who have tried to use the conflict in Viet-nam for partisan political profit. . . . Their pressure on the Johnson administration can only have negative effects on our posture toward achievement of a just settlement." The main obstacles to a peaceful settlement in Vietnam, are "the intransigence of the mainland Chinese government" and the "domestic opposition in the U.S. generated by the militaristic statements" of leading Republicans "who believe that temporary military success can or should be translated into military victory."[18]

In 1965, moderates and reformers forged a coalition that, though not supportive of Johnson's actions, was unwilling publicly to criticize him. Reformers still spoke out against the war, but they had little influence. Curtis Gans and Congressman Donald Edwards, a California Democrat, were two of the loudest reform voices in the ADA. While Gans and Edwards had very different backgrounds, they shared a critique of American foreign policy. Like other reformers, Gans admitted to holding "no brief for the North Vietnamese. If the war was immoral, it was because both Americans and North Vietnamese were losing their lives on something that wasn't worth fighting for." Since "the government in South Vietnam was not qualitatively different from the government in North Vietnam," the area, Gans asserted, "was very peripheral to American interests."[19]

Congressman Edwards, elected in April 1965 to the national chairmanship vacated by John Roche, was perhaps the organization's most outspoken opponent of the administration's Vietnam policy. His election to the ADA's highest office had little to do with his views on Vietnam, however, and much more with the organization's desire to have an elected official as its leader. Like other reformers, Edwards had little recollection of the New Deal, and when the ADA was joining forces with Truman in support of the Cold War, he was working with the other advocates of world government in the United World Federalist. Edwards believed that American foreign policy was deeply flawed and needed fundamental revision and that Vietnam was a logical result of those faulty assumptions. He disagreed with the fervent anticommunism of most liberals. "Communist revolutions are not *caused* by the communist doctrine," he told an American University audience in June 1965; "they are caused by disease and the lack of the decencies of life." Like his fellow reformers, he was moved by Kennedy's American University speech. That "immortal speech on world peace," he declared, "signified a new direction in American foreign policy." Edwards feared that rather than moving the country toward Kennedy's vision of a "peaceful world order," Johnson was accentuating the worst aspects of American policy. "We appear to be disassociating ourselves from a foreign policy whose matrix is the U.N. and instead giving increasing importance to unilateral power politics."[20]

Edwards wasted no time using his new position to force the organization to address the Vietnam problem head on. "If there is one thing I hope to achieve as chairman of ADA," he claimed at the September National Board meeting, it "is to generate a national debate on the issues of our time." American foreign policy, he said, is "sick" and will result "in more Vietnams and more Dominican interventions, if it is not cured." Edwards could not praise the great domestic achievements of the Johnson administration while ignoring its foreign policy. Although Johnson had transformed into law "much of the legislative programs of the American liberal community that had been awaiting action for decades," liberals could not, and according to Edwards should not, forgive Johnson's foreign policy mistakes. The "passage of Medicare," he said, "is greeted by liberals by 'Congratulations, but what about Vietnam,' or 'nice work on the education bill—but what about Santo Domingo?' " It is the liberals' responsibility "to convince our President that his imaginative and confident domestic philosophy must be matched by a wholly new and creative foreign policy." Edwards hoped to apply the same passion and commitment that worked so well for the civil rights movement to help bring an early end to U.S. involvement in the Vietnam War. "If we have learned anything in the past three years," he said, "it is that this country can be moved, and policies can be changed."[21]

As long as protest against the war was confined to the fringe of American politics, the ADA could successfully maintain its stature as an independent organization without losing its ties to the administration. However, protest against the war was growing in intensity and scope. Johnson's escalation of the conflict could not have come at a worse time. The integrationist phase of the civil rights movement was ending, and an army of somewhat disillusioned, and certainly more militant, young whites was moving back to college campuses in the North in search of a new cause to champion. The first teach-in at Ann Arbor acquired the same significance for the peace movement that the first sit-in at Greensboro had for the civil rights campaign. Born at the University of Michigan on March 24, 1965, the teach-in spread to hundreds of campuses that spring, culminating in the national teach-in in Washington, D.C., on May 15.

There was a heavy moral tone to the student dissent and to the themes of the teach-ins. Leaders of the Vietnam Day Committee at Berkeley invoked the Nuremberg ethic: "When the state acts immorally, it is the duty of the individual to refuse to participate in its immorality." The radical journalist Jack Newfield called the thrust of youthful protest "one generation's revolt against the last one's definitions of reality." By late 1965, students were planning mass demonstrations, burning draft cards, and chanting "Hey, Hey, LBJ, how many kids did you kill today?" The emerging radical critique charged that America was a sick society. The most obvious signs of this sickness were the Vietnam War and the reluctance of the government to meet the needs of the blacks and the poor. Unlike liberals who tried to distinguish between Johnson's enlightened domestic programs and his rash foreign policy, the young protesters saw a clear connection between the administration's increasingly cool support of civil rights and its suppression of nationalist movements abroad. "There is something sick," commented the University of Michigan daily newspaper, "about a nation that can deploy thousands of soldiers to go off shooting Vietcong . . . in the jungles but can't spare a few hundred to avert the murder of a minister by a used car salesman in Alabama." In perhaps the clearest statement of all, two radicals wrote in *Studies on the Left,* one of many New Left intellectual journals of the time, "The Administration [and its liberal ideologues] speak of civil rights and economic opportunity at home, just as they talk of democracy and self determination abroad; but whether it is in Harlem or Mississippi, Vietnam or the Dominican Republic, its policies are designed to solidify or secure the position of those classes and social groups already in power."[22]

The new radicals drew their inspiration not from the depression or the threat of fascism but from the "amorality, purposelessness, and lack of individual power in a technocratic society." Coming of age after 1956, many of the young leftists could not identify with the anti-Stalinism of Old Left spokesmen like the ex-Trotskyists Irving Howe and Dwight Macdonald or with labor leaders like Michael Harrington and Bayard Rustin. Of greater relevance was their shared experience in the civil rights movement, which much of the Old Left had watched from the sidelines. They also had different ideas about how to wage protest. The Old Left wanted to build a reformist coalition of labor, civil rights groups, churches, liberals, and intellectuals within the Democratic party. They argued that an effective peace movement needed to reach out and "gain the approval of more than the small band already committed to protest." "The Old Left," observed the author and activist Sidney Lens, "tends to mellow and seek bridges to liberalism, while a New Left comes to the fore to re-emphasize the need for independence from the Establishment." The visionary New Left wanted to create independent constituencies to oppose the establishment. The Old Left wanted to exclude Communists; the New Left argued that a movement fighting for the freedom of one group could not exclude another.[23]

In 1965 the ADA refused to sanction either the New Left tactic of civil disobedience or the Old Left commitment to respectable political protest. Curtis Gans, in an address to student leaders in Hawaii in November 1965, outlined the organization's critique of the New Left. He said that its "highly moral and highly simplistic" approach did not move beyond "moral outrage to political demand," lacked "cohesiveness," relied "too heavily upon demonstrations," and "failed to build bridges with other elements in the community that could be their natural allies." When Michael Harrington, Bayard Rustin, Norman Thomas, and Benjamin Spock organized a march on Washington on November 27, 1965, the ADA refused to participate. The organizers' objectives were modest: to put pressure on the Johnson administration to stop the bombing of North Vietnam, call for a cease-fire, halt the introduction of additional men and matériel, and declare its support of the principles of the 1954 Geneva accords—eventual withdrawal of all foreign military forces, prohibition against military alliances, peaceful reunification of Vietnam, and self-determination for the Vietnamese people.[24]

The ADA refused to participate in the march, although, according to Gans, a majority of the organization supported it. The problem, he said, was that "a few prominent individuals" raised concerns about the march that threatened to divide the organization. Tyler, along with two former national chairmen, Samuel Beer and Arthur Schlesinger, Jr., complained that the ADA *World* gave the appearance of endorsing the march by running an advertisement for it. In a letter to National Chairman Edwards, Beer and his coauthor Paul Seabury said that they found the idea of American domination of Southeast Asia "repugnant," but they added, "equally repugnant is the notion that the U.S. has no interests in Southeast Asia and no right to be there." An American withdrawal, they charged, will lead to "the complete collapse of a very unstable equilibrium and the risk of vastly enlarged conflict there." If America fails to honor its commitments in Southeast Asia, it will call into question similar commitments everywhere else in the world. While they did not accept the domino theory, "which says that when this goes all the rest goes," they also did not accept the "anti-domino theory, which says that it doesn't matter at all whether this one goes; that it has no subsequent effects." The more visible the protest movement in America becomes, they said, "the less inclined Hanoi is going to be to seriously negotiate." The goal of the march, Schlesinger recognized, is to achieve a "negotiated settlement in Vietnam," but the effect, he wrote, "will be to postpone progress toward that goal by persuading the Vietcong and Hanoi that domestic protest in the U.S. is about to cause a slackening of our military action or even a U.S. withdrawal." Like Beer and Seabury, Schlesinger feared the political consequences of getting involved in the protest. It will, he noted, "place a weapon in the hands of every enemy of the ADA in the country and enormously complicate the lives of people in politics who have collaborated with ADA."[25]

When the march turned out to be a success, Edwards was eager to reassure dissenters. The march, he wrote, was a "low-key, well-mannered demonstration by generally well-dressed, middle-aged, middle-class Americans carrying the message that this particular group emphatically suggests that more can be done by our government to honorably end the war in Vietnam." He told one critic that none of the sponsors advocated a policy of "get out of Vietnam." Edwards's letter did little to mollify critics, who feared that the ADA's involvement in the demonstration would forge in the public mind, a link between the ADA and the New Left. Liberals, Robert Scalapino warned, needed to retain their heritage of the Vital Center by distinguishing "themselves completely from the non-democratic Left and Right."[26]

The demonstration that Edwards hailed as "moderate" and "well-mannered" represented an important break in the evolving dissent against the war. Carl Oglesby, the leader of SDS, gave an electrifying speech that marked the final split between liberals and radical elements in the peace movement. Entitled "Liberalism and the Corporate State," it rejected any compromise with the establishment and blamed liberals for the embourgeoisement of blacks, the decal of the cities, the bureaucratization of the universities, and the distortion of national priorities. "This country, with its thirty-some years of liberalism, can send 200,000 young men to Vietnam to kill and die in the most dubious of wars, but it cannot get 100 voter registrars to go into Mississippi." Thereafter, liberals supplanted conservatives as a prime target for many leftist intellectuals.[27]

Events over the next eighteen months dashed any hope for an early resolution to the war. Johnson tripled the number of sorties flown over Vietnam, from 25,000 in 1965 to 79,000 in 1966. Not only did the bombing increase, but the targets changed, as American planes began bombing petroleum storage facilities and communications networks, raids that caused greater civilian casualties. Almost as important as the actions themselves was the devious way Johnson justified them. He never explained the shift from reprisal to "sustained pressure," or the change from defensive to offensive ground operations. His peace feelers were well publicized but also misleading. He said he was committed to a diplomatic settlement even though he knew that North Vietnam would not accept the one condition of a free and independent South Vietnam.

A CIA summary of air strikes showed that though hundreds of bridges, thousands of cars and trucks, and a majority of the oil installations had been destroyed, traffic was moving smoothly and no oil shortage existed. The bombing cost the United States nearly ten dollars for every dollar's worth of damage inflicted. Despite the overwhelming evidence that the bombing was unsuccessful, the generals continued to extol the air campaign as "highly effective." "Bomb, bomb, bomb—that's all they know," Johnson grumbled as he, lacking alternatives, authorized new targets. At the end of 1966 Harrison Salisbury, the *New York Times* assistant managing editor, in a series of detailed dispatches, reported that the "surgical" air strikes had in fact leveled many North Vietnamese cities and killed innocent civilians. Salisbury's reports, as one Pentagon spokesman said, made Johnson look like "a liar and deceiver" and only exacerbated the president's "credibility disaster."[28]

The antiwar movement in 1966 was, as one author has commented, "a flotilla of tiny craft becalmed in a sea of uncertainty." In January 1966, following the murder of Samuel Younge, a black SNCC worker shot and killed in Tuskegee, Alabama, SNCC issued a statement linking his murder to America's war in Vietnam. His death, it charged, "is no different from the murder of people in Vietnam." Both are "seeking to secure the rights guaranteed them by law. In each case, the U.S. government bears a great part of the responsibility for their deaths." Activists like the eighty-two-year-old A. J. Muste, and pacifist organizations like the War Resisters League and the Committee for Non-Violent Action, organized the second international days of protest on March 25–26, 1966, and engaged in sundry acts of civil disobedience. Norman Thomas declared that there was "no military victory in sight" and that any peace growing out of present American policy would be "a peace of death and destruction." Julian Bond, a staff member of SNCC, called for a closer relationship between the civil rights and peace movements, adding, "This relationship must be demonstrated and shown." Martin Luther King, Jr., complained, "The promises of the Great Society top the casualty lists of the conflict. The pursuit of widened war has narrowed domestic welfare programs making the poor—white and Negro—carry the heaviest burdens both at the front and at home."[29]

Antiwar sentiment was growing even within the staid Washington establishment. On January 31 Robert Kennedy, elected to the Senate in 1964, criticized the president for resuming bombing after a brief Christmas pause. The decision, he claimed, "may become the first in a series of steps on a road from which there is no turning back—a road that leads to catastrophe for all mankind." In April, Senator J. William Fulbright, the powerful chairman of the Senate Foreign Relations Committee, delivered a series of lectures at Johns Hopkins University in which he declared, the United States "is in danger of losing its perspective on what exactly is within the realm of its power and what is beyond it." In displaying an "arrogance of power," he continued, "we are not living up to our capacity and promise as a civilized example for the world." Walter Lippman predicted Johnson would eventually find himself "in a dead-end street" unless he reversed his Vietnam policy: "Gestures, propaganda, public relations, and bombing and more bombing will not work."[30]

The moderate group in the ADA, already frustrated with the war, now feared that public discord would give rise to another McCarthy-like hysteria and was dismayed that the bright hope for the Great Society was being dimmed by the shadow cast by the war. "One senses a feeling of frustration within the ranks of liberalism today," Rauh wrote William Connell, a

Humphrey aide. "It is not easy to see many of the social and economic proposals we have made over the years finally adopted into law and then fall short of their purpose for want of limited appropriations and inadequate implementation." "The Great Society," Schlesinger lamented in the summer of 1966, "is now, except for token gestures, dead."[31]

Schlesinger and other moderates moved away from their tacit support of the original commitment of troops in 1965, to a call for a negotiated settlement in which the NLF played a part in a coalition government—the position the reform liberals in the organization had advocated earlier. Only the traditionalist group, resisting any suggestion of allowing Communists into a coalition government, objected to this position. It was outnumbered, however, and by the spring of 1966 the organization regularly issued statements criticizing Johnson for his halfhearted peace gestures. The ADA deplored "the continuing intensification by the United States of the Vietnam military conflict which would better have been left to resolution by the people of Vietnam." It stated that the United States had "only a marginal interest in Vietnam, or at most a self-created interest," and called on Johnson to "promote achievement of negotiations among all parties to the conflict."[32]

At home, liberals watched as the war divided public opinion and forced cutbacks in many Great Society programs. Those who opposed the Great Society—and they were greatly strengthened by the 1966 congressional elections, in which the Republicans gained forty-seven seats in the House and three in the Senate—could now appeal to patriotism in their attacks on increased social spending. Senate Majority Leader Mike Mansfield said the watchword of the new Congress was "Stop, Look and Listen." House Majority Leader Carl Albert of Oklahoma warned, "We've run the gamut on new programs. Why, we've passed most of the bills we've talked about for the past 30 years. Now, we need to slow down. Besides, we have a war on our hands." "I view this election as a repudiation of the President's domestic policies," said the House Republican leader, Gerald Ford. "It's going to be rough going for him around here. Congress will write the laws, not the executive branch." According to the *Congressional Quarterly,* the poverty program lost forty-nine supporters; open housing, twenty-nine; and anti-inflation tax measures, twenty-two; meanwhile, anti-inflation spending cuts gained twenty supporters.[33]

Johnson, a meteorologist of the public mood, tailored his program to suit the times. Only once in his 1967 State of the Union Message, a thirteen-page single-spaced text, did he refer to the Great Society. Gone were youthful memories of poverty and the stirring calls for social justice. "The budget for 1967," said the president, "bears the strong imprint of the troubled world we live in." "The rate of advance in the new programs," he conceded, "has been held below what might have been." While he estimated the Vietnam War would require $10.5 billion, the War on Poverty was allotted only $1.6 billion, instead of the hoped-for $2.5 billion. The *Nation* claimed that Johnson's 1967 State of the Union Message reflected "the reality gap—the application of purely verbal remedies to the acute and worsening ills that afflict the country."[34]

The question the ADA had to confront in 1967 and thereafter was how to translate its growing frustration with the war into political action. The reform group, not satisfied with issuing declarations against the war, wanted the ADA to put public pressure on the administration. Its call to action now needed to be taken seriously because by late 1966 the reform group, using public frustration with the war, had dramatically increased its strength in the organization. Local chapters found that the ADA's opposition to the war attracted new members. As their numbers increased, the chapters became bolder, many of them imploring the national leadership to sever all ties with Johnson and to get to the forefront of the protest movement.

Many chapter representatives believed that younger people were turning to radicalism because liberals were not presenting them a real alternative. A meeting called "Communism as an American Obsession" had packed Claire Smith's living room for the Washington State chapter in the summer of 1966. "The war in Viet Nam is the wrong way to fight communism," declared Professor John Crow. Meyer Berger of the Pittsburgh chapter informed Shull in January 1967, "[There] is some feeling in the Chapter that the ADA has not taken a strong enough position or one of leadership with reference to the question of Viet Nam." Henry Sawyer, a board member from the Southeastern Pennsylvania chapter of the ADA, wrote Shull on February 2, 1967, to tell him that there was a consensus "that we should take a more active role in opposition to the Viet Nam war." He concluded, "There is no doubt that there is a marked rise in despair and concern in the ADA membership over the Vietnam war and a rise in general dove sentiment over what I sensed some months ago."[35]

Allard Lowenstein, a former student activist at the University of North Carolina at Chapel Hill, a past head of the National Student Association, and a civil rights activist in Mississippi, carefully orchestrated the discontent in the chapters. A thirty-seven-year-old attorney, Lowenstein was a burly ex-wrestler who, according to one observer, "could be found in a state of repose only after sensible people had been in bed for many hours." Lowenstein spent most of his time being a professional liberal. Using the local chapters and the Campus ADA as a base, he tried to persuade the national organization to lead a dump-Johnson movement.

At first Lowenstein was not anti-Johnson, but that changed after a January 1967 meeting with Walt Rostow, Johnson's chief theoretician on the war. Lowenstein said, "I found Rostow's position so arrogant, and so completely askew from my point of view, that there wasn't much we had to say to each other." Lowenstein recognized the danger of splitting the party, but the dangers of doing nothing would be worse, because the Democrats had no chance of winning with Johnson at the head of the ticket. His dump-Johnson campaign had two necessary parts: he had to fan the dump-Johnson fire in the grass roots, and he had to find his own candidate. Spending his own money and enlisting in his cause such other dissenters as Gerald N. Hill, the president of the California Democratic Council, and Harold Ickes, the son of FDR's secretary of the interior, Lowenstein moved to weld together the dump-Johnson sentiment."[36]

His appeal to the young made Lowenstein an attractive figure to many moderates in the ADA who feared that the organization was losing touch with the grass roots. For many middle-aged New Deal liberals on the National Board, Lowenstein provided a link between two generations, a chance for liberals to appeal to the new, baby-boom generation coming to political consciousness in the 1960s. Moderates and reformers combined forces at the ADA convention in April 1967 to get Lowenstein elected to the National Board. Galbraith, lobbying on Lowenstein's behalf, told a skeptical board member, "[Lowenstein] puts ADA in touch with a whole range of potential members and workers whom I fear we are in great danger of losing." Lowenstein, more than anyone else, Curtis Gans wrote, "speaks the voice of the membership of ADA." David Broder, a popular syndicated columnist, declared, "He brought more young people into American politics than any individual of our time." Representative Richard Miller of Massachusetts, who cast the deciding vote in favor of Lowenstein's election, confessed that he found Lowenstein to be "unimpressive," personally ambitious, and lacking "the national stature of other Vice Presidents of ADA." Still, he voted for him because, as he wrote Lowenstein afterward, "I am impressed by the fact that the median age of Americans today is 28; the average age of the group meeting last weekend was closer to 40." "There were precious few faces in the room," he continued, "which suggested the well springs of future leadership." Miller hoped that Lowenstein would "transfuse the liberal thought of two political generations."[37]

Once on the board, Lowenstein clashed repeatedly with Gus Tyler, the leading spokesman of the traditionalist group. Despite their common commitment to nonviolent change achieved through the established institutions of government, a generational chasm separated the two men. Tyler had associated with the workingman ever since his early years as a street corner agitator in Brooklyn during the depression. Raised by immigrant parents in New York's seamy Garment District, nurtured on great socialist thinkers, and disciplined by the radical labor movement, Tyler never lost his thirst for class struggle. Lowenstein, born in 1929, was only sixteen years old when Roosevelt died—too young to experience the misery of the depression. Lowenstein's training ground came later—during North Carolina's racial segregation troubles of the 1950s. His home was among the university crowd—the young and the educated.

Lowenstein and Tyler were formidable adversaries: both were spirited, animated, and articulate men, adroit in debate and passionate in conviction. The debates between them, always heated though rarely personal, reached a breaking point. "How," Gus Tyler asked, can liberals abandon the president who "has done more for liberal legislation" than any other president since Roosevelt. Liberals, he charged, had changed the rules in the middle of the game and blamed Johnson for not playing according to the new ones. Liberal thinking, Tyler claimed, shifted "away from economics to ethics and aesthetics, to morality and culture." "In the 1930's, one third of the nation was ill-clothed, ill-housed and ill-fed; today it is one fourth of the nation. The actual number of people affected is the same if not greater." Although the standard of living has increased, Tyler argued, so have expectations. "Senior citizens are no longer satisfied with a few dollars: they demand bigger pensions, hospitalization, free medicine, etc. Negroes are no longer satisfied with their old servile status: they expected more and they explode. . . ."[38]

Tyler had the support of most labor representatives on the National Board. I. W. Abel of the Steelworkers Union issued statements in support of Johnson's policy. David Dubinsky called upon the American people and all "liberty-loving people everywhere" to support the president for "his vision, determination and vigor." Dubinsky attacked liberals who criticized American policy but never found "time or reason to criticize the Communists." The Executive Committee chairman, Edward Hollander, claimed that the dump-Johnson movement was "a cry of frustration."[39]

The moderate wing, always leery of getting too far ahead of public opinion, felt, as the traditionalists did, that Lowenstein's proposal was too radical. Although moderates opposed the escalation of the war and had little love left for the president, they also believed, in Galbraith's words, that the ADA needed to maintain its "longstanding commitment to political realities." Through most of 1967, political realities dictated that the ADA work with the administration in seeking a "respectable" solution to the war. Moderates, while sympathetic to the reform liberals' critique of the war, could not ignore the political consequences of opposing an incumbent Democratic president. That could have changed if a strong candidate decided to challenge Johnson for the 1968 Democratic nomination, but in the spring of 1967 no such challenge appeared imminent. Many moderates still believed that Johnson was, in Galbraith's words, "a force of moderation" and would negotiate if there was a political consensus in support of such a position. Beginning in the fall of 1966, and continuing through most of 1967, Galbraith and Schlesinger, in public appearances, articles in the *New York Times Magazine,* and, in Schlesinger's case, a book entitled *The Bitter Heritage,* tried to build support for a negotiated settlement that would allow Johnson to deescalate the conflict. Both Schlesinger and Galbraith hammered home the same points: a policy of withdrawal would be as dangerous as one of escalation; the best way to protect American interests in Vietnam—and both believed that American prestige was on the line in Vietnam—was neither to escalate nor to withdraw but to establish a defensive perimeter in the urban areas of South Vietnam and hold on until the Communists agreed to negotiate. "Our national security may not have compelled us to draw a line across Southeast Asia where we did," Schlesinger wrote, "but, having drawn it, we cannot lightly abandon it. Our stake in South Vietnam may have been self-created, but it has nonetheless become real. Our precipitate withdrawal now would have ominous reverberations throughout Asia."

"Opposition to the war, if it were to be more than an act of personal protest," Galbraith wrote in his memoirs, "required a plan for ending it, one that would attract a political constituency." America had "no major national interest in Vietnam" and therefore had to keep its "risks in the region at a minimum." Although Vietnam is not a vital strategic concern, Galbraith claimed, "for domestic reasons, if for no other, we cannot walk out." With "the large manpower we have there," Galbraith and Schlesinger recommended, "we should hold, along with South Vietnam forces, the cities and a solid part of the countryside that is now friendly and make it just as secure as we possibly can." Galbraith called for a defensive U.S. posture in Vietnam—one including an end to all bombing, and negotiations with all parties involved. Galbraith, like Schlesinger, was willing neither to give up Vietnam nor to make sacrifices to keep it. While sanctioning ADA involvement in the "Negotiations Now!" campaign, a coalition of moderates who circulated petions calling for a cease-fire and negotiated settlement, they avoided association with any group that was out of the mainstream. Curtis Gans objected to the moderates' tactics, calling them a "slick attempt to coopt the peace movement." The "Negotiations Now!" campaign, Gans recalled, "gave the appearance of being against the war, when it really was not."[40]

William Bundy, Assistant Secretary of State for the Far East, responded to the Galbraith plan on behalf of the administration. The "enclave policy," Bundy charged, "has very little connection with reality, and particularly with the best evidence on the degree of Vietcong control within South Vietnam." Bundy claimed that according to North Vietnamese estimates, Communists controlled less than 35 percent of the countryside and none of the urban areas. Bundy also pointed out another serious flaw in the plan. Galbraith assumed that the North Vietnamese would accept a settlement that would deny the Communists control of all of South Vietnam. "Does Professor Galbraith really believe," Bundy asked, "that the Vietcong or the North Vietnamese would refrain from constant efforts to expand their areas of control, or would refrain from strengthening themselves to the maximum for this purpose?"[41]

Bundy's criticisms exposed the fatal flaw of the moderates' plan. No matter how suitable to the domestic political debate, their "respectable" solution had little relevance to the military situation in Vietnam. Moderates hoped to appeal to the broad mass of American voters by refusing to accept "defeat" in Vietnam and maintaining that an independent South Vietnam could be preserved with only limited American support. They also tried to attract the burgeoning peace movement with their calls for a "negotiated settlement" and a "peaceful solution" to the crisis. What they refused to accept was that the twin goals of negotiating a "peaceful solution" while also maintaining a free and independent government in South Vietnam were illusory so long as the North Vietnamese remained committed to their long-expressed goal of reunification. Shortly after 1967 the war would force moderates to choose between their perception of what was right and their recognition of what was possible.

The moderates had much in common with the reformers. Both groups expressed dissatisfaction with Johnson's handling of the war and anger over the cutbacks in Great Society programs. All feared that a continued escalation of the war would further divide Americans at home and create public hysteria that could lead to another McCarthy. Both factions looked to the young to provide new blood and new energy for the liberal movement. They called for the same strategy in Vietnam: stop the bombing and begin negotiations. But much also divided them. The Schlesinger group refused to entertain any move to dump Johnson without a viable presidential candidate. They also believed that Johnson, always the pragmatic politician, would deescalate if he thought there was political support for such a move. Lowenstein entertained no such hopes. For the moderates it was a matter of politics: How could the organization maintain the support of the young without alienating either the president or his supporters in the administration? For Lowenstein it was a question of both politics and morality. As he was so fond of repeating, "If a president is wrong but popular, political realities may make opposing him difficult, however right; if a president is right but unpopular, supporting him may be a duty, however difficult. But when a president is both wrong and unpopular, to refuse to oppose him is a moral abdication and a political stupidity."[42]

The moderates' immediate objective was to rally support for their peace plan and to reach an accommodation with the administration. Once again they turned to their old friend Hubert Humphrey. Although an early critic of the war, Humphrey underwent a conversion during a January 1966 trip to Vietnam. The trip, he confessed in his memoirs, "had in fact made me much more a supporter of our policy on Vietnam, and my public statements reflected my views." For most of the next year and a half, Humphrey told audiences that America had to "be firm in resisting the expansionist designs of the present rulers of China." Humphrey's nearly unquestioned loyalty to the president frustrated many liberals. The *New Republic* commented, "To expect him to moderate his enthusiasm is to expect sobriety from an alcoholic." Moderates in the ADA, however, still hoped to bring Humphrey around to their point of view.[43]

In April 1967 Rauh, at Humphrey's request, assembled ten liberals—including Schlesinger, Galbraith, Robert Bendiner, and James Wechsler of the ADA—at his house for a last-try dinner with the vice-president. After a few pleasantries Humphrey made the standard White House pitch about Vietnam. When he claimed that America's presence in South Vietnam had been the key factor in swinging the Indonesian government from pro-Peking neutralism to the anti-Communist side, Schlesinger blew up: "Hubert, that's shit and you know it. Those generals were just fighting for their lives, and would have done so whether we were in Vietnam or not."

Humphrey held his temper. He insisted that on military matters the president had to listen to the generals. Schlesinger recalled how the generals had misled Kennedy in the Bay of Pigs invasion. Did that mean, Humphrey asked Schlesinger, that he was better equipped than the generals to evaluate these matters? Schlesinger retorted, "I damn well do." But when Schlesinger kept demanding an overhaul of the State Department—"everybody in the State Department identified with Dean Rusk has to be thrown out," he declared—Humphrey finally raised his voice. "Arthur, these are your guys," he shouted. "You were in the White House when they took over. Don't blame them on us." Schlesinger did not answer. Although on good terms when the evening ended, they all went away convinced that if Humphrey had to choose between his old liberal constituency and the president, he would support the president. Rauh said later, "Most of us were struck by the sense that he was increasingly conscious of the dead-end into which his own political life might be headed as the result of the war."[44]

Other Johnson advisers, especially Marvin Watson, recognized the growing strength of the Lowenstein group in the ADA and tried to persuade Johnson to make symbolic overtures to Galbraith, Schlesinger, Rauh, and other liberals who opposed the war but not the president. However, Johnson, by the summer of 1967, was a deeply troubled man, physically and emotionally exhausted, and torn between his advisers. Not in the best frame of mind, he blindly lumped all liberals together as closet Kennedy supporters who were just waiting for the heir apparent to return and accept his throne. His one attempt to woo ADA liberals, his appointment of the former ADA national chairman John Roche as his liaison with the liberal community, backfired since Roche was by then a strong backer of the labor group that already supported the president's policies. Bill Moyers "quizzed Roche at length on his position" on Vietnam because he wanted to be certain he was for the administration. Moyers assured Johnson, "We are getting an honest Johnson supporter, although he is a very liberal fellow."

Roche, convinced Johnson had much stronger support in the liberal community than anyone realized, suggested "that the Administration keep in touch with its friends among the liberals." Roche's effort, however, gained few converts among moderates in the ADA. James Wechsler, who traveled in both Schlesinger's and Lowenstein's circles, commented that the president "had chosen a man equipped to provide more skillful language in the rationalization of existing policy." Roche, whose caustic personality and personal dislike for Schlesinger, Galbraith, and Lowenstein were well known, only confirmed Johnson's own paranoia and further isolated the president.[45]

Two questions confronted the ADA delegates who gathered for their annual convention in April 1967. The first one—how critical they should be of Johnson's Vietnam policy—was not going to be difficult. The organization would simply reiterate its opposition to the war. The second, far more difficult question was how the organization should manifest its disagreement with the administration. Would the ADA continue to hope to work with the Johnson administration in reaching a settlement of the war or would it break with Johnson and call on Democrats to look for another candidate in 1968? The convention gave an indication of which direction it would go when it elected Galbraith to succeed Don Edwards as national chairman. Although Galbraith was an outspoken critic of Vietnam, he was considered safe by all sides. Personally close to Lowenstein, whom he had lobbied hard to get on the board, Galbraith was also known to be fond of Johnson, which pleased the president's supporters.

In his acceptance speech Galbraith scrupulously avoided criticism of the administration. John Roche was so pleased by the tone of the speech that he recommended that the president "have an off-the-record session with him as soon as possible—alone." Roche properly identified Galbraith as a "restraining force within ADA."[46] Immediately after Galbraith's address, the four hundred delegates at the Twentieth Annual Convention, at the Shoreham Hotel in Washington, D.C., debated resolutions on the war and political policy. The convention passed a resolution expressing "disenchantment and dismay over many aspects of Administration policy in Vietnam and parallel retreat at home." It argued that the predominant blame for escalation lay with the United States and that the war had increased "in size, scope and barbarity." It condemned U.S. policy in Vietnam and called for a halt to the bombings of North Vietnam, a standstill truce, and recognition of the National Liberation Front as a party in negotiations and in the future political life of South Vietnam.

As expected, most of the serious fireworks came over the political policy resolution. Rauh offered a resolution that welcomed "the emergence of a serious liberal challenge to the administration's course in the ranks of the Republicans." Rauh said the resolution was designed "to say to Johnson 'you don't have the liberals of America in the bag.' " Another supporter, Robert Schwartz of New York, told the convention, "We don't believe that the more liberal aspects of Johnson's program can continue while the war goes on. Vietnam permeates everything this country does, at home and abroad." Lowenstein, in a passionate and moving concluding speech, spoke in favor of the Rauh resolution, saying that Johnson might be the first president in history to win by 60 percent of the vote in one election and lose by an even bigger margin in the next election.

Tyler, the chairman of the political policy committee, proposed a milder resolution that praised the legislative achievements of the Johnson administration, condemned Congress, opposed the administration's "slowdown" on domestic programs, and urged a speedy political settlement of the war in Vietnam. In the debate on the two resolutions, Tyler argued for the milder version, insisting that many in the liberal-labor coalition did not agree with the ADA position on the war and that the important thing was to keep the coalition together. Tyler claimed that adoption of the "strong statement of anger, protest and frustration against the President on Vietnam" would "mislead the liberal community."

As a compromise, the convention deferred the whole question indefinitely. It said, "ADA, of course, takes no position now with respect to the national elections of 1968," although Johnson's opponents did succeed in including an implicit threat in the statement "We are pledged to no man and no party; our commitment is to a sane peace and the advance of the cause of human justice and equality." The ADA also joined the efforts of the "Negotiation Now!" campaign, which sought to bring moderate and uncommitted Americans to support peace through negotiations by focusing attention on the United Nations and Secretary General U Thant's three points: a unilateral cessation of bombing of North Vietnam, a general deescalation of fighting in South Vietnam, recognition of the NLF's right to participate in negotiations and the future political life of South Vietnam.[47]

The compromise at the convention had a short life. At the next National Board meeting, in May, with only 40 of the 143 Board Members present, the reform group passed a resolution that went beyond the spirit of the convention. The ADA, it said, "expresses its intention to support in the 1968 election that candidate of either party, who offers a genuine hope for restraint in the conduct of the war in Vietnam and for its peaceful resolution on honorable terms, if such a candidate is presented to the American people." In tone, the statement was very similar to the one passed by the convention, confirming both the organization's commitment to work within the two-party system and its political independence. Yet, in one crucial respect, it went far beyond the previous statement because it made Vietnam the sole test of ADA support in 1968—exactly the position that Johnson's supporters on the board had argued against so vehemently.

The statement once again exposed the divisions in the organization. Gus Tyler organized a campaign to have the decision overturned and within a few weeks boasted 61 board members supporting his position. Vietnam, he said, should "not become the exclusive concern . . . of a liberal movement already divided on this question in the summer of 1967 when the slums are exploding in Tampa, Boston, Cincinnati, Cleveland, or—when the Middle East threatens to explode into a conflagration that would make Vietnam look like a wienie roast." The ADA's strength, Tyler and other traditionalists maintained, comes from its power "to mold the opinion of opinion makers not [from] its comic opera threats to withhold its vast votes from Johnson if he does not comply." Union representatives, who composed the largest voting group in ADA and "practically every one of whom has rejected the ADA resolution," are for the most part "talking about leaving ADA." "Does anyone seriously believe," he asked, "that Johnson could be bombed to the peace table by a resolution passed by two dozen people, dressed up as 143 board members in the press? If anything, this 'bomb' might blow up ADA, but not the White House." "This monomania," he concluded, "would isolate ADA not only from the mainstream of American politics, from the vast body of liberal voters in America, but even from the meaningful and influential elements that have been with ADA since its inception."[48]

Those who supported the statement believed that liberals needed to move beyond the New Deal coalition and appeal to the young, and they were afraid to tie themselves too closely to the Johnson administration. "Your conviction about preserving the old coalition," Loeb wrote Tyler, "assumes that the coalition of the past several decades will persist eternally. In any event, let us not forget that youth was part of that coalition, and you and I, Gus, are no longer youth." One of the questions raised by the resolution, Schlesinger said, is "whether ADA is going to have more influence if the administration can assume it has ADA in its pocket." "Really, Gus, the politics of sycophancy are played out," Schlesinger concluded, and if "ADA follows your policy . . . it will forfeit any right to be considered what you and I helped start twenty years ago—an independent liberal movement dedicated to justice and peace throughout the world."[49]

Events were conspiring to widen the divisions in the ADA. "Between Independence Day and Labor Day," wrote *Time,* "a profound malaise overcame the American people. A kind of psychological Asian flu, it has as its overt symptoms bewilderment about U.S. aims in Vietnam, impatience with the pace of the war and, increasingly, an unmistakable if still inchoate tide of opposition to the entire U.S. involvement in that costly, ugly, not so far-off conflict." In August, Johnson sent 45,000 more troops to Vietnam and asked for higher taxes to finance the war. And, though Defense Secretary Robert McNamara himself voiced criticism of the bombing, day after day the bombs continued to fall.[50]

The horror of the war, flashed into the homes of most Americans on the evening newscasts, was matched by that of the racial violence in the nation's cities. Flames tore through thirty cities—Omaha, Houston, Chicago, Nashville, Jackson, Boston, Tampa, Cincinnati, Atlanta, Buffalo, Kansas City, Hartford. In one week alone in August, forty-five people were killed and thousands injured, and property damage ran into the billions of dollars. Robert Kennedy called it the "greatest domestic crisis since the war between the states." Congress, reflecting a widespread fear among white America, passed stiff antiriot legislation but showed little inclination to waste time on civil rights. Senator Ernest Hollings of South Carolina called on the president to "invoke the necessary price, wage and commodity controls, shelve the 'Great Society' for now, and call up the needed units of reserves and National Guard."[51]

Demands for black power grew louder. H. Rap Brown urged blacks to "wage guerrilla war on the honkie white man." "White Americans are not going to deal in the problems of colored people," commented one civil rights leader, "when they're exterminating a whole nation of colored people." At the Riverside Church in New York City, Martin Luther King, Jr., called the United States the "greatest purveyor of violence in the world" and compared its use of new weapons in Vietnam to Nazi medical experiments. Roche concluded that King had "thrown in with the commies." King, Roche assured the president, "was inordinately ambitious and quite stupid" and had allowed himself "and his driving wife" to be "played like trout." Radicals were making clear that they believed that the violence at home and abroad stemmed from the same problem—the failure of democracy. Jack Newfield wrote after watching the Newark riots, "One cannot speak of Black Power, or the riots or even Vietnam, in a departmentalized vacuum. They are all part of something larger. We have permitted political power in America to pass from the people to a technological elite that manipulates the mass media and hoards nuclear weaponry. Representational democracy has broken down."[52] In Chicago over 2,000 radicals met at the National Conference for New Politics, where King once again drew parallels between domestic ills and involvement in Vietnam. The National Mobilization to End the War in Vietnam held marches in New York and San Francisco. From 100,000 to 400,000 people turned up in New York and 50,000 in San Francisco. Vietnam summer, patterned on Mississippi summer of 1964, recruited 10,000 volunteers for a public outreach program nationwide to build a solid base of antiwar support. Protest was no longer confined to a radical fringe. In July 1967 Thomas O'Neill of Massachusetts informed Johnson, "Within the past six months there has been a slow but constant change in the local Boston area on the Vietnam issue." The most striking aspect was that those protesting "were mainly from a solid middle class social and economic status and there was no evidence of youthful agitators."[53]

Senators who had earlier supported Johnson now expressed second thoughts. Vermont's George Aiken remarked, "When we follow a policy that does not work and has not worked, then it is time, perhaps, to try something else." Missouri's senator Stuart Symington, previously a hard-liner on the war, suggested that America "offer not only to stop the fighting in North Viet Nam but also the fighting in South Viet Nam, and start negotiations from there." Those who had opposed the administration policy from the beginning became even more strident in their criticisms. George McGovern called it a "policy of madness" that "brought us one step closer to World War III" and that would sooner or later envelop his "son and American youth by the millions for years to come."[54]

Between unrest over urban upheaval, the war, and the need to raise taxes, the president's popularity all but vanished. "If I got to believing all the things that had been written about me," Johnson said, "I would pack my suitcase and go home." The pollster Lou Harris showed that support for the war dropped from 72 percent to 61 percent in just a few months. Harris concluded, "The growing public disenchantment stems directly from the now dominant view that the war is not going better militarily."

These events of the summer of 1967 only hardened the convictions of the contesting factions in the ADA. The continued escalation and cries of protest convinced Lowenstein that the party would suffer a devastating defeat at the polls in 1968 if Johnson was the nominee. The radicalization of the peace movement and the growing friction in the civil rights movement convinced Schlesinger and Galbraith of the need for compromise and not for dramatic gestures. To Tyler the black unrest proved that liberals should be devoting their attention to the great unsolved domestic issues of poverty and racism and not be making divisive political decisions on the basis of foreign policy. The other issues that concerned the ADA in the summer of 1967—urban riots, taxes, crime—all swirled around the vortex of Vietnam. Not only did it dominate the attention of both the National Board and the Executive

Committee; it also pervaded the personal correspondence of all the key participants.

Each group viewed the riots, for example, in the larger context of the war and hoped the unrest would strengthen its position in the organization. In the ADA Executive Committee meetings held to discuss the summer's rioting, Roche reported that reformers made "the usual effort . . . to blame them on the war in Vietnam." Roche and other traditionalists found that logic "dubious," resting on the faulty assumption that "if there were no war, there would have been some sort of exponential increase in spending for poverty." "I suppose the temptation to tie our social problems to the war in Vietnam is virtually irresistible," Roche commented in June. "I fully expect cranberry growers to blame any bad crop on the war." Most moderates, although disturbed by Johnson's obsession with Vietnam and apparent indifference to the Great Society, were still reluctant to risk the president's wrath by joining forces with reformers. Consequently, Roche boasted to Johnson that his "faithful majority—present and voting—killed all such nonsense." Instead of attacking Johnson, the committee's resolution, written almost entirely by Gus Tyler, criticized the liberals' old nemesis—the conservative coalition in Congress. "A Congress that cuts poverty funds saves pennies on projects," the statement declared, "and loses millions to crime and chaos."[55]

The debate in the ADA came to a head at the September 1967 National Board meeting, where Lowenstein rallied his supporters in an effort to push through a dump-Johnson statement. The chapters and Campus ADA quickly fell in line with Lowenstein. Some chapters proposed resolutions that the ADA abandon Johnson and elect delegates to the Democratic convention pledged to oppose his candidacy. Johnson's nomination, they feared, "would have the same devastating effect on the Democratic Party that the nomination of Barry Goldwater had on the Republicans." The Northern California chapter was even more critical: "We hold President Johnson morally and politically responsible for the escalation of the war in Vietnam, and we will oppose his re-election for this reason alone." Elliott Abrams, the president of Campus ADA, wanted to steal some of the thunder from the more radical campus groups like SDS. He believed that "students want to work effectively in politics and that nothing would be more appealing to them, and more timely, than a dump Johnson resolution." They threw their support behind a resolution that read, "Since Vietnam, race and poverty are the moral tests of this generation, it is equally plain that moral Americans cannot support Lyndon Johnson. He must be rejected in the most practical way—electing delegates to the Democratic national Convention pledged to oppose his nomination in 1968."[56]

Gus Tyler countered with a more moderate proposal, calling on the ADA to dissociate itself from any third-party movement or from any movement committed to electing convention delegates opposed to Johnson, continue its campaign for "Negotiations Now!" and not permit "our involvement in Vietnam to become an excuse to deny domestic programs that our nation can afford." He offered a statement that Johnson should not be judged solely on the basis of Vietnam but rather as "the president who has promoted a wide range of liberal domestic legislation."[57]

Moderates like Schlesinger and Galbraith searched for a short-term remedy that would keep the reformers content without alienating labor. While unwilling to join a quixotic dump-Johnson movement, many moderates were losing patience with the president and had begun their own search for a candidate to oppose him. In September of 1967, lacking both the will to dump the president and a candidate to oppose him, moderates searched for a way to keep liberal ranks united. Rauh offered a plan he hoped would satisfy both the Tyler and the Lowenstein factions. It called on the ADA to organize a delegate peace caucus at the Democratic convention that would oppose the war but not Johnson. Rauh's "peace caucus" program was actually an attempt to defuse the more radical dump-Johnson movement that was gaining ground among ADA members. Roche believed that the proposal represented "a real strategic retreat" from "the 'Dump Johnson' line. . . ." "It reflects," he wrote Marvin Watson, "their collective political understanding that attacks on the President will be the route to disaster." Godfrey Hodgson has written that a more suitable description for the plan might have been "an argument against the disturbing talk on the part of Allard Lowenstein and others about organizing opposition to Lyndon Johnson's reelection." Rauh recognized that the dump-Johnson movement had considerable appeal, but he feared that by personalizing the issue, it would deny "the opportunity for participation to the many Democratic political leaders who want to join a peace effort inside their party but where position prevents their joining a 'dump Johnson' movement." More important, Rauh was afraid the Lowenstein plan would fracture "the liberal-labor-Negro coalition that had elected every liberal president and made possible every liberal advance since the 1930s." Rauh wanted the peace movement "to work with responsible figures in the Democratic party through the normal processes of politics and to demonstrate the true strength of the anti-war movement which will be obscured by the methods presently being suggested."[58]

Lowenstein criticized Rauh's proposal as too weak. "What the Rauh memorandum overestimates," he told the National Board, "is the effectiveness of the coalition around the *Negotiations Now!* campaign and what he underestimates is the depths of the national revulsion against the President." Dr. Norman Frankel, a New York psychiatrist, commented indignantly, "We say the policy in the war is madness, and then we support the principal madman." Rauh's compromise, however, seemed to point a way out of the dilemma and was overwhelmingly approved. Galbraith and other moderates found it attractive because it would give the ADA more leverage as the campaign approached. "As long as a liberal organization is uncommitted," Galbraith reasoned, "it has somewhat more influence on events."

According to Roche's analysis, which he gave to the president the next day, there were 90 members at the meeting: "About 20 on the nut fringe,"— his euphemism for Lowenstein—"40 in Rauh's center lump, and 30 with me." Schlesinger, he said, was "cooing like a dove in the Rauh caucus," while

Lowenstein was "left a querulous, bitching, pleading casualty." Roche looked forward to the possibility of "a lovely intestine brawl between the peace nuts and the Rauh entourage." Roche planned to stand on the sidelines with "his faithful thirty" and "throw some gasoline on the fire every time it threaten[ed] to die down."[59]

By September an uneasy truce had settled over the organization. While the lines of division were clearly drawn, Rauh's compromise provided a much needed opportunity for ADA's leaders to assess their position. They had no illusions that the compromise would have a long life. But there was hope that some dramatic breakthrough could cool the heated debate and quiet the sounds of discord.

9

Liberals and the 1968 Election

In the fall of 1967 Vietnam seemed only the most glaring symbol of a deep malaise affecting all of American society. *Newsweek* commented that the nation was experiencing ". . . one of the most histrionic autumns America had ever known." The symbols of revolt, James Reston said, "are merely the outlawed manifestations of a much deeper derangement in the life of the nation." "The State of the Union," wrote the columnist Kennedy Crawford in late 1967, "has never looked more chaotic than it does right now. Not since the depression have there been so many demonstrations of public discontent." Anxiety over the war did not translate into support for any particular policy, either withdrawal or escalation, but fostered a public mood of weariness, frustration and anger. "More and more," Secretary of Health, Education and Welfare John Gardner told a University of North Carolina audience in October, "hostility and venom are the hallmarks of any conversation on the affairs of the nation. Today, all seem caught up in mutual recriminations—Negro and white, rich and poor, conservative and liberal, hawk and dove, labor and management, North and South, young and old."[1]

Vietnam was the looking glass in which the nation saw itself in 1967. It was not an appealing sight. Despite American attempts to establish a secure government in South Vietnam, the nationalist revolution waged its own effective war against the American-supported regime. The air war escalated, as B-52's dropped their deadly cargo on oil installations, truck depots, and railroad yards around major North Vietnamese cities. General William Westmoreland routinely pursued his strategy of attrition, with a new series of search-and-destroy operations, and the enemy "body count" mounted astronomically. By the fall of 1967 the American troop commitment had reached nearly 500,000, an increase of 100,000 during the year. Over 13,000 Americans had already lost their lives in the war, and draft calls were exceeding 30,000 per month. American planes had dropped more than a million and a half tons of bombs. But the war remained deadlocked.[2] A Harris poll in October showed that only 31 percent of the Nation approved Johnson's handling of the war—a 15 percent drop in three months. Gallup reported that only 35 percent approved the president's overall job performance—down 10 percent from the preceding year.

Peace activists, seeing little noticeable effect from years of respectable dissent through teach-ins, rallies, and petitions, were becoming increasingly militant. A radical publication, the *Mobilizer,* which appeared in September, captured the new spirit: "We will fill the hallways and block the entrances . . . [in order to] disrupt the center of the American war machine. In the name of humanity we will call the warmongers to task." Intellectuals now saw, in the words of the *Village Voice* reporter Jack Newfield, an "evil link between internal and external violence." Noam Chomsky announced in the *New York Review of Books* that for the second consecutive year he was withholding half his income taxes to protest the war. Paul Goodman invited federal prosecution by acknowledging his efforts to aid and abet draft resistance. Andrew Kopkind declared, "Morality, like politics, starts at the barrel of a gun." On October 12, 1967, the *New York Review of Books* published a statement signed by 121 intellectuals and entitled "A Call to Resist Illegitimate Authority." The statement denounced the war on legal and moral grounds and pledged the signers to raise funds "to organize draft resistance unions, to supply legal defense and bail, to support families and otherwise aid the resistance to the war in whatever ways may seem appropriate." In October the antiwar movement staged a march on the Pentagon, later memorialized by Norman Mailer's *Armies of the Night.* One thousand angry students converged on the Pentagon in order to shut down "the American military machine" in one act of civil disobedience.[3]

By the early winter of 1967, it was obvious that the year coming to an end had dramatically altered the political landscape in America. Now even Congress was balking. According to *Congressional Quarterly,* from the time Johnson took office until the end of 1966, he got 655 of his 1,057 proposals enacted into law—a sensational 62 percent. But in 1967 Johnson lost on his tax surcharge, civil rights, anticrime, East-West trade, and legislative reorganization bills. Congress cut foreign aid by a record $1 billion, poverty funds by $300 million, model cities by $350 million. When Johnson finally asked, in August, for a 10 percent surcharge on income taxes to damp down the supercharged economy, the Arkansas Democrat Wilbur Mills, chairman of the House Ways and Means Committee, insisted on an equivalent cut in federal spending, which the president refused to make. Many could agree with the Yale economist James Tobin's dictum, "The butter to be sacrificed because of the war always turns out to be the margarine of the poor." In his 1968 State of the Union Message, Johnson received only one prolonged ovation, when he said, "The American people have had enough of rising crime and lawlessness in this country." Congress greeted his pleas for civil rights laws, enforcement of equal employment opportunity, and open housing with silence—a drastic change from the rousing applause that had met similar proposals just three years earlier.[4]

Rauh's well-intentioned attempt at compromise fell prey to the pervasive distrust that was sweeping the country. For many liberals the debate had moved beyond the point of compromise. The ADA's attempt to step just far enough to the left to maintain the loyalty of the reformers, without alienating administration supporters, only confirmed the suspicions of many liberals that the organization was too timid and too wedded to the administration. Mary McGrory wrote that the ADA delegates came to town "prepared to storm the White House. Instead they slipped a note under the door and told the President he better watch his step." One reader wrote the *New Republic* that Rauh's "muddleheaded thinking" was "characteristic of the intellectual bankruptcy of the old liberal establishment as typified by the Americans for Democratic Action." The *New Republic* itself called the proposal "peripheral" and "diversionary." The ADA, it editorialized, "finds the food poisonous but defers advertising for another cook." Jack Newfield accused Rauh of being "Lyndon Johnson's last fig leaf."[5]

The debate within the organization was heating up. Don Edwards told the Conference of Concerned Democrats, meeting in Chicago, that the Vietnam was "only a symptom of a sick and misguided view of our role in the world." "Unless a new direction is taken," he warned, "there will be other Vietnams." The Campus ADA's national chairman, Elliott Abrams, openly defied the National Board's decision to abstain from any dump-Johnson movement. "We will not be eunuchs," he said. Craig Pregillus, national director of CADA, said, "We can't officially endorse a 'dump Johnson' program, but that doesn't mean that CADA people won't participate on individual campuses."[6]

The ADA's decision in October also did not dampen Lowenstein's spirits. He was trying harder than ever to mold "dissident" and "concerned" Democrats into a national organization. Jetting across the country, he promised his audiences that he would soon have a candidate "of great prominence" who would announce before Christmas. His first choice was Robert Kennedy, but he was also considering George McGovern, who faced a hard fight for reelection to the Senate. "We have been in touch with leaders," he confirmed, "but none seem to want to commit themselves now. We are building a visible base of opposition to Mr. Johnson. The leaders will come along later."[7]

If Vietnam was a test of American democracy, as Schlesinger claimed, then many moderates were beginning to believe that democracy was failing. Perhaps the old coalition was too inflexible to permit necessary change; perhaps the traditional and reform agendas were incompatible. "Liberalism," Galbraith now concluded, "has gone slightly sour. . . . Its pace far too slow. And it has imposed upon us the painful task of escaping from old convictions that the principal American mission is to destroy communism." As he lost hope in creating a coalition that included both the traditionalists and the reformers, Galbraith recalled some years later, "the need for an anti-war candidate became even more urgent." He and Rauh joined Lowenstein in his desperate search for a candidate to oppose Johnson. McGovern was sympathetic but more concerned with his reelection in South Dakota. Kennedy was also not interested, but he suggested they see Eugene McCarthy, who immediately expressed interest and began testing the political waters.[8]

Born in a small Catholic community in central Minnesota in March 1916, McCarthy often displayed a paradoxical blend of humility and arrogance, idealism and pragmatism, detachment and involvement. Cultivated, quick-witted, and possessed of saturnine good looks, he tended to be too sophisticated and too stuffy to excite audiences. He valued his privacy. "There is a feeling about him," David Halberstam observed, "that while his voting record is liberal, his wit is more that of a conservative dwelling on man's imperfectibility." In nineteen years in Congress—ten in the House and nine in the Senate—McCarthy placed his stamp on very little legislation. Much to the liberals' consternation, he sometimes voted with special interests on issues like drug prices and oil depletion. "Gene," one friend commented, "is sometimes a little soft on minor issues." Many of his colleagues interpreted his sardonic humor as cynicism, his casualness as indifference or even laziness.[9]

Shortly after ten o'clock on the morning of November 30, 1967, the fifty-one-year-old McCarthy stepped into the Caucus Room of the Old Senate Office Building and announced that he intended to enter four presidential primaries. "I am concerned," he said in a matter-of-fact tone, "that the administration seems to have set no limits on the price that it is willing to pay for military victory." McCarthy planned to present his candidacy as an alternative to radicalism. In a speech at Macalester College, in St. Paul, Minnesota, McCarthy explained his reasons for opposing Johnson. "There is deep anxiety and alienation among a large number of people," he said, "so we have demonstrations and draft card burning and all the rest. Someone must give these groups entrance back into the political process." McCarthy contended that Johnson's offer to stop the bombing if North Vietnam would stop supplying its troops in the South was not a serious negotiating position: "It's like saying we'll stop eating for twenty-four hours if you'll stop breathing. It's not negotiable." The basic question that must be faced in 1968, he claimed, is whether "what is called our commitment in South Vietnam is morally defensible. . . . We must raise the essential moral question as to whether or not there is a proper balance in what we may gain in what is projected as victory. . . ." His position on the war was nearly identical with the ADA's: a halt to bombing, an immediate cease-fire in the South, and a negotiated settlement that gave the NLF a part in a coalition government.[10]

McCarthy enjoyed overwhelming support among the local ADA chapters. The New Jersey chapter found, shortly after Minnesota's "Man of La Mancha" announced his candidacy, that 93.0 percent of its members expressed disapproval of Johnson's Vietnam policy; that 75.0 percent were enthusiastic about McCarthy's candidacy; that 85.5 percent wanted "a clear-cut choice of a peace candidate within the Democratic party"; that 64.5 percent would support a third- or fourth-party candidate if neither party offered a peace choice; and that 93 percent demanded a "drastic reversal of national priorities." The New York chapter revealed that 63.3 percent felt that the ADA should endorse McCarthy, 60 percent that the ADA should oppose Johnson's nomination, and only 7 percent that the ADA should work for his renomination. The New York City chapter found that 76 percent of its members favored endorsing McCarthy.

The Philadelphia, Ann Arbor, Washington State, Northern California, and Baltimore chapters all voted unanimously for a McCarthy endorsement. Others, including Massachusetts, Connecticut, New York, Detroit, and Pittsburgh, conducted polls indicating strong but less than unanimous support for McCarthy. In Illinois the leaders said they would not vote for McCarthy even though they "candidly admitted membership would vote to endorse McCarthy." In Wisconsin the ADA chairman was also leader of the McCarthy committee. According to National Director Leon Shull's calculations, two-thirds of the ADA's membership wanted to endorse McCarthy.[11]

As public opposition to the war reached new heights and Johnson's popularity new lows, moderates saw little choice but to support McCarthy's candidacy. Many moderates believed that if liberalism was to present a viable alternative to radicalism, it needed to direct frustration with the war into responsible channels of dissent. In November, Rauh told a New York City Democratic group that unless a peace candidate ran in 1968, "the rioting at the Pentagon would look like a panty-waist tea-party. . . . We've got to turn this horrible frustration from the streets to the ballot box." Rauh argued that, since the ADA had taken a position against civil disobedience, if it did not endorse McCarthy, it "would have been in truth what the fellow-travelers and New Left have always wanted to paint us—total and complete captives of any Democratic Administration." The middle ground was no longer secure; if moderates were to maintain the loyalty of the young, they needed to abandon the old coalition. Labor's threats notwithstanding, much could be gained by such a move. As Galbraith remembered, "We just couldn't keep this organization going if we compromised on what so many people—and especially younger ones—regard as the key issues of principle." The war, James Wechsler wrote, "has fractured many 'coalitions'; it has also paved the way for new ones. . . . No matter what the consequences of the endorsement in terms of some labor relationships, the price of passivity would surely have been exorbitant."[12]

For many moderates support for McCarthy was a matter of conviction, not choice. McCarthy was not politically appealing, and he did not have a very encouraging voting record. But he was right on the single most important issue of 1968—Vietnam. "No one cared that McCarthy was awful on domestic affairs," Rauh recalled some years later. "He was right on the war, and the war was everything." He was a symbol of protest that moderates could no longer ignore. The day before McCarthy announced his candidacy, Shull wrote, "I can only tell you how much I wish Kennedy would run and that McCarthy would go back to being what he is—a negative, colorless Senator who makes high-sounding speeches and then votes wrong on many issues. However, if McCarthy announces he is running for the

Presidency I think we shall have to support him. The moral imperative, whatever that is, seems to require it."[13]

Moderates had no illusions about what a McCarthy endorsement would do to the ADA. When Rauh, meeting with labor representatives in the organization, asked, "What will you do if we endorse McCarthy?" the response was immediate and unanimous—"Pull out!" There was also an agonizingly painful side to the problem. Moderates were abandoning not only the most progressive president since FDR but also one of the organization's founding fathers, its most prestigious public figure, and, more important, a very close friend—Hubert Humphrey. Humphrey was not making it easier. He was lobbying his friends against an endorsement. When Rauh went to see the vice-president to explain to him why he was going on television the next day to endorse McCarthy, Humphrey went into one of his long monologues—this one lasted fifty-five minutes—trying to justify the war. When he finished, he glanced at Rauh and said, "Geez, Joe, I said a lot of things that were classified in order to persuade you not to do that." Rauh responded, "Well, you don't have anything to worry about. You talked so damn fast and said so much, I can't remember a thing you said." But Rauh nonetheless asserted, "I just can't believe we should be in a land war in Vietnam."[14]

If cautious liberals were to be led away from the security of the Democratic party, they wanted a candidate who had a reasonable chance of winning. But in the winter of 1968 McCarthy was not an effective candidate. "Let the unhappy, brutal truth come out," Jack Newfield wrote. "Eugene McCarthy's campaign is a disaster. . . . McCarthy's speeches are dull, vague, and without either balls or poetry. He is lazy and vain." "Eugene McCarthy is doing so badly," Roche informed the president, "that I am tempted to float a rumor that he is actually working for you to dispirit the peace movement." His campaign, Newfield said, "looks like just another effort by the ADA to promote a candidate for vice-president."[15]

The traditional group resisted any suggestion that the ADA should endorse McCarthy. With considerable conviction they continued to argue that an endorsement before the Democratic convention was politically unwise and probably in violation of the organization's mandate and that, more important, it was perniciously divisive. Reuther warned that "a primary endorsement would almost certainly alienate and offend members" and risk making the ADA "into a single-purpose organization" confronting "a future of reduced size and influence, and probably unable to revert effectively to its original purposes."[16] Hyman Bookbinder, a National Board representative of the American Jewish Committee, claimed that on the whole range of issues McCarthy did not measure up to Johnson. "Frankly," he said, McCarthy is "as ignorant as a Chicago *Tribune* editorial writer." Bookbinder also had strong ideas about the ADA's political role. "ADA's principal duty is to protect the very unique coalition it has sustained for over 20 years. I don't want to see it destroyed because of the current emotional situation over Vietnam." Since the ADA is probably going to have to choose between LBJ and the GOP anyway, he argued, "why make it difficult in September because we acted emotionally in February?" If liberals cannot unite behind Johnson, Gus Tyler feared, "America can be swept into a dismal abyss of prolonged reaction." Others, like James Loeb, opposed the endorsement for more practical reasons. Pleading for ADA's survival, Loeb concluded, "I have been for lost causes all my political life, and I am ready to be for some more. But never a cause so lost as this one, even before it starts."[17]

Leon Keyserling presented the most sustained and forceful argument against the endorsement. In the article "What Has Happened to the ADA," Keyserling expressed his frustrations with the changing political direction of the ADA's liberalism, its increased activism in political affairs at the expense of its Fabian role, and, perhaps most of all, his personal feeling of futility as he and many who still adhered to the Vital Center were pushed aside in favor of a "new" liberalism. By focusing so much of its attention on Vietnam, he argued, the ADA was ignoring many other issues that liberals should be addressing. It was the ADA, he said, and not the Johnson administration, that has "turned its back on progressive economic and social policies on the domestic front." He resumed his attack on Galbraith's celebration of an "affluent society" when economic misery was still widespread in America. "It is really hard to imagine where Mr. Galbraith was when he wrote all this," Keyserling blustered. "I believe he was in Switzerland. Even today, there are millions of American families who cannot afford a nutritious and balanced diet."[18]

McCarthy supporters received a big boost when on January 31, 1968, Communist troops launched an offensive during Tet, the lunar New Year. The Vietcong invaded the U.S. embassy compound in Saigon and waged bloody battles in the capitals of most of South Vietnam's provinces. Sixty-seven thousand enemy troops invaded more than one hundred of South Vietnam's cities and towns. While militarily a victory for the United States, the Tet offensive showed that no place in South Vietnam was secure, not even the American embassy. Coming after administration assurances that the war was being won, it dealt Johnson's credibility a final blow. In the six weeks after Tet, Walter Cronkite, *Newsweek,* the *Wall Street Journal,* and NBC News called for deescalation. McCarthy deftly exploited the loss of confidence in Johnson's credibility. He reminded audiences that the administration's repeated "hollow claims of programs and victories" in Vietnam had not proven accurate: "Only a few months ago we were told that sixty-five percent of the population was secure. Now we know that even the American embassy is not secure."[19]

After the Tet offensive, Johnson faced a more critical military choice. Westmoreland and the Joint Chiefs of Staff asked for 206,000 men, which would have brought the total to 750,000. The shock waves from Tet and the popular reaction converged with other forces bearing down upon the president. On one side treasury secretary Henry Fowler was pleading for an emergency tax boost to keep the dollar from collapsing under the withdrawal of confidence abroad. On another side Clark Clifford, recently appointed defense secretary, completing a review of U.S. strategic commitments, recommended that General Westmoreland's call for more troops not be accepted.

In the wake of the McCarthy candidacy and the Tet offensive, there was no doubt that the liberal press wanted the ADA to endorse McCarthy. The *New Republic* declared, "If the ADA makes this choice, it cuts its ties with the past, endangers its 20-year alliance with a coterie of influential labor leaders but opens the door to hundreds of thousands of 'grass-roots' liberals." Most would have agreed with TRB's observation that "if it did not support Senator McCarthy who was fighting for its program it might just as well have folded. . . ."[20]

The climactic board meeting was the best-attended in the organization's history, with only 18 of the 117 National Board members absent. On Saturday morning, February 10, Rauh introduced an unequivocal statement of support for McCarthy's candidacy. Rauh said that McCarthy was "a man on our side, with a 92% ADA rating in 19 years in Congress," that ADA offices and expertise could add "new drive, professionalization and legitimization" to the McCarthy challenge, and that "anything less would constitute abdication of the liberal position." The Rauh resolution never mentioned Johnson by name but said only that McCarthy has "dared to offer an alternative." "Only his candidacy," it added, "offers a banner around which those who oppose the deadly draft can rally. His calls for reason, reawakening and reappraisal embodies both the spirit and substance of positions repeatedly urged by ADA."[21]

Robert Bendiner and Edward Hollander responded with a resolution calling for local option. Local ADA chapters, it said, have "to take whatever political action they think desirable with respect to the Presidential candidacy of Senator Eugene McCarthy."[22] Bendiner and Hollander represented a small group of moderates who, while disenchanted with Johnson, refused to accept McCarthy. They probably would have voted to endorse Kennedy had he been a candidate. Their hope was simply to hold the organization together by avoiding an endorsement decision. Yet, especially after the Tet offensive, the question of endorsement had for most members taken on a symbolic importance beyond the mere calculus of electability.

According to a prearranged plan, Rauh withdrew his resolution in favor of Galbraith's proposal, which declared that the "ideas" McCarthy represented outweighed his limitations as a candidate. While putting the ADA on record as endorsing McCarthy, the Galbraith resolution allowed individual members to support publicly the candidate of their choice. They hoped that this toned-down statement would leave the less recalcitrant traditionalists with a reason to remain in the organization. Tyler contended that the ADA should make no endorsement and keep its options open. In attacking McCarthy, he used Jack Newfield's *Village Voice* articles criticizing the senator for having "fractionated the peace movement, blocked Bobby, and voted against tax reforms and drug regulation."[23]

Over eight hours of debate ensued. Those supporting a McCarthy endorsement argued that, whether or not McCarthy was successful, his campaign had a significance that went beyond the poll results. He was a symbol, "the only available symbol of protest" that the ADA had to grasp. McCarthy provided liberals with a respectable and responsible means of protest. What, they asked, did the organization have to lose? It did not have to worry about losing influence with the administration, because Johnson "never listened to his critics" anyway. If anything, the endorsement would "attract new blood among cynical and disenchanted youth." The administration's supporters contended that "the coalition was threatened and that the pullout of labor would mean the end of ADA." They attacked McCarthy's credibility as a candidate, arguing that he was a "one issue man" and that, if judged on all the issues, he could not be compared to the president. Carl Auerbach denied that the war was preventing the expansion of Great Society programs. The reaction against the Great Society occurred for political rather than economic reasons. It is, he exclaimed, an "injustice to American liberalism to depreciate what is actually being done while the war is going on." The traditionalists asked only that the ADA hold off making any endorsement until after both parties had held their conventions. They agreed that if McCarthy won the nomination, they would do everything possible to help him in the general election.[24]

Despite Tyler's sometimes emotional defense of the administration, the combined weight of moderate and reform forces overwhelmed the traditionalists and carried the day. The final vote was sixty-five to forty-seven in favor of endorsement. Critics pounced on the decision. "The coalition is finished," Tyler fumed. "Everything was all right when the ADA was a coalition of major unions and prominent individuals. Now, these new people have come." Keyserling said the decision was "very silly," adding, "I've never felt the ADA should take on the face of a political party. . . . It should function as a small group of intellectuals providing liberal ideas and backing liberal programs." Ben Fisher, a Pittsburgh chapter representative who voted against endorsement, said it made "the ADA a center for dissent instead of a center for liberal unity on a balanced progressive political program." Paul Porter, who twenty years earlier had helped coordinate ADA efforts with the Truman campaign, wrote Humphrey, "It was mostly in sorrow that I read of the deliberations of our cherished alma mater ADA (Adult Delinquents Association)."[25]

Three union presidents turned in their resignations in protest: I. W. Abel of the United Steelworkers of America, Louis Stulberg of the ILGWU, and Joseph Beirne of the Communications Workers of America. Most ADA leaders felt that Abel's resignation would have the sharpest impact because his 1.1-million-member union was a strong financial backer of the group. Neither Stulberg nor Beirne had contributed much money in recent years. Shull tried to convince those who resigned and those threatening to resign that the decision to support McCarthy applied only to the presidential primaries and that the organization had not made a choice for the general election. "The real decision which ADA has to make—the truly significant one—will come at the Convention and at the board meeting to be held in September after the national conventions are held."[26]

Despite Tyler's threats, David Dubinsky, the retired president of the ILGWU, retained his membership so that he could "work within the organization to change the position."[27] Four vice-presidents—Emile Benoit, Edward Hollander, Robert Nathan, and Marvin Rosenberg—fifteen board members, and a number of labor representatives issued a statement the week after the endorsement to signal their intention to stay in the ADA. Their main point was that "a working coalition of all liberal forces" was too important to be destroyed for the sake of one issue, although an important one. Among the labor leaders who stayed in the organization were Walter Reuther and Charles Cogen, president of the American Federation of Teachers; Leon Schachter of the Amalgamated Meat Cutters Union; Jake Clayman from the Industrial Union Department of AFL-CIO; Walter L. Mitchell, International Chemical Union; and Ralph Halsrein, United Packinghouse Workers Union.[28]

After the endorsement, many moderates feared that the labor defections could seriously upset the balance within the organization. "One can picture a situation," Rauh warned, "where the more conservative elements in ADA withdraw at the same time new and more radical elements are entering. Obviously that will shift the center of gravity inside the organization and those of us who have taken a middle course could very well lose influence." In order to prevent that from happening, the moderates appealed to the more progressive labor representatives to stay in the organization and help forge the nucleus of a new liberal coalition. Galbraith believed that intellectuals and the "scientific community" could join forces with the "disciplined troops" of progressive labor and form such a coalition. Galbraith was especially solicitous of Reuther's support. "You are the best labor leader in the country," he wrote the UAW head. "I think I probably classify as one of the better liberals. My thought is we had better stay in communication."[29]

One thing was certain—the McCarthy endorsement led to major organizational changes. Shull claimed the overall membership "grew by 6,000 in the few months following the McCarthy endorsement to a total of 60,000." A comprehensive study of ADA's organizational status conducted in August 1968 showed the effect the McCarthy endorsement had on the organization. Within just a few weeks after the February decision, 1,400 people had joined the ADA. The Southern California chapter alone gained 462 members as of March. In addition 4,000 people with no previous history of support gave money. Also, a mailing to 31,000 members produced an extraordinary 7.5 percent response, averaging $23.80 per contribution—the most successful fund-raising mailing in the ADA's history. Increased contributions allowed the organization to erase its troublesome debt and for the first time to establish a savings account.[30]

The ADA experience was not unique. Other liberal and peace organizations, especially those founded before 1960, nurtured on anticommunism and committed to moderate reform, faced very similar problems. The most glaring example was SANE—the National Committee for a Sane Nuclear Policy. Founded in 1957, this organization, like the ADA, refused to accept Communists and tried to build a broad-based reform movement. By 1967 Dr. Benjamin Spock, SANE's counterpart to Allard Lowenstein, organized the local chapters in revolt against the national leadership. The issue confronting SANE, the ADA, and many other liberal social movement groups was, as the disgruntled former executive director Donald Keys put it, should the organization "move to the left, becoming more radical and cooperating with extremist groups, in order to accommodate itself to the drift of many of its supporters who are going in this direction due to their anger and frustration over the war?" Or should it "continue attempting a dialogue and establishing communication with the undecided American Middle and maintain its efforts to construct conduits of influence that will reach to policy makers and government officials?"[31]

The ADA endorsement gave an added boost to the McCarthy campaign, which was beginning to make gains in the polls. The organization could not supply many votes; it was the symbol of an "established" liberal organization breaking away from the administration that was significant. Individual members gave McCarthy advice that he usually disregarded, while the local chapters worked with the McCarthy organization—where there was one.[32]

McCarthy reluctantly entered the first big primary of the season, in New Hampshire, believing that his brand of midwestern liberalism would have little appeal. Governor John King predicted that the president would "murder" McCarthy and his youth army. Instead, McCarthy polled a stunning 42.2 percent of the Democratic vote to Johnson's 49.4 percent and captured twenty of the twenty-four convention delegates. He galvanized feeling against the war, both among doves and among hawks who opposed Johnson's policy, into an upset victory against the incumbent president of his own party. The New Hampshire primary demonstrated Johnson's vulnerability and transformed McCarthy from a hopeless underdog into a serious challenger. "People have remarked that this campaign has brought young people back into the system. But it's the other way around," he told his adoring followers. "The young people have brought the country back into the system."

Four days after McCarthy's New Hampshire victory, Robert Kennedy entered the race. The younger Kennedy's political strategy was straightforward—to sweep the primaries, drawing such large crowds and showing such support at the polls that the convention delegates would have no choice but to support his nomination. Although Kennedy and McCarthy held similar positions on the war—a total bombing halt and the inclusion of the NLF in the peace talks—the two men were strikingly different, not so much in politics as in values and temperament. Kennedy was passionate and visceral; McCarthy, detached and cerebral. McCarthy was the unpartisan, WASP-ish looking (though he was, like Kennedy, Catholic) intellectual who presented cogent yet uninspiring discourses against the war; Kennedy was the tough Irish blue blood who expressed the moral trauma of blue-collar America. McCarthy drew his support from among the young, the affluent, the educated; Kennedy also appealed to these groups but was able to reach out and organize the poor, blacks, and ethnic Americans along class lines.[33]

The moderates in the ADA were personally close to Kennedy, who had been their first choice for opposing Johnson. Not only did they believe that Kennedy was the more compelling leader of the antiwar forces; they recognized that he, unlike any of the other candidates in the race, could also appeal to young reformers and working-class ethnics alike. But that was before the organization went on record as supporting McCarthy, and before McCarthy showed his political effectiveness in New Hampshire. Although a few prominent ADA members, most visibly Arthur Schlesinger, Jr., switched to Kennedy, for the time being most planned to continue to work with McCarthy, hoping that the two peace candidates would not bludgeon each other and leave Johnson, the real enemy, unscathed.

Kennedy had little support in the ADA outside of the moderate group. While a few of the traditionalists, like Walter Reuther, were personally close to RFK, many others had nothing but contempt for the junior senator from New York. John Roche described him as "demonic." "I don't think he knew a principle from a railroad tie," he said later. What irked Roche and other traditionalists was Kennedy's close links to the moderates in the ADA. Roche believed that many of the ADA's most prominent members, especially Schlesinger, Galbraith, and, to a lesser extent, Rauh, had transformed the ADA into "the bastion of the Kennedys in exile." Keyserling accused them of plotting, from the day President Kennedy was killed, "to regain their place in the sun of some future" Kennedy administration. "The Kennedys in exile were not interested in Vietnam," Roche charged later, "they were not interested in poverty; they were not interested in anything except getting a Kennedy back into the White House."[34]

Some of the reformers, like Allard Lowenstein, were fond of Robert Kennedy, but many believed he was too closely tied to the politics of the past. They were less forgiving than Lowenstein of Kennedy's early association with Joseph McCarthy's witch-hunt in the 1950s, of his indifference to the freedom riders in the South while he was attorney general, and of his apparently expedient decision to jump into the race after McCarthy had paved the way by winning in New Hampshire.

Never one to share center stage, Johnson had one more surprise in his bag of tricks. On March 31 he went before a national television audience to announce that he was ordering a temporary pause in the bombing. Was this another political ploy by the president to take the wind out of the sails of the McCarthy and Kennedy campaigns? As he closed, Johnson gave the answer that astonished the nation: "With America's sons in the fields faraway, with America's future under challenge right here at home, with our hopes and the world's hopes for peace in the balance every day, I do not believe that I should devote an hour or a day of my time to my personal partisan causes or to any duties other than the awesome duties of this office—the presidency of your country." His face grown gaunt and tired from years of strain, the president looked directly into the camera and declared, "Accordingly, I shall not seek, and I will not accept the nomination of my party, for another term as your president."[35]

Johnson's announcement of a bombing pause combined with his renunciation of another term raised hopes that the national nightmare was over. The hope proved short-lived. On April 4 a lone gunman shot and killed Martin Luther King, Jr., as he stood on the second-floor balcony of the Lorraine Motel in Memphis. King's death shocked the nation, for it marked not just the loss of a great leader but the end of the nonviolent civil rights movement to which King had dedicated his life. Even as the presidential contenders gathered for King's funeral services in the narrow pews of the steamy Ebenezer Baptist Church, in Atlanta, politics could not have been far from their minds. Each contemplated the consequences of Johnson's decision not to seek reelection and of King's assassination. The heaviest burden fell on Humphrey. The vice-president had responded cautiously to the news of Johnson's decision not to seek reelection. "I don't want to be destroyed again in a fight with the Kennedys," he told one aide. But McCarthy's April 2 victory in the Wisconsin primary convinced Humphrey that Kennedy and McCarthy would weaken each other, divide the peace forces, and leave the nomination to him. He had no intention of entering the primary contests. Not only had the filing date passed in many states, but he knew he could rely on the president's supporters to commit delegates to him, even if the other candidates won in the primaries. Humphrey's advisers were not concerned that his avoiding the primaries would create, as some observers were predicting, a damaging backlash from the young. While McCarthy and Kennedy were trumpeting the virtues of the New Politics, Humphrey seemed content with the Old. William Connell, a Humphrey aide, warned the vice-president not to "go overboard on the theory of the younger voter." "While it is important to note the increasing numbers of young voters," he said, "it is also important to note . . . that in 1968 almost three-fourths of those actually voting will be over 35. Only 25% of those who vote will be under 35."[36]

Three weeks after the announcement of Johnson's decision, on April 27, Humphrey made it official—he was a candidate for the presidency. While contending that he was the candidate who could unify the country, Humphrey, in one of his typical bouts of exuberance, uttered words that were to haunt him throughout the campaign. "Here we are," he exclaimed, obviously exhilarated by the enthusiastic applause of a partisan crowd, "just as we ought to be, the people, here we are, in a spirit of dedication, here we are, the way politics should be in America, the politics of happiness, the politics of purpose, and the politics of joy." Humphrey's attempt to inject joy into a campaign marred by divisive debates over a war in Vietnam rang hollow. This gaffe, however, did not inhibit his march to the nomination. Two days after he entered the race, his campaign staff boasted that 1,200 of the 1,312 delegates needed for the nomination were already committed to or leaning toward Humphrey.[37]

Johnson's decision, and the simultaneous announcement of a bombing halt and new peace negotiations, undermined McCarthy's and Kennedy's most compelling issue, leaving them engaged in an increasingly bitter personality fight. After winning uncontested primaries in Connecticut and Pennsylvania, McCarthy prepared to tackle Kennedy in Indiana and Nebraska in May. Kennedy won significant, though not overwhelming, victories in both, but McCarthy breathed new life into his campaign by handing Kennedy his first defeat in Oregon.

When the ADA met for its Twenty-first Annual Convention on May 17–21 in Washington, it was a different organization from the one that had met just the year before. Few labor representatives were present, the delegates were younger, and many were attending for the first time and were there for one reason—the ADA's endorsement of McCarthy. Humphrey and Kennedy supporters were still present, but they were a distinct minority. In order to avoid another split at the convention, Shull recommended that the organization reendorse McCarthy but also say "something nice" about Kennedy and Humphrey in order not to tie their hands if one of them were to get the nomination. The five hundred delegates followed Shull's advice, passing a resolution that proclaimed, "[McCarthy] has made political participation a viable course for thousands of politically alienated Americans, both young and old. He has talked sense to the American people on foreign and domestic issues." They congratulated Kennedy for having the courage to oppose the war, and praised Humphrey as "a dynamic and innovative figure in American liberalism."[38] With most of the hard-core traditionalists absent, there were no more of the heated debates and emotional fireworks that had marred previous debates over political policy.

Following the endorsement Rauh was asked to represent the organization at a large McCarthy rally in Madison Square Garden. When Rauh announced to the jam-packed hall, "Four hours ago the ADA voted to endorse the candidacy of Senator Eugene McCarthy," the crowd went wild. Rauh has remembered thinking at the time that the crowd obviously considered the ADA a more important and influential organization than it actually was.[39]

After the convention, liberals turned their attention to the big California primary on June 4. A poor showing in a televised debate made McCarthy and his aides prepare themselves for defeat. As McCarthy sat alone in his hotel room watching the disappointing returns and drafting a congratulatory telegram, Kennedy was ending his victory speech from the rostrum of his headquarters at the Ambassador Hotel, near downtown Los Angeles. After his last words—"I think we can end the divisions within the United States, the violence"—Kennedy was escorted directly behind the speaker's platform through a gold curtain toward a kitchen that led to the press room. As he passed through the kitchen, he was met by Sirhan Sirhan, a deranged Jordanian nationalist, who fired two fatal shots at Kennedy. Twenty-five hours later, without ever regaining consciousness, Robert F. Kennedy died.

Kennedy's death assured Humphrey of the nomination. In the middle of June a *New York Times* poll gave Humphrey 1,600 delegates, considerably

more than the 1,312 needed for the nomination. Yet Humphrey's goal was to
make the nomination worth winning. In order to do that, he needed to convince people that his candidacy was independent of the administration and
that he was more than just a mouthpiece for Johnson. A *Wall Street Journal*
headline summed up Humphrey's dilemma—"Vice President Tries, But Can't
Shed Image as the President's Boy." He considered a number of steps to drive
the point home, including resigning the vice-presidency. Eventually, he agreed
to the less dramatic step of trying to put some light between his and Johnson's positions on the war. When, in July, Humphrey and his advisers drew
up a statement on Vietnam that called for an unconditional end to the bombing, Johnson refused to accept it. "Hubert, if you do this, I'll just have to be
opposed to it, and say so." They were strong words from a man whose patronage Humphrey still needed. Perhaps more convincingly, Johnson said
such a statement would damage the very delicate peace negotiations taking
place in Paris.[40]

It was clear that McCarthy no longer had any stomach for campaigning.
"McCarthy did not resign his candidacy after the Kennedy Assassination,"
one former staff member commented; "he left his lottery ticket in the big barrel to await the hand of God." After Kennedy's death, McCarthy's quirky
personality became even more puzzling, his manner more indifferent. He refused to campaign in the New York primary, causing one of his organizers to
comment, "McCarthy didn't throw cold water on the New York primary—he
pissed on it." Although he kept a heavy speaking schedule, mostly in non-
primary states, he spoke "more about the Democratic party than about [his]
own campaign." By the summer of 1968 his candidacy, which had once inspired such hope in New Hampshire, was devoid of leadership and degenerat-
ing into factional dispute.[41]

When the Democrats arrived in Chicago for their convention, they found
a city prepared for war. Humphrey had asked earlier to have the convention
moved to Miami Beach, but Johnson, who retained personal control over the
convention machinery, decided to stick with Chicago. In early August, Humphrey had written to Mayor Richard Daley urging him, to no avail, to provide
a hall for the thousands of protesters who were planning to descend on the
city. As the convention opened in August, about ten thousand protesters were
matched against Mayor Daley and his police force equipped with billy clubs,
tear gas, and mace and backed up by five thousand National Guardsmen. It
was, Galbraith observed, "an occasion of brutality and horror."

During the convention the ADA strategy was to work for McCarthy but
to avoid involvement in any effort to disrupt the proceedings. Realizing that
Humphrey would probably be the nominee, it did not want to do anything
that would make working with him any more difficult than it was already going to be. "Our differences with the Humphrey forces," Rauh said, "will be
only on Vietnam policy. We will do everything not to exacerbate our differences." In previous conventions the ADA had refused to pursue issues at the

expense of party unity. But this year was different. "In politics," Galbraith recalled about the organization's strategy, "one usually fights in order to compromise. . . . But there are times when one must be completely adamant, and this was one. The war was the transcendent issue. Compromise would not only have cost us the confidence of our own supporters, it would have provided sanction for those saying the war must go on." The top priority was to marshal all of the ADA's resources in support of the McCarthy candidacy. Beyond that they would push for a liberal platform, a credentials fight, and a democratization of the rules for the selecting of delegates.[42]

Despite Rauh's claim that the ADA would do nothing to exacerbate its differences with Humphrey, he, along with Galbraith and Leon Shull, did exactly that by distributing a letter to delegates at the convention reaffirming their support for McCarthy and expressing dissatisfaction with Humphrey. McCarthy, they said, rescued the party from the "worst error in modern times." Humphrey, on the other hand, "is the candidate of the past—of a past and a policy that the people have rejected." "Consistent with our deep belief in the politics of issues and ideology," they said, "we can come to no other conclusion than to oppose the nomination of Vice President Humphrey."[43]

The letter upset a number of vice-chairmen. Nathan was furious that ADA officers would, in the name of the organization, take a public position that was "so totally incompatible with and so substantially contrary to the position taken at a national convention." The "unwarranted and unjust charge," he argued, "could upset the fragile truce within the ADA and seriously split the organization once again." "Can't you resist," Hyman Bookbinder pleaded with Galbraith, "being caught up in this horrible lynch spirit against one of ADA's former Chairmen?"[44]

Liberal stubbornness on the issue of the war made it necessary for Humphrey to reach a compromise with the peace forces. A coalition of peace groups, including the ADA, drew up a minority plank calling for "an unconditional end to all bombing of North Vietnam"; negotiated phased withdrawal of U.S. and North Vietnamese troops; negotiations with the NLF; and a lowering of offensive operations to allow for an early withdrawal of foreign forces. Humphrey's aides felt sure that he could accept the language. "There's not ten cents of difference between this and the vice-president's policy," said one of them. Just to be on the safe side, Humphrey cleared the language with Secretary of State Dean Rusk and the presidential adviser Walt Rostow, both hawks. When Johnson caught wind of what Humphrey was doing, he told the platform committee to sink it. Before Humphrey even had a chance to explain his position to the president, the committee voted sixty-five to thirty-five to endorse Johnson's Vietnam policy. The peace delegates donned black armbands and joined in a mournful chorus of "We Shall Overcome" as the convention recessed until evening for the nomination. The irony of Humphrey's situation was stunning. Twenty years earlier he had led a minority challenge against the Democratic establishment and won a famous victory for the ADA's civil rights plank. Young and combative, he was the self-proclaimed leader of the "new" liberalism. Now, older and cautious, Humphrey was part of the establishment and could not muster the courage to challenge a president whose patronage he needed for his political survival. Although his philosophy had changed little, to many younger liberals Humphrey symbolized "the last hurrah" of the old order.

After the turbulent Vietnam debate, delegates turned their attention to the business of nominating a candidate for the presidency. At the same time the area outside the amphitheater turned into a battleground. Inside, angry delegates gathered around television screens to watch scenes of flailing police batons. Standing at the podium to nominate McGovern, Abraham Ribicoff denounced "Gestapo tactics in the streets of Chicago." The violence overshadowed Humphrey's nomination on the first ballot and his choice of Maine's Lincolnesque Edmund Muskie as his running mate. Outside, demonstrators hurled bricks, bottles, and nail-studded golf balls at the police lines. Never known for their restraint, the Chicago cops flailed blindly into a crowd of three thousand. No one accused the police of discrimination that night. They savagely beat hippies, yippies, liberal Democrats, newsmen, journalists, clergymen, and anyone else within striking distance.

As the campaign commenced, Humphrey needed to solve the problem that lay at the heart of his political difficulties—the public's perception that he was just a mouthpiece of the administration. "My most serious dilemma," Humphrey said at the time, "is how on the one hand do you chart an independent course and yet at the same time not repudiate the course of which you've been a part." Hecklers and angry demonstrators followed him everywhere. At the same time, his Republican opponent, former Vice-President Richard Nixon, was free to frame the issues as he wished for the constituency he most coveted—the "decent," white, middle-class people who were growing daily more conservative and alienated. "If you want your President to continue the do-nothing policy toward crime, vote Humphrey," Nixon said. "If you want to fight crime, vote for Nixon." Humphrey, he declared, "sat on his hands and watched the U.S. become a nation where 50% of American women are frightened to walk their city streets at night."[45]

Like Truman in 1948, Humphrey also had to deal with a strong third-party challenge, this time from the right. George Wallace of Alabama, seeking the presidency on the American Independent party platform, had been a hero in the South ever since he first tried to block admission of black students into the University of Alabama in 1963. In 1968 he sought to expand his base in the North by pitching his appeal to the "average man in the street, this man in the textile mill, this man in the steel mill, this barber, this beautician, the policeman on the beat." A dour little man, a ranting orator who seemed intentionally to mangle his syntax and mispronounce words, Wallace had an appeal that was blatantly racist and anti-intellectual. Wallace crept upward in the polls—to 11 percent in February, 14 percent in May, 16 percent in July, 21 percent in late September. He was actually running ahead of both Nixon and Humphrey in the South. His greatest gains were among labor. A survey of blue-collar workers in Gary, Indiana, revealed that 38 percent intended to vote for Wallace. He won a landslide victory by collecting 62 percent of the vote in a UAW presidential poll in a local Nashville branch of the UAW.[46]

Trailing by 15 percentage points in the polls on the last day of September, Humphrey went on nationwide television from Salt Lake City. He announced that if elected he would temporarily cease bombing North Vietnam. It was not a radical departure from the president's policy, but it was a move in that direction. "It was just enough to give a little light between the president's position and mine, but without jeopardizing his," Humphrey later explained. Afterward the cacophony of perpetual heckling faded away. A sign in Chicago promised, "If you mean it, we're with you." On the offensive for the first time, Humphrey, with his usual exuberance, pursued a three-pronged strategy. He tried to blunt Wallace's appeal to the workingman by portraying the governor as a dangerous extremist and an enemy of organized labor; he put Nixon on the defensive by challenging him to debate; and he emphasized the themes of trust and togetherness, which he felt the American people wanted to hear. Suddenly, the campaign picked up.

Humphrey's speech gave Rauh the rationale he needed to propose that the ADA finally endorse Humphrey for president, despite continued resistance from the local chapters. Jack Justice, speaking for the Southeastern Pennsylvania chapter of the ADA, claimed that a majority of the chapters wanted the ADA to refrain from endorsing any candidate for president, "but to challenge Vice President Humphrey to conduct a campaign that [would] give ADA cause to reconsider his candidacy before election day." He claimed that 70 percent of the members supported his position, that 25 percent wanted to endorse Humphrey immediately, and that a few wanted to endorse Dick Gregory. Other chapters expressed similar feelings. The Queens chapter poll of its members found that "14 favored an immediate endorsement of the Humphrey ticket, 44 wanted endorsement qualified by a clear statement of ADA's opposition to the war, 13 favored no endorsement, while 4 presented other options including support of Nixon." The IVI board meeting on September 14 found its members split on the issue, with twenty-one voting to endorse Humphrey and twenty-one recommending no action. The Northern California chapter instructed its delegates to oppose any action "that could be interpreted as approval of the Johnson-Humphrey Administration, and specifically to oppose the endorsement of Hubert Humphrey."[47]

Encouraged by Humphrey's Salt Lake City speech, Rauh believed he had enough support to overwhelm the opposition. He opened the October 5 National Board meeting by calling for the adoption of a resolution that endorsed Humphrey with reservations. The statement declared that while Humphrey had moved "substantially" in the direction of the ADA, the organization was "still far from satisfied" with his position on Vietnam. It encouraged Humphrey to "separate himself from the Johnson-Rusk errors of the past" and "from the reactionary elements within the Democratic Party." Liberals, it said, should endorse Humphrey because of his strong support for minority rights and racial equality, because a number of liberal senators and congressmen depended on the success of the national ticket, and because he chose Muskie as his running mate.

Other members proposed substitute resolutions. One board member offered a proposal of "passive support" for Humphrey. According to this resolution, the ADA would not endorse Humphrey, would recognize him as the best among available candidates, and would instead concentrate its efforts on the election of congressional and state officers. Another representative offered the alternative of "no endorsement." His resolution read, "To endorse candidates of smoke-filled rooms after we had endorsed the people's choice would be to refute the people's choice, and to refute the voice of the new politics in favor of the professional politicians' choice, the voice of the old politics." Humphrey, protested Kenneth Wentworth of the New York chapter, was "not the fiery liberal we once knew, but a passionate defender of our vicious policy in Vietnam."

After eighteen members spoke in favor of a Humphrey endorsement, Galbraith ended the discussion. He then read telegrams from prominent liberal officials, like Joseph Clark and Wayne Morse, and a moving personal letter from Humphrey asking for ADA's support. After lunch the votes were read. The "passive support" substitute lost, twenty-five to sixty, and the "no endorsement" proposal lost, seventeen to sixty-seven, but the Rauh resolution for Humphrey passed, seventy-one to sixteen.[48]

Following the meeting the national office rushed copies of the endorsement resolution to all chapters, with a covering memo urging them "to move promptly and vigorously to implement this resolution by fully engaging in the campaign on behalf of Hubert Humphrey's candidacy." Although the ADA was now officially behind Humphrey, there was still little enthusiasm for his candidacy. Schlesinger and Galbraith, two of the most outspoken opponents of the war, did the bare minimum to mobilize their antiwar supporters to Humphrey's cause. In press releases they did the least they could to fulfill their obligations as good Democrats while remaining true to their ideals. Galbraith told the *Boston Globe* political editor Robert Healy that he favored endorsement of Humphrey because of their friendship. He added, "I don't hold to the theory of an Old Nixon and a New Nixon: one Nixon is enough for a lifetime." Schlesinger released a statement on October 24 endorsing Humphrey. "If we don't have Mr. Humphrey as President," it said, "we will have Mr. Nixon."[49] Those who did work actively for Humphrey, like Joseph Rauh, found themselves pushed aside by conservative supporters. Rauh's brief fling with the Humphrey entourage came to an abrupt end when Governor John Connally of Texas, during a Humphrey tour of the state, warned the vice-president that he would refuse to ride in the same plane with Rauh. Recognizing that Connally's support was more crucial than Rauh's advice, Humphrey ungraciously expelled Rauh from his inner circle.[50]

By October 21 Humphrey had cut Nixon's lead to only 8 percentage points and was gaining. "We've done the best job we could," Humphrey told reporters two weeks later, as he arrived at his home in Minneapolis to hear the election results. His best, however, was not enough. His defeat was agonizingly narrow: Nixon won 31,770,000 votes, or 43.4 percent of the total, compared with Humphrey's 31,270,000, or 42.7 percent, while 9,906,000 voters, or 13.5 percent, chose Wallace. The following morning a graceful Humphrey strolled into a ballroom filled with tearful supporters, to read his concession statement. His face bearing the anguish of defeat, his eyes brimming with tears, the "Happy Warrior" told his faithful listeners, "I shall continue my personal commitment to the cause of human rights, of peace, and to the betterment of man. . . . I have done my best. I have lost. Mr. Nixon won. The democratic process has worked its will, so now let's get on with the urgent task of uniting our country."

A close study of the debates in the ADA sheds light on why the war had such a traumatic effect on liberalism. The war exposed a tension at the heart of the Vital Center. Liberals who had come to prominence after World War II tried to strike a balance between their commitment to abstract ideals of social justice and their sense of the politically possible. This tension was built into the ADA's organizational framework. Its founders wanted the ADA to function, in Schlesinger's words, "not only in the field of policy but in the field of politics." This meant that "sometimes a sense of practical possibility" kept it "from pushing issues as hard as a more strictly intellectual organization might have done." Irving Howe, after observing the ADA's 1954 convention, called attention to this same duel role, commenting that the organization was torn between its desire to reform and its need to be "respectable." On most of the controversial issues where the ADA's view of what was right clashed with its sense of what was possible, it had favored the latter. During the Joseph McCarthy period, most ADA members opposed the prosecution of Communists under the Smith Act, but they feared that public opposition would further alienate them from the Democratic party and thus chose not to publicize their dissent. In the 1950s the organization, torn between its backing of Adlai Stevenson, who it believed had the best chance of defeating Eisenhower, and its commitment to a strong civil rights plank, backed away from full support of civil rights out of fear that it would split the Democratic party and destroy its chances at the polls.

The Vietnam War proved fatal for the Vital Center because it upset the delicate balance between politics and vision. The war accentuated the differences within the organization, by providing the young reformers with a dramatic and pervasive cause, which they used to challenge the moderate leadership of the Schlesinger-Galbraith faction. Also, as the cost of the war increased and victory seemed further away than ever, as the protest at home appeared to undermine the legitimacy of democratic government in America, the ADA's moderate leadership reluctantly concluded that the organization's future depended on the hopes of the new reformers. Moderates, confident that American institutions needed only incremental repair, had for twenty years subjected their ideas to the test of politics. By 1968 they were so disillusioned with the war, frustrated with labor, alienated from the Johnson administration, and impressed by the activism of the young that they abandoned their claims of moderation and balance and pursued instead, for the first time, the politics of vision. While they did not repudiate the essential elements of their faith, liberals did redefine their role in society.

There was a striking contrast between the liberals who founded the ADA in 1947 and those who gained control after 1968. The anti-Communist liberals who gravitated toward the ADA in the 1940s had been disappointed with Roosevelt's policy of neutrality; they were impatient to lead the nation into war against Hitler and wanted the United States to assume the responsibility of a great military power. Many were former socialists who, encouraged by America's wartime productivity, found new faith in capitalism. The reform liberals who captured the ADA in 1968 were eager to extract the United States from an unjust war and restless to limit America's global commitments. They were socialists who had repudiated the limited welfare state, independent Democrats who had lost faith in the Democratic party. Like many of the independent liberals of the 1930s, ADA reform liberals hoped, through the force of their ideas, to change political attitudes, restructure political institutions, and reforge a new coalition. Once again, they failed.

10

Epilogue: Liberal Dilemmas, 1968–1985

Vietnam destroyed the tenuous balance between politics and vision that had united liberals in the postwar era. Liberals espousing the New Politics hoped that by standing firm on the side of vision they could entice the growing army of the young to join a new reform coalition. Political realities in the 1970s and 1980s frustrated these hopes. By proposing a farsighted reform agenda, the New Politics liberals divorced themselves from mainstream opinion and appeared unresponsive to the fears and anxieties of most voters. Jolted by America's stagnant economy and declining power in the world and frustrated by a lack of political leadership, many Americans turned to conservative solutions to their problems. By the time of Ronald Reagan's second inauguration, the ADA and the New Politics were struggling to survive, having been pushed to the fringe of American politics.

Richard Nixon's election in 1968 marked the end of eight years of Democratic rule and symbolized America's disillusionment with liberal reform. Liberals found themselves under assault from all sides. From the left, intellectuals, students, and minorities complained about liberal complicity in waging an immoral war in Vietnam and creating an indifferent bureaucracy that resisted change. Liberals had hoped that the McCarthy endorsement would prove that liberalism was still a "demanding faith" and thus undercut support for radical change. In fact, McCarthy's subsequent defeat in the primaries, Humphrey's nomination, and Nixon's election only confirmed radicals' suspicion that American society was rigid and incapable of change. Liberalism, critics charged, became a ruse for buying off discontent with meaningless palliatives. Jack Newfield declared, "The liberals seem willing to pay the ransom of a little repression in order to get the movement off their backs."[1]

From the right came charges from an emerging "silent majority"—working-class Americans who reasserted their sense of patriotism, commitment to the work ethic, and desire for "law and order." The silent majority appeared everywhere—*Time* named "The Middle Americans" as its "Man and Woman of the Year" for 1969—yet no one was sure who the Middle Americans were. Some observers defined them in cultural terms. *Newsweek*'s Karl Fleming

225

noted that middle Americans felt "threatened by a terrifying array of enemies: hippies, Black Panthers, drugs, the sexually liberated, those who questioned the sanctity of marriage and the morality of work." Others defined them in economic terms—blue-collar workers, lower-echelon bureaucrats, and white-collar employees who earned between $5,000 and $15,000 a year. The typical middle American, the columnist Stewart Alsop wrote, is a union worker "making around $9,000 a year" who is outraged that "the rich liberals are insisting that *his* children be bused across town to achieve racial balance, or that *his* suburb be invaded by blacks in subsidized housing, while the affluent liberal sends his children to private schools and lives in a comfortable apartment or in exurbia."

It was recently emerged social issues that proved most troubling for many Americans. "If radical critics of America were alienated from the values of mobility, achievement, and responsibility that characterized the dominant culture," William Chafe has written, "many middle-class Americans were equally alienated from those who questioned customs they had been taught to cherish." Black protest in the streets violated middle-class ideas of law and order, student antiwar demonstrations disturbed their sense of patriotism, the proliferation of alternative lifestyles—gay rights, feminism—offended their sense of decency, while affirmative action and busing challenged their notion of fairness.[2]

No one was sure what the long-term effect of these attacks would be, but most observers were certain they meant the demise of New Deal liberalism. The 1968 election proved, Stewart Alsop concluded confidently, that "American liberalism, New Deal style, doesn't work very well any more." William Pfaff, writing in *Commonweal,* contended that "the established liberal leadership of this country" was "sterile at best, and at worst a destructive force in opposition to change." The former Nixon adviser Kevin Phillips predicted that Nixon's election "bespoke the end of the New Deal Democratic hegemony and the beginning of a new era in American politics." "The question for the immediate future," observed *Time,* "is how the party will attempt to construct a new coalition in view of the wholesale defection of the South, the disaffection of many middle-income families, the revolt of many liberals and young voters."[3]

Many former liberals, finding this analysis persuasive, formed the Coalition for a Democratic Majority (CDM). Norman Podhoretz, editor of *Commentary* magazine, argued that "the purpose of CDM was to challenge the influence of the New Politics movement within the Democratic Party." The rise of the "New Class"—what Michael Novak called the Know-Everythings—created a crisis of authority in America by attempting to promote an adversary culture. Neoconservatives, who placed themselves in the reform tradition of Roosevelt, Truman, Kennedy, and Johnson, believed that the New Politics group perverted New Deal liberalism. While the New Politics emphasized neo-isolation, equality of condition, and redistribution, the neoconservatives believed that the United States "should continue to play an active role in the defense of freedom throughout the world," that society should be "based on equality of opportunity," and "that further economic growth was possible and that it was also necessary to ensure the continued prosperity of the already prosperous and the future prosperity of the presently poor." Although unable to agree on a coherent social philosophy, most neoconservatives stressed market mechanism and fewer government programs to solve social problems.[4]

The ADA, however, learned different lessons from the 1960s. After 1968, ADA liberals reassessed many of the assumptions of the Vital Center. The war had altered the balance of power in the organization. Most traditionalists, who had always kept the ADA anchored in the political mainstream, left the organization after the McCarthy endorsement. Some, like Leon Keyserling, John Roche, and Paul Seabury, joined the Coalition for a Democratic Majority and became prominent in the neoconservative movement. Those who stayed found themselves relegated to the role of exclaiming, "I told you so." "Anyone who was alive during the past year knows that the ADA precipitated the dismantling of the Liberal coalition and helped head it towards its defeat," a disgruntled traditionalist wrote Galbraith. "Indeed, the only accomplishment you can boast of is the election of Nixon." Another member referred to the ADA's role as "arrogant, dishonest, irresponsible, stupid and incredible." John Roche commented drolly that the ADA "took the trip to Disneyland and while it was there the people of the United States put Richard Nixon in the White House." Gus Tyler continued to argue that liberals should be addressing economic issues, not social problems, suggested that the New Politics make room for the working man, and predicted a redefinition of liberalism that would reaffirm the "Roosevelt accords."[5]

Tyler, however, was now arguing from the outside. Within the ADA, moderates and reformers ruled without opposition after 1968. By 1969 there were few differences between them. Moderates bcame disillusioned with liberalism during the debates over the Vietnam War, just as reformers had been frustrated during the civil rights struggles in the early 1960s. Both groups believed that the New Politics was not only morally correct but politically farsighted as well. Most would have agreed with Lowenstein when he noted, "[The] one good thing about the war is that it peeled off a lot of assumptions, and caused us to see things we had never seen before. We began to realize the need for total overhaul of many aspects of the entire system, from foreign policy to the tax structure." The war, commented Dolores Mitchell, "was the catalyst that brought underlying dilemmas to the surface." It "has shattered the social compact under which we were trying to make a better society."[6]

The ideas of Arthur Schlesinger, Jr., like those of most moderates, underwent an important transformation after 1968. The war and the assassinations of John and Robert Kennedy and Martin Luther King, Jr., forced Schlesinger to reassess the Vital Center. In 1970 he admitted that he had underestimated how anxiety, the growth of large bureaucracies, and the quickening pace of technological change could transform society. The velocity of history, he now argued, "is far too great for our inherited ideas and institutions to make the requisite adaptations." Schlesinger conceded that he had "accepted a little too easily the idea that the stimulation of economic growth through the magic of fiscal policy could solve our main economic problems." Keynesianism was not enough, he confessed; "structural reform, a price-wage policy, income redistribution, public service employment, the rationing of gross growth and the protection of the environment against uncontrolled technology will all be necessary if we are to move toward a decent society."[7]

In 1969, moderates and reformers alike had to face an uncomfortable reality. Most of the programs that the ADA had advocated in 1947—civil rights legislation, an expanded welfare system, and increased defense spending—were law in 1969. Yet poverty persisted, America was at war in Vietnam, and the country had elected a conservative Republican president and appeared in open rebellion against liberalism. Had liberalism failed? Most ADA leaders contended that what liberalism needed was more vision and less politics. The old liberalism was too accommodating to the prevailing political climate. If liberalism was to be successful, they maintained, it needed to be bolder, more penetrating, and less compromising.

Consequently, there was a dramatic change in both the tone and the substance of ADA statements after 1968. The criticism of American society was more trenchant; the language, sharper; the programs it advocated, bolder. The organization no longer identified with the aspirations of the middle class. It now saw that class to be in conspiracy with conservatives to poison the environment and enslave the poor. After 1968 the organization identified with the disfranchised and the disinherited. "In a nation of unparalleled affluence," it charged,

> millions of citizens—blacks, Mexican Americans, Puerto Ricans, American Indians, and poor whites—continue to live under the yoke of deprivation and discrimination. Children grow up hungry and ill, adults lack decent jobs, families struggle for survival in slum housing in dangerous neighborhoods, and cities continue to rot. Our values as a nation continue to be distorted. Our economy fabricates new material wants and a credit system to satisfy them instantaneously while the environment deteriorates and our air and streams are poisoned.

The ADA demonstrated little concern for middle-class anxiety over busing, law and order, or affirmative action. It supported busing, gay rights, the equal rights amendment for women, and court-enforced affirmative action.

ADA foreign policy underwent a similar transformation after 1968. For the first time the organization advocated a complete withdrawal from Vietnam. The foreign policy commission at the 1969 convention offered a resolution calling for "an immediate cessation of offensive military operations" and a "drastic reduction in the strength of American forces." After a spirited debate, the delegates rejected that resolution and instead adopted, by a two-to-one margin, a minority resolution calling on the administration to withdraw all American troops. The organization moved away from its belief in spheres of influence and emphasized vague notions of world law as a means of ensuring peace. The ADA advocated "development of a regime of enforceable world law to insure peaceful settlement of international disputes, immediate elimination of international armed conflict, and the international recognition of human rights." Its attention shifted away from East-West conflict and toward North-South dialogue. While it expressed strong support of détente and arms control, its main concern was with initiating a "fundamental restructuring of U.S. foreign policy" that would address "the needs and demands of the poorest countries."[8]

A similar change took place in the organization's economic program. The ADA, no longer captivated by Keyserling economics, now called for a "massive redistribution of wealth and power in America," which involved "effective democratic control over the economic organization of the country." Along with government-guaranteed full employment, the ADA advocated a guaranteed national income, a government-guaranteed $5 billion jobs program, increases in federal spending on education to $30 billion over four years, and construction of six million low- and moderate-cost housing units over six years. It also insisted on a 50 percent increase in Social Security benefits and on national health insurance. The ADA's convention resolutions became barely distinguishable from the Socialist party platform. Socialists like Michael Harrington, who was elected to the ADA National Board in the early 1970s, believed that this change in liberalism presented an opportunity for liberals and Socialists to forge a new coalition. "For better or worse," he claimed, "I think we have carved out a socialist presence in the democratic left of this country." Leon Shull confirmed that a close relationship existed between the ADA and democratic Socialists. "There was not a bit of difference between the ADA and Socialist party on economic issues in the 1970s," he commented. Although the ADA supported socialist economic reforms, it refused, much to Harrington's dismay, to identify itself with democratic socialism. "Why is it," Harrington complained, "if these liberal organizations urge essentially social democratic programs that they have so steadfastly refused any social democratic identification?"[9]

With its bold new foreign and domestic policy positions, the ADA counted on young reformers to replenish the organization and fill the void left by labor. As a first step it elected Joseph Duffey, director of the Center for Urban Studies at the Hartford, Connecticut, Seminary, and a strong backer of Eugene McCarthy, to succeed Galbraith as ADA national chairman. Galbraith jokingly called Duffey's election a move "not to bridge the generation gap but to jump it." Duffey informed the convention that he identified "with those who tried the system last year" and who "view that system with skepticism, yet who continue with a cautious will to persist, with great longings for a new America, and with a sober, chastened hope for meaningful change." Duffey recognized that he was of a generation different from that of most of ADA's leaders—he was fourteen years old when the ADA was founded in 1947. He spoke about how much problems had changed: "Then the poor and disinherited needed others to speak for them. Now they are increasingly able to speak for themselves." Before, liberals "looked to the federal government to deliver us from the provincialism and smallness of local tyranny and indifference." In 1969 the same "federal bureaucracies have become rigid and unresponsive." "For two decades," he declared, "ADA has advocated change. The question now is whether ADA itself can change."[10]

Despite its bold programs, the organization had no intention of abandoning its political responsibilities. After 1968, most ADA members believed that vision also made for good politics. Some ADA leaders hoped that the middle class could eventually be persuaded to support the organization's reform agenda. Shull, for example, thought that liberals had to convince the middle-class Americans that they had "more in common with poor black youths, welfare mothers, and the unemployed than with Richard Nixon's affluent hard-core Republicans." Liberals, he contended, need to inspire confidence in liberal solutions, to convince voters that the problems that concern them most "CAN be solved with liberal programs and WILL NOT be solved with conservative programs and no-programs." Shull did not suggest how liberals would accomplish this feat. For the most part, Shull's reaction was instinctive; raised as a Socialist with strong ties to the labor movement, he could not conceive of a reform movement that did not include the middle class.[11]

Shull and most other ADA leaders still believed that the Democratic party offered the best hope for change. They hoped to restructure the party and make it more responsive to its liberal elements. When the Democratic national chairman Fred Harris announced in early 1969 the creation of the McGovern commission to study party reforms, the ADA initiated an intense lobbying campaign to convince the commission that the Democratic party must draw support from "the black, the poor, and the young and the millions of workers and intellectuals who share their objectives." Stacked with other reformers who shared the ADA's perspective, the committee established a de facto quota system that forced state parties to select representative delegations to the national convention.[12]

The Republicans, however, had a more effective plan for reaching the middle class. Richard Nixon tapped the ground swell of frustration and resentment and attempted to use it in a governing coalition. As a candidate in 1968, Nixon had attacked compulsory school desegregation. Once in office he instructed the Department of Health, Education and Welfare to intervene in favor of school boards attempting to slow down the process of desegregation. Calling upon "the great silent majority" to back his policies at home and abroad, the president treated the plight of blacks and urban centers with indifference, demonstrated in part by his half-hearted enforcement of civil rights laws. One NAACP official commented, "For the first time since Woodrow Wilson, we have a national administration that can be rightly characterized as anti-Negro." Attorney General John Mitchell tried to prevent extension of the 1965 Voting Rights Act, urged "preventive detention" of suspected criminals, and prosecuted antiwar demonstrators in highly visible public trials. Meanwhile, Vice-President Spiro Agnew attacked the news media and intellectuals as "vicars of vacillation," "nattering nabobs of negativism," and "an effete corps of impudent snobs" who encouraged a "spirit of national masochism." He traveled around the country flailing at "ideological eunuchs," "merchants of hate," "parasites of passion," and campus protesters who took "their tactics from Castro and their money from Daddy."

For liberals the 1972 election results provided chilling proof of Nixon's success in reaching the "silent majority." The Democrats nominated their most liberal candidate, Senator George McGovern of South Dakota. Taking advantage of the new nominating rules that increased activist influence in the party, McGovern defeated the front-runners Hubert Humphrey and Senator Edmund Muskie of Maine for the nomination. Many of the issues that endeared McGovern to liberals—guaranteed income, immediate withdrawal from Vietnam—annoyed moderate Democrats and independents. He did not help his cause with a series of blunders. He chose as his running mate Senator Thomas Eagleton of Missouri, yet, when it was reported that Eagleton had suffered a series of nervous breakdowns, McGovern gradually nudged him off the ticket. A crafty Nixon, helped by the October announcement "Peace is at hand," crushed McGovern, polling 45.9 million votes to McGovern's 28.4 million. He won 60.8 percent of the popular vote and swept 521 electoral votes, losing only Massachusetts and the District of Columbia.

McGovern's loss came as a cruel blow to the ADA. "The devastating defeat suffered by Sen. McGovern has given dedicated liberals solemn pause," wrote one disgruntled member. "The November election has compelled me to admit that the American citizenry, by and large, is far less progressive than I had hoped." Another member commented, "Our fatal inadequacy has been our inability to understand the dynamics of change. . . . The hard fact is that change is deeply disturbing to people who are trying to hold on to the little they have, or make their way up the plastic ladder."[13] The ADA played no visible role in the campaign. Some political observers made note of the organization's declining stature as a political pressure group. "ADA used to be a home for labor leaders, professors and ladies who felt uncomfortable and were not welcome in machine politics," remarked a onetime aide to former Senator Joseph Clark. "Now it's not a home for labor or for kids either. It's neither the new left nor the old left. The kids probably laugh at it. Nobody takes it seriously."[14]

Politically ineffective and unable to attract new members, many of the local chapters languished. An internal study of the organization conducted in March 1974 found that all chapters had "severe financial problems." Many chapters, it discovered, had "sizeable deficits, or were working with no budget at all. In some cases, the fulltime staff had not been paid for several months." Most chapters were "inactive" and their membership numbers "dwindling." Only the Southern California, Chicago, Minnesota, Pittsburgh, Philadelphia, Oregon, and Massachusetts chapters were strong and viable. The District of Columbia, Detroit, Southern New Jersey, New York, Cleveland, and Independent Voters of Illinois chapters were functioning but "not viable." Almost half of the other chapters were "weak" and existing on paper only. They included the Northern California, Hawaii, Iowa, Baltimore, Missouri, Northern New Jersey, Nassau County, Ohio State, Columbus, Dayton, and Texas chapters.[15] With labor leaders gone and chapters barely surviving, the national organization's debt rose to $50,000 in the early 1970s. Only emergency measures—freezes on hiring and on already meager salaries and temporary production cuts in the ADA *World*—saved the organization from bankruptcy.

The ADA suffered other jolts during the decade. Johnson's abuse of presidential power had forced liberals to rethink their faith in the presidency as an instrument of social change. White House involvement in a clumsy attempt to break into the Democratic national headquarters in the Watergate complex on June 17, 1972, exacerbated this problem. Although Nixon's press secretary called the break-in "a third-rate burglary" and although the president declared that he had conducted a careful investigation that revealed "no one in the White House staff, no one in this Administration presently employed, was engaged in this very bizarre incident," investigators discovered a trail of illegal activity and cover-up that led directly to the president. On August 8, 1974, faced with impeachment, Nixon resigned in disgrace. Nixon's resignation left the presidency in the hands of an inexperienced Gerald Ford, whom Nixon had appointed vice-president a few months earlier.[16]

The abuse of presidential authority during the Johnson and Nixon years not only forced liberals to reassess their faith in the presidency but also contributed to the erosion of public trust in government. The pollster Daniel Yankelovich noted in 1977 that the percentage of the populace that trusted the government declined from 80 percent in the late 1950s to about 33 percent in 1976. More than 80 percent of the public expressed distrust in political leaders, 61 percent believed something was morally wrong with the country, and nearly 75 percent felt that it had no impact in the decisions of government. While the ADA was advocating greater government involvement in all aspects of life, most Americans were expressing skepticism about public institutions, thus widening the gap between the liberal vision and political realities.

Economic dislocation during the decade also undermined public support for liberal programs. From 1975 until 1980 the nation experienced for the first time what became known as stagflation—the simultaneous increase of unemployment and inflation. When the annual rate of inflation reached 11 percent in 1975, unemployment swelled to nearly 9 percent. By the early 1980s real discretionary income per worker had declined by 18 percent since 1973. The average price for a new single-family house more than doubled in the seventies, while the cost of basic necessities rose 110 percent. The conservative columnist George Will commented, "Inflation is a great conservatizing issue."

Foreign policy reverses contributed to the confusion. Americans, who had always controlled their own economic destiny, found themselves sitting in endless gas lines because Middle Eastern oil-exporting nations decided to punish the United States for its support of Israel during the Yom Kippur War of October 1973. President Nixon warned the American people that they needed to face "a very stark fact: We are heading toward the most acute shortage of energy since World War II." The greatest shock, however, came on April 29, 1975, when Communist tanks rolled through the gates of South Vietnam's capital in Saigon. As the red-and-yellow Vietcong flag flew triumphantly from the balcony, Americans realized they had lost their first war.

Political leaders seemed incapable of contending with these problems. In 1976 the Democrats nominated Jimmy Carter, an obscure peanut farmer and one-term governor of Georgia. Carter hoped to avoid getting caught in the internal bickering of the Democratic party by telling all groups what they wanted to hear. His "New Foundation" appealed to conservatives because of its promise to streamline government and cut wasteful spending; liberals were excited about the prospect of tax reform, the SALT II agreement, and national health insurance. Carter's Republican opponent also failed to inspire enthusiasm. One month after assuming office, Ford had issued a "full, free, and absolute" pardon of Nixon for "all offenses against the United States." He vetoed a wide range of important legislation—federal aid to education, health care, and a school lunch program. Also, his obsession with inflation at a time of rising unemployment led to the highest unemployment rate since 1941 and a dramatic decline in the gross national product. Personalities, not issues, animated the election. For a small majority of Americans, Carter had the more appealing personality. Carter polled 40.8 million votes, to Ford's 39.1 million—or 50.1 percent of the total, to Ford's 48 percent. He squeaked out a 297–240 victory in the electoral college.[17]

Carter found that governing required more than symbolic gestures and good intentions. Unfamiliar with Washington's ways, he alienated natural allies like House Speaker Thomas "Tip" O'Neill; he declared the energy problem "the moral equivalent of war" and then failed to pass an energy program. Economic problems also contributed to Carter's downfall. When inflation, which stood at a modest 4.8 percent a year in 1976, had skyrocketed to 12 percent by March 1980, Carter turned to conservative fiscal and monetary policy—tightening the money supply and promising to submit a balanced budget for fiscal 1981. Yet, Carter was haunted by his campaign pledge never to "use unemployment and recession as a tool to fight inflation." The cruelest blows, however, came from abroad. On November 9, five hundred angry young Iranians occupied the American embassy in Teheran and held one hundred Americans hostage. One month later the Soviet Union invaded Afghanistan.

Carter's response to these crises underscored the nation's sense of impotence. In dealing with Iran, Carter contemplated his limited choices while Iranian militants burned American flags and shouted anti-American slogans. In April the president decided on a daring commando raid, but the attempt failed when two helicopters collided while refueling on an Iranian desert. In Afghanistan the president resorted to more bluster, yet even less action. While calling the invasion the "greatest threat to world peace" since the Cuban missile crisis, Carter imposed a grain embargo on Russia and discouraged American athletes from participating in the Olympic Games in Moscow scheduled for the summer of 1980. The contrast between Carter's harsh words and mild actions seemed to emphasize the nation's feeling of helplessness.

The ADA condemned Carter for his vacillating leadership and conservative economics. Senator George McGovern blasted Carter at the ADA convention in May 1977, claiming that though liberals wanted "to be able to applaud the President's record," they would not become "a cheering section for tinkering symbols signifying nothing." Rauh was even more blunt. Carter's New Foundation, he declared, is "the conservative doctrine of donothingism dressed up in five-dollar words. It's not a New Deal, or a Fair Deal, or even a Square Deal. It's a Bum Deal for the nation!"[18] When the debate shifted to foreign policy questions, however, the ADA had little to say. About Iran the organization released a vague statement, accusing the president of having "inflicted upon himself" the "greatest foreign policy crisis" of recent years, but did not explain why it arrived at that conclusion or how the situation could have been avoided. The organization condemned the Soviet Union for its invasion of Afghanistan but also criticized Carter for his provocative response.[19]

The ADA's criticism of Carter stemmed in large part from its basic disagreement with his domestic policy, but a feeling of isolation from the administration no doubt contributed to the organization's bitter tone. "Feeling Left Out" was the way the *New Republic* described the ADA's relationship with the Carter administration. While the organization always had difficulty working with a Democratic president, its problems with Carter were especially acute. Truman, following the advice of Clark Clifford, believed that liberals wielded great political clout, so he courted their favor. Kennedy turned to liberal intellectuals to provide inspiration for his New Frontier. Even Lyndon Johnson, a rural Texan who had shown nothing but contempt for liberals, realized he required liberal support for his Great Society programs. Carter, however, did not need liberals or the ADA. Not only was the public mood hostile to liberal reform, but Carter was a provincial southerner who ran for office as an outsider promising to streamline programs that liberals had helped to create.

In November 1979 Senator Edward Kennedy, who had cast a long shadow over Democratic presidential politics for over a decade, announced that he was a candidate for the presidency. The last surviving son of modern America's most famous political family told a partisan crowd in historic Faneuil Hall in Boston' North End, "This country is not prepared to sound retreat. It is ready to advance. It is willing to make a stand. And so am I." To many liberals Kennedy emerged as a progressive white knight—a charismatic leader who, because of family name and broad popular appeal, would forge a new coalition of New Politics liberals and working-class Americans. "What we see emerging from the Draft Kennedy movement," Shull declared, "is a strong coalition of liberals and labor, and tremendous support from usually non-political, non-activist citizens." Just as many liberals had turned to Robert Kennedy in 1968 to pull together the disparate elements of the Democratic party, so they believed that Edward Kennedy's personal magnetism could surmount the divisions in 1980. Once again they were to be proven wrong.[20]

Kennedy hoped to make leadership and economic problems the major themes of his campaign, since voters seemed most concerned about these in the summer and early fall of 1979. However, the dramatic events in Iran and Afghanistan changed the political agenda and undermined Kennedy's candidacy. Instinctively, Americans rallied around the president, leaving Kennedy without an issue or a cause. Kennedy was also weighed down by questions about his character stemming from his involvement in a fatal 1969 car accident. Of the first nineteen primaries and caucuses, Kennedy won only Massachusetts and Alaska. Victories in Connecticut and New York in March kept his candidacy alive, but Carter continued to collect delegates and close in on the nomination. Although Kennedy won five of seven primaries on "Super Tuesday"—including the important ones in California and New Jersey—Carter amassed enough delegates to clinch the nomination. Kennedy fought Carter to the end, but in July the Democratic convention nominated Carter for a second term.

In August the Republicans nominated Ronald Wilson Reagan, a former New Deal Democrat and ADA founding member who had repudiated his liberal heritage while Truman was still in the White House. By 1966, when he was elected governor of California, Reagan had become one of the bright lights of the Republican party's right wing, a Barry Goldwater with charm. In 1980 Reagan told the Republican National Convention that he would "renew the American spirit and sense of purpose." He called for a "new beginning" that included large reductions in personal income taxes, cuts in unnecessary social spending (Reagan was intentionally vague on what was not necessary), and massive increases in defense spending. His program revealed the contradiction in the public mind. Reagan offered the country an image of an earlier America confident and strong, committed to the old verities and sure of its future. He captured the themes that liberals had long conveyed but had abandoned after 1968: optimism, faith in economic growth, and supreme confidence in American military might.

Although the possibility of a Reagan presidency horrified most liberals, it did produce one positive side effect for the ADA: it helped bring labor back into the organization. Actually, the ADA had begun luring labor leaders much earlier. In March 1975 it established the "Democratic Conference," which provided a home for labor leaders who were still concerned with liberal causes but did not want to be directly associated with the ADA. Pressing economic issues in the later half of the 1970s also helped the ADA's reconciliation efforts. Liberals and labor had always found it easier to work together on economic issues than on either foreign policy or social issues. Labor, like liberalism, had fallen on hard times in the 1970s and was searching for new allies. Foreign competition, technological changes, and a less receptive public climate worked to undermine union gains. Many of the largest and most influential unions—the Steelworkers, the UAW, the Machinists—faced

serious hardship. Most jobs in the 1970s existed in the service sector—
retailing, high technology, and clerical work. Also, while craft unions remained predominantly male, women accepted two-thirds of all jobs that
opened during the decade. Management took advantage of a less tolerant public attitude to force concessions from unions. Concession bargaining eroded
union wage levels, and many unions reluctantly accepted "two-tier" wage
structures.

The ADA's 1979 convention witnessed the largest labor turnout since the
split in 1968. William Wynn, president of the United Food and Commercial
Workers, joined other union representatives, including William Winpisinger
of the International Association of Machinists, Keith Johnson of the International Woodworkers of America, and Charles Perlik of the Newspaper Guild.
"Labor participation in ADA is at its greatest level in over ten years," declared Leon Shull. "A new liberal-labor coalition that will dominate the politics of the 1980's is being built."[21] Speaker after speaker at the convention
emphasized the need for unity. While the "deep divisions which resulted from
Vietnam will not leave the progressive movement unscarred," Wynn told the
convention, liberals and labor have "healed most of the old wounds and are
ready once again to give battle in our strongest and most effective position—
that of solidarity." Senator Carl Levin gave the ADA similar advice. Liberals
needed to unite, he charged, rather than focus on "the sin and transgressions"
of fellow members: "You would have thought that we learned that lesson in
1968 when some sat on their hands too long and allowed a liberal leader like
Hubert Humphrey to fall short in his drive for the Presidency. Because he
was only partly pure, we allowed this country to be polluted by the policies
and politics of the Nixon Administration." Liberals could no longer afford
such exercises in futility. "What value does it serve other than generating internal dissension and further reducing our already decimated ranks?"[22]

This new, smaller labor contingent lacked the stature and influence that
Reuther and Dubinsky had commanded. United by political necessity, liberal
intellectuals and labor leaders remained unsure of each other's intentions. Labor, leery of liberal advocacy of sensitive social issues and skeptical of the
intellectuals' political acumen, hoped that by nudging the organization away
from its pretense of nonpartisanship it could revitalize the ADA as a political
force in the nation's political life. Liberals, wary of labor's partisanship and
uncertain of its agenda, realized that working-class support was essential to
building a sustained reform movement.

The choice the ADA faced in the 1980 presidential election revealed the
beleaguered state of liberalism. It had to choose between a president it had
rejected and a candidate it despised. John Anderson, a former Illinois Republican congresman running on an independent ticket, presented an unalluring
alternative. At a September 1980 National Board meeting, Schlesinger and
Rauh led a large group that opposed an ADA endorsement of Carter. Instead,
they wanted the organization, for the first time in its history, to refrain from
endorsing a candidate for the presidency. "Endorsing Reagan, of course,
would be unthinkable," they charged in a joint statement, "and endorsing

Carter would undermine ADA's credibility, demonstrate that we never really meant what we said about him these past four years, and give final validation to the public perception of ADA as part and parcel of the Democratic party ready to endorse anyone running on the Democratic ticket." Rauh and Schlesinger received unexpected support from Victor Reuther, who deviated from the labor line to support the call for no endorsement. "We must maintain our integrity in the political system and not allow ourselves to become a party for the power brokers," he said. Some of the larger chapters—IVI, New York, Pittsburgh, and Maryland—agreed. Those supporting a Carter endorsement, which included most of the labor contingent, recalled the lessons of 1968. "Let's not elect R.R. through an abdication of our responsibility to endorse Carter," commented one member. It was fear of Ronald Reagan that inspired many of those who wanted the ADA to endorse Carter. "We must, by any means necesary, defeat Ronald Reagan," declared a worried board member. Persuaded by this practical appeal, the board voted overwhelmingly for a Carter endorsement. The *Washington Post* columnist Colman McCarthy charged, "In backing Carter, after three years of correctly denouncing him, ADA has said that its appetite for idealism is not so strong after all."[23]

Capitalizing on popular frustrations, Reagan won a respectable 51 percent of the popular vote, an overwhelming forty-four state, and a staggering 489 electoral votes. Carter finished with 41 percent of the popular vote, six states, and 49 electoral votes. The Republicans took control of the Senate and made substantial gains in the House. Liberal stalwarts like Birch Bayh in Indiana, George McGovern in South Dakota, Frank Church in Idaho, and John Culver in Iowa went down to defeat. Reagan ate into every traditional liberal voting bloc. He captured an estimated 41 percent of the union vote, won the Catholic vote 46 percent to 42 percent, and split the Jewish vote. Almost 25 percent of all Democrats crossed over to vote for Reagan. Only blacks and Hispanics remained faithful to the Democrats. Carter was the first Democratic president since Grover Cleveland in 1888 and only the tenth sitting president in U.S. history to be voted out of office. Republicans were quick to conclude that the election represented a fundamental political realignment. "Our old enemy liberalism had died," declared William Rusher of the *National Review*. Senator Orrin Hatch claimed that the election marked the overthrow of "fifty years of liberal government."[24]

Once again, the ADA played a negligible role in the election. Many liberal candidates feared that an ADA endorsement would be political suicide. In most cases, however, the fact was that no one really cared what the ADA had to say about the election. "You have to understand," New York's colorful mayor, Ed Koch, confided to a friend in 1981, "ADA was formed in the late forties, as I recall by Mrs. Roosevelt and Hubert Humphrey, in order to prevent the radical left from taking over the Democratic Party. Now, what is interesting and almost ludicrous is that the ADA has *become* the radical left in the Democratic Party. They are a fringe element. Who cares about ADA? I don't."[25]

The 1980 election results revealed the gravity of the ADA's predicament.

Its policy positions remained farsighted and independent of the Democratic party; at the same time the organization appeared more willing to work within the party to achieve its reforms. However "correct" the ADA's solutions, they were far removed from both the public mood and the political debate. The organization attempted to have it both ways—to be visionary in proposing farsighted solutions to the nation's economic woes and to be practical by rebuilding its ties with labor and endorsing electable candidates. In reality, however, the ADA's vision undermined its political credibility, while its desire to work with the Democrats robbed the organization of its independence.

Believing he had received a "mandate for change," Reagan set out to reverse the growth of the federal government and improve America's stature in the world. He pushed through Congress a three-year, 25 percent reduction in personal income taxes, made deep cuts in many social welfare programs, and embarked on a massive increase in defense spending. Whether stimulated by his policies or not, the economy, after suffering the worst recession since the 1930s, bounced back in 1983. Unemployment leveled off at 7.5 percent—exactly what it was when Reagan took office. The annual rate of inflation fell from 11.7 percent to 4.2 percent in 1984. Perhaps the greatest legacy of Reagan's "supply-side" economics, however, was a crippling deficit, which threatened to grow above $200 billion by the end of the decade. In foreign policy Reagan sent American military aid to El Salvador, overthrew a leftist government on the tiny Caribbean island of Grenada, and attempted to subvert the leftist government of Nicaragua. He followed through on his promise to take a hard line with the Russians. He deployed cruise and Pershing missiles in Europe, scrapped SALT II, and promoted an ambitious nuclear defense system in space. Reagan showed contempt for other issues dear to liberals. He appointed the controversial James Watt secretary of interior and helped him in his fight to permit drilling in wilderness areas, accelerate coal leasing, halt the acquisition of national parkland, and open the continental shelf to oil and gas exploration. He named another conservative, Anne Burford, head of the Environmental Protection Agency. Burford quickly slashed funds for enforcement, monitoring, and research. Although neither survived Reagan's first term, they left their imprint on government policy. The Reagan administration also abandoned the government's commitment to affirmative action and proposed to provide tax credits to private schools practicing discrimination. It backed away only after the Supreme Court declared such action unconstitutional.

Reagan's presidency stirred considerable soul-searching among liberals. Confronted by Reagan's successful legislative program and his strong standing in the polls, many liberals believed it was time to move beyond their New Deal heritage. Senator Paul Tsongas of Massachusetts, a leader of a group of "neoliberals" who advocated a compromise between liberal values and conservative methods, told the ADA convention in 1980, "Liberalism is at a crossroads." Either it will change to meet the demands of the 1980s "or it will be reduced to an interesting topic for Ph.D.-writing historians." Liberals need to appeal, he insisted, to a new generation that never knew "the anger that fed the liberal cause." Tsongas engaged National Director Leon Shull in a debate at the convention. Shull insisted, "The essence of liberalism is the use of government to intervene on behalf of people." Tsongas disagreed. "I don't think government is where it's at," he retorted. "The Johnson-Humphrey Great Society approach is that government does work, but I think government has a deadening impact." Tsongas accused the ADA of being "mired in yesterday's truisms." Shull concluded, "To say these are old battles is not an excuse to stop fighting them."[26]

The ADA did not heed Tsongas's advice. Instead, it combined sharp rhetorical attacks on the president with strong advocacy of an alternative economic policy. Reagan inspired the harshest language the ADA had used since its fight against Joe McCarthy in the 1950s. "Under the guise of fighting inflation and rebuilding the U.S. economy," the ADA charged, "President Reagan is attempting a complete transformation of the role of the federal government." Reagan's budget and tax program, it claimed, "is fundamentally a transfer of resources from those with little to those who already have more than enough." The Massachusetts congressman Robert F. Drinan, the ADA's new national chairman, accused Reagan of "trying to create a new and frightening America . . . where the government favors the wealthy, virtually eliminates income taxes on corporations, refuses to enforce the civil rights laws, and turns its back on environmental reforms required for the health of its citizens."[27]

The guiding economic principle of both the ADA and the democratic Left in the 1980s was "economic democracy"—democratic control of investment, democratization of the workplace, and democratic local planning. The ADA's economic program called for, among other things, a commitment to full employment and creation of a national industrial policy board responsible for economic planning. "Clearly we reject the rigid, centralized, and authoritarian planning characteristics of the Soviet Union," declared Drinan. "But our vast economic problems cannot be left to the pressure of countless private interests operating independently for their own private purposes in the marketplace." To allocate money to rebuild America's decaying roads, airports, and basic urban systems, the ADA called for creation of an infrastructure financing bank. It also advocated a restructured tax program to provide greater benefits to the poor and middle class, as well as strict antitrust enforcement. "Until we institute democratic national planning directed toward the goal of full employment, we will have to take individual emergency measures to deal with each immediate crisis," Shull wrote.[28]

In the Democratic primaries of 1984, as in those of 1980, the organization endorsed the candidate with the best chance of winning rather than the one with the most liberal record. The former ADA national chairman George McGovern advocated a 25 percent reduction in defense spending as well as increased domestic spending. Walter Mondale, on the other hand, had established himself as the clear frontrunner by trimming his liberal sails. He advocated a 4 percent increase in defense spending and a budget reduction plan that would freeze social spending. While McGovern had a minuscule popular following, and no organization, Mondale had assembled a political jugger-naut fueled by endorsement from many prominent Democrats and labor orga-nizations, including the AFL-CIO.

The choice between Mondale and McGovern presented the ADA with a classic dilemma: it could stand on principle alone and endorse McGovern, or it could compromise its vision for the sake of influence. Congressman Barney Frank of Massachusetts championed Mondale's cause at the January 1984 National Board meeting. "If this is therapy, then vote for George McGovern," he declared. "If you're trying to elect a president, then vote for Walter Mon-dale." A still feisty Joseph Rauh disagreed, charging that the ADA's role was "not to be realistic" but to be idealistic. "I'm appalled," he declared, that ADA would consider endorsing "a candidate in the middle. If ADA is true to its role of liberalism, it will endorse from the left, or it won't endorse at all." Actually, Rauh hoped for a postponement so he could raise the question at the convention, where the labor delegation exercised less influence. But labor was not Rauh's only opponent. The board voted down Rauh's proposal and on the next vote decided two to one to endorse Mondale. For the second time in four years, Rauh lost a vote on presidential endorsement. "I can't re-member the last time the AFL-CIO and the ADA endorsed the same candi-date," commented Frank. "Its a sign that Democrats have healed the breach of the Vietnam War."[29]

Mondale had an easier time convincing liberals that he was presidential timber than he did voters. The interest-group politics Mondale had learned so well in his days in the Minnesota Farmer-Labor party, and from his mentor Hubert Humphrey, did not strike a responsive chord in the American public in 1984. Even though he chose a woman, Representative Geraldine Ferraro of New York, as his running mate, Mondale never established himself as an independent and forceful leader who would stand up to special interest groups to which he was indebted. Reagan carried forty-nine states and won 59 per-cent of the popular vote and an astonishing 525 electoral votes. Mondale was left with 41 percent of the popular vote—just a little more than Barry Gold-water received in 1964 and George McGovern in 1972—and 13 electoral votes. While Reagan's victory in 1980 resulted from voter dissatisfaction with Carter, his smashing triumph in 1984 represented a great personal triumph.

Reagan's victory confirmed liberals' worst fears and moved the ADA closer to an alliance with labor and the Democratic party. Appropriately, when Leon Shull resigned as national director in January 1985, the organiza-tion chose Ann Lewis, formerly political director of the Democratic National Committee, to replace him. Lewis has an unabashed belief in a liberal-labor coalition and close association with the Democratic party. "I do not believe it is possible to be effective in American politics today," she claims, "by being detached or neutral from the two major parties." A dynamic leader and in-spirational advocate of the New Politics, Lewis is committed to maintaining the organization's ideological integrity. Yet, when it comes to politics, she believes that the ADA's self-proclaimed policy of independence is no longer relevant to the political climate. The debate in 1985, she declares, "is more polarized; there are no liberal Republicans for the ADA to appeal [to]; all the liberals are in the Democratic party." The basic question the ADA has to confront, she argues, is "How do we function most effectively for the issues we care most about?" For Lewis, and many other ADA leaders, the time has come for the ADA to abandon the fiction of bipartisanship and discard its claims of independence in favor of effective political action. Unfortunately, as the organization nears its fortieth birthday, it appears to have neither.[30]

It has become fashionable for observers to mourn the death of liberalism in America. "I do not recall a time when the prospects for the left in America have looked quite so dim," lamented Dennis Wrong in *Dissent*. William Schneider, writing in the *New Republic,* warned that in 1985 liberals are in the same position "as the French aristocracy at the time of the Bourbon Restoration. We can pretend that nothing has happened, but the *ancien régime* is dead." Already historians have begun autopsies on the corpse of liberalism. Alonzo Hamby has written that "the failure of the Carter presidency was yet another indication of the exhaustion of liberalism."[81]

For twenty years liberals, with their limited reform agenda and stifling fear of conservative reaction, were convinced that accommodation was the best way to go. On the major issues they cared about most—civil liberties, civil rights, economic growth, and foreign policy—ADA's leaders thought it best to mute their internal differences and work for incremental change. In the late 1950s, as the red scare faded from memory and the political atmosphere became more conducive to reform ideas, moderates and traditionalists began bickering openly about the direction liberalism should take in the coming decade. By 1960, as they were being called upon to devise new programs for the nation, liberals were divided and confused.

Liberalism began unraveling even before the tragedy of Vietnam, but the war fractured liberal ranks by heightening tensions present in liberalism since the mid-1950s; it polarized the factions and made compromise and consensus—key tenets of the liberal faith—impossible. Vietnam was to liberalism what slavery was to the Civil War. As the historian Avery Craven has written, the Civil War was "the symbol and carrier of all sectional differences." All the other questions that divided liberals were consumed in the larger debate over the war. Furthermore, the debate over Vietnam forced liberals to redefine modern liberalism, to reconsider its agenda, and to rethink the coalition originally forged under very different circumstances during the Great Depression. The liberalism that emerged after 1968, while still in the mainstream of American politics, was changed in substantive ways.

Moderates and traditionalists alike were correct is assessing the consequences of endorsing McCarthy in 1968. Traditionalists accurately predicted that the coalition's effectiveness would be impaired by a split with labor. Yet, they were blind to the long-term generational changes that were gradually making that coalition obsolete, and they underestimated the moral impact the war was having on a whole generation of younger Americans. Moderates correctly perceived that the New Deal reform agenda, and the political coalition that sustained it, had lost much of its vitality. However, they underestimated the resiliency of established institutions and overestimated the potential impact of the reformers. In the end, although the ADA suffered politically by endorsing McCarthy, it could not have survived without supporting him. The organization paid the political price for choosing vision. Since the mid-1970s the ADA's leaders have tried to become more visionary in presenting alternatives to counter the popular appeal of conservative ideas, while also being more pragmatic, reestablishing their political legitimacy, and reforging their ties with labor. They are finding, however, that their vision often gets in the way of their politics. The organization's unflinching commitment to unpopular causes has left it isolated and alienated, on the periphery of the political landscape.

In the mid-1980s the ADA and liberals in general are searching for a new faith that will assuage their conscience and also win them votes. Still scarred by the experience of the 1960s, liberals are torn between their commitment to a just society and their desire to propose solutions that are politically acceptable. Neoconservatives and, to a lesser extent, neoliberals have attempted to redress the balance in favor of political realities. Liberals, they argue, must return to the glory days of Camelot when "hardheaded" realism and political pragmatism guided their thought. The New Politics liberals, represented by the ADA, disagree; by giving in to public pressure, they charge, Vital Center liberals forfeited any chance of initiating real reform. Neither side has found a way out of the dilemma. Neoconservatives and neoliberals have overestimated the ability of their moderate reform agenda to achieve their optimistic vision of a just society. The ADA's "new liberalism," while intellectually consistent, has failed the test of politics.

While liberals attempt to redress the balance between politics and vision, conservatives—united behind the charismatic leadership of Ronald Reagan— have tightened their grip on the popular imagination. Reagan's success is due in part to his charming personality. His infectious smile and perpetual optimism provide him a public persona unequaled since Roosevelt. Although Reagan is more popular than his policies, the public finds attractive the compelling simplicity of his vision; his ability blithely to dismiss most of the issues—poverty, racism, militarism—over which liberals agonize. Reagan has remained committed to the political values of the Vital Center, the same ones he held as a founding member of the ADA in 1947. Reagan is wedded to the lessons of Munich, convinced of America's mission to fight communism, and certain of the social benefits of economic growth. Reagan may have temporarily reestablished a new Vital Center, but most liberals believe his legacy will be short-lived. When Reagan's revolution crashes on the shores of reality, as his critics predict, a question remains: Will liberals be prepared to offer an alternative?

It is unclear what role the ADA will play in the liberals' attempts to redefine their faith. The organization bears the psychological and political scars from years of battles, and it has lost much of its youthful energy and enthusiasm. Many younger liberals mistakenly perceive the organization as tied too closely to the mistakes of the "old" liberalism; yet many older liberals believe it has become too radical, moved too far from the political mainstream in America. Ironically, many of its founding fathers, including Arthur Schlesinger, Jr., and Joseph Rauh, believe that the ADA has outlived its usefulness and should retire quietly and allow a new organization to fill the vacuum.

Despite these problems, the ADA persists. Taking advantage of liberal antipathy toward Reagan, it has gained support from a wide range of progressive forces, including socialists, feminists, gay rights advocates, environmentalists, and a handful of bread-and-butter unionists. Its budget, approaching one million dollars in 1985, has doubled since 1979.[32] As always, the organization has benefited from a small and very competent national staff that has lost none of its commitment to liberal causes.

These gains, however, cannot hide the reality that the organization is only a shadow of what it was before 1968. The large and robust chapters that provided the organization with fresh talent and local influence have disappeared. General membership, which has risen slightly since 1981, is still dismally low (most estimates place it between five and eight thousand), while active members—those who organize rallies, make phone calls, lobby congressmen—have dwindled to fewer than a thousand. For two decades prominent national figures like Eleanor Roosevelt and Hubert Humphrey were actively involved in the organization, while others, among them Harry Truman, Adlai Stevenson, John F. Kennedy, and even Lyndon Johnson, participated by appearing at Roosevelt Day Dinners, entertaining ADA delegations, or sending messages to the annual convention. In recent years, however, even liberal politicians have perceived the ADA as extreme in temperament and ineffective in practice and have thus tried to avoid association with the organization. Once the largest and perhaps most respected liberal organization in national politics, the ADA has been eclipsed by newer, more effective groups. Today even liberals pay little attention to what the ADA has to say.

Few of those who gathered at the Willard Hotel in January 1947 believed that the organization they were founding would be active almost forty years later. The prime movers of the earlier years—Schlesinger, Rauh, Loeb, Niebuhr, and Dubinsky—are no longer active in the organization, and no one of similar stature has taken their places. The liberalism they once espoused, with its emphasis on gradualism and consensus, has also given way to a more probing philosophy that seeks significant institutional change. While the names and the ideas have changed, the obstacles liberals must face have remained the same. Confronted by a resilient and conservative political culture, liberals have been forced either to temper their vision and accommodate the prevailing consensus or stand firmly on principle and sacrifice influence. Impaled on the horns of this dilemma, liberals must confront the travail of redefinition.

NOTES

Works listed in the bibliography have been cited in shortened form in the notes. Use has also been made of the following abbreviations:

ADA Papers	Americans for Democratic Action Papers, Wisconsin State Historical Society, Madison, Wisconsin
ADA Papers (NO)	Americans for Democratic Action Papers, National Office, Washington, D.C.
CF	Correspondence File
COHP	Columbia Oral History Program, New York, New York
DDEL	Dwight D. Eisenhower Library, Abilene, Kansas
FDRL	Franklin D. Roosevelt Library, Hyde Park, New York
GC	General Correspondence
HSTL	Harry S. Truman Library, Independence, Missouri
JFKL	John F. Kennedy Library, Boston, Massachusetts
LBJL	Lyndon B. Johnson Library, Austin, Texas
LC	Library of Congress, Washington, D.C.
MF	Mayoralty File
MSHS	Minnesota State Historical Society
NR	*New Republic*
NYPL	New York Public Library, New York, New York
NYT	*New York Times*
PF	Political File
PPF	President's Personal File
SCPC	Swarthmore College Peace Collection, Swarthmore, Pennsylvania
SF	Senatorial File
SHC-UNC	Southern Historical Collection, University of North Carolina, Chapel Hill, North Carolina
UC	Unprocessed Collection
WRLLUA	Walter Reuther Library of Labor and Urban Affairs, Detroit, Michigan
WSHS	Wisconsin State Historical Society, Madison, Wisconsin
YUL	Yale University Library, New Haven, Connecticut

Preface

1. Hodgson, *America in Our Time*, 7.
2. Hartz, *The Liberal Tradition in America;* Boorstin, *The Genius of American Politics;* Hofstadter, *The Age of Reform;* Bell, *The End of Ideology.*

245

3. Alan Brinkley, "Writing the History of Contemporary America: Dilemmas and Challenges," *Daedalus* (Winter 1984), 121–41.

4. Brinkley, *Voices of Protest;* David Kennedy, *Over Here: World War I and American Society* (New York: Oxford Univ. Press, 1980); Patterson, *America's Struggle against Poverty.*

5. Kennedy, *Over Here,* 35.

6. Seymour Martin Lipset, "Social Structure and Social Change," in Peter M. Blau, ed., *Approaches to the Study of Social Structure* (New York: Free Press, 1975); Sheldon Wolin, *Politics and Vision* (Boston: Little, Bown, 1960).

7. A very broad definition of liberalism is employed here. While liberals did not always speak with one voice, they did accept a common language. Allowing for differences in emphasis and nuance, liberal thought in the immediate postwar period rested upon two premises: that America needed to assume the position of a world power in order to prevent the expansion of Communist influence abroad and that economic growth and gradual change of national institutions achieved within a capitalist system offered the best hope for domestic prosperity. To state that the ADA is representative of postwar liberal thinking is not to imply that all liberals subscribed to the organization's position on particular issues. Indeed, some prominent liberals never joined the ADA and disagreed with its stance on controversial issues. Despite occasional differences, however, the ADA, more than any other group or organization, attracted the nation's leading liberal figures and helped shape the guiding principles of postwar liberal thought.

8. With the exception of their religious background, most ADA members had much in common with earlier reformers. See, for example, George Mowry, *The California Progressives* (Berkeley: Univ. of California Press, 1951); Hofstadter, *The Age of Reform;* Robert H. Wiebe, *The Search for Order, 1877–1920* (New York: Hill and Wang, 1967); Samuel Hays, "The Politics of Reform in Municipal Government in the Progressive Era," *Pacific Northwest Quarterly* (1964), 157–169. For a more cynical view, see Christopher Lasch *The New Radicalism in America: The Intellectual as a Social Type* (New York: Knopf, 1965), and *The Agony of the American Left.* The organization's strong Jewish character is also not surprising. Jews, who had long been excluded from mainstream American politics, became a welcome addition to the New Deal coalition. Roosevelt appointed Jews to important government positions and maintained friendships with many prominent Jewish figures. Beyond that, Jews enthusiastically supported most of his foreign and domestic policy initiatives. Roosevelt led the nation into war against the Nazis at a time when world Jewry itself was threatened; at home he was responsible for initiating the early welfare state—an idea long popular with many Jews. Even more than most Americans, Jews felt a great sense of loss at Roosevelt's death and were determined to keep his policies alive.

9. The reform group in the ADA is tied closely to the emergence of the "New Class" in postwar liberalism. Most scholars have traced the roots of the New Class to the development of a postindustrial service economy and the proliferation of mass education. Critics have argued that the New Class has fostered an "adversary culture" that attempts to undermine the capitalistic pillars of contemporary society. "Large segments of the broad, new upper-middle classes, including the professional and managerial categories, who are the most affluent, secure, and closely associated with advanced culture and technology, increasingly cease to defend business values," commented the political scientist Everett Carll Ladd. See B. Bruce-Briggs, ed., *The New Class?* (New Brunswick, N.J.: Transaction Books, 1979). Especially

interesting are the essays by Norman Podhoretz, Jeane Kirkpatrick, Everett Carll Ladd, and Daniel Bell.

10. The leading approach to the sociological study of social-movement organizations has been Max Weber's and Robert Michels's model of organizational transformation. According to this approach, when an organization attains an economic and social base in society and when a bureaucratic structure replaces the original charismatic leadership, the organization will lose much of its social vision. Newer studies have replaced this view of an "iron law of oligarchy" with a more complex model that emphasizes the uniqueness of the process of organizational change. Since the reformers used democratic means to gain control of the organization in the 1960s, a study of the ADA seems to support the findings of the newer studies. See H. J. Gerth and C. W. Mills, *From Max Weber: Essays in Sociology* (New York: Oxford Univ. Press, 1946); Robert Michels, *Political Parties* (Glencoe, Ill.: Free Press, 1949); Mayer Zald and Roberta Ash, "Social Movement Organizations: Growth, Decay and Change," *Social Forces* (March 1966), 327–40; Joseph Gusfield, "Problems of Generations in an Organizations Structure," *Social Forces* (May 1957), 323–30; Peter B. Clark and James Q. Wilson, "Incentive Systems: A Theory of Organizations," *Administrative Science Quarterly* (June 1961), 129–66.

11. Gus Tyler, "Puncturing the Liberal Illusion," *New Leader* (March 3, 1969), 6–8.

1. Communists, Anti-Communists, and the Cold War

1. Tugwell, *The Stricken Land*, x. Leuchtenburg, *In the Shadow of FDR*, 4.

2. Bowles, *Tomorrow without Fear;* John Morton Blum, *V Was for Victory* (New York: Harcourt Brace Jovanovich, 1976); Hamby, *Beyond the New Deal*, 17.

3. Stone, *The Truman Era*, xv; Leuchtenburg, *In the Shadow of FDR*, 21.

4. Hamby, *Beyond the New Deal*, 68–79.

5. Gaddis, *The Origins of the Cold War*, 198–244.

6. *Time* (Feb. 18, 1946), 29–30; Gaddis, *The Origins of the Cold War*, 300–303.

7. Halle, *The Cold War as History;* Yergin, *Shattered Peace;* Hugh DeSantis, *The Diplomacy of Silence: The American Foreign Service, the Soviet Union, and the Cold War, 1933–1947* (Chicago: Univ. of Chicago Press, 1980); Vojtech Mastry, *Russia's Road to the Cold War: Diplomacy, Warfare, and the Politics of Communism, 1941–1945* (New York: Columbia Univ. Press, 1979); Messer, *The End of an Alliance.*

8. Starobin, *American Communism in Crisis*, 21; Irving Howe and Lewis Coser, *The American Communist Party: A Critical History* (Boston: Beacon Press, 1957).

9. Hamby, *Beyond the New Deal*, 33–38.

10. "Russia in Europe," *NR* (Jan. 24, 1944), 105; J. Alvarez Del Vayo, "Report from Moscow," *Nation* (Aug. 17, 1946), 175; Max Lerner, "Who Can Build the New World?" *NR* (Sept. 16, 1946), 323–24; Michael Straight, "Fixing the

11. *Time* (Sept. 30, 1946), 23.

12. Hamby, *Beyond the New Deal*, 25.

13. Henry Wallace, "Memorandum to the President," July 1946, Wallace Papers, Microfilm Edition, Univ. of Iowa, Reel 41, Frames 761–72; Goldman, *Crucial Decade and After*, 36–39; Hamby, *Beyond the New Deal*, 127–34; Donovan, *Conflict and Crisis*, 222–28.

14. TRB, "Washington Wire," *NR* (Sept. 30, 1946), 399; ibid., 396; Freda Kirchwey, "The Challenge of Henry Wallace," *Nation* (Sept. 28, 1946), 339.

15. Walker, *Henry A. Wallace and American Foreign Policy*, 107.

16. Fox, *Reinhold Niebuhr*; Fox, "Reinhold Niebuhr and the Emergence of the Liberal Realist Faith, 1930–1945," 244–65; Charles W. Kegley and Robert W. Bretall, *Reinhold Niebuhr: His Religious, Social, and Political Thoughts* (New York: Macmillan, 1956); Niebuhr, *The Children of Light and the Children of Darkness*.

17. Adam Clymer, "Union for Democratic Action; Key to the Non-Communist Left" (Undergraduate thesis, Harvard College, 1958), 1–5.

18. "Four Years of UDA," n.d., ADA Papers, Ser. 1, Box 9.

19. Robert Pierce, "Liberals and the Cold War: Union for Democratic Action and Americans for Democratic Action" (Ph.D. diss., Univ. of Wisconsin at Madison, 1979), 40. Loeb described his experiences in his unpublished autobiography, at WSHS.

29. "Four Year of UDA," ADA Papers, Ser. 1, Box 9; Hal Siegel to Murray Gross, Oct. 20, 1940, ibid., Box 5; *NYT* (April 19, 1940); Norman Thomas to Frank Zeidler, June 19, 1941, Thomas Papers (NYPL), GP, Box 21.

21. "UDA Press Release," June 25, 1941, and Loeb to Biemiller, June 25, 1941, both in ADA Papers, Ser. 1, Box 18; UDA Bulletin, Aug. 1941, ibid., Box 35.

22. Wechsler, *The Age of Suspicion*, 212.

23. "Memorandum on Win the Peace Conference," ADA Papers, Ser. 1, Box 4; James Loeb, "Progressives and Communists," *NR* (May 13, 1946), 699.

24. James Loeb, Oral History, FDRL, pp. 24–25.

25. Schlesinger, "The U.S. Communist Party," 84–96.

26. Niebuhr, "The Fight for Germany," 65; Niebuhr, "Our Chances for Peace," 1; Lash, *Eleanor*, 73; Joseph and Stewart Alsop, "The Liberals and Russia," *NR* (Sept. 16, 1946), 321; Joseph and Stewart Alsop, "Tragedy of Liberalism," 68–72.

27. Barnard, *Walter Reuther and the Rise of the Auto Workers*; Cormier and Eaton, *Reuther*; Jean Gould, *Walter Reuther: Labor's Rugged Individualist* (New York: Dodd, Mead, 1972); Irving Howe, *The UAW and Walter Reuther* (New York: Random House, 1949); Keeran, *The Communist Party and the Auto Workers Unions*.

28. McAuliffe, *Crisis on the Left*, 12–13; Nelson Lichtenstein, *Labor's War at Home: The CIO in World War II* (New York: Cambridge Univ. Press, 1983); Starobin, *American Communism in Crisis*; Shannon, *The Decline of American Communism*; Isserman, *Which Side Were You On?*

29. Oshinsky, *Senator Joseph McCarthy and the American Labor Movement*, 94–95.

30. Haynes, *Dubious Alliance*.

31. Gieske, *Minnesota Farmer-Laborism*, 307–25.

32. Donovan, *Conflict and Crisis*, 259.

33. Wechsler, *The Age of Suspicion,* 210–11.

34. *NYT* (Dec. 30, 1946), 1, 9.

35. *NYT* (Jan. 5, 1947), 5.

36. Rauh interview, June 1985; Rauh, "Government by Directive," 326.

37. Arthur Schlesinger, Jr., "Prophet for a Secular Age," *New Leader* (Jan. 24, 1972), 11–14; Schlesinger interview, Oct. 1985.

38. Lash, *Eleanor,* 75–84.

39. Reinhold Niebuhr, "The ADA and the Liberal-Democratic Movement in the Past Decade," n.d., Niebuhr Papers (LC), Box 1; Lilienthal, *The Journals of David Lilienthal,* 527; Hamby, *Beyond the New Deal,* 161.

40. "Notes of January 4, 1947, UDA Conference," ADA Papers, Ser. 2, Box 71.

41. "Minutes of the January 4, 1947, Conference," ADA Papers, Ser. 2, Box 71; Rauh interview, Dec. 1985.

42. Ibid.

43. Ibid.

44. Rauh interview, Dec. 18, 1985; Rauh, Oral History, FDRL, p. 4.

45. *NYT* (Jan. 4, 1947), 1. Among those observing the convention were a couple of agents from the Federal Bureau of Investigation. FBI Director J. Edgar Hoover feared that, despite its public declarations of anticommunism, the ADA would work with the PCA to unite the Popular Front. The director informed the New York office, "Although the Americans for Democratic Action have stated they will not admit Communists to its membership, an examination of the press accounts reflects that several individuals who have previously affiliated with the Communist movement through its front programs are affiliated with this organization." Consequently, Hoover demanded that "consideration should be given to the possibility that this organization may cooperate on issues of mutual interest with the Progressive Citizens of America which should eventually unite the progressive movement." Although the agents reported to Hoover, "We believe that the ADA may be sincere in their anti-communist program," Hoover remained unconvinced. For the next fifteen years he required local FBI offices to observe and report on all ADA activities in their area. Although the FBI never gathered any evidence to support a full-scale investigation, it did collect over 10,000 pages of information on the ADA. Director to New York, "Progressive Citizens of America, Americans for Democratic Action: Internal Security," Feb. 7, 1974. Documents received through the Freedom of Information Act.

46. Loeb to David Williams, Jan. 7, 1947, ADA Papers, Ser. 1, Box 19.

47. Charles Sellers to ADA National Board, May 20, 1947, ADA Papers, Ser. 2, Box 81.

48. James Loeb to Executive Committee, Spring 1947, ADA Papers, UC; William R. Burke to Melvyn Douglas, June 19, 1947, Douglas Papers (WSHS), Box 3.

49. "Statement on ADA and PCA," March 14, 1947, ADA Papers, Ser. 2, Box 30.

50. Frances Cousens, "Americans for Democratic Action: A Study in Middle Class Political Behavior" (M.A. thesis, Wayne State Univ., 1951), 70; Frederick W. Grupp, "Social Correlates of Political Activists: The John Birch Society and the ADA" (Ph.D. diss., Univ. of Pennsylvania, 1968), 102–5. A survey conducted by the Survey Research Laboratory at the Univ. of Wisconsin in Sept. 1965 confirmed these earlier findings. The survey found that 97% of the membership was

male; 33% belonged to the Jewish faith; over half had college degrees beyond the bachelor's; 76% lived either in the East or Midwest; and 82% categorized themselves as either middle or upper class.

51. Thomas Amlie to Robert McGill, April 1947, Amlie Papers (WSHS), Box 63; Bowles to Eleanor Mishnun, March 26, 1948, Bowles Papers (YUL), Box 31.

52. Straight, *After Long Silence; NYT* (Jan. 5, 1947), E7, and sec. 4, p. 7.

53. Freda Kirchwey, "Mugwumps in Action," *Nation* (Jan. 18, 1947), 61–62; Henry Wallace, "The Enemy Is Not Each Other," *NR* (Jan. 27, 1947), 22–23.

54. Schlesinger to Wilson Wyatt, Feb. 21, 1947, ADA Papers, Ser. 2, Box 95.

55. *The Public Papers of the Presidents of the United States: Harry S. Truman, 1947,* 176–80; Wittner, "The Truman Doctrine and the Defense of Freedom," 161–88; Lawrence S. Wittner, *American Intervention in Greece, 1943–1949* (New York: Columbia Univ. Press, 1982); Kuniholm, *The Origins of the Cold War in the Near East.*

56. *NYT* (March 14, 1947), 3; Markowitz, *The Rise and Fall of the People's Century,* 236; Henry Wallace, "The Fight for Peace," *NR* (March 24, 1947), 12.

57. *NYT* (March 30, 1947), 46.

58. Minutes of the Foreign Policy Committee, National Conference, March 30, 1947, ADA Papers, Ser. 2, Box 71.

59. Minutes of the Foreign Policy Committee, National Conference, March 30, 1947, ADA Papers, Ser. 2, Box 71; Charles Bolte, "Democratic Assembly," *Nation* (April 12, 1947), 424.

60. "Notes on the Foreign Policy Discussion," March 30, 1947, ADA Papers, Ser. 2, Box 71.

61. Domestic Policy Resolutions, March 1947, ADA Papers, Ser. 2, Box 71.

62. ADA Constitution and By-Laws, March 1947, ADA Papers, Ser. 2, Box 71.

63. Washington, D.C., Chapter, "Report of the Conference of the ADA," April 16, 1947, p. 3. ADA Papers, UC.

64. See Freeman, *The Politics of the Women's Liberation Movement.*

65. "Report of the Committee on Economic Stability," April 1947, Galbraith Papers (JFKL), GC, Box 10.

66. Leon Keyserling to James Loeb, May 22, 1947, ADA Papers, Ser. 2, Box 30; Edwin Nourse to Chester Bowles, June 2, 1947, Bowles Papers (YUL), Box 40, File 288; Nourse to Loeb, June 1947, Gilbert Papers (FDRL), Box 2, Folder 4.

67. *Nation* (May 24, 1947), 617; *NR* (May 26, 1947), 7.

68. Henry Wallace, "Too Little Too Late," *NR* (Oct. 6, 1947), 11.

69. Hamby, *Beyond the New Deal,* 193; ADA *World* (July 1947).

70. "Statement of ADA on the Marshall Plan," Executive Committee Minutes, ADA Papers, Ser. 2, Box 34.

71. Loeb to Harold Stein, "ADA Projects on the Marshall Plan," Jan. 2, 1948, ADA Papers, Ser. 2, Box 59.

72. House Select Committee on Lobbying Activities, July 11–12, 1950. In preparation for its testimony, the ADA completed a thorough review of its financial resources and expenses. Most of the material covered the organization's activities in 1949 and 1950, but there is some valuable information for 1947.

73. Notes of discussion following Treasurer's Report, Sept. 20, 1947, ADA Papers, Ser. 2, Box 65.

2. The ADA, Wallace, and the 1948 Election

1. *NYT* (June 17, 1947), 1; Hamby, *Beyond the New Deal,* 206.

2. MacDougall, *Gideon's Army,* 208, 229–38.

3. Starobin, *American Communism in Crisis,* 143–57; De Caux, *Labor Radical,* 518–19.

4. *Newsweek* (March 1, 1948), 17; *NYT* (Feb. 18, 1948), 1.

5. James Loeb to David Williams, June 10, 1947, ADA Papers, Ser. 2, Boxes 58, 94; James Loeb, "Report to the National Board," Sept. 20, 1947, ibid., Box 65.

6. ADA Press Release, Dec. 30, 1947, ADA Papers, Ser. 3, Box 87.

7. Lee, *Truman and Taft-Hartley,* 49–105.

8. Herbert Harris, "What Taft Taught Labor," *NR* (Aug. 18, 1947), 21–24; Lee, *Truman and Taft-Hartley,* 15–232.

9. "The Quarter's Poll," *Public Opinion Quarterly* (Winter 1947–48), 639–84.

10. CIO-PAC, "Third Party: Red Ally of Reaction," Textile Workers Union of America Papers (WSHS), COPE-PAC, Box 481.

11. Clark Clifford, "Memorandum for the President," Nov. 19, 1947, Clifford Papers (HSTL), PF–1948 Election.

12. *Time* (Jan. 19, 1948), 19; *Newsweek* (Jan. 19, 1948), 20; *NYT* (Jan. 19, 1948), 1.

13. J. Howard McGrath, "Memorandum," Jan. 19 and 27, 1948, J. Howard McGrath Papers (HSTL), PF–1948 Election.

14. Loeb to Jensen, June 11, 1948, ADA Papers, Ser. 2, Box 58; Humphrey to Henderson, March 24, 1947, Humphrey Papers (MSHS), MF.

15. Bowles to Humphrey, March 17, 1948, Bowles Papers (YUL), Box 49; Humphrey to Henderson, March 24, 1947, Humphrey Papers (MSHS), MF.

16. Bowles to Shull, March 5, 1948, Bowles Papers (YUL), Box 40.

17. Humphrey to Henderson, March 24, 1947, Humphrey Papers (MSHS), MF.

18. "Notes on the Convention," March 1948, ADA Papers, Ser. 4, Box 12; Willard Shelton, "ADA's Dilemma: HST or GOP; Convention in Philadelphia," *NR* (March 1, 1948), 9.

19. "Notes on the Convention," March 1948, ADA Papers, Ser. 4, Box 12. The ADA's indecision disappointed some prominent anti-Stalinist intellectuals, who feared that its equivocating on dumping Truman would only help Wallace. "Why in hell doesn't ADA come out for a liberal candidate to put up against Truman for the Democratic nomination," complained Dwight Macdonald. "The convention's stand was dismal: neither yes or [*sic*] no on Truman, and no other candidate in sight. If ADA is just part of the Truman forces, what's the use of it? No wonder Henry steals all your thunder." Dwight Macdonald to Arthur Schlesinger, Jr., Feb. 28, 1948, Macdonald Papers (YUL), Box 45, File 1109.

20. Loeb to Humphrey, April 14, 1948, ADA Papers, Ser. 2, Box 58.

21. *Newsweek* (Feb. 16, 1948), 24–25.

22. "Numerical Breakdown of ADA Membership," June 6, 1948, ADA Papers, Ser. 2, Boxes 26, 27, 34.

23. House Select Committee on Lobbying, July 13, 1950, 1–98.

24. Loeb to Humphrey, March 10, 1948, and Humphrey to Henderson, March 24, 1947, both in Humphrey Papers (MSHS), MF.

25. Loeb, Memorandum to National Board, March 15, 1948, ADA Papers, Ser. 2, Boxes 66, 74.

26. Ibid.

27. Executive Committee Minutes, March 18, 1848, ADA Papers, Ser. 2, Box 34.

28. ADA *World* (March 2, 1948), 1.

29. Tucker to Chapters, March 29, 1948, Reuther Papers (WRLLUA), Box 472, File 2.

30. "Revolt against Truman," *Nation* (April 3, 1948), 367; *Newsweek* (April 5, 1949), 12; *NYT* (March 17, 1948), 1.

31. Goldman, *The Crucial Decade and After,* 82–83; *Vital Speeches* (July 1, 1945), 549–50.

32. Franklin D. Roosevelt, Jr., Press Release, March 26, 1948, ADA Papers Ser. 2, Box 74; Leon Henderson, Memorandum, March 27, 1948, ibid., Box 34.

33. William Batt to Clark Clifford, April 15, 1948, Clifford Papers (HSTL), PF, Box 20.

34. "Statement on Political Policy." April 27, 1948, ADA Papers, Ser. 2, Box 34.

35. Executive Committee Minutes, May 1, 1948, and "Memo re the Availability of General Eisenhower," April 27, 1948, both in ADA Papers, Ser. 2, Box 34.

36. Henderson to Executive Board, Nov. 22, 1947, ADA Papers, Ser. 2, Box 34.

37. Loeb to Executive Board, Nov. 22, 1947, ADA Papers, Ser. 2, Box 34.

38. Loeb to Walls/Nevins, Feb. 14, 1949, ADA Papers, Ser. 3, Box 18; Batt to Clifford, April 15, 1948, Clifford Papers (HSTL), PF, Box 20.

39. Andrew Biemiller, "Notes on the Democratic Presidential Nomination," June 1948, ADA Papers, Ser. 2, Box 26.

40. *NYT* (July 6, 1948), 1, 21; (July 10, 1948), 1; (July 11, 1948), 2; Rauh interview, Dec. 1985.

41. *New York Times* (July 11, 1948), 2; *Time* (July 19, 1948), 21.

42. Humphrey, *The Education of a Public Man,* 111.

43. "Clark Clifford Draft of the Democratic National Platform," Elsey Papers (HSTL), Democratic Party Platform, 1948 File.

44. Martin, *Civil Rights and the Crisis of Liberalism,* 84; Rauh interview, Nov. 29, 1983.

45. ADA *World* (Aug. 7, 1948), 1: Ferrell, *Off the Record,* 141–43.

46. Brock, *The Americans for Democratic Action,* 98.

47. *Newsweek* (July 26, 1948), 20.

48. Jack Kroll, "Day-to-Day Account of the Activities of the CIO-PAC at the Democratic National Convention," Kroll Papers (LC), Box 7.

48. Irene Sagan to Loeb, Aug. 13, 1948, ADA Papers, Ser. 2, Box 66; Brock, *The Americans for Democratic Action,* 131.

50. *Newsweek* (Aug. 2, 1948), 17–19.

51. Bruce Bliven, Oral History, COHP, p. 50.

52. Starobin, *American Communism in Crisis,* 180–86; Hamby, *Beyond the New Deal,* 230–32; Henry Wallace, Oral History, COHP, vol. 75, p. 5118.

53. Henderson to Executive Board, Nov. 22, 1947, and Loeb to Executive Board, Nov. 22, 1947, both in ADA Papers, Ser. 2, Box 34; Loeb to Walls/Nevins, Feb. 14, 1949, ibid., Ser. 3, Box 18.

54. Johannes Hoeber, Oral History (HSTL), 57–66.

55. Ibid., 22.

56. Loeb to Harris, April 23, 1947, ADA Papers, Ser. 2, Box 58; Foster, *The Union Politic,* 106.

57. Andrew Biemiller, "The Political Situation among Union Leaders and Members Today," Nov. 28, 1947, ADA Papers, Ser. 2, Box 26.

58. Foster, *The Union Politic,* 91–92.

59. "Henry Wallace: The First Three Months of His Campaign," and "Henry Wallace: The Last Seven Months of His Campaign," ADA Papers, UC.

60. Loeb Testimony before the PCA, July 22, 1948, ADA Papers, Ser. 2, Box 27.

61. *Time* (Nov. 1, 1948), 22.

62. *NYT* (Nov. 4, 1948), 1, 28.

63. Historians disagree about the role the Wallace campaign played in the decline of the Communist party. Joseph Starobin, a former party member, believes that the campaign was the main culprit. The party, he has charged, by compromising its position in the CIO and destroying its reputation for political expertise, opened the way for vicious attacks from liberals and labor. David Shannon has argued that while the Wallace campaign weakened the party, external pressures—namely, prosperity, the Cold War, and anticommunism—dealt the fatal blow. Michael Belknap has maintained that the party's "suicidal reaction" to the Smith Act prosecutions led to its demise. See Starobin, *American Communism in Crisis;* Shannon, *The Decline of the Communist Party;* Belknap, *Cold War Political Justice.*

64. Wechsler, *Reflections of an Angry Middle-Aged Editor,* 55; MacDougall, *Gideon's Army,* 638; Yarnell, "Liberals in Action," 260–73.

65. Haynes, *Dubious Alliance.*

66. Hamby, *Beyond the New Deal,* 257–58.

67. Most scholars view 1948 as a "maintaining" election. Truman won by rallying just enough of the New Deal coalition to squeak by his lackluster Republican opponent. Richard S. Kirkendall, "Election of 1948," in Arthur M. Schlesinger, Jr., and Fred L. Israel, eds., *History of American Presidential Elections, 1789–1968* (New York: Chelsea House, 1971), 3099–145; Lubell, *The Future of American Politics.* Divine, "The Cold War and the Election of 1948," 90–110, has tried, unsuccessfully, I feel, to demonstrate that Cold War issues critically influenced the voters.

68. Studies done by Truman's research staff indicate that Wallace never had the widespread support liberals feared. A comprehensive poll completed in April 1948 reported that, five months after Wallace announced his candidacy, his support remained at just 7 percent. In most areas, the report stated, "Wallace's strength does not alter the fact that the Democrats have a plurality. While Wallace voters are more frequent in important areas; even in these areas the Democratic vote is still greater than the Republican." Wallace's appeal was restricted to two groups: black and Jewish voters. Since the black vote responded "almost univocally to the specific policy towards minorities," it would appear that the ADA's campaign to link Wallace to the Communists had little meaning to black voters. The ADA probably struck the strongest blow against Wallace by pushing for its strong civil rights plank at the convention. The study found Jewish support for Wallace "diffuse and based on a variety of factors." It is possible that the ADA's campaign against Wallace had some impact on Jewish voters, but there is no evidence to indicate that it was a deciding force. "The Wallace Voter and the 1948 Election," Clifford Papers (HSTL), Polls-Miscellaneous, Box 21.

3. The Dilemma of Power: The ADA and National Politics, 1948–1952

1. "Report on ADA National Convention, October 4, 1949," ADA Papers, Ser. 4, Boxes 2, 3.

2. "Summary of ADA Financial Outlook," May 2, 1949, ADA Papers, Ser. 2, Boxes 37, 66.

3. "The ADA Convention," *NR* (April 17, 1950), 13.

4. Rieve to Hoffman, Jan. 26, 1951, ADA Papers, Ser. 2, Box 83; Rieve to Humphrey, Jan. 1951, Humphrey Papers (MSHS), MF.

5. Schlesinger, *The Vital Center.*

6. "Next Steps in the Fair Deal," *NR* (March 7, 1949), 23.; Jonathan Stout, "Which Way for ADA?" *New Leader* (March 5, 1949), 1–3.

7. "Next Steps in the Fair Deal," *New Republic* (March 7, 1949), 23.

8. David Lloyd, "Notes on A.D.A. Convention, Chicago, April 8-9-10, 1949," PPF (HSTL), Box 590, Folder 4752; Robert Bendiner, "Politics and People," *Nation* (April 23, 1949), 461–62; Gus Tyler, "New Trends in ADA," *New Leader* (June 15, 1950), S-1, S-4.

9. I. F. Stone, "Has the ADA Stopped Being a Truman Front?" *New York Daily Compass* (April 6, 1950), 5; David Lloyd, "Notes on ADA Convention, Chicago, April 8-9-10, 1949," PPF (HSTL), Box 590, Folder 4752.

10. Chalmers M. Roberts, "Liberals & Power," *Washington Evening Star* (Jan. 17, 1949).

11. "Annual Message to Congress on the State of the Union, January 5, 1949," *Public Papers of the Presidents of the United States, Harry S. Truman, 1949,* 1–8.

12. "The Shape of Things," *Nation* (Jan. 15, 1949), 57; "The Fair Deal Begins," and "Washington Wire," both in *NR* (Jan. 31, 1949), 3; "Harry Truman on His Own Now," *NR* (Jan. 24, 1949), 5.

13. *Time* (Jan. 17, 1949), 13.

14. Quoted in Gosnell, *Truman's Crises,* 466.

15. "Minutes of the National Board Meeting," Dec. 1949, ADA Papers, Ser. 2, Box 66.

16. Schlesinger to Joe Rauh and Jim Loeb, Jan. 25, 1950, ADA Papers, UC.

17. James Loeb, Radio Address, March 15, 1949, ADA Papers, Ser. 2, Box 58; "Notes on the 1949 Convention," ADA Papers, UC.

18. "Next Steps in the Fair Deal," *NR* (March 7, 1949), 3–6; Hamby, *Beyond the New Deal,* 331.

19. "Memorandum from Charles M. La Follette on the Full Employment Conference," July 19, 1949, ADA Papers, Ser. 5, Box 28; Ser. 2, Box 52.

20. ADA *World,* Sept. 22, 1949; Hamby, *Beyond the New Deal,* 332–33.

21. *NYT* (Jan. 21, 1949), 4.

22. Blair Bolles, "The Fallacy of Containment," *Nation* (March 19, 1949), 329; "The North Atlantic Pact," *NR* (Feb. 14, 1949), 5–6; Walter Millis, "An Inevitable Commitment," *Nation* (March 19, 1949), 325.

23. ADA *World,* Feb. 1949; Memorandum, "ADA Action on the North Atlantic Treaty," ADA Papers, UC.

24. David Lloyd, "Notes on A.D.A. Convention, Chicago, April 8-9-10, 1949," (HSTL), PPF Box 590, Folder 4752; I. F. Stone, "The ADA—Third Force or Truman Stooge," *New York Daily Compass* (April 3, 1950), 5.

25. Donovan, *Tumultuous Years*, 66; Acheson, *Present at the Creation*, 257.

26. Cohen, *America's Response to China*, 202–5; Donovan, *Tumultuous Years*, 82–86; *Time* (Jan. 16, 1950), 15; (Jan. 23, 1950), 9–10.

27. Borg and Heinrichs, *Uncertain Years;* Blum, *Drawing the Line.*

28. Andrew Roth, "China: The Communists' Plan," *Nation* (Jan. 5, 1949), 156–58; John Fairbank, "Toward a New China Policy," *Nation* (Jan. 1, 1949), 5–8; Hamby, *Beyond the New Deal*, 367.

29. "The Collapse of Nationalist China," Oct. 5, 1949, ADA Papers, Ser. 4, Box 6.

30. In the margin, Humphrey scribbled a note to his aide: "He's right." It appears that when Humphrey's aide Max Kampelman prepared a fairly stern response to McDowell, Humphrey requested that he destroy the first draft and write a new letter. "I wonder if your first two paragraphs aren't just a little bit too firm and harsh," he wrote in the margin. "Art is a pretty good guy, basically I find myself in substantial agreement with his position. I think his emphasis is a little heavier than I would make it. Just turning this back for your re-consideration." Humphrey, "Memo to Max," Feb. 18, 1950, Humphrey Papers (MSHS), MF. In the new draft Humphrey emphasized that he shared many of McDowell's "own convictions on foreign policy and . . . differed with some . . . liberal colleagues on many of the same issues."

31. McDowell to Marx Lewis, Dec. 14, 1950, Humphrey Papers (MSHS), MF.

32. *NYT* (June 26, 1959), 1.

33. Cohen, *America's Response to China*, 208.

34. Berger, *A New Deal for the World*, 76; *Nation* (July 1, 1950), 1; Hamby, *Beyond the New Deal*, 403–06; *NR* (July 8, 1950), 24; Sevareid, *In One Ear*, 134.

35. John W. Spanier, *The Truman-MacArthur Controversy and the Korean War* (Cambridge, Mass.: Belknap Press, 1959).

36. Reinhold Niebuhr, "Tentative Analysis on United States Foreign Policy to Be Used as Basis of Discussion at National ADA Board Meeting, Dec. 8–9, 1950," Dec. 8, 1950, ADA Papers, Ser. 2, Box 66.

37. "Text of Resolution," Dec. 9, 1950, ADA Papers, Ser. 2, Box 66.

38. "Minutes of the National Board Meeting," June 17–18, and Sept. 23, 1950, ADA Papers, Ser. 2, Box 66; Gus Tyler to Andrew Rice, Feb. 16, 1951, ADA Papers, *UC.*

39. ADA *World* (Feb. 1951; March 1951); Andrew Rice, "Report to ADA National Board," Oct. 5, 1951, ADA Papers, Ser. 2, Box 66.

40. *NYT* (March 22, 1947).

41. Belknap, *Cold War Political Justice;* Richard Freeland, *The Truman Doctrine and the Origins of McCarthyism* (New York: Knopf, 1971); Harper, *The Politics of Loyalty.*

42. Arthur Schlesinger, Jr., "What Is Loyalty? A Difficult Question," *NYT Magazine* (Nov. 2, 1947), 7, 48–51; ADA *World* (Dec. 1947); "Statement by the National Board of ADA Concerning Loyalty Investigations of Federal Employees," Sept. 19, 1947, ADA Papers, *UC.*

43. James A. Wechsler, "The Remington Loyalty Case," *NR* (Feb. 28, 1949), 18–20; ADA *World* (Feb. 1949).

44. ADA *World* (April 20, 1949).

45. David Caute, *The Great Fear* (New York: Simon and Schuster, 1978), 187–88.

46. La Follette to J. Howard McGrath, Oct. 21, 1949, and John Gunther to Charles La Follette, Oct. 27, 1949, both in ADA Papers, Ser. 2, Box 56.

47. Rauh to Executive Committee Members, Nov. 3, 1949, ADA Papers, *UC*.

48. O'Keefe to La Follette, Dec. 29, 1949, ADA Papers, *UC*.

49. Daniel S. Gillmor, "Guilt by Gossip," *NR* (May 31, 1948), 15–16.

50. Rovere, *Senator Joe McCarthy*, 3; see also Phillips, *The Truman Presidency;* Thomas Reeves, *The Life and Times of Joe McCarthy: A Biography* (New York: Stein and Day, 1983); Oshinsky, *A Conspiracy So Immense.*

51. Oshinsky, *A Conspiracy So Immense,* 103–14.

52. ADA *World* (March 20, 1950).

53. See L. L. Laughton to D. M. Ladd, Jan. 3, 1950, Declassified FBI documents obtained under the Freedom of Information Act. There are numerous other letters of individuals inquiring whether the ADA was a "communist front organization." In most cases, however, the name of the correspondent has been blotched over.

54. ADA *World* (Oct. 1950).

55. Ibid. (Nov. 1950).

56. Ibid. (Oct. 1951; Oct. 1952).

57. Smith to National Board, Dec. 9, 1952, ADA Papers, Ser. 2, Box 66; Ser. 5, Box 51.

58. "What the Court Has Destroyed," *NR* (June 18, 1951), 5.

59. "For Consideration of the ADA Executive Committee," June 26, 1951, Western Union to Loeb, June 11, 1951, Biddle to Loeb, June 8, 1951, all in ADA Papers, Ser. 5, Box 61.

60. Loeb to Chapters, June 12, 1951, ADA Papers, Ser. 5, Box 61.

61. Schlesinger to Rauh and Wechsler, June 22, 1951, ADA Papers, Ser. 5, Box 61.

62. "Proposed Statement by ADA National Board," June 27, 1951, ADA Papers, Ser. 5, Box 61.

63. Biddle to National Board, July 17, 1951, ADA Papers, Ser. 5, Box 61.

64. The only exception in the labor ranks was Joseph Beirne of the Communications Workers. Hugo Ernst expressed sympathy with the thrust of the statement even though he did not want his name used, because he was "now in the course of cleaning up the Communist situation in one of our largest locals in New York." He noted, "I am afraid that such publicity may handicap me in achieving my objectives." Interestingly, although Schlesinger expressed strong opposition to the statement, he voted "present." See National Board Meeting Notes, July 1951, Ser. 5, Box 61.

4. The ADA, Adlai Stevenson and Civil Rights, 1952–1956

1. Galbraith, *A Life in Our Times,* 289.

2. "Adlai Stevenson and Alger Hiss," *Commonweal* (Aug. 22, 1952), 475; David Caute, *The Great Fear* (New York: Simon and Schuster, 1978), 80.

3. Max Ascoli, "These Moderate Elections," *Reporter* (Sept. 6, 1956), 9; Martin, *Civil Rights and the Crisis of Liberalism,* 98–100.

4. Martin, *Civil Rights and the Crisis of Liberalism,* 96.

5. James Loeb, Oral History HSTL, 18–21; Loeb, Oral History, FDRL, vol. 2, pp. 24–25.

6. Montgomery to Reuther, July 2, 1952, Reuther Papers (WRLLUA), Box 430, File 21.

7. Niebuhr to Stevenson, March 1952, Stevenson Papers (Princeton Univ.), CF 267; Schlesinger to Stevenson, March 25, 1952, ibid., CF 271; ADA *World* (Aug. 1952).

8. Gunther to Trentlyon, Feb. 19, 1952, ADA Papers, Ser. 2, Box 35.

9. There was, however, a clear difference. The 1944 plank was deliberately blurred and ambiguous, exhorting Congress to "exert its full constitutional powers to protect those rights." The 1948 plank called for specific measures—poll-tax abolition, antilynching legislation, integration in the armed services, and the FEPC. The 1944 platform included only a two-sentence statement on discrimination: "We believe that racial and religious minorities have the right to live, develop and vote equally with all citizens and share the rights that are guaranteed by our Constitution. Congress should exert its full constitutional powers to protect those rights." The vague wording satisfied southerners who wanted to reserve such matters as poll-tax repeal, antilynching, and fair-employment-practices legislation for state rather than for federal action. The 1948 platform was far stronger, spelling out the president's "courageous stand" on civil rights and calling on Congress to support the president in "guaranteeing" basic and fundamental rights, such as "the right to equal opportunity of employment." See "A Civil-Rights Plank," *NR* (May 12, 1952), 6.

10. "Text of Statement of the National Board of ADA," n.d., ADA Papers, Ser. 2, Box 66.

11. "Statement on the 1952 Elections," May 18, 1952, ADA Papers, *UC*, p. 1; Alan Barth, "The Democrats and FEPC," *Reporter* (Aug. 5, 1952), 13–16.

12. James Loeb, unpublished autobiography, Loeb Papers (WSHS), 218–20.

13. "The Shape of Things," *Nation* (Aug. 9, 1952), 3; "Draft Proposal on Endorsement Statement," Aug. 8, 1952, Reuther Papers (WRLLUA), Box 430, File 22, p. 3. Shull to Nathan, Aug. 11, 1952, ADA Papers, UC; "1952 ADA Endorsement of Stevenson-Sparkman Ticket," ADA Papers, Ser. 2, Box 66.

14. *Wall Street Journal* (July 26, 1952); Edwin A. Lahey, "Labor, Adlai and Ike," *NR* (Aug. 9, 1952).

15. Anne A'Hare McCormick, "Confidence Is Rekindled," *NYT* (July 25, 1952), 12; William S. White, "Democrats Take a Lesson to Heart," *NYT* (July 27, 1952), sec. 4, p. 5; Anthony Leviero, "The New and Fair Deals: A New Phase in Prospect," ibid., p. 4.

16. On Stevenson's opinion of Keynes, Galbraith said, "Our candidate had heard of Keynes but largely from people who supposed him subversive. Stevenson's own views on economic policy, to the extent they existed, had been formed at Princeton thirty years before in an economic atmosphere dominated by a stalwart resistance to the twentieth century. It was his uneasy suspicion that Keynesian economics as reflected in the Employment Act of 1946 was a dubious excuse for the budget deficits of the Roosevelt and later Truman years." Galbraith, *A Life in Our Times*, 296–97.

17. Ibid., 295.

18. Montgomery to Reuther, "Stevenson on Civil Rights," Aug. 1, 1952, Reuther Papers (WRLLUA), Box 430, File 21, pp. 1–2.

19. Leo Lerner to George Ball et al., Aug. 15, 1952, Adlai Stevenson Papers (Princeton Univ.), CF 323; "Memorandum to Chapters on Volunteers for Stevenson," ADA Papers, UC.

20. See *Washington Times-Herald* (Dec. 13, 1949), 22; (Nov. 22, 1949), 67.

21. Republican National Committee, "Americans for Democratic Action," 1952, Republican National Committee Papers (DDEL), Box 5, Folder ADA.

22. *Washington Post* (Oct. 20, 1952), 5; *Washington Star* (Oct. 28, 1952), 6; (Nov. 7, 1952).

23. Washington Chapter to Gunther and Kansas City Chapter to Gunther, both in ADA Papers, Ser. 5, Box 29.

24. Stevenson to Dick, Aug. 8, 1952, in Johnson, *The Papers of Adlai Stevenson,* 37.

25. A. W. Hall to Stevenson, March 2, 1953, Stevenson Papers (Princeton Univ.), CF 373; Davis R. B. Ross, "The Democratic Party, 1945–1960," in Arthur M. Schlesinger, Jr., ed., *History of U.S. Political Parties* (New York: Chelsea House, 1973), 2694.

26. James E. Doyle, "Working Paper for ADA National Board Discussion of Political Program," Sept. 26–27, 1953, ADA Papers, Ser. 5, Box 21; Ser. 2, Box 67.

27. Loeb, "ADA Convention Policy," n.d., ADA Papers, UC.

28. Ibid.

29. Reinhold Niebuhr, "Notes," Feb. 28, 1956, Niebuhr Papers (LC), Box 11.

30. Lash, *Eleanor,* 241–42.

31. Niebuhr to Norman Thomas, Dec. 5, 1956, Niebuhr Papers, Box 12, GC; Goldman, *The Crucial Decade and After,* 283; *Washington Post and Times Herald* (July 31, 1955), A-12.

32. Parmet, *The Democrats,* 121–25; Martin, *Civil Rights and the Crisis of Liberalism,* 117–36.

33. *Boston Herald* (Dec. 13, 1953); *Boston Globe* (Dec. 13, 1953); *Boston Post* (Dec. 17, 1953); *Newark Star Ledger* (Sept. 16, 1956).

34. Parmet, *The Democrats,* 106.

35. Smith to Mitchell, Dec. 18, 1953, Mitchell Papers (HSTL), Box 8, pp. 1–3; Tyler to Dubinsky, Jan. 18, 1954, Dubinsky Papers (ILGWU), Box 279, Folder 1A.

36. *NYT* (Jan. 15, 1954), 15.

37. Mitchell to Stevenson, Jan. 5, 1954, Stevenson Papers (Princeton Univ.), CF 397; Mitchell to Barnard, Jan. 1954, Mitchell Papers (HSTL), Box 8, p. 2.

38. Mitchell to Barnard, Jan. 1954, Mitchell Papers (HSTL), Box 8, pp. 2–3.

39. Stevenson to Gertrude Eli, Jan. 11, 1954, Stevenson Papers, (Princeton Univ.), CF 397.

40. The following year the Court adopted a "go slow" approach to the *Brown* decision by requiring local judges to determine the pace of segregation and demanding only that a "prompt and reasonable start toward full compliance" be made. See Sitkoff, *The Struggle for Black Equality,* 23–24.

41. Chafe, *The Unfinished Journey;* William Leuchtenburg, "The White House and Black America: From Eisenhower to Carter," in Namorato, *Have We Overcome?* 121–46; Martin, *Civil Rights and the Crisis of Liberalism,* 117–18. Arthur Schlesinger, Jr., to Walter Lippmann, March 8, 1956, Lippmann Papers (YUL), Box 101, File 1902.

42. Harry Ashmore to Stevenson, March 30, 1956, Stevenson Papers, (Princeton Univ.), CF 505.

43. Quotation in Martin, *Civil Rights and the Crisis of Liberalism,* 120;

"Memorandum from Meeting between Butler, Rauh and Gunther," n.d., ADA Papers, UC, pp. 1–3.

44. "Confidential Report of Conference," May 13, 1955, ADA Papers, UC, pp. 1–4.

45. Lewis to National Board, n.d., Beer Papers (JFKL), Box 2, pp. 1–3.

46. James Reston, "A Return Engagement," *NYT* (Aug. 8, 1956), 11; James Reston, "Stevenson's Move Left," *NYT* (Aug. 9, 1956), 16; Martin, *Civil Rights and the Crisis of Liberalism,* 239.

47. "Minutes of ADA Board Meeting," Chicago, Aug. 11, 1956, ADA Papers, Ser. 2, Box 67.

48. "Notes on Civil Rights Meeting," Aug. 15, 1956, ADA Papers, UC.

49. Richard Amper, "Mrs. Roosevelt Aids Stevenson," *NYT* (Aug. 3, 1956), 6.

50. Anthony Lewis, "Humphrey Urges Patience on Bias," *NYT* (Aug. 13, 1956), 19.

51. Robert Nathan, Aug. 1956, "Some Observations and Highlights on the Democratic National Convention in Chicago," ADA Papers UC; Rauh interview, Dec. 18, 1985.

52. Parmet, *The Democrats,* 144; Goldman, *The Crucial Decade and After,* 296.

53. Arthur Schlesinger, Jr., "The First Ten Years of ADA," ADA *World* (May 1957).

54. Dronsick to Zalles, Nov. 7, 1952, and Auerbach to Loeb, Oct. 21, 1948, both in ADA Papers, UC.

55. See the debate between Norman Thomas and Robert Nathan in the *Progressive* (Sept. 1954), 8–13.

5. The ADA, Eisenhower, and Liberalism in the 1950s

1. Wittner, *Cold War America;* Alexander, *Holding the Line.*

2. A number of new studies have attempted to revise traditional interpretations of Eisenhower as, in the words of Arthur Schlesinger, Jr., "a genial, indolent man of pied syntax and platitudinous conviction." Among the finer revisionist works are Robert Griffith, "Dwight D. Eisenhower and the Corporate Commonwealth," *American Historical Review* (Feb. 1982); Ambrose, *Eisenhower;* Herbert Parmet, *Eisenhower and the American Crusades* (New York: Macmillan, 1972); Elmo Richardson, *The Presidency of Dwight D. Eisenhower* (Lawrence: Regents Press of Kansas, 1979). These works should be read in conjunction with Arthur Schlesinger, Jr., "The Ike Age Revisited," *Reviews in American History* (March 1983), 1–11.

3. Arthur Schlesinger, Jr., to Walter Lippmann, Jan. 10, 1958, Lippmann Papers YUL, Box 101, File 1902; Galbraith, *A Life in Our Times,* 304.

4. Oshinsky, *A Conspiracy So Immense,* 235–36, 256–67.

5. Francis Biddle, Press Release, April 1953, ADA Papers, UC.

6. ADA *World* (Dec. 1953; June 1954).

7. Ibid. (June 1953); Hollander to Nathan, June 11, 1954, ADA Papers Ser. 2, Box 67. ADA membership figures are sketchy and sometimes contradictory. The figures cited here are for active members who had paid their yearly dues. The figures that the organization cited in its public statements included inactive mem-

bers—those who expressed some interest or perhaps were members at one time but had allowed their membership to expire. When inactive members are included the ADA's membership more than doubles, to between 28,000 and 30,000 members. Olga Tabaka to Vi Gunther, Aug. 31, 1955, ibid., Box 52; "Chapter Membership," Aug. 4, 1960, ibid., Box 29. The latter document has figures on chapter membership for selected years during the 1950s.

8. *Chicago Sun-Times* (April 11, 1954).

9. Solberg, *Hubert Humphrey,* 157–59.

10. "Outlawing the Communists," *NR* (Aug. 30, 1954), 6–7; "Who Should Be Censured?" *Nation* (Aug. 21, 1954), 45; Carey McWilliams, "A Can of Worms," *Nation* (Aug. 28, 1954), 163–65.

11. Rosenberg to Humphrey, Sept. 16, 1954, Humphrey Papers (MSHS), SF, 1949–54.

12. Arthur Schlesinger, Jr., *New York Post,* Aug. 29, 1954; Schlesinger to Humphrey, Sept. 14, 1954, Humphrey Papers (MSHS), SF, 1949–54.

13. Humphrey, "Memo to Max," Humphrey Papers (MSHS), SF, 1949–54.

14. Frank Serri to National Board, Jan. 20, 1955, ADA Papers, Ser. 2, Box 67.

15. Howe, "Liberalism—A Moral Crisis," 109.

16. Hollander to Humphrey, Sept. 17, 1954, Humphrey Papers (MSHS), SF, 1949–54.

17. Oshinsky, *A Conspiracy So Immense,* 457–64; Goldman, *The Crucial Decade and After,* 274–79.

18. ADA *World* (June 1954).

19. Quotation in Oshinsky, *A Conspiracy So Immense,* 483; ADA *World* (Nov. 1954).

20. ADA *World* (Dec. 1954).

21. *NR* (March 28, 1955), 3–4.

22. *Washington Star* (March 21, 1955); *Washington Post and Times-Herald* (March 21, 1955), 1, 5; *Daily Worker* (March 23, 1955); Charles Murphy to Rauh, March 22, 1955, Murphy Papers (HSTL), Box 33, Folder ADA.

23. Howe and Schlesinger, eds., *Guide to Politics, 1954,* xi–xiv.

24. Ibid., 9–13.

25. Leon Keyserling, "For a National Prosperity Budget," *NYT Magazine* (March 25, 1956), 12–13, 36. Keyserling expounded on the same themes in "Less for Private Spending?" *NYT Magazine* (May 23, 1960), 15–16.

26. ADA Platform, 1956, "Domestic Policy Statement," ADA Papers, Ser. 6, Box 3, File 39.

27. Robert Nathan, "Memo," Sept. 17, 1956, ADA Papers, Ser. 2, Box 64.

28. 85th Congress, Subcommittee on Fiscal Policy of the Joint Economic Committee, April 1958; House Subcommittee on Housing of the Committee on Banking and Currency, March 1957.

29. Divine, *Eisenhower and the Cold War,* 33–39; Ambrose, *Rise to Globalism,* 221.

30. Karnow, *Vietnam,* 128–239; Herring, *America's Longest War,* 1–72.

31. Divine, *Eisenhower and the Cold War,* 85–88.

32. ADA *World* (Oct. 1953).

33. Nathan to Executive Committee, "Review of U.S. Foreign Policy," Aug. 19, 1953, CIO Secretary-Treasurer Papers (WRLLUA), Box 157, File ADA, 1953; ADA *World* (April 1953).

34. ADA *World* (Nov. 1954).

35. Ibid. (Jan. 1955).

36. "Draft Foreign Policy Statement," ADA National Board, June 5, 1955, ADA Papers, Ser. 2, Box 67; ADA *World* (April 1954).

37. "Partnership for Freedom," 1955, ADA Papers, UC.

38. "Legislative Newsletter," July 18, 1955, ADA Papers, UC; ADA *World* (May 1955).

39. ADA *World,* (May 1954).

40. Ibid. (Sept. 1954).

41. Ibid. (June 1954).

42. "ADA National Board Statement on Geneva," Oct. 10, 1955, ADA Papers, Ser. 2, Box 67.

43. Reinhold Niebuhr, "ADA Statement on Foreign Policy," Nov. 30, 1955, Niebuhr Papers (LC), Box 1, ADA File.

44. Hollander to Nathan and Schlesinger, Sept. 14, 1956, ADA Papers, UC.

45. ADA *World* (Nov. 1956).

46. Robert Nathan, "An Agenda for Liberals," Sorensen Papers (JFKL), Box 1; Joseph Rauh, "Keynote Address, 11th Annual ADA Convention," May 17, 1958, ADA Papers, Ser. 4, Box 11.

47. Reinhold Niebuhr, "Lunik and Ike's Budget," *New Leader* (Jan. 26, 1959), 7.

48. *Time* (Nov. 17, 1958), 30.

49. ADA *World* (Nov. 1958); *Washington Post and Times-Herald,* (Dec. 3, 1958).

50. National Board Minutes, Jan. 25, 1958, ADA Papers, Ser. 2, Box 67.

51. ADA *World* (June 1958).

52. William V. Shannon, "ADA: The Price of Success," *New York Post* (May 18, 1958), M7.

53. Wechsler, *Reflections of an Angry Middle-Aged Editor,* 65; "Income Survey, 1957," "Financial Statements, 1950–1959," and "Financial Statement for Year Ended December 31, 1959," all in ADA Papers, Ser. 2, Boxes 36, 38.

54. Wechsler, *Reflections . . . ,* 67.

55. Arthur Schlesinger, Jr., "Death Wish of the Democrats," *NR* (Sept. 15, 1958), 7–9.

56. Arthur Schlesinger, Jr., "Which Road for the Democrats," *Reporter* (Jan. 20, 1953), 31–34; "Stevenson and the American Liberal Dilemma," 24–29; "The Future of Liberalism," *Reporter* (May 3, 1956), 8–11; "Where Does the Liberal Go from Here?," *NYT Magazine* (Aug. 4, 1957), 7–8, 38.

57. Galbraith, *The Affluent Society,* xxiii–xxiv; *A Life in Our Times,* 335–40.

58. Galbraith later called this idea the greatest error in the book: "I didn't realize how enormous would be the public costs of congested existence in the modern metropolis, costs made greater by the migration of the socially unprepared from the poor rural areas. I didn't see that a minimally tolerable social balance in New York City would require public outlays far beyond any imagined at that time." See *A Life in Our Times,* 336–37.

59. Keyserling to Galbraith, June 9, 1960, Galbraith Papers (JFKL), Box 38.

60. Leon Keyserling, "Eggheads and Politics," *NR* (Oct. 27, 1958), 13–17; "Galbraith and Schlesinger Reply to Leon Keyserling," *NR* (Nov. 10, 1958), 14–15; "Leon Keyserling on Economic Expansion," *NR* (Nov. 17, 1958), 16–17.

61. Keyserling to Schlesinger, Aug. 26, 1959, Galbraith Papers (JFKL), Box 38.

62. Keyserling, "Eggheads and Politics," 13–17.
63. Robert Lekachman, "Liberals and the U.S. Economy," *New Leader* (Jan. 26, 1959), 4–6.
64. These differences were not limited to the ADA. The Democratic Advisory Committee, a liberal policy group established after the 1956 election to provide ideas for the Democratic nominee in 1960, experienced similar disagreements. Keyserling, "Eggheads and Politics," 14–15; "Schlesinger and Galbraith Reply to Leon Keyserling," *NR* (Nov. 10, 1958), 14–15.
65. Arthur Schlesinger, Jr., "Soviet-American Relations," Jan. 7, 1960, ADA Papers, Ser. 3, Box 50; Ser. 2, Box 67.
66. David Lloyd to National Board, "Soviet-American Relations," Jan. 7, 1960, ADA Papers, Ser. 2, Box 67.
67. "ADA National Board Meeting," Jan. 24, 1960, ADA Papers, Ser. 2, Box 68.

6. The ADA and the Kennedy Administration

1. Robert Nathan, Oral History, JFKL, pp. 6, 19; Joseph Rauh, Oral History, JFKL, pp. 3–5.
2. Parmet, *Jack,* 465–78, 499–518; Taylor to Saltonstall, Jan. 25, 1960, and Taylor to Sorenson, Nov. 29, 1959, both in Sorensen Papers (JFKL), Campaign File, Box 23.
3. Solberg, *Hubert Humphrey,* 206–8; Theodore White, *The Making of the President, 1960* (New York: Atheneum, 1961), 78–97.
4. Solberg, *Hubert Humphrey,* 211; White, *The Making of the President, 1960,* 97–114.
5. Schlesinger, *A Thousand Days;* Robert Nathan, Oral History, JFKL, p. 14.
6. "An Important Message to All Liberals," Sorensen Papers (JFKL), Campaign Files, Box 23; Loeb to Humphrey, June 26, 1960, Humphrey Papers (MSHS), SF, National Politics, 1960.
7. Bowles later confirmed that he played a minor role in the campaign: "I was window-dressing, and Kennedy didn't really feel he needed this assistance. . . . In the last analysis I had very little to do with speech-writing or the general development of Kennedy's campaign." Parmet, *Jack,* 513.
8. Gunther to Rauh, Aug. 26, 1960, ADA Papers, Ser. 2, Box 69.
9. "Minutes of the National Board Meeting," Aug. 27, 1960, ADA Papers, Ser. 2, Box 69.
10. Auerbach to Rauh, July 16, 1960, and Rauh to Auerbach, July 26, 1960, both in Beer Papers (JFKL), Administrative File 1; "Minutes of the National Board Meeting," Aug. 27, 1960, ADA Papers, Ser. 2, Box 69.
11. Beer Notes, n.d., Beer Papers (JFKL), Administrative File 1; Schlesinger to Kennedy, Aug. 30, 1960, President's Office File, Special Correspondence: Schlesinger (JFKL), Box 32.
12. Arthur Schlesinger, Jr., to Senator Kennedy, Aug. 30, 1960, Galbraith Papers (JFKL), Box 74; Beer to Kennedy, Aug. 30, 1960, Beer Papers (JFKL), Box 5.
13. Robert Schwartz to Kennedy, Oct. 26, 1960, ADA Papers, UC; Galbraith, *A Life in Our Times,* 386.
14. Parmet, *JFK,* 8.

15. Halberstam, *The Best and the Brightest,* 50–51; Rowland Evans, Jr., "In Washington," *New Leader* (Jan. 22, 1962), 3; Parmet, *JFK,* 85.

16. For a complete list of ADA members in the Kennedy administration, see Robert Hartman's excellent series on the ADA that appeared in the *Los Angeles Times* in Sept. 1961. In particular see "The ADA: Its Impact on the New Frontier," *Los Angeles Times* (Sept. 3, 1961), 3.

17. Parmet, *JFK,* 353.

18. Brauer, *John F. Kennedy and the Second Reconstruction;* Burner, *The Torch Is Passed.*

19. Sundquist, *Politics and Policy,* 254–59; Parmet, *JFK,* 249–52; Brauer, *The Second Reconstruction,* 11–29, 61–88; Matusow, *The Unraveling of America,* 60–75.

20. V. Lewis Bassie, "Myth of Guaranteed Prosperity," *Nation* (June 3, 1961), 471; Parmet, *JFK,* 66.

21. Parmet, *JFK,* 91–95; Sundquist, *Politics and Policy,* 34–40; Matusow, *The Unraveling of America,* 30–45; Schlesinger, *A Thousand Days,* 570–83.

22. Lewis Paper, *The Promise and the Performance: The Leadership of John F. Kennedy* (New York: Crown, 1975); Walton, *Cold War and Counterrevolution;* Parmet, *JFK.*

23. *Time* (Sept. 8, 1961), 20; *Time* (March 9, 1962), 19; Parmet, *JFK,* 201–3; Schlesinger, *A Thousand Days,* 749–68.

24. Oscar Gass, "Political Economy and the New Administration" *Commentary* (April 1961), 277–87; Seymour Harris, "Kennedy Economics," *NR* (Sept. 18, 1961), 19; TRB, "What Should Kennedy Do?" *NR* (March 6, 1961), 2, and "Get What You Can," *NR* (May 29, 1961), 2.

25. Galbraith, *A Life in Our Times,* 372–73.

26. Beer Notes, May 19, 1961, Beer Papers (JFKL), Subject File 3.

27. Ibid.; Marvin Rosenberg to Mrs. Marshall Field, May 9, 1961, ADA Papers, Ser. 2, Box 36.

28. Robert Nathan, Oral History, JFKL, pp. 22–24; Joe Rauh, Oral History, JFKL, pp. 101–2; "Minutes of the National Board Meeting, Feb. 11–12, 1961," ADA Papers, Ser. 2, Box 68.

29. ADA *World* (May 1961); Schlesinger Address to ADA Convention, 1961, ADA Papers, UC.

30. ADA *World,* May 1961; James Wechsler, Keynote Address, 1961, ADA Papers, Ser. 4, Box 14.

31. ADA *World,* May 1961.

32. Rauh to Schlesinger, May 19, 1961, Beer Papers (JFKL), CF 1. In 1965 Robert Kennedy revealed that the administration took more notice of ADA actions than it showed publicly. He told an ADA banquet in 1965 that when he was in the White House he thought " 'Goddamn-Joe-Rauh' was one word." As much as Rauh exasperated Kennedy, the president, as Arthur Schlesinger has noted, "liked and admired him none the less." Kennedy once remarked to Ben Bradlee that Rauh was "the only one [of the professional liberals] I care about." Rauh interview, June 1985; Arthur Schlesinger, Jr., letter to author, Dec. 26, 1985; Ben Bradlee, *Conversations with Kennedy* (New York: Norton, 1975), 71.

33. Seymour Harris, "Kennedy's Economics," *NR* (Sept. 18, 1961), 19–21; "President Kennedy's Economics," *NR* (Oct. 30, 1861), 13–14; Leon Keyserling, "Old Economics on the New Frontier," *Progressive* (Sept. 1961), 21–23; "J.F.K.

Economics: Should We All Stand Up and Cheer?" *NR* (Oct. 9, 1961), 13–14; "Letter to the Editor," *NR* (Nov. 27, 1961), 23.

34. *Newsweek* (April 16, 1962), 29–30; "1962 Convention Resolutions," ADA Papers, Ser. 4, Box 14.

35. John Roche, "The Limits of Kennedy's Liberalism," *New Leader* (Oct. 1, 1962), 9–11.

36. *Time* (May 4, 1962), 25; ADA *World* (Oct. 1962); *New York Journal American* (Jan. 25, 1962); *Chicago Daily Tribune* (March 14, 1962); *Washington Times-Herald* (Sept. 26, 1962, and Dec. 6, 1961); *Freedom Press* (Sept. 19, 1962). Actually, the most systematic attack came after the election, in May 1963, when the *National Review* attempted to blame Kennedy's liberalism on ADA influence. "Many of the ideas aired in the White House these days are ADA ideas; much of the intellectual atmosphere is formed by 'ADAism.' " "The ADA ideology will continue to exert powerful pressures," James Burnham warned, "as long as a large number of its members hold policy and advisory posts—pressures sufficient, possibly, to decide the direction in which our country is to travel." Burnham, "Does ADA Run the New Frontier?" *National Review* (May 7, 1963), 335–62.

37. Kennedy, *Thirteen Days*.

38. ADA *World* (Oct. 1962). Following the Cuban missile crisis, John Roche wrote a personal letter to Humphrey expressing his views of it. "What the President has got to remember is that Khrushchev has never been educated on the underlying vitality of our dedication to freedom," Roche said. "Stalin got stopped cold by Truman and Dean Acheson, but Khrushchev came in during the catatonic years of American policy. My guess is that it took that shrewd bastard about five minutes to size Eisenhower up as a dope and Dulles as a rhetorician with a fundamentally isolationist orientation who if it came down to risking Chicago or New York to save Berlin, would welch." The Soviets, he went on to say, have "no Gotterdammerung Complex, and confronted by a stonewall they will, I am convinced, back up." Kennedy, he charged, reacted personally to Khrushchev's double cross with the missiles. "He seemed to feel an American boy's sense of fury at being double-crossed whereas I (for instance) would take for granted that Khrushchev would double-cross us and plan on that basis." Roche to Humphrey, Oct. 25, 1962, ADA Papers, UC.

39. McDermont to Hollander, Roche, Wentworth, and Williams, Oct. 4, 1962, ADA Papers, UC.

40. Beer to Todd Gitlin, Jan. 12, 1962, Beer Papers (JFKL), CF; "Reply to Advocates on Unilateral Initiatives," Sept. 1962, ibid., Subject File; ADA *World* (Jan. 1962); John Roche, "Memo to Today's 'Young Radicals,' " *NYT Magazine* (Oct. 14, 1962), 17, 110–14.

41. *Time* (May 17, 1963), 23–25; (June 7, 1963), 17; Lewis, *King*, 171–209; Schlesinger, *RFK and His Times*, 317–42; Parmet, *JFK*, 260–76; Brauer, *John F. Kennedy and the Second Reconstruction*, 180–264; Sundquist, *Politics and Policy*, 259–65.

42. Matusow, *The Unraveling of America*, 40–53; Sundquist, *Politics and Policy*, 40–56.

43. Herring, *America's Longest War*, 73–107; Karnow, *Vietnam*, 240–331; Schlesinger, *A Thousand Days*, 491–508.

44. ADA *World* (Feb. 1963); *Washington Post* (Dec. 19, 1962); National Board Minutes, ADA Papers, Ser. 2, Box 69; 1963 Convention Resolutions, ibid., Ser. 4, Box 14.

45. Joseph Rauh, "Personal Reflection on the Civil Rights Bill of 1964," July 1964 (MS in author's possession); Schlesinger, *RFK and His Times,* 375.

46. ADA *World* (May 1963).

47. Gans interview, June 1985.

48. Beer to Hollander, Feb. 26, 1963, Beer Papers (JFKL), ADA File.

49. Pollack to Beer, July 25, 1961, Beer Papers (JFKL), CF 5; Edward Eichler to Arthur Schlesinger, March 16, 1962, Schlesinger Papers (JFKL), Subject File 3; "Background Memorandum: Observations about ADA Drawn from Conversations between the Officers and ADA Leaders," ca. 1963, ADA Papers, UC; Wechsler, *Reflections . . . ,* 57–58.

50. David Williams, "The Care and Feeding of Revolutions," *Progressive* (Oct. 1961), 16–19; Delson, "Convention Background Paper—World Domination or World Cooperation," ADA Papers, Ser. 4, Box 14; "Total Disarmament Now," New Jersey ADA, Lloyd Papers (HSTL), Box 18, Folder 2; Arthur Waskow, "Notes Toward an ADA Foreign Policy Resolution," ADA Papers, Ser. 4, Box 14.

51. Williams to Beer, Oct. 10, 1960, and April 20, 1961, Beer Papers (JFKL), Box 5.

52. Wentworth to Board of Directors," ca. Jan. 1963, ADA Papers, UC; Wechsler, *Reflections* 57–58; Pollack to Beer, July 25, 1961, Beer Papers (JFKL), CF 5; Edward Eichler to Arthur Schlesinger, March 16, 1962, Schlesinger Papers (JFKL), SF 3; Eichler to Hollander, March 1, 1963, ADA Papers, UC.

53. See John L. Saltonstall, Jr., to Theodore Sorensen, March 10, 1960, Sorensen Papers (JFKL), Box 23.

54. Lambert to Gunther, April 12, 1963, Derek to Howard, April 15, 1963, both in ADA Papers, UC.

55. Robert Hartman, "Views on ADA," *Los Angeles Times* (Sept. 5, 1961), 6.

56. See "Background Memorandum Observations . . . ," ca. 1963, ADA Papers, UC; "Financial Statement for December 31, 1961," "Statement of Income," April 1962, and "Financial Statement as of July 30, 1963," all in ADA Papers, Ser. 2, Box 38; Gunther to National Board, Oct. 6, 1962, and Violet Gunther, "ADA-Staff Reorganization," Jan. 28, 1963, both in ADA Papers, UC.

57. Una Corbett to National Board, June 23, 1962, ADA Papers, UC; Arthur I. Waskow, "Notes toward an ADA Foreign Policy Resolution," and Washington, D.C., Chapter, "Resolutions on Domestic Policy," 1961, both in ADA Papers, Ser. 4, Box 14.

58. Myerson to Organization Committee, Sept. 6, 1963, "Notes Caustic and Otherwise," ca. 1963, both in ADA Papers, UC.

7. The ADA, Lyndon Johnson, and the Great Society

1. Ted Lewis, "Political Problems," *Nation* (Dec. 14, 1963), 409; Goldman, *The Tragedy of Lyndon Johnson,* 618; Anthony Lewis, *NYT* (Nov. 24, 1963), 6E.

2. *Time* (Sept. 23, 1966), 5.

3. Wicker, *JFK and LBJ,* 153–60; Miller, *Lyndon,* 234; Goldman, *The Tragedy of Lyndon Johnson,* 27; Dugger, *The Politician;* Divine, *Exploring the Johnson Years.*

4. Lowenstein to President, Nov. 27, 1963 (LBJL), Name File, Lowenstein.

5. Anthony Lewis, *NYT* (Nov. 24, 1963); Sitkoff, *The Struggle for Black Equality,* 165; Bottone, "The Push beyond Liberalism," 35–45; Turner, "The

Black Man's Burden," 215–19; Parenti, "White Anxiety and the Negro Revolt," 35–39.

6. Sitkoff, *The Struggle for Black Equality*, 167–78.

7. Hollander to Roche, Nov. 18, 1963, "Proceedings of 17th Annual Convention of ADA, May 15–17, 1964," both in ADA Papers, UC.

8. Gans to Shull, "Atlantic Trip," Nov. 20, 1964, ADA Papers, UC.

9. *The Public Papers of the Presidents of the United States, Lyndon B. Johnson, 1964*, 8–10.

10. Joseph Rauh, "Reflections on the Civil Rights Act of 1964" (MS in author's possession).

11. Ibid., 11–13.

12. Ibid., 14–18.

13. *Time* (May 25, 1964), 33; (June 19, 1964), 15–18; (June 22, 1964), 25–26.

14. *Nation* (June 8, 1964), 567; ADA *World* (June 1964).

15. Anne Romaine interview of Joseph Rauh, transcript in Romaine Papers (WSHS); Gans to Shull, "Atlantic Trip," Nov. 20, 1964, ADA Papers, UC.

16. *NYT* (Aug. 23, 1964), 1.

17. Sitkoff, *The Struggle for Black Equality*, 179–86.

18. Joseph Rauh, Oral History LBJL, 14–35; Romaine interview of Joseph Rauh, Romaine Papers (WSHS); Carl Solberg, *Hubert Humphrey*, 239–56.

19. Carson, *In Struggle*, 54, 123–29; Sitkoff, *The Struggle for Black Equality*, 179–86.

20. Miller, *Lyndon*, 267; *The Public Papers of the Presidents of the United States, Lyndon B. Johnson, 1964*, 112–17.

21. Miller, *Lyndon*, 557–58; Matusow, *The Unraveling of America*, 56–59.

22. ADA *World* (Feb. 1964).

23. Galbraith, "Let Us Begin," 17–26; Leon Keyserling, "Poverty and the Economy," *Nation* (June 7, 1965), 615–17.

24. *Time* (Jan. 1, 1965), 14; Miller, *Lyndon*, 363.

25. Galbraith, "Let Us Begin," 17–26.

26. Leon Keyserling, Oral History, LBJL, 9–10. Gardner Ackley wrote the president on December 17, 1964, to dispute Keyserling's ideas. "As always," he wrote, Keyserling "exaggerates the amount of slack in our economy, and cares little about price stability relative to the goal of full employment. He overlooks and minimizes many problems." Yet, Ackley admitted, "there is a certain amount of truth on his side," and it is "probably good for us to be exposed to this criticism from the left as a counterbalance to equally one-sided attacks from the right." Three weeks later, Heller suggested that Johnson use Robert Nathan as a "counterforce" to Keyserling. Nathan, wrote Heller, "is the most reasonable, effective, and friendly ally we have in the liberal camp. . . . He can make the difference between opposition and support among very influential liberals." See Ackley to President, Dec. 17, 1964, EX Welfare (LBJL), Box 25; Heller to President, Jan. 8, 1964 (LBJL), Name File, Leon Keyserling.

27. Leon Keyserling, "The Great Society; A New Kind of Balance Sheet Is Needed," *NR* (June 22, 1965), 11–14. Despite these trenchant criticisms, Keyserling remained an admirer of Johnson and of his programs. "I am increasingly encouraged by the main direction of your policies," he wrote Johnson in June 1965, "even though I at times express reservations about some of the details." See Keyserling to Johnson, June 11, 1965 (LBJL), Name File, Keyserling.

28. Keyserling, "Poverty and the Economy," 615–17.

29. "Proceedings of 17th Annual Convention of Americans for Democratic Action," May 15–17, 1964, and Domestic Policy Resolution, "Poverty in America," May 16, 1964, both in ADA Papers, UC; ADA *World* (Feb. 1964).

30. ADA *World* (Feb. 1964).

31. Humphrey, *The Education of a Public Man*, 288–309.

32. See Galbraith, *A Life in Our Times*, 245.

33. "Goldwater Attacks on LBJ, HHH, and JFK," DNC-Research Division (LBJL), Box 161.

34. "Opening Campaign Address at Lockport, N.Y., by Representative William E. Miller," Sept. 5, 1964, Page Wilson, Oct. 10, 1962, and "Fact Sheet on Charges by . . . Miller against Americans for Democratic Action," Sept. 14, 1964, all in ADA Papers, UC; *Congressional Quarterly* (Sept. 17, 1964), 2139–40; *Congressional Weekly Report* (Sept. 18, 1964), 2185–87.

35. "Republican National Committee Memo," ADA Papers, UC.

36. ADA *World* (Dec. 1964).

37. Arthur Schlesinger, Jr., "Keynote Address," April 2, 1965, ADA Papers, UC.

38. ADA *World* (Dec. 1964).

39. "On the Side of Change," *NR* (Jan. 30, 1965), 5.

40. ADA *World* (Feb. 1965).

41. Goldman, *The Tragedy of Lyndon Johnson*, 266.

42. *Time* (Jan. 29, 1965), 19.

43. ADA *World* (March 1965).

44. Ibid. (Feb. 1965).

45. Ibid. (Dec. 1965).

46. Matusow, *The Unraveling of America*, 159.

47. Sitkoff, *The Struggle for Black Equality*, 188–97; Lewis, *King*, 264–96; *Time* (March 19, 1965), 23–28.

48. *NYT* (March 17, 1965), 27.

49. "Press Release" Feb. 8, 1965, ADA Papers, UC; ADA *World* (April 1965).

50. *The Public Papers of the Presidents of the United States, Lyndon B. Johnson, 1965*, 840–43.

51. Carson, *In Struggle*, 160–64.

52. *Newsweek* (Aug. 30, 1965), 13–21; Matusow, *The Unraveling of America*, 360–62; *Time* (Aug. 20, 1965), 15–17.

53. ADA *World* (Aug. 1965).

54. Ibid. (Dec. 1965).

55. Ibid. (Sept. 1965).

8. The Agony of Dissent: Liberals and Vietnam, 1965–1967

1. David Halberstam, "McCarthy and the Divided Left," *Harper's* (March 1968), 32–44; Hodgson, *America in Our Time*, 275.

2. Goldman, *The Tragedy of Lyndon Johnson*, 467–81.

3. Humphrey, *The Education of a Public Man*, 313–53; May, *Lessons of the Past*, 114.

4. Johnson ignored the warnings of Clark Clifford and George Ball. "We won't get out," Ball predicted in 1965; "we'll double our bet and get lost in the

rice paddies." As the political scientist Larry Berman has concluded, Johnson "believed that to accept Ball's advice would be political suicide and result in political paralysis for the next four years." Herring, *America's Longest War*, 143; Berman, *Planning a Tragedy*, 145–46; "Meeting on Vietnam," July 21, 1965, National Security File (LBJL), Country File, Vietnam.

5. Herring, *America's Longest War*, 108–44; Karnow, *Vietnam*, 387–426; Miller, *Lyndon*, 458–66; *Time* (Aug. 6, 1965), 17–18.

6. "The Only War We've Got," *Nation* (Aug. 24, 1964), 66; "DeGaulle and Asia," *Nation* (Feb. 17, 1964), 157; "Get Off the Escalator," *NR* (Dec. 18, 1965), 5–6; "War in Asia—Why?" *NR* (Aug. 7, 1965); Reinhold Niebuhr, "Roosevelt and Johnson: A Contrast in Foreign Policy," *New Leader* (July 19, 1965), 8; "Less and Less Unconditional," *NR* (Dec. 6, 1965), 429; "Candor, Credibility, Confidence," *Nation* (Dec. 6, 1965), 429; "The Message," *Nation* (Feb. 1965), 182.

7. *Time* (April 16, 1965), 23–24; (June 4, 1965), 15–16; *Newsweek* (Aug. 30, 1965), 21; (Sept. 27, 1965), 27–28. Powers, *Vietnam*, 41–42; *Time* (June 25, 1965), 25; *Newsweek* (Aug. 2, 1965), 15–16.

8. "Vietnam—A Way Out," *NR* (Oct. 3, 1964), 5; Zaroulis and Sullivan, *Who Spoke Up*, 46.

9. John Roche, "Convention Speech," April 3, 1965, ADA Papers, UC; "A Professor Votes for Mr. Johnson," *NYT Magazine* (Oct. 24, 1965), 162–70.

10. Lowenstein, "Notes," ca. 1965, Lowenstein Papers (SHC-UNC), File 4843.

11. Arthur Schlesinger, Jr., "Address to the 1965 ADA National Convention," ADA Papers, UC.

12. Reinhold Niebuhr, "Consensus at the Price of Flexibility," *New Leader* (Sept. 27, 1965), 18–20; "Roosevelt and Johnson: A Contrast in Foreign Policy," ibid. (July 19, 1965), 5–8; "Pretense and Power," ibid. (March 1, 1965), 6–7; Stone, *In a Time of Torment*, 234.

13. Shull interview, June 28, 1985.

14. "Foreign Policy Commission Resolution, May 15–17, 1964," and "Proceedings of 17th Annual Convention of Americans for Democratic Action, May 15–17, 1964," both in ADA Papers, UC.

15. Lowenstein, Untitled Speech. ca. 1965–1966, Lowenstein Papers (SHC-UNC), File 4843; Miller, *Lyndon*, 488.

16. Rauh interview, June 1985; Halberstam, *The Best and the Brightest*, 695.

17. "Draft Resolution on the Dominican Republic," May 14, 1965, ADA Papers, UC.

18. "ADA Statement on President's Speech," July 30, 1965, and "National Board Resolution, Sept. 25, 1965," both in ADA Papers, UC.

19. Gans interview, June 27, 1985.

20. Edwards speech at the Institute for World Affairs, American University, June 24, 1965 (unpublished text obtained through Congressman Edwards's Washington office); Edwards interview, June 28, 1985.

21. Edwards to National Board, Sept. 25, 1965, ADA Papers, UC.

22. Tom Hayden, "The Ability to Face Whatever Comes," *NR* (Jan. 15, 1966), 16–18; "The Nation Apathetic," *Nation* (March 29, 1965), Dellinger, "The March on Washington and Its Critics," 6; Aronowitz and Weinstein, "The New Peace Movement," 8–12.

23. Newfield, *A Prophetic Minority*, 74–82; Lens, "The New Left and the

Establishment," 7–10; Lynd, "Coalition Politics or Nonviolent Revolution," 18–21; Howe et al., "The Vietnam Protest," 12–13.

24. Curtis Gans to Leon Shull, Nov. 12, 1965, ADA Papers, UC; "Call for Mobilization in Washington," Gus Tyler Papers (ILGWU), Box 39, File 2; Norman Thomas to John Roche, March 5, 1965, ADA Papers, UC.

25. Beer and Seabury to Edwards, Oct. 20, 1965, Schlesinger to Edwards, Oct. 21, 1965, Tyler to Gans, Nov. 15, 1965, and Gans to Tyler, Dec. 6, 1965, all in ADA Papers, UC.

26. Edwards to Scalapino, Nov. 30, 1965, and Scalapino to Edwards, Dec. 21, 1965, both in ADA Papers, UC.

27. Oglesby, "Let Us Shape the Future," 11–14; Vogelgesang, *The Long Dark Night of the Soul,* 99.

28. Miller, *Lyndon,* 427–73; Powers, *Vietnam,* 171–73.

29. *NYT* (May 16, 1966), 1; (June 4, 1966), 20.

30. Kearns, *Lyndon Johnson and the American Dream,* 309–17; Zaroulis and Johnson, *Who Spoke Up?,* 71–74; Powers, *Vietnam,* 116–18; Robert Sherrill, "The Democratic Rebels in Congress," *Nation* (Oct. 10, 1966), 341–46.

31. Rauh to William Connell, Feb. 2, 1966, ADA Papers, UC; Arthur Schlesinger, Jr., *The Bitter Heritage* (Boston: Houghton Mifflin, 1967), 50.

32. "Foreign Policy Resolution—Vietnam," April 24, 1966, ADA Papers, UC.

33. Matusow, *The Unraveling of America,* 206–7; "The War President," *NR* (July 16, 1966), 5–6; "Crisis of Color," *Newsweek* (Aug. 22, 1966), 38.

34. "A Message of Defeat," *Nation* (Jan. 23, 1967), 99.

35. Sawyer to Shull, Feb. 2, 1967, Washington State Chapter, Summer 1966 Newsletter, and Berger to Shull, Jan. 13, 1966, all in ADA Papers, UC.

36. For general accounts of Lowenstein's activities during this time, see Stone and Lowenstein, eds., *Lowenstein.* Harris, *Dreams Die Hard,* and Hodgson et al., *American Melodrama.* Richard Cummings, in his recent Lowenstein biography entitled *The Pied Piper: Allard Lowenstein and the Liberal Dream,* contends that Lowenstein worked secretly with the CIA. Most of his evidence, however, is impressionistic and, in my opinion, unconvincing. For specific references concerning his activities in the ADA, see Gans to Shull, March 16, 1967; Galbraith to Conway, May 12, 1967; and Gans to Shull, April 11, 1967, all in ADA Papers, UC. SHC-UNC houses a rich collection of Lowenstein's personal papers.

37. Gans to Shull, April 11, 1967, and Galbraith to Conway, May 12, 1967, both in ADA Papers, UC. Miller to Lowenstein, May 31, 1967, Lowenstein Papers (SHC-UNC). The Broder quotation is displayed on the cover of Stone and Lowenstein, eds., *Lowenstein.*

38. Tyler, "Johnson and the Intellectuals," 35–45; Tyler to Galbraith, May 25, 1967, Beer Papers (JFKL), Box 2; Tyler to Schlesinger, June 15, 1967, and Tyler to Goodwin, June 15, 1967, both in ADA Papers UC; Tyler to Galbraith, May 23, 1967, and Tyler to Wechsler, July 7, 1967, both in Beer Papers (JFKL), Box 2.

39. David Dubinsky, "Resist Aggression Wherever It Occurs," *Free Trade Union News* (Aug. 1967), 3–5; ADA *World* (Dec. 1967).

40. Galbraith, *A Life in Our Times* 181–83; Arthur Schlesinger, Jr., "A Middle Way out of Vietnam," *New York Times Magazine* (Sept. 6, 1966), 47–48, 111–20; Schlesinger, Press Conference, March 8, 1967, ADA Papers UC; Gans interview, June 27, 1985.

41. William Bundy, "Bundy Comments on Galbraith's Plan," *New York Times Magazine* (Nov. 12, 1967), 31, 132–35.

42. Lowenstein, Untitled Speech, ca. 1967, Lowenstein Papers (SHC-UNC).

43. Humphrey, *Education of a Public Man,* 301–52; Solberg, *Hubert Humphrey,* 285–300; "Old Hubert," *NR* (March 12, 1966), 7.

44. Solberg, *Hubert Humphrey,* 306–7; Eisele, *Almost to the Presidency,* 252–55.

45. See Humphrey to Johnson, Sept. 13, 1967, Watson Papers (LBJL), Vietnam Folder, Box 32; Marvin Watson to Johnson, March 29, 1967, Ex Pl (LBJL), Box 1; Moyers to President, Sept. 7, 1966, Office Files of the President (LBJL), Box 11; Roche to President, Jan. 23, 1967, Ex Pl (LBJL), Box 1.

46. Roche to Johnson, April 1967, Watson Papers (LBJL), Roche memos.

47. "Notes on the Convention," April 1967, ADA Papers, UC.

48. Tyler to Galbraith, May 25, 1967, Beer Papers (JFKL), Box 2; Tyler to Schlesinger, June 15, 1967, and Tyler to Goodwin, June 15, 1967, both in ADA Papers, UC; Tyler to Galbraith, May 23, 1967, and Tyler to Wechsler, July 7, 1967, both in Beer Papers (JFKL), Box 2.

49. Loeb to Tyler, June 17, 1967, Dubinsky Papers (ILGWU), Box 142, File 9; Schlesinger to Tyler, June 13, 1967, ADA Papers, UC.

50. *Time* (Sept. 8, 1967), 13–15.

51. Powers, *Vietnam,* 229–51; Zaroulis and Sullivan, *Who Spoke Up?* 119–48, *Time* (Aug. 4, 1967), 12–15.

52. Lewis, *King,* 354–89; *Time* (April 21, 1967), 20–22; (May 12, 1967), 17–18; (July 20, 1967), 9–15; Roche to Johnson, Ex Pl (LBJL), Box 3; Newfield, "Black Power," 222.

53. Powers, *Vietnam,* 229–31; Zaroulis and Sullivan, *Who Spoke Up?* 119–48; O'Neill to President, July 18, 1967, ND 19/CO 312 (LBJL); *Time* (Aug. 4, 1967), 12–15.

54. *Time* (Aug. 11, 1967), 9–10.

55. Roche to John Spiegel, June 26, 1967, and Roche to President, Aug. 1, 1967, both in Office Files of the President, John Roche (LBJL); Executive Committee, "Statement on the Riots," July 27, 1967, ADA Papers, UC.

56. Schwartz Amendment, National Board Meeting, Sept. 23, 1967, and Northern California Chapter, Sept. 19, 1967, both in ADA Papers, UC.

57. Gus Tyler, "Political Action for ADA," Sept. 23, 1967, ADA Papers, UC.

58. Roche to Marvin Watson, Aug. 2, 1967 (LBJL), National Security File, Defense, Box 227; Joseph Rauh, "Proposal to Maximize Support for an End to the War in Vietnam," Sept. 1967, and National Board Minutes, Sept. 1967, both in ADA Papers, UC; *NR* (Oct. 28, 1967), 34–36; Cohen to Rauh, Sept. 6, 1967, ADA Papers, UC.

59. Allard Lowenstein, "Comments on the Rauh Memorandum," Sept. 1967, Lowenstein Papers (SHC-UNC); Roche to Johnson, Sept. 25, 1967, Watson Papers (LBJL), Roche memos.

9. Liberals and the 1968 Election

1. *Newsweek* (Nov. 27, 1967), 25, 47; *Time* (Sept. 8, 1967), 14; (Oct. 27, 1967), 23–33; (Nov. 3, 1967), 15–17; "The Sense of Crisis," *Nation* (Nov. 13, 1967), 485–86; Zaroulis and Sullivan, *Who Spoke Up?,* 123–48; Powers, *Vietnam,* 229–51; *Newsweek* (Sept. 11, 1967), 19–20.

2. Karnow, *Vietnam,* 474–514; Herring, *America's Longest War,* 145–82; Miller, *Lyndon,* 491–99; *Time* (Sept. 22, 1967), 19–20.

3. *Time* (Sept. 8, 1967), 13–14; (Jan. 5, 1968), 13–22; (Jan. 26, 1968), 11–13; *Newsweek* (Sept. 4, 1967), 17–21; (Oct. 9, 1967), 23–25; (Oct. 30, 1967), 20–21; (Nov. 13, 1967), 31–32; Powers, *Vietnam,* 229–51; Zaroulis and Sullivan, *Who Spoke Up?,* 123–48.

4. *Congressional Quarterly* (Dec. 15, 1967), 2515–16; (Jan. 5, 1968), 1–4; *NYT* (Jan. 11, 1968), 1; *Time* (Jan. 5, 1968), 13.

5. "ADA Defers," *NR* (Oct. 7, 1967), 5; Mary McGrory, "Part-Way with LBJ," *New York Post* (Sept. 25, 1967), 18.

6. *Colorado Daily* (Oct. 5, 1967), 4.

7. Frederick Klein, "Liberal 'Shaker' Edges to Limelight," *Wall Street Journal* (Nov. 1, 1967), 16.

8. Arthur Schlesinger, Jr., "Vietnam and the 1968 Election," Speech to the National Assembly for *Negotiations Now!* Oct. 8, 1967, ADA Papers, UC; Galbraith, *A Life in Our Times,* 487–90.

9. Matusow, *The Unraveling of America,* 389–93; Parmet, *The Democrats,* 249–50; Eisele, *Almost to the Presidency,* 27–42, 71–86, 256–82; Hodgson et al., *American Melodrama,* 68–77.

10. *NYT* (Dec. 1, 1967).

11. "ADA Chapters on McCarthy Candidacy," Jan. 31, 1968, "New Jersey Newsletter," March 1968, and "News from New York State ADA," all in ADA Papers, UC.

12. James Wechsler, "Behind ADA's McCarthy Vote," *New York Post* (Feb. 12, 1968), 33; Powers, *Vietnam,* 251.

13. Shull to Swadish, Nov. 29, 1967, ADA Papers, UC.

14. Rauh interview, Nov. 1983.

15. Jack Newfield, "A Time of Plague," *Village Voice* (Dec. 28, 1967), 5, 40–41; Roche to Johnson, Dec. 18, 1967, Watson Papers (LBJL), Roche memos.

16. Walter Reuther, in his statement to the ADA regarding the McCarthy endorsement, stressed that endorsing a candidate in a national primary would "constitute an abrupt deviation from the essential purposes and past practices of the organization." Yet, his brother Victor, in a private memo, reminded him that he had voted in favor of an Eisenhower-Douglas endorsement in April 1948. Victor to Walter, Jan. 25, 1968, Reuther Papers (WRLLUA), Box 472, File 1.

17. Bookbinder to Galbraith, Jan. 10, 1968, and Loeb to Galbraith, Dec. 12, 1967, both in ADA Papers, UC; Tyler, "Liberal Crisis," *New Leader* (Oct. 23, 1967), 3–5.

18. Keyserling to National Board, "What Happened to the ADA," Jan. 1968, ADA Papers, UC. Keyserling originally planned to publish his thoughts in the ADA *World.* Leon Shull rejected the article because "relatively little of the article is addressed to the question at issue; whether ADA should support or oppose the 'dump Johnson' movement." The article is devoted mainly to "picking to pieces *The Affluent Society* which scarcely requires reviewing . . . ten years later," and partly "to a reprint of a disagreement with Arthur Schlesinger in 1956 which scarcely needs reprinting today." Keyserling responded by printing over a hundred copies at his own expense and distributing them to the National Board. Leon Shull, "Notes," Feb. 7, 1968, ADA Papers, UC.

19. Karnow, *Vietnam,* 523–66; Powers, *Vietnam,* 284–94.

20. "ADA's Option's," *NR* (Dec. 23, 1967), 6–7; TRB, "If Not LBJ, What?" *NR* (Feb. 24, 1968), 3.

21. Rauh Resolution, Feb. 10, 1968, ADA Papers, UC.

22. Hollander Resolution to National Board, Feb. 10, 1968, ADA Papers, UC.

23. Quirk, "ADA and LBJ," *Commonweal* (Feb. 1968), 643.

24. Auerbach to Galbraith, Feb. 23, 1968, and Detroit Chapter Minutes, Feb. 19, 1968, both in ADA Papers, UC.

25. *NYT* (Feb. 11, 1968), 1; Fisher to Shull, Feb. 19, 1968, ADA Papers, UC; Paul Porter to Humphrey, Feb. 12, 1968, Humphrey Papers (MSHS), SF.

26. *NYT* (Feb. 13, 1968), 1; Shull to Fisher, Feb. 26, 1968, ADA Papers, UC.

27. Dubinsky to Daniel, Feb. 15, 1968, Dubinsky Papers (ILGWU), Box 142, File 9. Evelyn Dubrow, Dubinsky's alternate on the board, was upset that Dubinsky decided to stay after she had stated publicly that he would resign. She wrote Dubinsky that he should resign since President Stulberg and the general executive board of ILGWU, at its Florida meeting said they would dissociate themselves from ADA if it reendorsed McCarthy. Dubrow to Dubinsky, Feb. 15, 1968, ibid., File 8.

28. *NYT* (Feb. 14, 1968), 26; (Feb. 16, 1968), 18; (Feb. 20, 1968), 54.

29. Rauh to William Dodds, Feb. 28, 1968, Reuther Papers (WRLLUA), Box 435, File 4; Galbraith to Reuther, March 15, 1968, ibid., Box 472, File 2.

30. Shull to Dewitt, Sept. 18, 1968; National Director's Report to National Board, Dec. 7, 1968, and Brown to Shull, Aug. 30, 1968, both in ADA Papers, UC; Rauh interview, Dec. 18, 1985.

31. Donald Keys, "SANE's Wayward Drift to the Left," Keys Papers, SCPC, Box 1.

32. Rauh interview, November 1983.

33. Parmet, *The Democrats,* 249–51; Schlesinger, *RFK and His Times,* 842–57; Hodgson et al., *American Melodrama,* 127–41; Eisele, *Almost to the Presidency,* 299–321; Kennedy had a higher ADA rating from 1965 through 1967 than McCarthy. Kennedy scored 94% in 1965, yet for both 1966 and 1967 he had a perfect score. McCarthy earned a 82% for 1965, a 90% for 1966, and only a 62% in 1967. Robert Yoakum, "Kennedy and McCarthy," *NR* (May 11, 1968), 23–27.

34. John Roche, Oral Interview LBJL, p. 7; Leon Keyserling, "What Happened to the ADA?" April 1967, ADA Papers, UC.

35. Solberg, *Hubert Humphrey,* 317–23; Miller, *Lyndon,* 508–13.

36. William Connell to the Vice-President, July 5, 1967, Humphrey Papers (MSHS), Vice-Presidential Files, 1965–68.

37. Solberg, *Hubert Humphrey,* 325–28; Eisele, *Almost to the Presidency,* 322–41.

28. Shull to Galbraith, May 10, 1968, ADA Papers UC. The *NR* estimated that 60% of the delegates favored McCarthy, compared with 25% for Hubert Humphrey and 15% for Robert Kennedy. "ADA Looking Ahead," *NR* (June 1, 1968), 8.

34. Rauh interview, Dec. 18, 1985.

40. Eisele, *Almost to the Presidency,* 322–43; Carl Solberg, *Humphrey,* 339–54.

41. Solberg, *Hubert Humphrey,* 339–54; Schlesinger, *R.F.K. and His Times,* 876–918; Eisele, *Almost to the Presidency,* 340–41.

42. Executive Committee Minutes, July 16, 1968, and Galbraith, *A Life in Our Times,* 503; Shull, "1968 Political Convention," July 24, 1968, both in ADA Papers, UC.

43. Galbraith, Shull, and Rauh, "Delegate Letter," July 1968, ADA Papers, UC.

44. Nathan to Board, Aug. 22, 1968, and Bookbinder to Galbraith and Shull, July 31, 1968, both in ADA Papers, UC.

45. Solberg, *Hubert Humphrey*, 355–71; Zaroulis and Sullivan, *Who Spoke Up?*, 175–208; Sidney Blumenthal, "Made in Minnesota," *NR* (Aug. 6, 1984), 19.

46. Victor Riesel, "Inside Labor," *Nashville Tennessean*, March 23, 1968, Reuther Papers (WRLLUA), Box 435, File 4; Matusow, *The Unraveling of America*, 423–26; Frady, *Wallace*.

47. SEP Chapter, "Press Release," Sept. 18, 1968, "Report on Election Questionnaire," Oct. 3, 1968, Drake to Shull, Sept. 25, 1968, and "Resolution to National ADA Board," Sept. 6–7, 1968, all in ADA Papers, UC.

48. National Board Meeting, Oct. 1968, ADA Papers, UC.

49. ADA *World* (Nov. 1968). *Boston Globe* (Oct. 16, 1968). Arthur Schlesinger, Jr., Oct. 24, 1968, ADA Papers, UC.

50. Rauh interview, Dec. 18, 1985.

10. Epilogue: Liberal Dilemmas, 1968–1985

1. "A New Sensibility Rooted in Rebellion," *Liberation* (Aug.-Sept. 1969), 20.

2. The Supreme Court played an important role in establishing affirmative action programs and busing. After the 1964 Civil Rights Act prohibited discrimination on the basis of race or sex, President Johnson ordered executive agencies to take "affirmative action" to guarantee enforcement. Initially, lower courts interpreted the order to mean that employers must actively recruit minority candidates; later, however, the Supreme Court, in a series of decisions, expanded on these decisions to allow hiring quotas for minorities. The Court first accepted busing as a means of desegregation in *Swann* v. *Charlotte-Micklenbury Board of Education* in 1970. While the Court established a general framework for busing, it delegated to district judges and the circuit courts authority for devising specific desegregation plans. Stewart Alsop, "Labor and the Liberals," *Newsweek* (Nov. 22, 1971); Richard Schier, "Can the Democrats Learn from Defeat," *Intellect* (July–Aug. 1975), 13–16; Richard Rogin, "Joe Kelly Has Reached His Boiling Point," in Murray Freedman, ed., *Overcoming Middle-Class Rage* (New York: Westminster Press, 1971); Chafe, *The Unfinished Journey*, 336.

3. *Newsweek* (Jan. 13, 1969), 88; Phillips, *The Emerging Republican Majority; Time* (Nov. 15, 1968), 20; William Pfaff, "Repudiation Now." *Commonweal* (Oct. 18, 1968), 79–80.

4. Podhoretz, *Breaking Ranks*, 344.

5. It is interesting to note, however, that though many traditionalists joined the neoconservative ranks, Tyler did not. Some years later Tyler moderated many of his foreign policy views. "As far as I was concerned the Soviet Union and China were one," he recalled. "I believed that if we let the Communists take South Vietnam, they would then move into South Korea and all of Southeast Asia would follow. I realize now that I was wrong." While he never again associated with the ADA, Tyler has maintained strong ties with the liberal movement since 1968. William Stern to Galbraith, Jan. 15, 1969, ADA Papers, UC; *National Journal* (Sept. 5, 1970), 1923; Tyler interview, Oct. 1985.

6. James Reichley, "The Time Bomb inside the Democratic Party," *Fortune* (Feb. 1972), 126–31, 172–74; ADA *World* (April–May 1972).

7. ADA *World* (April–May 1972).

8. *Washington Star* (June 8, 1969); "1969 Policy Platform," ADA Papers (NO), UC.

9. ADA Domestic Policy Platform, 1969, 1970, 1971, 1972, ADA Papers (NO), UC; Shull interview, June 28, 1985; Harrington interview, April 1985; Michael Harrington, "Say What You Mean," *Nation* (May 25, 1974), 648–51.

10. *Washington Post* (June 9, 1969), A8; "Acceptance Speech," June 8, 1969, ADA Papers (NO), UC.

11. ADA *World* Nov.–Dec. 1972; Leon Shull, "Joe and Gene and ADA," Nov. 28, 1973, Fraser Papers (MSHS).

12. ADA *World* (Oct.–Nov. 1970; Dec. 1971).

13. Ibid. (Jan. 1973).

14. *National Journal* (Sept. 5, 1970), 1923.

15. Keith Haller to Richard Sachs et al., "Some Observations on ADA's Organizational Structure," March 11, 1974, Fraser Papers (MSHS), ADA File.

16. Theodore White, *Breach of Faith: The Fall of Richard Nixon* (New York: Atheneum, 1975); Robert Woodward and Carl Bernstein, *The Final Days* (New York: Simon and Schuster, 1976); Gerald Ford, *A Time to Heal: The Autobiography of Gerald Ford* (New York: Harper and Row, 1979).

17. Martin Schram, *Running for President, 1976* (New York: Stein and Day, 1977); James T. Wooten, *Dasher: The Roots and Rising of Jimmy Carter* (New York: Summit Books, 1978); Jimmy Carter, *A Government as Good as Its People* (New York: Simon and Schuster, 1977); *Time* (Oct. 4, 1976), 14.

18. ADA *World* (March–April 1979).

19. *NYT* (Jan. 20, 1980), 19.

20. ADA *World* (Nov. 1979).

21. ADA Press Release, June 15, 1979, ADA Papers (NO), UC.

22. William Wynn Address to 1979 ADA Convention, June 23, 1979, and Keynote Address of Carl Levin, June 23, 1979, both in ADA Papers (NO), UC.

23. "Liberals and Carter," *NR* (Sept. 27, 1980), 8–9; Rauh to Shull, Oct. 24, 1980, and Schlesinger to Evans, Oct. 10, 1980, both in ADA Papers (NO), UC.

24. Germond, *Blue Smoke and Mirrors.*

25. Ed Koch, *Mayor: An Autobiography* (New York: Warner Books, 1985), 324.

26. Paul Tsongas, *The Road from Here: Liberalism and Realities in the 1980s* (New York: Knopf, 1981); *NYT* (June 15, 1980), 14.

27. "For Your Information," April 1981, and Press Release, June 3, 1983, both in ADA Papers (NO), UC.

28. ADA Press Release, Oct. 10, 1982, ADA Papers (NO), UC; *Dissent* (Spring 1983), 162.

29. *Philadelphia Inquirer* (Jan. 15, 1984); Rauh interview, Dec. 18, 1985.

30. Lewis interview, June 1985.

31. Dennis Wrong, "How Critical Is Our Condition?" *Dissent* (Fall 1981), 414–24; William Schneider, "Half a Realignment," *New Republic* (Dec. 3, 1984), 19; Hamby, *Liberalism and Its Challengers,* 352.

32. These are rough estimates gathered by an analysis of comparative assets-and-liability statements over the past six years. The organization claims not to have accurate information on membership or budget for recent years. See Amy Isaacs Files, ADA National Office, Washington, D.C.

BIBLIOGRAPHY

Manuscript Collections

Americans for Democratic Action Papers. WSHS.
  —Legislative File, 1947–65.
  —Administrative File, 1947–65.
  —Serial File, 1947–65.
  —Chapter File, 1947–65.
  —Unprocessed Collection, 1965–72.
Americans for Democratic Action Papers. Unprocessed Collection. National Office, Washington, D.C.
Americans for Democratic Action, Southeastern Pennsylvania Chapter. Temple University, Philadelphia, Pa.
Anlie, Thomas. WSHS.
Beer, Samuel. JFKL.
Bowles, Chester. YUL.
Clark, Jack. HSTL.
Clifford, Clark. HSTL.
Democratic National Committee Papers, 1945–52. HSTL.
Democratic National Committee Papers, 1952–64. JFKL.
Democratic National Committee Papers, 1964–68. LBJL.
Douglas, Melvyn. WSHS.
Elsey, George. HSTL.
Edwards, Donald, Washington, D.C.
Fraser, Donald. MSHS.
Galbraith, John Kenneth. JKFL
Gilbert, Richard. FDRL.
Halsted, Anna Roosevelt. FDRL.
Humphrey, Hubert. MSHS.
———. LBJL.
Isaacs, Amy. ADA National Office, Washington, D.C.
Jackson, Gardner. FDRL.
Johnson, Lyndon B. White House Central File. LBJL.
———. Confidential File. LBJL.
Kennedy, John F. White House Central Office Files. JFKL.
Keys, Donald. SCPC.
Kroll, Jack. LC.
Lippmann, Walter. YUL.
Loeb, James. WSHS.
Lowenstein, Allard. SHC-UNC.
Lubin, Isador. FDRL.

Macdonald, Dwight, YUL.
McGrath, J. Howard. HSTL.
Niebuhr, Reinhold. LC.
Mitchell, Stephen. HSTL.
Montgomery, David. WRLLUA.
Murray, Philip. Catholic University of America, Washington, D.C.
Republican National Committee Papers, 1952–61. DDEL.
Reuther, Walter. WRLLUA.
Reuther, Victor. WRLLUA.
Roche, John. LBJL.
Roosevelt, Eleanor. FDRL.
SANE Papers. SCPC.
Schlesinger, Arthur, Jr., JFKL.
Sevareid, Eric. LC.
Sorensen, Theodore. JFKL.
Stevenson, Adlai. Princeton University, Princeton, N.J.
Textile Workers Union of America. WSHS.
Thomas, Norman. NYPL.
Truman, Harry S. White House Central Files. HSTL.
Union for Democratic Action Papers. WSHS.
Watson, Marvin. LBJL.

Oral Histories

Baldwin, C. B. COHP.
Batt, William. HSTL.
Bliven, Bruce. COHP.
Hoeber, Johannes. HSTL.
Keyserling, Leon. LBJL.
Loeb, James. HSTL.
———. FDRL.
Lowenstein, Allard. SHSW.
Nathan, Robert. JFKL.
Rauh, Joseph. FDRL.
———. LBJL.
———. JFKL.
———. Georgetown University, Washington, D.C.
Roche, John. LBJL.
Schlesinger, Arthur, Jr., LBJL.
Shull, Leon. Georgetown University, Washington, D.C.
Wallace, Henry. COHP.

Interviews

John Roche. Boston, Mass., February 1982.
Leon Keyserling. Washington, D.C., January 1983.
Robert Nathan. Washington, D.C. January 1983.
Joseph Rauh. Washington, D.C., January 1983; June 1985; December 1985.
Leon Shull. Washington, D.C., April 1983; June 1985.
John Kenneth Galbraith. Cambridge, Mass., November 1983.

William Leuchtenburg. Chapel Hill, N.C., November 1984.
Michael Harrington. Providence, R.I., April 1985.
Curtis Gans. Washington, D.C., June 1985.
Ann Lewis. Washington, D.C., June 1985.
Gus Tyler. New York, October 1985.
Arthur Schlesinger, Jr. New York, October 1985.
Amy Isaacs. Washington, D.C., March 1986.

Journals and Newspapers

Commentary, November 1945–August 1985.
Commonweal, January 1945–December 1968.
Nation, January 1945–August 1985.
New Leader, January 1946–May 1968.
New Republic, January 1945–August 1985.
New York Times, January 1946–August 1985.
Newsweek, January 1945–August 1985.
Progressive, January 1947–May 1968.
Time, January 1945–August 1985.

Selected Books and Articles

Aaron, Henry. *Politics and the Professors: The Great Society in Perspective.* Washington, D.C.: Brookings, 1978.
Acheson, Dean. *Present at the Creation.* New York: Norton, 1969.
Alexander, Charles. *Holding the Line: The Eisenhower Era, 1952–1961.* Bloomington: Indiana Univ. Press, 1974.
Alsop, Joseph, and Stewart. "Tragedy of Liberalism." *Life* (May 20, 1946), 68–72.
Ambrose, Stephen. *Eisenhower.* New York: Simon and Schuster, 1984.
———. *Rise to Globalism: American Foreign Policy since 1938.* London: Penguin Press, 1971.
Aptheker, Herbert. "Task Force ADA." *Mainstream* (June 1948), 28–34.
Aronowitz, Stanley, and James Weinstein. "The New Peace Movement." *Studies on the Left* (Summer 1965), 8–15.
Barkin, Solomon, and Albert Blum. "Is There a Crisis in the American Trade-Union Movement?" *Annals of the American Academy of Political and Social Sciences* (Nov. 1963), 16–24.
Barnard, John. *Walter Reuther and the Rise of the Auto Workers.* Boston: Little, Brown, 1983.
Barnett, Lawrence. *Gambling with History: Ronald Reagan in the White House.* Garden City, N.Y.: Doubleday, 1983.
Belknap, Michael. *Cold War Political Justice.* Westport, Conn.: Greenwood Press, 1977.
Bell, Daniel. *The End of Ideology.* New York: Free Press, 1960.
Berman, Larry. *Planning a Tragedy: The Americanization of the War in Vietnam.* New York: Norton, 1982.
Bernstein, Barton. "Henry A. Wallace and the Agony of American Liberalism." *Peace and Change* (Fall 1974), 62–67.

————. "Stripping Away Liberals' Self-Deception." *Center Magazine* (March–April 1981), 41–44.

————. *Towards a New Past*. New York: Pantheon, 1968.

Blum, Robert M. *Drawing the Line: The Origins of the American Containment Policy in East Asia*. New York: Norton, 1982.

Boorstin, Daniel. *The Genius of American Politics*. Chicago: Univ. of Chicago Press, 1953.

Borg, Dorothy, and Waldo Heinrichs. *Uncertain Years: Chinese American Relations, 1947–1950*. New York: Columbia Univ. Press, 1980.

Bottone, Sam. "The Push beyond Liberalism," *New Politics* (Spring 1964), 35–45.

Bowles, Chester. *Promises to Keep: My Years in Public Life, 1941–1969*. New York: Harper and Row, 1971.

————. *Tomorrow without Fear*. New York: Simon and Schuster, 1946.

Brauer, Carl. *John F. Kennedy and the Second Reconstruction*. New York: Columbia Univ. Press, 1977.

Brinkley, Alan. *Voices of Protest: Huey Long, Father Coughlin and the Great Depression*. New York: Random House, 1983.

Brock, Clifton. *The Americans for Democratic Action: Its Role in National Politics*. Washington, D.C.: Public Affairs Press, 1962.

Burner, David. *The Torch Is Passed: The Kennedy Brothers and American Liberalism*. New York: Atheneum, 1984.

Burnham, James. "Does the ADA Run the New Frontier?" *National Review* (May 7, 1963), 355–62.

Cannon, Lou. *Reagan*. New York: Putnam, 1982.

Capps, Walter. *The Unfinished War: Vietnam and the American Conscience*. Boston: Beacon Press, 1982.

Caro, Robert. *The Years of Lyndon Johnson: The Path to Power*. New York: Knopf, 1982.

Carson, Clayborne. *In Struggle: SNCC and the Black Awakening of the 1960s*. Cambridge: Harvard Univ. Press, 1981.

Chafe, William H. *The Unfinished Journey*. New York: Oxford Univ. Press, 1986.

Clecak, Peter. *America's Quest for the Ideal Self: Dissent and Fulfillment in the 60s and 70s*. New York: Oxford Univ. Press, 1983.

Coffey, John. *Political Realism in American Thought*. Lewisburg, Pa.: Bucknell Univ. Press, 1977.

Cohen, Warren. *America's Response to China: An Interpretative History of Sino-American Relations*. New York: Wiley, 1971.

Cormier, Frank, and William Eaton. *Reuther*. Englewood Cliffs, N.J.: Prentice-Hall, 1970.

Cummings, Richard. *The Pied Piper: Allard Lowenstein and the Liberal Dream*. New York: Grove Press, 1985.

Dallek, Robert. *Ronald Reagan: The Politics of Symbolism*. Cambridge: Harvard Univ. Press, 1984.

De Caux, Len. *Labor Radical: From the Wobblies to the CIO*. Boston: Beacon Press, 1970.

Dellinger, David. "The March on Washington and Its Critics." *Liberation* (May 1965), 6–7, 31.

Diggins, John. *The American Left in the 20th Century*. New York: Harcourt Brace Jovanovich, 1973.

Divine, Robert. "The Cold War and the Election of 1948." *Journal of American History* (June 1972), 90–110.

———. *Eisenhower and the Cold War.* New York: Oxford Univ. Press, 1980.

———. *Exploring the Johnson Years.* Austin: Univ. of Texas Press, 1981.

Donovan, Robert J. *Conflict and Crisis: The Presidency of Harry S. Truman.* New York: Norton, 1977.

———. *Tumultuous Years: The Presidency of Harry S. Truman, 1949–1953.* New York: Norton, 1982.

Dugger, Ronnie. *The Politician: The Life and Times of Lyndon Johnson.* New York: Norton, 1982.

Eisele, Albert. *Almost to the Presidency.* Blue Earth, Minn.: Piper Press, 1972.

Erickson, Jan, and Robert Coles. *Middle Americans.* Boston: Little, Brown, 1971.

Evans, Rowland, and Robert Novak. *Lyndon B. Johnson: The Exercise of Power.* New York: New American Library, 1966.

Ferrell, Robert. *Off the Record: The Private Papers of Harry S. Truman.* New York: Harper and Row, 1980.

Fiedler, Leslie. *An End to Innocence: Essays on Culture and Politics.* New York: Stein and Day, 1972.

Foster, James Caldwell. *The Union Politic: The CIO-PAC.* Columbia: Univ. of Missouri Press, 1975.

Fox, Richard. *Reinhold Niebuhr: A Biography.* New York: Pantheon, 1986.

———. "Reinhold Niebuhr and the Emergence of the Liberal Realist Faith, 1930–1945." *Review of Politics* (1976), 244–65.

Frady, Marshall. *Wallace.* New York: New American Library, 1968.

Freeman, Jo. *The Politics of the Women's Liberation Movement.* New York: Longmans, 1975.

Fried, Richard M. *Men Against McCarthy.* New York: Columbia Univ. Press, 1976.

Gaddis, John. *The Origins of the Cold War.* (New York: Columbia Univ. Press, 1972.

———. *Strategies of Containment.* New York: Oxford Univ. Press, 1982.

Galbraith, John Kenneth. *The Affluent Society.* Boston: Houghton Mifflin, 1976.

———. *American Capitalism: The Concept of Countervailing Power.* Boston: Houghton Mifflin, 1952.

———. "Let Us Begin: An Invitation to Action on Poverty," *Harper's* (Aug. 1964), 17–26.

———. *A Life in Our Times.* New York: Ballantine, 1982.

Gambs, John S. *John Kenneth Galbraith.* Boston: Twayne Publishers, 1975.

Gelb, Leslie, and Richard Betts. *The Irony of Vietnam: The System Worked.* Washington, D.C.: Brookings, 1979.

Germond, Jack. *Blue Smoke and Mirrors: How Reagan Won and Why Carter Lost the Election of 1980.* New York: Viking, 1981.

Gieske, Millard. *Minnesota Farmer-Laborism: The Third-Party Alternative.* Minneapolis: Univ. of Minnesota Press, 1979.

Goldman, Eric. *The Crucial Decade and After: America, 1945–1960.* New York: Viking, 1960.

———. *The Tragedy of Lyndon Johnson.* New York: Dell, 1969.

Gosnell, Harold. *Truman's Crises: A Political Biography of Harry S. Truman.* Westport, Conn.: Greenwood Press, 1980.

Griffith, Robert. "The Politics of Anti-Communism: A Review Article." *Wisconsin Magazine of History* (Summer 1971), 299–308.

———. *The Politics of Fear*. Rochelle Park, N.J.: Hayden, 1970.

———. "Truman and the Historian: The Reconstruction of Postwar American History." *Wisconsin Magazine of History* (Autumn 1975), 20–50.

Halberstam, David. *The Best and the Brightest*. New York: Random House, 1972.

———. "The Man Who Ran against Lyndon Johnson." *Harper's* (Dec. 1968), 47–66.

———. *The Unfinished Odyssey of Robert Kennedy*. New York: Random House, 1969.

Halle, Louis J. *The Cold War as History*. London: Chatto and Windus, 1967.

Hamby, Alonzo. *Beyond the New Deal*. New York: Columbia Univ. Press, 1978.

———. "Henry A. Wallace, the Liberals and Soviet-American Relations." *Review of Politics* (April 1968), 153–69.

———. *Liberalism and Its Challengers*. New York: Oxford Univ. Press, 1985.

———. "The Liberals, Truman and FDR as Symbol and Myth." *Journal of American History* (March 1970), 859–67.

———. "The Vital Center, the Fair Deal, and the Quest for a Liberal Political Economy." *American Historical Review* (June 1972), 653–78.

Harper, Alan D. *The Politics of Loyalty*. Westport, Conn.: Greenwood Press, 1969.

Harrington, Michael. *The Other America*. New York: Macmillan, 1962.

Harris, David. *Dreams Die Hard*. New York: St. Martin's, 1983.

Hartz, Louis. *The Liberal Tradition in America*. New York: Harcourt, Brace and World, 1955.

Haynes, John Earl. *Dubious Alliance: The Making of Minnesota's DFL Party*. Minneapolis: Univ. of Minnesota Press, 1984.

Hero, Alfred O. *The Reuther-Meany Foreign Policy Dispute*. New York: Oceana Publications, 1970.

Herring, George. *America's Longest War*. New York: Wiley, 1979.

Hicks, Granville. "Liberalism in the Fifties." *American Scholar* (Summer 1956), 283–96.

Hodgson, Godfrey. *America in Our Time: From World War II to Nixon, What Happened and Why*. New York: Random House, 1976.

Hodgson, Godfrey, Lewis Chester, and Benjamin Page. *American Melodrama*. New York: Viking 1969.

Hofstadter, Richard. *The Age of Reform*. New York: Knopf, 1955.

Howe, Irving. "Liberalism—A Moral Crisis I. The ADA: Vision and Myopia." *Dissent* 2 (Spring 1955), 107–13.

Howe, Irving, et al. "The Vietnam Protest." *New York Review of Books* (Nov. 25, 1965), 12–13.

Howe, Quincy, and Arthur Schlesinger, Jr., eds., *Guide to Politics, 1954*. New York: Dial Press, 1954.

Humphrey, Hubert. *The Education of a Public Man*. Garden City, N.Y.: Doubleday, 1976.

———. "A Reply to Rex Tugwell." *Progressive* (April 1949), 7–9.

Isserman, Maurice. *Which Side Were You On?* Middletown, Conn.: Wesleyan Univ. Press, 1982.

Johnson, Haynes. *In the Absence of Power*. New York: Viking, 1980.

Johnson, Lyndon. *The Vantage Point.* New York: Holt, Rinehart and Winston, 1971.

Johnson, Walter. *The Papers of Adlai Stevenson.* Vol. 4. Boston: Little, Brown, 1974.

Karnow, Stanley. *Vietnam: A History.* New York: Viking, 1983.

Kearns, Doris. *Lyndon Johnson and the American Dream.* New York: Harper and Row, 1977.

Keeran, Roger. *The Communist Party and the Auto Workers Unions.* Bloomington: Indiana Univ. Press, 1980.

Kennedy, Robert. *Thirteen Days.* New York: Norton, 1969.

Kirkendall, Richard, ed. *The Truman Field as a Research Field: A Reappraisal.* Columbia: Univ. of Missouri Press, 1974.

Kuniholm, Bruce. *The Origins of the Cold War in the Near East: Great Power Conflicts and Diplomacy in Iran, Turkey, and Greece.* Princeton: Princeton Univ. Press, 1980.

Ladd, Everett Carll, Jr., "Liberalism Upside Down: The Inversion of the New Deal Order." *Political Science Quarterly* (Winter 1976/77), 577–600.

Lasch, Christopher. *The Agony of the American Left.* New York: Knopf, 1969.

Lash, Joseph P. *Eleanor: The Years Alone.* New York: Norton, 1972.

Lee, R. Alton. *Truman and Taft-Hartley: A Question of Mandate.* Lexington: Univ. of Kentucky Press, 1966.

Lekachman, Robert. "Too Little of Everything." *New Leader* (Feb. 15, 1965), 3–5.

Lens, Sidney. "The New Left and the Establishment." *Liberation* (Sept. 1965), 7–10.

Leuchtenburg, William. *In the Shadow of FDR.* Ithaca, N.Y.: Cornell Univ. Press, 1984.

Levenstein, Harvey. *Communism, Anti-Communism and the CIO.* Westport, Conn.: Greenwood Press, 1981.

Lewis, David. *King: A Biography.* Urbana: Univ. of Illinois Press, 1978.

Lewy, Guenter. *America in Vietnam.* New York: Oxford Univ. Press, 1978.

Libros, Hal. *Hard Core Liberals: A Sociological Analysis of the Philadelphia Americans for Democratic Action.* Cambridge, Mass.: Schenkman, 1975.

Lilienthal, David. *The Journals of David Lilienthal: The Atomic Energy Years, 1945–1950.* New York: Harper and Row, 1964.

Lipset, Seymour, and William Schneider. *The Confidence Gap: Business, Labor, and Government in the Public Mind.* New York: Free Press, 1983.

Lipset, Seymour Martin, and John H. M. Laslett. *Failure of a Dream? Essays in the History of American Socialism.* Garden City, N.Y.: Doubleday, 1974.

Lubell, Samuel. *The Future of American Politics.* New York: Harper, 1951.

Lynd, Staughton. "Coalition Politics or Nonviolent Revolution." *Liberation* (June–July, 1965), 18–21.

McAuliffe, Mary. *Crisis on the Left.* Boston: Univ. of Massachusetts Press, 1976.

MacDougall, Curtis. *Gideon's Army.* New York: Marzani and Munsell, 1965.

Markowitz, Norman. *The Rise and Fall of the People's Century.* New York: Free Press, 1973.

Martin, John Fredrick. *Civil Rights and the Crisis of Liberalism: The Democratic Party, 1945–1976.* Boulder, Colo.: Westview Press, 1979.

Matusow, Allen J. *The Unraveling of America.* New York: Harper and Row, 1983.

May, Ernest. *Lessons of the Past.* New York: Oxford Univ. Press, 1973.

Messer, Robert L. *The End of an Alliance: James F. Byrnes, Roosevelt, Truman, and the Origins of the Cold War.* Chapel Hill: Univ. of North Carolina Press, 1982.

Miller, Merle. *Lyndon: An Oral Biography.* New York: Putnam, 1980.

Morris, Charles. *A Time of Passion: America, 1960–1980.* New York: Harper and Row, 1984.

Morton, Marian J. *The Terrors of Ideological Politics: Liberal Historians in a Conservative Mood.* Cleveland: Case Western Reserve Univ. Press, 1972.

Moynihan, Daniel. *Maximum Feasible Misunderstanding.* New York: Free Press, 1970.

Namorato, Michael. *Have We Overcome? Race Relations since Brown.* Jackson: Univ. of Mississippi Press, 1979.

Newfield, Jack. "Black Power." *Partisan Review* (Spring 1968), 221–22.

———. *A Prophetic Minority.* New York: New American Library, 1966.

Niebuhr, Reinhold. *The Children of Light and the Children of Darkness.* New York: Scribner, 1960.

———. "The Fight for Germany." *Life* (Oct. 21, 1947), 65–67.

———. "For Peace, We Must Risk War." *Life* (Sept. 20, 1948), 38–39.

———. *The Irony of American History.* New York: Scribner, 1952.

———. "Our Chances for Peace." *Christianity and Crisis* (Feb. 17, 1947), 1–6.

Novak, Michael. *The Rise of the Unmeltable Ethnics.* New York: Macmillan, 1972.

Oglesby, Carl. "Let Us Shape the Future." *Liberation* (Jan. 1966), 11–14.

O'Neill, William. *A Better World.* New York: Simon and Schuster, 1982.

———. *Coming Apart.* New York: Quadrangle Books, 1971.

Oshinsky, David. *A Conspiracy So Immense.* New York: Free Press, 1983.

———. *Senator Joseph McCarthy and the American Labor Movement.* Columbia: Univ. of Missouri Press, 1976.

Parenti, Michael. "White Anxiety and the Negro Revolt." *New Politics* (Winter 1964), 35–39.

Parmet, Herbert. *The Democrats.* New York: Macmillan, 1976.

———. *Jack: The Struggles of JFK.* New York: Dell, 1980.

———. *JFK: The Presidency of John F. Kennedy.* New York: Dell, 1983.

Patterson, James T. *America's Struggle against Poverty.* Cambridge: Harvard Univ. Press, 1981.

———. *Paths to the Present.* Minneapolis: Burgess, 1975.

Pells, Richard. *The Liberal Mind in a Conservative Age.* New York: Harper and Row, 1985.

Phillips, Cabel. *The Truman Presidency.* London: Macmillan, 1966.

Phillips, Kevin. *The Emerging Republican Majority.* New Rochelle, N.Y.: Arlington Books, 1969.

Podhoretz, Norman. *Breaking Ranks.* New York: Harper Colophon Books, 1979.

Powers, Thomas. *Vietnam: The War at Home.* Boston: Hall, 1984.

Rauh, Joseph. "Government by Directive—A Case History." *Harvard Law Review* (Nov. 1947), 88–111.

Reichley, James. *Conservatives in an Age of Change: The Nixon and Ford Administrations.* Washington, D.C.: Brookings, 1981.

Reeves, Richard. *A Ford, Not a Lincoln.* New York: Harcourt Brace Jovanovich, 1975.

Rovere, Richard. *Senator Joe McCarthy.* New York: Harcourt, Brace, 1959.

Rowan, Herbert. "Kennedy Economists." *Harper's* (Sept. 1961), 25–32.

Scammon, Richard, and Benjamin Wattenberg. *The Real Majority*. New York: Coward-McCann, 1970.

Schlesinger, Arthur M., Jr. *The Crisis of Confidence*. Boston: Houghton Mifflin, 1969.

———. *The Imperial Presidency*. New York: Atlantic Monthly, 1973.

———. *The Politics of Hope*. Boston: Houghton Mifflin, 1962.

———. *RFK and His Times*. Boston: Houghton Mifflin, 1978.

———. "Stevenson and the American Liberal Dilemma." *Twentieth Century* (June 1953), 24–29.

———. *A Thousand Days*. Boston: Houghton Mifflin, 1965.

———. "The U.S. Communist Party." *Life* (July 29, 1946), 84–96.

———. *The Vital Center*. Boston: Houghton Mifflin, 1949.

Scoble, Harry. *Ideology and Electoral Action*. San Francisco: Chandler, 1967.

Sevareid, Eric. *In One Ear*. New York: Knopf, 1952.

Shannon, David. *The Decline of American Communism*. Chatham, N.J.: Chatham Bookseller, 1959.

Sitkoff, Harvard. *The Struggle for Black Equality*. New York: Hill and Wang, 1981.

Solberg, Carl. *Hubert Humphrey: A Biography*. New York: Norton, 1983.

Starobin, Joseph. *American Communism in Crisis, 1943–1947*. Cambridge: Harvard Univ. Press, 1972.

Sternsher, Bernard. *Consensus, Conflict, and American Historians*. Bloomington: Univ. of Indiana Press, 1975.

———. "Liberalism in the Fifties: The Travail of Redefinition." *Antioch Review* (Fall 1962), 315–31.

Stewart, John. *One Last Chance: The Democratic Party, 1974–1976*. New York: Praeger, 1974.

Stone, Gregory, and Douglas Lowenstein, eds. *Lowenstein: Acts of Courage and Belief*. New York: Harcourt Brace Jovanovich, 1983.

Stone, I. F. *In a Time of Torment*. New York: Viking, 1967.

———. *The Truman Era*. New York: Monthly Review Press, 1953.

Straight, Michael. *After Long Silence*. New York: Norton, 1983.

Stueck, William W. *The Road to Confrontation: American Policy toward China and Korea, 1947–1950*. Chapel Hill: Univ. of North Carolina Press, 1981.

Sunquist, James. *Politics and Policy: The Eisenhower, Kennedy and Johnson Years*. Washington, D.C.: Brookings, 1968.

Thurow, Lester. *The Zero Sum Society*. New York: Penguin, 1980.

Tugwell, Rexford. *The Stricken Land: The Story of Puerto Rico*. Garden City, N.Y.: Doubleday, 1947.

Turner, Charles B. "The Black Man's Burden: The White Liberal." *Dissent* (Summer 1963), 215–19.

Tyler, Gus. "Johnson and the Intellectuals." *Midstream* (Aug.–Sept. 1967), 35–45.

Unger, Irwin. *The Movement: A History of the New Left, 1959–1972*. New York: Dodd, Mead, 1974.

Vogelgesang, Sandy. *The Long Dark Night of the Soul*. New York: Harper and Row, 1974.

Walker, J. Samuel. *Henry A. Wallace and American Foreign Policy*. Westport, Conn.: Greenwood Press, 1976.

Walton, Richard. *Cold War and Counterrevolution: The Foreign Policy of John F. Kennedy.* New York: Viking, 1972.

———. *Henry Wallace, Harry Truman, and the Cold War.* New York: Viking, 1976.

Wechsler, James. *The Age of Suspicion.* New York: Random House, 1953.

———. *Reflections of an Angry Middle-Aged Editor.* New York: Random House, 1960.

Wicker, Tom. *JFK and LBJ: The Influence of Personality on Politics.* New York: Penguin, 1969.

Wilkinson, J. Harvey. *From Brown to Bakke: The Supreme Court and School Integration, 1954–1978.* New York: Oxford Univ. Press, 1979.

Wills, Gary. *Nixon Agonistes: The Crisis of the Self-Made Man.* Boston: Houghton Mifflin, 1970.

Wilson, James Q. *The Amateur Democrat: Club Politics in Three Cities.* Chicago: Univ. of Chicago Press, 1962.

Windmiller, John P. "The Foreign Policy Conflict in American Labor." *Political Science Quarterly* (Summer 1967), 205–34.

Wittner, Lawrence S. *Cold War America.* New York: Praeger, 1974.

———. "The Truman Doctrine and the Defense of Freedom," *Diplomatic History* (Spring 1980), 161–88.

Wyatt, Wilson. "The Application of the Truman Doctrine." *New Leader* (April 26, 1947), 1–3.

Yankelovich, Daniel. *New Rules.* New York: Bantam, 1982.

Yarnell, Allen. *Democrats and Progressives.* Berkeley: Univ. of California Press, 1974.

———. "Liberals in Action: The ADA, Henry Wallace, and the 1948 Election." *Research Studies* (Dec. 1972), 260–73.

Yergin, Daniel. *Shattered Peace: The Origin of the Cold War and the National Security State.* Boston: Houghton Mifflin, 1977.

Young, James P. *The Politics of Affluence.* San Francisco: Chandler, 1968.

Zaroulis, Nancy, and Gerald Sullivan. *Who Spoke Up?* Garden City, N.Y.: Doubleday, 1984.

Government Publications

The Public Papers of the Presidents of the United States: Harry S. Truman. Washington, D.C.: GPO, 1963.

The Public Papers of the Presidents of the United States: John F. Kennedy. Washington, D.C.: GPO, 1964.

The Public Papers of the Presidents of the United States: Lyndon Johnson. Washington, D.C.: GPO, 1968.

U.S. Congress. House. Select Committee on Lobbying. *Lobbying, Direct and Indirect,* pt. 6, *Americans for Democratic Action,* July 11–12, 1950. 81st Cong. Washington, D.C.: GPO, 1950.

U.S. Congress. House. Subcommittee on Housing of the Committee on Banking and Currency. *Housing Act of 1958,* March 1957. 85th Cong. Washington, D.C.: GPO, 1957.

U.S. Congress. House. Ways and Means Committee. *Social Security Legislation,* June 1958. 85th Cong. Washington, D.C.: GPO, 1958.

INDEX